MY HIJACKING

MY HIJACKING

A Personal History of
Forgetting and Remembering

MARTHA HODES

HARPER

An Imprint of HarperCollinsPublishers

HarperCollins books may be purchased for educational, business, or sales promotional use. For information, please email the Special Markets Department at SPsales@harpercollins.com.

FIRST EDITION

Library of Congress Cataloging-in-Publication Data has been applied for.

ISBN 978-0-06-269979-4

23 24 25 26 27 LBC 5 4 3 2 1

For Catherine, my hero
For Bruce, as ever and always

CONTENTS

Author's Note   ix

WHAT HAPPENED? 1

PART ONE: No Memory of Knowing 11

PART TWO: Never Coming Back 43

PART THREE: See, It Wasn't That Bad 85

PART FOUR: It Could Have Gone a Thousand Ways...... 193

PART FIVE: A Matter of So Much Importance 253

Acknowledgments   311

Notes   319

Works Consulted   361

AUTHOR'S NOTE

Although my research encompassed conversations with family members and friends, accounts of fellow hostages, and communications and meetings with fellow hostages, this narrative, and the views expressed here, are fully and only my own.

MY HIJACKING

WHAT HAPPENED?

———

We were flying from Tel Aviv to New York on a September day in 1970. I had turned twelve in June, Catherine would turn fourteen in December. We were flying alone because our mother lived in Israel and our father lived in America.

We boarded at six o'clock in the morning, but instead of landing in New York that evening, we ended up as hostages in the Jordan desert. Our plane was one among several hijacked by the Popular Front for the Liberation of Palestine, in the most spectacular episode of air piracy the world had yet seen. My sister and I were among those held inside the plane for six nights and six days. After we came home, there was no debriefing by authorities. No teacher sent us to a school guidance counselor, and no one took us to a therapist. Our parents never told us what it was like for them. My best friend wanted to know everything, but I didn't want to talk about it.

I kept on flying, shrugging off my unease. My sister and I went back to Israel the next summer. In high school, I flew to Poland on a choral tour. In college, I flew to London to begin a five-month solo backpacking trip. I flew to Paris and Rome during graduate school to visit friends, and to Madrid to join my mother on tour with a dance company. When I got a job in California, I flew back and forth to New York several times a year. When I got a job back in New York, I flew often to Los Angeles to visit my in-laws. Researching books and delivering lectures, I flew around the United States, to the Caribbean, Great Britain, Europe, Australia.

Then came 9/11. Tuesday, September 11, 2001, was the first day of school at New York University, where I was starting my eighth year as a professor. I loved teaching nineteenth-century US history, opening up past worlds for my students and introducing them to the art and craft of historical research: formulating the best questions, considering multiple experiences and points of view, scrutinizing the evidence both critically and with empathy. I wondered that morning whether the students in my 9:30 class would care about our studies, whether the group would be lively or dull. Just before I left my apartment, an enormous boom shook the building. Startled, I nonetheless dismissed the sound as the backfiring of an outsize truck. On the street, I joined a knot of people facing south, heads upturned. Smoke flowed from the upper floors of the North Tower of the World Trade Center, and within moments an orange ball of fire burst from the South Tower. Someone said, "Now we know it wasn't an accident."

Uncomprehending, I proceeded to class. Everyone on my attendance roster showed up and sat in the chairs I'd arranged in a semicircle. As if in a trance, I began to go over the syllabus. My seminar that semester was called Travel and Travelers in American History, and I told the students that we would study the experiences and observations of travelers both within and beyond the United States. The students followed along, obedient in their own states of stupor, until an hour later someone opened the door of our windowless classroom to say that both towers had fallen. Class dismissed, we climbed out of the West Fourth Street basement and emerged into a world transformed.

A month later, I was on my way to the University of Michigan to give a lecture. I alerted my host that I reserved the right to turn around on the jetway if I couldn't bring myself to board the plane, a warning she accepted without question. There was no need to reveal anything more, since in October 2001 people all over the world were afraid to fly. Soon after takeoff, passengers peered out the windows at the gaping hole in the ground. Some cried quietly through the flight, others prayed visibly. For the first time in thirty years, other people were acting the way

I always felt on airplanes. That's when memories of the hijacking began to intrude.

Still more years passed, in which I wrote books and articles about other people's lives, often in one way or another about grief and loss. Then, nearly forty-five years after our return from the desert, I broached the subject with my sister. Close as we had been as children, Catherine and I often struggled as grown-ups to maintain the intimacy that helped us survive back then. Did the hijacking have anything to do with that? Catherine hadn't thought about it "for years and years," she told me, "almost as if it was insignificant or didn't happen," but after 9/11 she too had found herself thinking and talking about it more than in all the years before. Sometimes when she did, she would shake or have trouble breathing.

That's when I realized how little I remembered. Right away I wrote down everything I could conjure. My memories were murky, and there wasn't much. My hastily recorded impressions felt haphazard and jumbled, confusing and chaotic.

When I thought about what happened up in the air, fragmented images came to mind. *Sitting by the window, Catherine in the middle seat. Two people running up the aisle, shouting. The old lady in our row crying out, "My pills! My pills!" Catherine helping her find the bottle in her purse. Watching out the window as the plane reversed course. A stewardess moving Catherine and me to first class, where we fell asleep in the big seats. An announcement coming over the loudspeaker about our new captain, about putting our hands behind our heads, and about landing in a friendly country. The copilot coming out of the cockpit with his hands up and a gun at his neck.*

When I thought about landing in the desert, I saw hazy pictures and heard faint voices. *Someone apologizing to us. A Palestinian doctor walking down the aisle, a nice, smiling man. The copilot telling us that our captors promised "no bodily harm." Watching our captors carrying dynamite onto the plane.*

Of the first day in the desert, I could call up only a single disconnected picture. *At daylight, some passengers leaving. A woman wearing a sari walking up the aisle, carrying her suitcase.*

Amid the blank spaces there was one longer memory, a frightening one that I'd never succeeded in erasing. *Lining up in the aisle as it grows dark on the second night. A commando at the front of the plane looking at the passport my sister and I shared. The man asking why we were in Israel. Catherine saying we were visiting our grandparents, not saying anything about our mother. The man asking if we were Jewish. Catherine saying yes. The commandos boarding the hostages into vans, then making us get off the vans. Standing huddled together in the darkness and cold, the commandos surrounding us in a circle, holding guns. Wondering if they would shoot us.*

Straining to recall our days and nights on the plane brought random, floating images. *Two friendly young grown-ups sitting behind us, and the old rabbi sitting in front of us. Foozie, nineteen years old, watching out for us and making us laugh. Eating pita and hard-boiled eggs. Dipping my hands into perfumed water in a red plastic tub outside the bathrooms. People digging trenches in the sand under the plane to drain the toilets. Our captors smiling and hugging, with grown-up hostages angry because they weren't allowed to visit the new hostages on another plane that had just landed. Seeing water on the horizon. Learning that the tanks in the distance were the Jordanian army. Studying the costumes of the dolls in the airline's mail-order catalog.*

Some of the impressions were happy—the ones I never minded remembering. *Singing the hit song "Leaving on a Jet Plane," and everyone laughing. Cords from the life rafts turning into jump ropes, and a smiling Palestinian man leaping in, playing with the children, hostages cheering. The commandos passing out postcards and telling us to write to our government. Mark, the guy sitting behind us, making us laugh by cursing President Nixon on his postcard.*

A few more fragments summoned a vague sense of anxiety. *Watching a hostage, a young woman, arguing in Arabic with the commandos. The Palestinians bringing the checked luggage out to the desert floor, tops of suitcases open, and Mark worrying about the Israeli flag he'd spread out over his clothes. Hearing that they were taking away everything made in Israel, and a commando taking away a photograph I'd tucked into my diary, then giving it back to me. One of the women commandos pointing her gun at me.*

Another vivid image brought with it a memory of feeling curious. *A sheaf of rough off-white pages, the words typed, double-spaced. Some of the* grown-ups calling the pages propaganda. Reading the opening salutation, "Ladies and gentlemen." Reading an apology that interested me.

Sometime after that came another grim shard. *The old rabbi who sat in front of us being taken off the plane. All the men being taken off the plane, leaving only women and children as hostages.*

When I tried to recall leaving the desert, the images felt just as arbitrary. *Boarding vans, an armed commando inside. Sand turning to road. Children and grown-ups clapping and cheering as we passed by, a boy in the crowd smiling a wide smile right at me. Arriving at the Intercontinental Hotel in Amman, a dazzling white building. Being surrounded by a thicket of newsmen and cameras, and Catherine telling a reporter, "Now I am going to thank God and have a bath." Foozie and some of the others never showing up at the hotel. Sleeping in a different hotel, in a big room with stone tiles and iron beds. Someone telling us to lie on the floor if we heard shooting. One of the girls in our room smoking a cigarette and telling us that her mother had recently died. Throwing away the clothes I'd worn in the desert.*

I remembered that after the capital city of Amman came the island of Cyprus. *Staying a night in a hotel with a curving staircase, where the bellman gave us a carton of cigarettes. Operators in a room with switchboards, connecting released hostages with their relatives.*

About our arrival home, I could envision only a few disjointed scenes. *Applauding as the wheels thudded down at Kennedy Airport. Walking along a sealed-off jet bridge so we didn't have to talk to reporters anymore. Peering into a sealed-off room, crowded with newsmen and camera equipment. Watching the six-year-old girl who had been all alone on our flight greeted by her parents. My father bolting into view.*

I could stir up only one image of being back home. *Lying in bed for a long time, feeling like I was in an airplane.*

For the first time ever, I wanted to know more. I wanted to know what happened to me when I was twelve years old, traveling with my sister, hijacked and held hostage. I wanted to know what happened up in the air, when we landed, and inside the plane stranded in the desert. I wanted to know what happened when we left the desert and when we got home. I wanted to know what happened to my family, caught in that world-historical event. I wanted to know what I couldn't remember and all that I was unaware of at the time. I wanted to connect the twelve-year-old girl who buried as much as she could to the grown-up struggling to understand what happened to that girl.

Telling the stories of our own lives, how can we answer the questions we think to ask later on, after the passage of so much time? A historian by trade, I wanted to do more than excavate my own memories. With a scholar's passion for evidence and accuracy, I wanted to compare recollections, compare documents, and compare recollections and documents with each other. As a hostage I had quelled memories and emotions; as a historian I wanted to search for facts and feelings, to provide meaning for everything that had happened to me and my family.

I dug farther into my own memories, and I put my memories together with Catherine's. I began to talk with my parents, taking note of my father's carefully scripted stories, my stepmother's more nuanced versions, my mother's misty memories. I found mementos my father had saved, some in my old room, some in his self-storage unit over on Eleventh Avenue. I talked with childhood friends, rekindling snuffed-out conversations about a topic I hadn't mentioned in decades. I searched for teachers from the distant past and asked what they remembered. I asked friends from high school, college, and beyond if I'd ever even told them I'd been hijacked. The answers surprised me, then didn't.

Meeting with my literary agent one autumn day, I told her I'd begun to think about a long-ago event in my life. In Wendy Strothman's Greenwich Village office, I was speaking matter-of-factly when the dog slumbering at her feet roused himself, padded over to my chair, and placed his front paws on my knees. Solemnly and searchingly, his face looked into mine.

"What's going on?" I asked Wendy, petting her friendly goldendoodle.

"Farley can tell when someone's in distress," she said. The dog had sensed something I had not, which turned out to be another clue.

I visited archives, read news coverage, and watched television broadcasts. I read the manifestos of my captors and listened to their narratives, past and present. I met and conversed with fellow hostages. I went back to the places where everything happened.

I knew I could never piece together a seamless story of the hijacking because different people's experiences varied so greatly. It mattered where you were sitting on the plane, whom you talked to, what you heard, what you overheard, and what you slept through. It mattered what you knew about the history of Palestine and the history of Israel, and what you thought about that history. It mattered if you were a crew member or a passenger, a grown-up or a child. For a child, it mattered if you were flying with a grown-up or flying alone. Mine could not be the story of any other hostage, including even my own sister, nor could it be the story of my captors. I could strive only to tell my own story of the hijacking in the truest possible way.

The question loomed: Why did I remember so little? When Catherine and I got home, we said we knew "everybody" on the plane, but in newspaper photos and television footage I recognized only a few faces. In an effort to fill in some of the blanks, I read a book I'd studiously avoided: David Raab, one of the few hostages I remembered, had published *Terror in Black September: The First Eyewitness Account of the Infamous 1970 Hijackings*, focusing much of his archival research on the international negotiations. As I read, I marked the margins with "remember" and "don't remember," the latter far outweighing the former.

I suspected some of the reasons for my limited memories: because everything had happened such a long time ago, because I was a child then, because human memory can erase trauma. All of that was true, but I would also come to find answers that felt more important, more compelling.

Another question also kept me company: What could remembering tell me? Strikingly missing from my own memories of the hijacking was a sense of fear that seemed suitable to the circumstances. Had I ever felt afraid? I couldn't remember. Could reconstructing the hijacking recover feelings that had been lost to me? When I corresponded with David, he had a question of his own for me. He was interested to know, he said, "how the hijacking may have affected your life." I wanted to know that too.

Almost as if it was insignificant or didn't happen, Catherine had said, and that described how I felt too. I'd submerged the hijacking so deeply that it felt nearly unreal, except for a single, persistent intimation. It would begin with an uncharacteristic procrastination around making an airline reservation, followed by sustained anxiety throughout the task, the completion of which signaled a commitment to board a plane. Entering an airport always—*always*—had me choking back tears, as did the sound of wheels hitting a runway. I held back every time, afraid that without such vigilance, there would be no end to the tears. For her part, Catherine rarely flew at all. Across the decades, I'd mastered the skill of not thinking about the origins of any of that.

If I researched the hijacking as a historian, could that stamp out the absurd sense that it had never happened at all? David Raab didn't remember Catherine and me directly, but we do appear briefly in his book. The airline had informed the State Department of our allergies to dust and animals, and tracing David's footnote, I found the telegram that mentioned us as "two children . . . still held on aircraft." Reading our names, first in David's book, then in the original document, the thought swam into my mind: *We must have been there.* That was a start. Could recovering the feelings that accompanied the hijacking make real something that felt unreal?

Two documents would prove crucial to my quest.

Packed away in a closet, inside a carton full of bound volumes and spiral notebooks, I found what I was looking for. Embossed in cheap gold ink on the red plastic cover, the words DIARY 1970 were partially rubbed away. I'd written every day during our desert sojourn, setting down a little over a thousand words altogether. That was the first document.

Then, in an unmarked folder in an overstuffed filing cabinet in my father's apartment, I came upon a newspaper interview that Catherine and I had given six days after our return. When I eventually located the original tape, I listened to a disjointed, sometimes inaudible, sometimes cacophonous conversation.

"The first three days, I was terrified," Catherine says on the tape, "and then I felt hopeless, and then I was terrified, and I was hysterical, and then—"

"Were you that bad?" That's my father's voice.

"I was."

"She wasn't." That's me.

"I was!"

"You weren't that bad."

"I was terrified the first few days, and so was everybody else on the plane."

"Were you terrified, Martha?" my father asks.

"I was fine."

"No you weren't," my sister contradicts me. "That's a lie!"

"I wasn't terrified!"

"Yes you were!"

The diary and the tape: those two documents, most of all, would help answer the questions I wanted to solve. Why did I remember so little? And what could remembering tell me?

Part One

NO MEMORY OF KNOWING

1

Sunday before sunrise. Everything is dark and quiet in our Tel Aviv neighborhood. We packed the night before, and now my mother helps us close the tops of our identical hard-sided gray suitcases. She is wearing her long nightgown. Because she has the new baby, only our Israeli stepfather will be seeing us off. At Lod Airport, not much more than a single building, we come to an ascending stairway with a big BON VOYAGE sign hanging above. From there travelers must proceed alone, and usually when we arrive at that stairway in early September, my mother puts on her sunglasses. She is crying because she has to say goodbye to us for a long time.

I like that memory. Something about it parallels my favorite book in the summer of 1970. My stepfather had given us *The Little Prince*, with an intriguing cover illustration of a young boy standing on a barren planet with a miniature volcano. First my stepfather read the story to us, then I read it myself, enchanted by the lonely aviator narrator whose plane crashed in the desert, and the downcast boy wanderer he met there. That boy, the little prince, bids farewell to a temperamental flower, a rose he loves very much. "Of course I love you," the rose tells the little prince. "It is my fault that you have not known it all the while." She implores the boy to be happy and asks him not to linger, "for she did not want him to see her crying." I read the book twice more until I had it nearly memorized. In my diary I wrote, "It is FANTASTIC!"

In the narrow Boeing 707, a single aisle divides two rows of three seats each. The sky over Tel Aviv is already bright and cloudless when

Catherine and I settle in. Somewhere in the nonsmoking section near the front of tourist class, my sister takes the middle seat, next to an elderly woman. The window seat is mine.

I am wearing my favorite bell-bottoms, patterned with red and gold swirls. My mother bought them for me at Bloomingdale's during a visit to New York the winter before. She had come to rehearse for the Martha Graham Dance Company's two-week season, performing the starring role in *Phaedra*. "In the evening we saw Mom dance," I wrote in my diary. "It was GREAT!"

When I watched my mother dance, was she speaking to me without words? Was she saying to me the same thing as when she put on her sunglasses at the Tel Aviv airport at the end of each summer? I did not know.

"She's leaving the day after tomorrow," I wrote in my diary. Two days later, in purposefully shaky handwriting, I wrote "Mom left for Israel," then drew a teardrop underneath. During that visit, my mother bought Catherine a pair of bell-bottoms too, which she is also wearing on the plane. My sister's swirls are pink and orange.

Sixteen hours later, we will touch down at John F. Kennedy Airport. My father will be waiting for us. It will be late afternoon, and it will still be Sunday, September 6.

I unfold a goodbye note from one of our Israeli friends, who instructed us not to read her message until we boarded the plane. "Good luck to you and have a good fly," Ani has written. "Please come back quickly." I pass the note to Catherine and open my diary.

Writing in script with curlicue capitals, I record the number of our flight (TWA 741), the time of our departure (6:00 a.m.), and where the plane will stop before landing in New York (Athens, then Frankfurt). We took the exact same flight home from Israel the previous summer—same number, same time, same stopovers—and a calamity ensued. Catherine and I lost track of time in the Frankfurt airport and missed the connecting flight to New York. "Darlings," my mother wrote, "I was *very, very* upset to get your father's letter." She assured us that she would keep feeding the stray cat we had befriended and named Perdita—"lost" in Italian. "We miss you terribly," she wrote. "You poor little perditas."

Recalling that mishap, I write in my diary, "This whole flight is jinxed!"

This time, though, we safely reboard. From there, it will be another eight hours until we reach New York. In my diary, I write, "*So* long!!!!"

Takeoff from Frankfurt is right on schedule, at 11:02 a.m. Less than an hour later, as we soar over Belgium, the captain announces an altitude of twenty-eight thousand feet, with Brussels visible on the left. The purser is selling headsets for the movie. The stewardesses are taking meal orders and selling drinks.

I hear a commotion: shouting that sounds angry, words I do not understand. Now a woman is running up the aisle. A man follows, both of them shouting. Some passengers think a husband and wife are having a violent argument, others that the woman is airsick, running to the bathroom to vomit. I see only a blur, but Catherine sees the man's gun. Others see the nickel-plated revolver too, along with the woman's finger inserted through the ring of a hand grenade.

"I hope it's not the Arabs!" gasps the old lady sitting in our row, her small frame rigid, her creased forehead signaling agitation. Clutching her heart, she moans, "My pills! My pills!" prompting Catherine to rummage through her handbag. The old lady warns my sister, who is crying as she searches for the medicine, to take off the Jewish star hanging on a slim gold chain around her neck. Catherine obeys, letting the necklace slip between the seats, to be lost for good. When Catherine and I look around, we see faces, six across each row, visibly alarmed.

The purser still thinks the man and woman are fighting with each other, and he runs after them, clapping a hand on the man's shoulder. The man turns, points his gun, and shouts, "Get back! Get back!"

"Oh, my God!" the purser cries out. "I don't believe it!" Sweating with fear, he crouches behind the bulkhead that divides first class from tourist class.

Just in front of the curtain that leads to the first-class cabin, the man and woman turn to face the passengers, shouting "Hijack! Hijack!"

First-class passengers watch the man direct one of the stewardesses to the flight deck, brandishing his gun and demanding to be let in, with the words, "This is a hijack." Crews have ways to signal emergencies, and the stewardess raps out a code, yelling to the pilots. The flight engineer opens the door to find a rattled stewardess crying out, "It's a hijacking!" She then pivots, composes her face, strides through first class, slips through the curtain, and walks unhurriedly down the tourist-class aisle.

The word *hijack*, I know, is nearly synonymous with Cuba, referring to American protestors or Cuban exiles seizing airplanes as stunts or pranks. Just that summer, Monty Python's Flying Circus recorded a comedy sketch of crew and hijacker wisecracking together in a cockpit, and even Cuban leader Fidel Castro has joked about hijacking. Maybe we will take a Caribbean detour—everyone knows about inconvenienced flyers compensated with lavish dinners and Cuban cigars in fancy hotels. Some of the grown-ups figure everyone will have a drink in Havana before heading home. Kids imagine missing a day or two of school. I think of my father, awaiting our arrival with his usual exuberance. How will he know that we might be late, and how sad will that make him?

Not everyone thinks of Havana, though. Like the old lady in our row, some worry about where we might be heading. Two men who work for the US Department of Defense use pocket knives to remove sensitive pages from their notebooks. Tearing them to bits, they swallow some and will soon flush the rest down an airplane lavatory. A little boy, seated nearby, asks his mother why the men are eating paper.

Passengers trade guesses. Is it a prank? Have a couple of fellow travelers lost their minds? Will everyone die? People speak urgently, if quietly, some exchanging phone numbers and pledging to notify family members should only some of us survive. One man pictures his parents watching the news on television and finding out that he died. Others envision their own deaths.

"Where are we going?" passengers plead with the cabin crew. "What's going to happen to us?" A stewardess, smiling and speaking calmly, says there are two people in the cockpit speaking with the captain. All around Catherine and me, passengers scan the seat-pocket route maps, wondering, *Morocco? Algeria?* Some note the position of the sun and identify the landmasses and waters below: Italy's Apennine Mountains, the shimmering Aegean. We are heading east, and a passenger who is himself a pilot confirms that the aircraft is also flying south.

Soon a woman's voice comes over the loudspeaker, which I record this way in my diary: "Good afternoon ladies & gentlemen. I am the new pilot who has taken command of your TWA flight. Keep calm. Please cooperate and put your hands behind your head." Catherine and I copy the other passengers, raising arms and lacing fingers. I wonder why the woman does not tell us to put our hands *over* our heads, the way robbers do. But she is not trying to prevent the passengers from drawing weapons; instead, she needs all of us to brace for impact, in case something goes wrong in the cockpit. I plead with God, begging him to save my life and Catherine's. What will my father do without us?

Catherine and I are both looking forward to the new school year. I am excited about starting seventh grade at Hunter High, an all-girl public school with an admissions test, along with lots of my friends from Hunter Elementary. Catherine has auditioned for the acting program at the High School of Performing Arts and will be entering ninth grade there. "I'll have *3* acting classes a day!!" she wrote to our mother over the winter. "*Fantastic*, isn't it?"

But out the window I have already seen our plane turning, the earth spinning around, those eight hours till home expanding into an indefinite amount of time. Catherine wonders if it will take another eight hours for the captain to let the hijackers off wherever they want to go. As we fly back in the other direction, the cabin becomes quiet. The two of us again copy our fellow passengers, lowering our hands. As the captain steers his hijacked aircraft back across the coastline of the eastern Mediterranean, passengers close their eyes to doze, to forget, to compose letters to God.

The male hijacker orders everyone out of first class, obliging crew members to pull out the armrests between tourist-class seats to accommodate four or five to a row. The hijacker moves in and out of the cockpit, standing by the lavatory or walking up and down the first-class area, smoking cigarettes. He summons a stewardess to join him, and while they puff together, he teaches her a few Arabic words and congenially shows her how his hand grenade works. He offers the flight engineer a smoke too, and carelessly lets his gun protrude from his pocket while using both hands to light his own cigarette. Next he orders the stewardesses to continue with the long-ago-interrupted beverage service, and the crew declares all drinks free, which is standard policy during hijackings.

Headsets will be complimentary too, but the captain does not want the plane's interior darkened, so the stewardesses fib that the projector is broken. Catherine and I had been eager to watch the movie, a Hollywood remake of the 1950s musical *Paint Your Wagon*, about the California gold rush. My father had danced in the chorus of the Broadway show, then understudied for six weeks when the lead dancer broke his ankle. I wanted to imagine my father dancing.

A stewardess comes by and, without explanation, shepherds Catherine and me into an empty first-class row. Catherine lets me take the window as usual, this time with the added incentive to shield her younger sister from any activity in and around the cockpit. The wide cushions feel like beds to two girls who awakened before sunrise on a morning now incalculably far away. Right before I fall asleep, I see it: the copilot, his naturally kind face wearing an expression of suffering and solemn resignation, emerging from the cockpit with his hands up and the barrel of a gun against his neck. It is an image that will remain fixed in my mind for the rest of my life.

Some five hours later, a second loudspeaker announcement awakens me. Again the woman identifies herself as our new pilot, and again she instructs us to place our hands behind our heads, this time in preparation for a potentially dangerous landing. She does not name our destination, but she says the words "friendly country" and "friendly people."

Behind the cockpit door, the captain faces the challenge of landing an aircraft in unknown territory, in rapidly falling darkness. Near our first-class seats, the male hijacker is still standing, and the stewardesses have to convince him to take a seat and fasten the seat belt. Below, some sort of runway comes into view, dimly lit with vehicle headlights and what looks like flares or smudge pots. Miniature trucks and figures move about. The landing is a "greaser": very smooth, with no damage to the aircraft. Local time is 6:40 p.m., about a quarter hour before sunset.

I let Catherine appraise the situation. Leaning past me, she peers out the window at billows of dust and sand, which look like smoke. Commandos on the ground have fashioned a makeshift runway by lining up barrels filled with sand and diesel-soaked rags, and the blazing torches light up people in military uniforms with rifles and machine guns, which makes it look like a war. Crew and passengers are relieved to be on solid ground, but the absence of real runway lights and airport terminal buildings is unsettling.

If fear fills the inside of the plane, outside there is a celebration. A crowd claps, waves, and cheers euphorically. They sing, dance, and fire weapons into the air. Someone props a ladder from the back of a truck up to the plane's front exit. The man and woman who took over our flight climb down, triumphant heroes welcomed by their comrades, melting into the outdoor throng. People dressed in fatigues in turn ascend the ladder, armed with flashlights and rifles, lanterns and machine guns. Some are boys no more than fourteen or fifteen years old, and some are young women with short hair.

Claiming the first-class section as their headquarters, the commandos order Catherine and me back to tourist class, and we return to our seats next to the old lady.

Listening to my captors, I absorb both apology and explanation. A woman named Hallah Joseph, dressed in an army uniform, says that we are "safe and welcome" in the country of Jordan, and that the Popular Front for the Liberation of Palestine regrets the inconvenience they have caused us. A man named Bassam Abu-Sharif is sorry too that the Popular Front has hijacked us. He explains his organization's motives, speaking about liberating his country from occupation by Israel, and talks about the strategy of exchanging all of us for Palestinians imprisoned in Israel and in other countries. Unable to make sense of a history I do not know, I translate his words to myself only as *We're sorry to trouble you, but we hope you understand our point.*

Less than an hour after we land, with the plane's batteries dead, the only illumination inside the aircraft comes from the fiery torches and the glimmering headlights of the trucks outside. Armed men and women walk the aisles and guard the exits. As if we have arrived at a real airport, the guards distribute landing cards, offering the beams of flashlights by which to write our names and addresses, which Catherine does for both of us. When they instruct everyone to forfeit their passports, Catherine hands over the single booklet we share. It is in her name, with me listed as a minor. In the single photo we stand side by side, Catherine taller.

That first night too, our captors declare their cause by way of slogan cards distributed to the passengers, which we read by the faint light of the few lanterns they have brought on board. Printed on stiff cardboard in English, and in smaller type in Arabic, the most generic message, attributed to Mao Zedong, reads, "To link oneself with the masses one must act in accordance with the needs and wishes of the masses." Another card, more specific, reads, "The fact that imperialist interests are linked with the existence of Israel will make our struggle against Israel a struggle against imperialism." A third card, bearing words attributed to Vladimir Lenin, presents our captors' viewpoint most strongly: "The idea of a Jewish nation is an erroneous Zionist idea and reactionary in essence." Catherine and I slip our set of cards, with their confusing words, into our tote bags.

Soon a roaring sound pierces the nighttime quiet, deafening thunder rolling across the ground, with no rain following. It turns out to be the landing of another hijacked plane—what sounds like thunder is their captain putting his engines in reverse to avoid crashing into us.

Our stewardesses serve dinner and distribute milk and water supplied by our captors, particularly mindful of babies and young children. With an ambulance at the ready, a nice Palestinian doctor from the Red Crescent walks the aisles, inquiring if anyone needs medical attention. The cabin crew, in their double role as hostages and airline staff, set about making everyone as comfortable as possible.

The copilot—the man I saw with a gun held to his neck right before I fell asleep up in the air—stands in the aisle to address the passengers. His face kind and earnest, he tells everyone that he does not know how long we will be held, that we could be held indefinitely, but that our captors have promised "no bodily harm." Quickly I memorize those words, for this is the story I plan to tell everyone when I get home: despite the weapons all around me, I was not afraid because the nice copilot told us right away that we would not be harmed. In another imprinted memory, though, I watch the commandos carry thick yellow cables—the cables in the image may be fabricated—the faces of the men expressionless as they go about their task. Although I determine somehow that this is dynamite, there is no memory of accompanying emotion, only the sense of a child intently watching every move.

That evening, as Catherine takes in the scene outside, as she fills out our landing cards and puzzles over the slogan cards, and as she helps her little sister settle in for the night, she vows to herself that she will never let the two of us be separated.

2

D awn seeps into the airplane. Was yesterday a dream?

No. We have slept on the plane. Sand stretches into an unforgiving distance, a flat landscape, dry and cracked, low hills far away, and beyond that, miles of nothing. People marvel at the vastness around us. ("At sunrise the sand is the color of honey," observed the aviator in *The Little Prince*. "One sits down on a desert sand dune, sees nothing, hears nothing.") It is Monday, Labor Day at home, the last day of summer for schoolchildren. My friends will be starting seventh grade tomorrow.

The first two hijacked planes in the Jordan desert. We were inside the TWA plane, on the left.

[Nik Wheeler/Corbis Historical via Getty Images]

Viewed from afar, the two stranded jetliners broil and shimmer. Up close, sunshine brightens a bustling scene. Jeeps and ambulances. Triangle-shaped tents. Children and dogs. A red, green, and black flag propped upright in a metal container. Hulking armored personnel carriers. Men and women with guns, wearing boots, some wearing kaffiyehs around their heads, some wearing bullet-laden belts, sashes across their chests, knives and grenades visible. Camels and a camel herder in the distance. Tanks on the horizon. Trenches about a hundred yards out, and commandos digging more trenches—for antiaircraft guns, or so we cannot escape, or, some fear, for our graves.

A local representative from the International Red Cross, permitted by the commandos to board our plane, implores us not to be afraid, assuring us that he is making contacts for our release. One of the hostages has a transistor radio that picks up a signal from the open aircraft door, and another, a college student who speaks Arabic, translates the broadcasts. That is how we learn of two more Sunday hijackings, besides ours and the Swissair jet now parked behind us: an El Al takeover was foiled in midair, and a Pan American jet exploded at the Cairo airport as soon as passengers and crew evacuated.

Sometime during that first day, a select group of passengers from both desert planes are allowed to leave, loaded into vans waiting on the desert floor. I watch carefully as a woman wearing a sari passes our row, memorizing her gait and expression in case Catherine and I should next be chosen. She moves purposefully and wears a neutral expression, as if a single wrong twitch might provoke the commandos to send her back to her seat. I will be sure to copy her demeanor if our turn comes, and I know that Catherine, a better actress than I, will do the same.

Taking cues from our fellow hostages, Catherine and I feel apprehensive about being Jewish. That is why Catherine obeyed the old lady in our row who told her to take off her Jewish-star necklace.

As the sun begins its descent that second night in the desert, I am happy to receive a hot meal: chicken, green beans, and potatoes, along with grapes and bananas. The stewardesses pour hot tea. Then, after dinner on Monday night, I tell my diary, came "the most frightening moment."

I remember the hostages lining up in the plane's narrow aisle. When it is our turn, a commando sitting behind a makeshift table in the first-class lounge consults our shared passport, the one confiscated the night before. Wearing a serious expression and speaking in clear, clipped English, he asks questions. *Are you American? Are you Israeli citizens? Why were you in Israel? Are you Jewish?* Catherine speaks for both of us. Yes, we are American. We are not Israeli citizens. We were visiting our grandparents in Israel. (It is true that our grandparents had moved to Israel a year earlier, and I, standing silently at my big sister's side, admire her for eliding the fact that we were really in Israel visiting our mother, which seems far more serious.) Yes, she says, we are Jewish.

The commandos then order some of the hostages off the plane, including Catherine and me, and board us onto vans. If we are on our way home, as I hope, then the whole ordeal will have amounted only to one night and one day. Abruptly and mysteriously, though, the commandos soon order the hostages off the vans. We stand huddled together on the desert floor, guards surrounding us in a circle, weapons at their sides. No one seems to know why any of this is happening, or why they suddenly changed their minds. The night air is chilly, and I hear whispers among the grown-ups about concentration camps. I wonder if someone will give an order to shoot. When we return to the plane, not everyone returns with us. Some have been driven away in the vans, and Catherine had seen three girls crying because one of them was being released, but not the other two. Catherine is pretty sure that only the released girl is not Jewish.

Our first day in the desert turns into another, which will turn into another, then another, then another.

Waking up the second morning, Catherine and I learn that some of the male passengers are missing, men who had been there when we fell asleep after the ordeal on the desert floor the night before. The rest of us—still nearly a hundred hostages—spread out in tourist class, and the old lady on the aisle finds somewhere else to sit, giving Catherine and me our own row. We entertain ourselves by imitating her heart-clutching cry, *My pills! My pills!* Our mockery helps interrupt the sense of dread all around us. From radio reports and from the commandos comes information about demands and deadlines and consequences.

Two questions intrude on my determination to remain calm: What is going to happen to Catherine and me, and what will happen to my father if we never come home?

Gathered around a radio one day, a group of commandos suddenly appear ecstatic. I watch them embracing and shaking hands, slapping one another on the back, their faces expressing joyous disbelief. We have been in the desert for three nights and two days when our guards order copilot Jim Majer into the cockpit to assist with the landing of another aircraft searching for the desert runway. A dot in the sky becomes a point, then a plane, then a roaring jet. Their captain makes such an expert landing, passing both planes and circling back, that hostages inside our plane cheer. Our TWA jet now stands between two others: the Swissair right behind us and the British BOAC at a right angle to us, its nose pointed to the southeast.

Armored vehicles, trucks, and jeeps approach the new prey as their hijackers alight to an enthusiastic welcome: more than a hundred commandos tossing their hats and guns, jumping up and down, dancing. Catherine and I do not have a direct view of the commotion from our side of the plane, so we lean over to peer out the windows across the aisle. When our guards explain that these new hostages will hasten the release of everyone, some feel hopeful, even if we also feel bad for the new arrivals. Passengers on our plane want to visit the new hostages, to console them, but our captors refuse, and the grown-ups' faces around me display consternation.

Because it is so hot during the day, male crew members shed jackets, ties, and socks, and the stewardesses wear only the dark-colored sleeveless shifts of their summer uniforms. Women cut off the sleeves of their dresses, and people lose track of their shoes. Then, as night swallows day, desert temperatures plunge to near freezing, prompting us all to don whatever extra clothing we have, while the crew provides makeshift blankets by slicing and distributing the curtains that divide first class from tourist class.

Nighttime's glacier makes us yearn for daytime's oven. As the sun climbs upward again, our yearnings reverse. Strong desert winds periodically whip up dry particles to create rolling sand walls, and twice the sandstorms come, the tan powder clouds pouring inside before anyone can get the exits sealed. The dust enters our eyes and ears, noses and mouths, making it hard to breathe, and when commandos come on board afterward, we see sand trimming their eyelashes, eyebrows, and beards. Until the storm passes, the plane remains sealed and suffocating.

Fear suppresses our appetites, at least at first, which is when meals are most plentiful, since there is still leftover airline food, and the International Red Cross flies in boxed lunches from Switzerland. Pita is the staple provided by our captors, filling and familiar. To go with it, there are hard-boiled eggs (stamped "Bulgaria"), tomatoes, cheese, or jam, though as the days pass the bread becomes "hard as a rock," I tell my diary, and eventually most of the fillings run out. On occasion there are olives and figs, grapes, apples, bananas, watermelon, and canned corned beef, but as I lament another day, "Mainly we live on water & hard boiled eggs!" As the days go on, meals become scarcer and sparser. As I write another time, "More bread & water. Oh dear!"

Thirst is a problem too. Water comes from two trucks that the commandos have driven out to the airstrip. At first we get a half cup every two hours, and when the Red Cross later brings in mineral water, every three hostages share a single bottle, refilled halfway twice a day.

Early along, mothers contrive diapers out of the first-class cloth napkins and the thin material intended for passengers' resting heads (Catherine and I count seven infants and fifteen toddlers on board), while women and older girls contrive sanitary napkins out of cloth supplied by the Palestinian Red Crescent. In place of running water, the commandos fill up large red plastic containers from the water truck parked outside, sweetening it with cheap-smelling perfume. Some of it is to help flush the toilets, but you can also dip in your hands for a semblance of a rinse. Cigarette smoke permeates the cabin as well, as commandos, crew, and passengers, including the teenagers, light up without regard for the plane's nonsmoking section.

The commandos do not want us to get sick, but they do want us to understand their lives as refugees by experiencing a modicum of their own sufferings. Tipping a plastic tub of dirtied water, one might say, "This is how we have to wash every day." When hostages take their worries about hungry children to the Palestinian doctor, he reminds them, if gently, "Our children are always hungry."

Catherine and I think all the hostages are like one big family, an ideal community, where everyone puts others before themselves.

"We have many, many adult & children friends," I write in my diary. For children, I list Tikva first. She is my age, traveling with her mother and four brothers. Her father is at home in New Jersey, awaiting the return of his whole family. After that, I name Susie, a little older than Catherine, traveling with her two younger brothers, unaccompanied by their parents. Among the children I also list Foozie, even though she is nineteen years old, probably because Catherine and I consider her our best friend on the plane. A college student from Brooklyn, whose real name is Fran (her nickname began in elementary school, as Foozle McDoozle, she explains cheerfully), she has slightly buck teeth, a sweet voice, and straight black hair that she pulls into a high ponytail in the desert heat. She is funny and shrewd, a wisecracking, compassionate soul.

Among the adults I list Mark and Mimi, sitting in the row behind us, both traveling home from Israel. Mark, a student at the University of Wisconsin, has curly brown hair and makes us laugh. Mimi, from Brooklyn, is going into her senior year at George Washington University. She is tall with blond hair and seems brave. A self-described hippie, Mimi met Mark standing in line for the bathroom the night we landed in the desert. Right away pegging him as funny and "alternative," she switched over to his row. Knowing that Mark and Mimi can see anything that happens to Catherine and me feels reassuring.

I write down a few more names, both children and grown-ups, followed by "etc.," certain that I will never forget anyone. I record first names only. Except for Foozie Chesler, I do not learn anyone's last name.

Since Jewish hostages seek guidance from the several rabbis on board, Catherine and I witness a lot of hubbub around the old man seated in the row ahead of us. I want to pray, but without Hebrew school instruction, without Sabbath-eve blessings around our dinner table on Friday nights, either in New York or Tel Aviv, I have no formal training in pleading with God. When I formulate prayers in my mind or in the pages of my diary, they feel strained.

Most of our captors are nice to Catherine and me, and we especially like Hallah Joseph, the head commando on our plane. A good English speaker in her early thirties, she plays with the little kids, talks to everybody, and answers everyone's questions. Most of the male guards are nice too. One day when Catherine's diary is resting on her tray table, one of the men spies the heart she has drawn on the back cover, enclosing her name with the name of the Israeli boy she liked that summer. Eyes twinkling, he exclaims, "Romantic!" Another time one of the commandos catches Catherine wiping away tears. "Don't cry," he says in a way that feels fatherly. "We have children too."

One of our grown-up friends explains that it is the commandos' job to keep us safe but also to scare us, and Catherine thinks they do a good job of keeping us scared. Sometimes they tell us that our lives rest in the hands of our governments, that "your government better decide soon," that our government has forgotten about us, does not care about us. All this makes some of the American hostages angry—at the Popular Front, but also at President Richard Nixon for prolonging our captivity. We laugh when we hear one hostage say, "I'm going to go to Washington and kick somebody in the face!"

Catherine and I dislike one particular commando. She is Palestina, named to represent the cause of her people, and other hostages fear her too. She keeps her weapon visible, rarely pointed toward the floor, and walks up and down the aisle making accusations like "You're an Israeli soldier!" When she guards the lavatories, Catherine just won't go ("Oh, the way she looked at you!" my sister remembered). Once when I come out of the bathroom, Palestina points her gun right at me and says, staring coldly, "Now *get* back to your seat." I compose my face to display no alarm, making sure to walk slowly enough not to betray any emotion. As Mark explains to us, "She's just walking around filled with hate, that's all."

Vanquishing my unease is also tough when I hear the Arabic-speaking college student—born in Sudan, she is a descendant of that country's chief rabbi—arguing with our captors. I do not know what they are saying, but I can tell she is talking back, and my admiration mixes with anxiety. As for Mark, he tells the commandos that he agrees they are being screwed over by America, and when they pass out postcards so we can plead with our governments to honor their demands, he writes to Nixon, opening with the salutation, "Dear Bastard," which sets Catherine and me into a fit of giggles. When Mark reads his message aloud, the commandos applaud. Catherine and I are not sure, though. Is Mark telling the truth, or is he protecting himself and his fellow hostages?

Darkness brings peace to some. Catherine finds the desert night beautiful, with all the stars visible. The few kerosene lamps supplied by the commandos shed only a faint glow, and the near pitch blackness makes it possible to blank out my surroundings, which makes it easier to wall off my trepidations. Catherine and I curl up in our seats, while smaller children stretch out on the floor or kneel, resting their heads on the cushions. Soon enough, though—too soon—the sun rises again.

One day, I write in my diary, the commandos order us "to give up all products made in Israel." That means, I elaborate, "anything like printed books, photos taken with Israeli cameras, key chains, ANYTHING!" I agonize that the commandos will confiscate my diary, the precious record of summer in Israel with my mother. Instead, a commando finds my photograph of Gerry—"not pronounced Jerry, but G as in girlfriend," I wrote to Jody, my best friend at home—his name and the word "Israel" written in Hebrew on the back. I told Jody about dancing slow with him at a party, drawing a helpful diagram with stick figures ("like this or closer"), and I cannot wait to show her Gerry's easy grin. "He's 12, handsome, fun & adorable," I gushed. The picture of the handsome boy makes me feel like a teenager, but when a commando sees the Hebrew lettering and takes it away, I dissolve into a little kid, crying in the lap of a stewardess. Witnessing my burst of tears, the offending commando soon walks back down the aisle, holding the photograph by one corner, as if not wishing to smudge it. Apparently he has consulted with his comrades, and with a rueful expression he returns it, abating my embarrassing tears.

Later, when our captors remove all our checked luggage from the cargo hold and lay out all our suitcases on the sand, Mark broods about the Israeli flag spread out on top of his clothes. I have grown used to his joking and laughing, and now he has turned quiet, which makes me uncomfortable, his somber face and downcast eyes another troubling image I am unable to erase from memory.

Even with some of the original passengers gone, the plane still feels crowded. It seems like there are a thousand little kids running around screaming, and taking care of them is, for some, one way to quicken the hours. Our aircraft holds perhaps twenty-five children under the age of fourteen, including the seven babies, along with acutely restless toddlers and youngsters; ten of us, counting Catherine and me, are unaccompanied. Parents gather at the front of tourist class, constructing cribs out of cartons found in the galley kitchens, and teenage girls assist mothers, holding, feeding, and changing infants. At the back of the plane, older teens organize games, improvise lessons, tell stories, and sing songs with the bigger kids.

At twelve and thirteen, Catherine and I are too old to gather with the little ones, not quite old enough to assume the role of teachers or hang around with the teenagers, and not quite young enough for the crew to dote on us. Flying from one parent to the other, we are with neither. Despite the names I have listed in my diary, my real friends are at home, at school without me. Inside the plane, my diary listens without judgment to my restrained and partial record of each day, and I find a whole host of silent friends in the dolls for sale in the pages of the in-flight catalog available in my seat-back pocket. I study them intently. I name each one and conjure them to life.

Going outside also helps time pass, the expansive desert landscape offering a dramatic change from the aircraft's airless interior. When our captors allow it, we make our way down the ladder, holding on to a rigged-up rope to steady ourselves, commandos assisting the young children and the mothers carrying babies.

Outside, I see that we are surrounded by machine-gun emplacements, pointing away from the aircraft. Gazing back at our metal quarters, I see too that the commandos have painted the fuselage with the letters *PFLP* in red and black. A slogan is painted in English: "Down with imperialism, Zionism & Israel," camera-ready for television audiences. A woman commando—one of three on our plane—gives out bottles of warm orange soda, while men use the water truck to hose down the sand to keep it from blowing. Grown-ups stroll back and forth. Children are keen to run around. When an especially energetic two-year-old is not dunking his hand into a puddle of oil, he tries valiantly to sneak through the legs of the surrounding guards. An older boy, aware of the boundaries, jogs in place. The only desert shade comes from the wings of the giant marooned airplanes.

Catherine and I walk with Foozie, who explains that the line visible on the horizon is the Jordanian army, inside their tanks, which I now understand is a different army from the one to which our captors belong, and the one at which our captors' machine guns, wedged in the sand, are pointed. On the horizon, past the tanks, I see shimmering water—are we on an island? Others at first think we are surrounded by lakes, and one of the hostages sees sailboats in the distance. Foozie explains that the water is a mirage. I have learned about mirages in elementary school, and a commando is pointing out the phenomenon to some of the other children, explaining their scientific workings. Other commandos give piggyback rides to little kids.

One day, sitting in the shade under an airplane wing, someone starts a round of John Denver's "Leaving on a Jet Plane," which the folk trio Peter, Paul and Mary made into a hit single that year. I know that the generic ballad about leaving home has become an anthem for young men drafted and sent to Vietnam, uncertain if they will ever return. A top-forty song among the troops, the lyrics speak also to their wives and sweethearts, who sing along to the words, "tell me that you'll wait for me." Since Frank Allen, the student purser on our plane, is supposed to get married the next weekend, I think the line, "When I come back, I'll wear your wedding ring" must have special meaning for him. Loud voices among the singing hostages—I can still see Mark sitting on the sand, grinning—change the words to "living on a jet plane," which Catherine and I think is hilarious, and everyone is laughing as we sing the line "Don't know when I'll be back again," which some people change to "Can't wait till I take off again."

I can see myself too, sitting under the wing, in my red-and-gold bell-bottoms and long-sleeved white button-down shirt, smiling and singing. I am not lost in the moment, though, since at the same time I am composing a narrative in my head, describing the scene to people at home. Not to a lot of people, mainly just to my father, so he will know that we were not too sad or afraid. Eventually the merriment proves too much for our captors, who order us to stop.

Another day, the crew thinks to inflate the aircraft's brightly colored life rafts. Copilot Jim Majer carries each 145-pound raft on his back, and after the crew tosses them down, Frank Allen inflates them, inviting the children to climb inside. Adults climb in too, to tell stories and sing and clap with the little ones. The crew gives out candy and gum from the supply bags inside the rafts, and flight engineer Al Kiburis disconnects the buoys at the end of the retention lines and passes them around as rubber balls. A commando joins in, cheerfully blocking a catch and tossing a ball to someone else. Even better, people turn the yellow connection lines, meant for tying rafts together in a water landing, into jump ropes. As two hostages spin the rope, others line up, including one of the commandos, a strapping man, smiling as he leaps in, belt clanging and military boots thumping. The gathered hostages marvel at his playfulness.

These are the tolerable moments, the ones I make absolutely sure to remember.

3

When I awaken at sunrise on Friday, my friend Tikva, in a nearby row, is crying hard. We have now slept five nights on the plane, and this morning ten more hostages are gone, including Tikva's seventeen-year-old brother, David. Mark is gone too, leaving Mimi alone in the row behind us, devastated. Catherine and I have both slept through the nighttime removals all around us.

Our morning disquiet is greeted with a powerful sandstorm. Before the crew and commandos can get the exit doors shut, great quantities of sand and dust have blown into our grounded ship. Soon the sealed interior is a broiling hundred degrees, with people coughing and wheezing, our eyes burning. The commandos who come on board after it is over look like they are made of sand. When the desert settles back into its flat monotony, hostages—there are still some 270 of us on the three planes—look out the windows to see vans arriving. Are we being released? Or are we going to be taken somewhere else?

Meanwhile, the guards inside our plane seem on edge, brusque and distracted. Even the affable Palestinian doctor has turned cold. Before long, the commandos instruct all of us to bring our belongings, in an orderly fashion, to the front of the plane, then decree that we return to our seats, as they once again inspect our carry-on bags.

In the uneasy atmosphere of missing men, unfriendly captors, and luggage searches, distractions seem in order. Tikva's mother, whose eldest son has been taken away, shares her perfume, prettying up the Jewish women for Friday night. An ad hoc committee organizes a talent show, in which I am sure Catherine will perform. In the meantime she sticks by Foozie, the two of them preparing a Sabbath-eve program, and I stick by both of them, comforted by their voices and plans. They are the two people who will keep me safe, along with copilot Jim Majer, who said that no one would harm us. Around me, fellow hostages wonder if our captors are going to blow us up soon.

The commandos distribute brown envelopes with sheaves of typed pages inside. Confined to my seat, I turn to the new reading material with interest. It opens with an apology, and I imagine the words spoken by the nice Palestinian doctor, even though he now appears uncharacteristically aloof. I like apologies, especially from grown-ups who make children sad.

I do not understand everything I read, but the parts I do understand fit with conversations I have heard around me all week. Even though some of the adults call the handouts propaganda, Catherine thinks the material is effective at explaining the Popular Front, making clear that the Palestinians have "so many people against them, including the Jordanians," as she will put it later.

The sun is setting, the plane darkening. "Tonight is Shabbat," I write in my diary, using the Hebrew word for the Sabbath, feeling bad for the "many kosher people who cannot eat the little food given out." Some of the observant Jews ask the crew for candles, but they have none to offer. A commando inquires into the cause of distressed voices and, in a turn of kindness after the day's hostilities, donates a few. A woman lights them—she is the mother of two missing rabbi brothers—then allows flight engineer Al Kiburis to blow them out instantly, for fear of starting a fire. Even though people have been smoking on the plane all week, everyone is much more nervous now, thinking about explosives. Dinner brings leftovers from lunchtime, until suddenly the commandos supply tomatoes and cooked green beans, then give out candy to the children.

All of this happens right before the commandos take the rest of the men away.

Among them is the old rabbi in the row ahead of us. When it is his turn to disembark, he wishes the remaining hostages a "guten Shabbos."

Good Sabbath. "Poor man!" I write in my diary. "It was the first time in his life that he broke the Sabbath."

There are about a hundred of us left inside. Some feel sure the commandos will never blow up a plane full of women and children. Others worry that our guards will quickly exit and do just that. The approaching night feels menacing, even to a child adept at suppressing fear. In the dark, Catherine and I sit by one of the open exit doors with our Foozie. She is smart, and she will know what to do if anything happens. The three of us again take in the beauty of the darkened desert, liquid black ink spilled over every edge of the sky's page. We talk about God, and we talk about *The Little Prince.* The little prince found the desert beautiful, and Foozie finds the desert beautiful too, and mysterious. She thinks that when God gets depressed, he goes there. "When we cry, our tears are wet," she says. "His are turned to sand." Gazing out at the desert, she thinks, *How much God must cry.* For Foozie, the claustrophobia is strangely magnified—even with so many hostages gone, it feels to her like there is not "enough wall space for all those people to start climbing all at once."

The stewardesses, ever fulfilling their roles, help everyone settle in for a sixth night, some of us finally able to stretch across three seats. Even so, Foozie takes the middle seat in our row so that Catherine and I can each lean on one shoulder. With only women and children remaining, further anxieties surface. Most of our captors are men. Armed men engaged in warfare historically spell danger for women. Those who are whispering around me must think all the children are asleep. Involuntarily I listen, and involuntarily words materialize in my mind. *The women are talking about rape.*

Foozie has accepted a pink pill from the Palestinian doctor, to help her sleep through the fear of the night ahead. Deep into the darkness she climbs over Catherine and begins walking up the aisle, sure that Al Kiburis has offered her a seat in first class. Midway, she realizes that she is hallucinating—Al is gone—and turns back to settle in between Catherine and me again.

The next morning, the commandos tell all of us to get ready to depart for good. Around me, my fellow hostages are oddly quiet, as if displays of exuberance might prompt our captors to change their minds. Or maybe it is the memory of Monday night's sudden return to the aircraft that leaves us unsure of what will happen next. Catherine and I exchange addresses and telephone numbers with Foozie, looking forward to seeing her back in New York, in case we are really going home.

As others trade information, some also bid amicable farewells to the commandos, a few exchanging addresses with them too. Some of our captors pick up young children to hug them goodbye. Before descending the ladder, for what I hope is the last time, we each have to sign our name and answer questions about our point of embarkation and reason for traveling, our nationality, home address, and—again—religion. For the second time, Catherine does the work for both of us, sticking to the story about visiting our grandparents and repeating that we are Jewish. A commando apologizes one last time and wishes everyone good luck. Around me I notice the continued lack of exultation, which tempers my own cautious hopes of soon seeing my father.

Down on the desert floor, our guards direct Catherine and me to the first van in a convoy. Our driver wears a khaki uniform and a maroon beret, which Catherine understands signifies the Jordanian army. The front passenger seat is reserved for a Popular Front commando, armed with a machine gun. Looking out the window of the van, the planes appear to Catherine as three silver dragonflies perched on the horizon. Staring hard at our aircraft, she can see a figure, a woman, leaning out of an exit, high above the ground. Catherine is afraid the commandos are going to blow up the planes with some of the hostages still inside. I do not look around at all.

I am trying to feel hopeful, but I can tell that Catherine is scared, and I see that one of the women in our van is crying. No one tells us where we are going, or why. Catherine thinks the commandos have removed the hostages because the planes are too unsanitary. She is not sure if we are going to a hotel or to a prison. She also thinks about what the commandos told us about Israel torturing their Palestinian prisoners, and now she fears that, wherever they are taking us, they might torture us. She also worries that when we get to our destination, someone might try to separate us, so she uses the time during the drive to plan how she can stop that from happening. For my part, I work to stop the spinning of all scenarios except for the loop that plays in my head, of my sister and me running toward our father. Skillful by now, I deploy hope to halt fear.

Our driver starts the engine, the tires kicking up dusty sand. Riding out of the desert, following a truck filled with armed commandos, we hear a series of booms. It should be obvious what causes the sound, but I am not sure, nor do I turn around or let myself imagine the three airplanes behind me exploding into flames. Copying our fellow passengers, Catherine and I crouch down.

The convoy keeps moving, our van in the lead, over a ridge and through a mile or two of sand and gravel. Catherine wonders if the Jordanian soldiers milling around along the route will cause any trouble, but they do not, at least not for our van. When our driver reaches a paved road, he slows down as people gather around the vehicle. Some stare. Others clap and cheer. A few smack the sides. I peer into the face of a smiling boy—a face I will ever after recall—unsure if he and his friends are celebrating our captivity or our release. Catherine feels like a prisoner of war. We know about POWs from the Vietnam War, and we have seen pictures in *Life* magazine of captured American soldiers paraded and reviled. With our friends at home, we wore political buttons appealing for their release.

Some two hours later, our van is the first to arrive at our destination, following directly behind the army truck carrying Popular Front commandos, four of them standing tall, their long weapons held straight at their sides. Through a megaphone, a woman sings in Arabic. I do not know what message she is conveying.

As soon as Catherine sees the Jordan Intercontinental Hotel, with flags of different nations fluttering out front, she feels a measure of relief. I think the building is beautiful, its boxy seven stories made of white cement and glass, balconies forming a grid of squares across the facade. Between the van and the hotel arises a forest of camera lenses, tripods, and microphones, a herd of reporters pressing against us on all sides.

"This morning we were piled into buses," I write in my diary. "We were going to Amman, to a hotel. Then maybe to New York tomorrow! Thank God! Thank God! We all left in groups in little trucks. Our truck was the first to drive up to the hotel! Jesus! Reporters, TV cameras, other cameras, microphones, EVERYTHING! This one guy took around 25 pictures of me in a row." If our ordeal is really over, I decide, it will be my mandate to craft everything that has happened into an adventure story. Since the ending is going to be happy, I can even mix in a few scary moments.

The Intercontinental is at the center of a city caught in an unofficial war between Jordanian forces and Palestinian resisters, but I do not register any of that. Perhaps it is hard to detect the signs of the battle-ravaged interior because there is so much pandemonium. Some commandos threaten to smash the cameras of newsmen who are rudely closing in on released hostages, while others helpfully hold babies. Some young children sleep sprawled atop suitcases, while others run around unrestrained. Or maybe I consciously ignore the evidence of warfare because I know it is something I do not want to remember.

While I stay quiet, Catherine speaks into a reporter's microphone. "At first we didn't know what they wanted of us and that scared us," she says.

"What are you going to do now?" another reporter asks.

"Now I am going to thank God and have a bath," she says. Her answer will become the *New York Times* Quotation of the Day, which my father will clip and save forever.

When a young boy chimes in that "the reason everybody got scared was that they went up and down the aisle with their guns," Catherine tells him firmly to be quiet, believing that information too incendiary. Not only are the men still missing, but Catherine had spied the young woman still inside the airplane, and Foozie and Mimi and the young woman who knows Arabic have not shown up at the hotel. In my diary I write, "When we got inside, Catherine & I were interviewed by *Time* magazine & later by the *New York Times*!!!!"

After the reporters leave the two of us alone, we remain in the lobby, wondering when we can go home, or if we cannot leave right away, where we will sleep that night. We want to call our parents, but there does not seem to be any way to do that. Lavish amounts of food stretch out before us, so we help ourselves and make our way to a pocket of serenity, a terrace with dark red cloths covering a row of tables adorned with vases of flowers. Waiters wear red jackets. Men wear suits. Incongruously, guests relax, sipping drinks and smoking. Catherine feels relieved and numb. In my diary I write, "We had a nutritious meal!" and then add, having listened to the ruckus around me, "I think they blew up TWA. Gosh!"

Reunited with our suitcases, Catherine and I leave the Intercontinental with a group of girls and women. We are shown to a second-floor room at the Shepherd Hotel, along with Susie and two others from our plane: a thirteen-year-old girl and a woman who celebrated her twenty-eighth birthday in the desert. Five beds have been crowded into the chamber, but the ceilings are high and the stone floor refreshingly cold. A balcony looks out over the street, and best of all, we each take a turn soaking in the tub. I drop my red-and-gold bell-bottoms into a wastebasket. I feel sad that my favorite pair of pants are too dust-infested ever to wear again, but I also know that I would never want to wear them again anyway.

Someone has instructed us not to stand out on the balcony because of the fighting in the streets and to lie on the floor if we hear gunfire. Later that night we disobey, watching distant flashes of orange from the balcony. In my diary, I make no mention of the sounds of war.

Susie is preoccupied, distressed to be apart from her two younger brothers, who have been taken to a different hotel. The other girl in our room, forlorn too, tells us that her mother died less than a year earlier. The woman, whose husband is missing, keeps to herself. Overlooking the anguish of my companions, I write in my diary that we four girls sang songs and talked. I judge the evening to be "really nice" and write that I miss Gerry, wondering if he knows what happened to me. Then, in an effort to appear less frivolous, I cross out Gerry's name and substitute my father, mother, and stepmother.

When the telephone rings at 6:15 the next morning, Susie answers to find someone from TWA on the line. "We're leaving at seven thirty for New York," she announces, and I record in my diary that we all "scrambled to get ready." In another van of released hostages, a Jordanian soldier again at the wheel, we ride this time to the Amman airport. On the way, our driver informs us that we will be flying only to Cyprus that day, but I do not let that diminish my good cheer.

"We took an AIRPLANE, not a JET," I tell my diary. "Catherine, Sue & her 2 brothers & I were sent to the Regina Palace!" I find the name of the Nicosia hotel enchanting, and Catherine finds the pink bougainvillea cascading down the sand-colored walls beautiful. Someone directs the two of us to a special room where operators plug wires into a switchboard. Neither Catherine nor I, nor my father nor my stepmother, will remember anything about that phone conversation. We call our mother too, and none of us will remember much about that either, except that my mother remembers Catherine saying she had to go because a reporter wanted to interview her. My mother also remembers that it was too late for her to come see us in Cyprus, since we would be flying home to New York the next day, plus she had the new baby.

The clusters of exclamation points in my diary signal my relief and delight, even though by now Catherine and I know that, along with the missing men, five girls and women from our flight are unaccounted for. In a letter to God that I record in my diary, I express gratitude that Catherine and I are free, then plead for the remaining hostages, then thank God again. Ever perplexed about how to ask a divine favor, I cross out the prayer. "Now, the only thing I want," I write, "is that the men return & Foozie & the 4 other girls." We know nothing of their fate, and no one else does either.

For the TWA flight to New York on Monday morning, September 14, Catherine and I choose identical favorite dresses from our suitcases, sleeveless navy-blue mini shifts. The aircraft's unsoiled interior seems remarkable, the airplane food tastes like paradise, and we revel in the complimentary treats: slippers and candy for everyone, toys for the little children, drinks for the grown-ups. As we reboard after a stopover in Rome, Catherine and I laugh with the others when a little boy delights in greeting the captain with the words, "Hi, Jack!" Just before takeoff, two crew members tear up the aisle to knock on the cockpit door, calling out, "Open up, open up!" Hearts pound as visions of the hijackers replay in our collective minds, but it turns out only that one of the aircraft doors is not properly latched. "You've got to be very careful with this group," a passenger warns. "Don't do that again!"

The movie, free this time, is *Tell Me That You Love Me, Junie Moon*, starring Liza Minnelli as a disfigured burn victim searching for a soulmate. With her short dark hair, forthright manner, and unconventional life, she reminds me of my mother, and I study Junie Moon all through the film, her grit mixing with her despair.

We are about to touch down. It is just after midnight in New York, which is early morning in Jordan. Had it been another day in the desert, the hostages' breakfast and sanitation committees would be getting started, the rising sun just beginning to bake the airplane. But we are not in the desert anymore. As we taxi into Kennedy Airport, I open my diary. "As the wheels hit the ground great cheers & clapping arose," I write. "It was so great."

I envision seeing my father instantly, but relatives who have come to meet the hostages are nowhere in sight. Instead, there are two ways to proceed. If you want, you can enter an enclosed room with bright lights and cameras. Inside, there is a press conference already under way, and I see a young boy in a red turtleneck and horn-rimmed glasses speaking into TV-station microphones. Or you can keep walking, through a sealed corridor where, for once, no reporters can intrude. Catherine and I keep walking, through the red-carpeted passageway with its curving walls, surveying the chaotic crowd in the waiting area ahead. I catch sight of the youngest unaccompanied child from our plane, a six-year-old girl, who has just found her parents. She is clutching a stuffed animal nearly too large for her grasp, and I feel a jab of sadness that her parents had to give her a big present.

I see my father before he sees us. His expression is serious, and he is so pale that the words *white as a sheet* leap into my mind. Then he sees us and bolts forward, and Catherine sees him too, his expression changing instantly from grave to beaming, now waving at us wildly. Catherine waves back before the uneasiness comes over her. She has never seen him so gaunt, his eyes two dark circles from afar. He breaks into a run, and so do we, the scene I had imagined so many times coming to life. My father folds his arms around both of us at the same time.

"Oh, Dad!" Catherine says. "We were so worried about you!"

My stepmother stands by, astonished that the two of us are so calm, "no crying, no tears, ready to go." ("Nothing about him," said the aviator in *The Little Prince*, "gave any suggestion of a child lost in the middle of the desert.")

In bed that first night, I try to silence the hum inside my head that replicates the sensation of a low-flying airplane: a buzzing and an ever-so-slight side-to-side motion. I will stay mostly in bed for nearly a week, each day and night a counterweight to each of the days and nights in the desert. Staring at the cracked plaster of my bedroom ceiling, where I long ago invented a map of imaginary islands and waterways, I lie there with the hum, my tiny room a hovering aircraft carrying me nowhere.

"There are millions of things I want to tell you," I wrote to Jody in August. "Let's have a date and tell each other lots of things that we won't tell the other girls." I assured her I would tell her "EVERYTHING in detail in September," but after I get home, in the early morning hours of Tuesday, September 15, I no longer want to tell Jody *everything*, that expansive promise suddenly far too carefree to encompass all that has since come to pass. Jody has seen the TWA passenger list in the *New York Times*, where Catherine and I were listed as "Hodes, Miss" and "Hodes (child)," and now she takes to calling me Hodes-Child, which we both find amusing. It is a way to acknowledge *everything* without talking about anything.

So many people call during those first days at home—relatives, friends from school, family friends and acquaintances—that my father has to take the telephone receiver off the hook "and just quiet things down," Catherine says, because we are "having a hard time getting our equilibrium back." Everyone wants to know what happened up in the air and in the desert. If I had to, I could talk about the friends we made, the nice Palestinian doctor and the nice commando who jumped rope with the children, even the scarcity of food and the disgusting bathrooms.

People want to know about the most harrowing parts too, though: the deadlines our captors imposed and the attendant threats to our lives. Those are the parts I do not want to talk about. When I think back now, conjuring those first days at home, lying in my bed, I have no memory of knowing about any of that.

Part Two

NEVER COMING BACK

4

When my parents found out that our plane had been hijacked, did either of them consider why their children had boarded a plane, alone, to travel from Tel Aviv to New York in the first place?

After Catherine and I returned home, letters with our mother would mention the hijacking only obliquely. When I ask, so many decades later, what September 6, 1970, was like for her, she recalls the experience as best she can. My stepfather, also a dancer, was at rehearsal. My mother was at home with her new baby, reading the Sunday *Jerusalem Post*, Israel's modest six- or eight-page English-language newspaper. Perusing that day's issue, I see that she would have read reports of "Jordanian-terrorist" clashes, scattered gunfire in the city of Amman, and army artillery fire aimed at a Palestinian refugee camp, with the *Post* harshly criticizing King Hussein I of Jordan for yielding to the Palestinian resistance. Later, on the radio, she heard a BBC announcement that an El Al flight had foiled a hijacking.

Thank God the children aren't on El Al, she thought.

Then the telephone rang. That's her most vivid memory.

"This is TWA calling," a woman's voice said. "Are you the mother of two unaccompanied children, Catherine Hodes and Martha Hodes, on TWA Flight 741?"

"Yes," my mother said, "I am."

"I regret to inform you that the flight"—the words well up from my mother's memory so many years later—"is being diverted by unknown hostile persons."

"What does *that* mean?" my mother asked.

"The flight is in the process of being hijacked."

"No," my mother corrected the caller, "that was an El Al flight." *What an idiot*, she thought, furious at such inconsiderate carelessness. *Calling me by mistake, as if my children were on that flight!*

"No," the woman countered, "both planes were involved in"—again the words rise from my mother's memory—"interrupted flight plans."

There couldn't be two hijacked planes, my mother insisted to herself, still irritated, but the woman kept talking. The information had not yet been released to news sources, but TWA was informing relatives of the passengers, and the airline promised to remain in contact. No one knew the plane's altered destination.

Frantic now, my mother called my stepfather, who immediately returned from the studio. Together with the baby, they hurried to the American embassy, a massive concrete citadel a fifteen-minute walk toward the beach. My mother had frequented the embassy while pregnant, ordering hamburgers and milkshakes from the restaurant and settling into the reading room filled with English-language magazines. That Sunday, a man in charge of the families of hijacked American passengers helped my mother call my father in New York.

Suddenly it seemed as if all Tel Aviv knew that Linda Hodes's daughters were being held hostage on a hijacked plane in the Jordan desert. Dancers, friends, neighbors, and acquaintances streamed into the apartment, bestowing food, extending condolences, milling about, and speculating as to our fates. As everyone conversed in rapid Hebrew, my mother retreated to the bedroom with the baby. My stepfather, serene by nature, alternately played host to the visitors and stole into the bedroom to try to calm her down. So as not to think about the planes blowing up, my mother wondered whether we were hungry or cold and hoped that we hadn't witnessed any violence in the air or on the ground. Now her poor little perditas were truly lost.

The whole scene—confined inside the apartment, with a ceaseless stream of guests depositing heaps of food—made it feel as if she were caught unawares in the Jewish ritual of shiva, where mourners stay home for seven days while friends and neighbors visit, bearing meals.

"It felt as if you were already dead," she tells me.

As for my father, I already know most of his story. Across the years he has formulated a narrative and stuck to it, and when I ask again, he easily recites it. In his story, he is calm and in control.

Sunday, September 6, was going to be a full day. My father had recently created Ballet Team as a young-audience company, which meant rising before dawn to bring his show into schools, getting disadvantaged kids interested in dance. On Labor Day weekend the company was doing something different, performing at the New York Dance Festival in Central Park. The skies were fair, perfect for an afternoon at the outdoor Delacorte Theater, and my father's eleven dancers would open the Sunday matinee. As soon as they were off-stage and his equipment packed up, he'd drive out to Kennedy Airport to pick up his girls.

Coffee brewing, he caught a news break on the radio: TWA Flight 714 had been hijacked. He consulted his appointment book just to be sure, relieved to find that our flight number was close but not the same. Then came a second news break. Correction: TWA Flight 741.

Immediately my father dialed the airline. Someone confirmed the hijacking out of Frankfurt and gave him a special telephone line with operators available around the clock. Soon he had three phone numbers: the airline, with the names of three people assigned to track all the passengers; the State Department; and the Red Cross. Decades later, in a soot-smothered carton in my father's self-storage unit, I unearth a folder labeled "Hijack," into which my father had slipped a scrap of paper, the names and numbers captured in his neat hand.

TWA—OX5-6700 ext. 2620, D. Turner, Miss Hundley, Mr. Dolman.

These were Dee Turner, Judith Hundley, and Don Dolman, three among the many reservation agents who hastily volunteered to run the improvised "hijack desk" at the airline's midtown Manhattan offices. Every couple of hours, each volunteer was to call designated relatives to deliver any new information or correct any media inaccuracies. The volunteers reassured the families and, one explained, "on occasion, cried with them." Dreading the possibility of bad tidings, some wondered how they might convey the worst news possible.

State Dept.—202-632-3172, Mr. Davis.

That was Lieutenant General Benjamin O. Davis Jr., retired Air Force officer and a pilot who commanded the all-Black Tuskegee Airmen in World War II, becoming the highest-ranking African American in the armed forces. Within weeks of the hijacking, President Nixon would appoint Davis as director of civil aviation security at the US Department of Transportation.

Red Cross—Mr. Bighinatti, 202-857-3535.

This was Enso Bighinatti, a disaster relief specialist with the Red Cross. Also a World War II vet, he served as a radio gunner on a B-24 bomber and was held prisoner of war after Germans shot down his plane.

My father wanted to fly to Jordan. He wanted to travel out to the desert, find us, and take us home. Where to turn? He called Martha Graham, his dear friend from the many years he served as a principal in her modern dance company. Martha in turn called Baroness Bethsabée de Rothschild in Israel, who offered to pay my father's airfare.

The phone rang, my mother calling from the American embassy in Tel Aviv. She thought my father would have more information because the American press was less secretive than the Israeli press, but my father thought my mother would have more information because Israel was closer to Jordan. The man at the American embassy told my father not to travel to Jordan—it was far better to let unaccompanied children fade into the background. Someone at the State Department, maybe Benjamin Davis, agreed, ultimately convincing my father that such a move would only call unnecessary attention to us. Nor would it do any good for the hijackers to learn that Catherine and I possessed even the most remote proximity to Rothschild wealth, absurd as that was, given the stack of unpaid bills in my father's dilapidated New York apartment.

My father decided to go on with the show. He owned two transistor radios, and New York had two all-news stations, so while he packed up costumes and props he tuned one radio to each station and listened to both at the same time, learning the fates of the Swissair, El Al, and Pan Am flights. Driving to Central Park in his red Volkswagen bus, he decided to keep the news from his dancers. They had a performance to do, and there was no sense distracting them.

I'd heard this story from my father a great many times across the years when I located one of the dancers who had performed that day. Clay Taliaferro, a sensitive six-foot-five company member who grew up in Virginia in the 1940s with only segregated schools and theaters available to him, went on to a distinguished career as a principal with the José Limón Dance Company. I phrased my question to Clay this way: "On Sunday, September 6, 1970, Ballet Team performed a matinee at the Delacorte Theater in Central Park. On that same day, my sister and I were on a hijacked plane. Does that ring any bells for you?" In response, Clay told me his own story.

That afternoon in Central Park, he saw something unusual in my father: a forced smile, a too-intense focus, a hint of frenetic movement as he set up the stage. *This is not our Stuart*, Clay thought. The other dancers could tell something was wrong too. At first some of them wondered if they had done something to make my father angry, but among themselves they noted the morning's shocking news reports and confirmed that Stuart's daughters were in Israel for the summer, coming home to start school. Worried, they worked extra hard to get everything right in each dance.

But my father hadn't said anything, so the dancers didn't bring it up either. After the show, following my father's lead, they asked him to join them for a meal.

"I'd love to," he said, "but I have to go home to keep tabs on the hijacking. My daughters are on one of those planes."

So it was true. "You let us do the show without even mentioning that your daughters had been hijacked!"

"I could see no good reason not to," my father said, taking refuge in the imperative that the show must go on.

I have another interpretation, though. Dance was, for my father, both solace and prayer. If his daughters were to die, the world would stop. If he kept going, if dancers kept on dancing, the world would not stop, and his daughters would come home.

Years later, Clay describes my father's demeanor that day as "searching for some way to be with his daughters, somewhere far, far away." As for the Ballet Team dancers, Clay says, "We all were Stuart that afternoon."

Early along in our conversations, my mother tells me that she felt she had brought this misfortune upon us, which means she had in fact been thinking, back then, about why Catherine and I were on that plane. If my father felt any bitterness toward my mother for creating the circumstances that made Catherine and me hostages in the desert, he never admitted those feelings to me, nor, I am sure, to himself.

What about me? Talking with my parents, I wonder: Sitting inside an airplane, held hostage in the desert, did I think about why Catherine and I had to board that plane from Tel Aviv to New York?

My family was different from other families, different even from my few friends whose parents were also divorced, since those friends lived with their mothers. Among the mothers who attended school events and parent-teacher conferences, or who dropped off and picked up kids from birthday parties, Stuart was often the sole father. As one of my elementary school friends told me many years later, "I think the fact that your parents lived in two different countries was almost as strange to me as your being hijacked." Since my parents almost never talked with us about the divorce and their subsequent arrangement, it was easiest to dismiss uncomfortable emotions that none of us wanted to acknowledge anyway. By the time I boarded the flight home from Israel at twelve years old, I was adept at banishing disagreeable feelings.

My mother's childhood was not happy. It took her own mother, Lily, so long to get dressed in the morning that even a little girl mesmerized by her neglectful parent eventually lost interest. Although Lily Margolies clad herself in stockings, slip, suit, knotted scarf, and jewelry, she mostly stayed home, reading the *New York Times* in an armchair by the fourth-floor window of 15 West Eleventh Street, rising only to refill her scotch and soda. Over the years, the drinks became straight scotches—"her eraser of choice," my mother called it. Lily puffed on cigarettes through an elegant cigarette holder, and at Schrafft's she cut her cold cheese sandwich with a knife and fork, in white-gloved hands. She was, my mother once said, a polite guest in her own life.

My mother's father, Bert, worked in public relations for a garment workers' union, then took his skills to United Artists and Alfred Hitchcock ("Hitch," my grandparents called him). Sometimes he was a delightful parent, entertaining the children with wordplay ("Finitch your spinach!"). Mostly, though, he was tyrannical, making dinnertime a cycle of criticism: of Lily, of the children, of the whole world ("Ignoramuses, Stalinists, and pansies!"). For each of her husband's affairs, Lily extracted a new dress.

Young Linda found a surrogate mother at the modern dance studio a block away. There she saw a pale woman with dark hair, red lips, and reddened eyes that made it seem as if she had been crying. To the nine-year-old girl, she was a tragic and alluring Snow White. "Do you know what *Linda* means?" Martha Graham spoke directly to the little girl, not to the girl's mother, who had brought her there. "It means *beautiful* in Spanish." When this fantastic woman took the little girl's hand, the girl thought, *If she were to kiss me I might fall asleep for a hundred years*, reversing the effects of the prince's kiss in the tale of Sleeping Beauty. Every day at the Dalton School, Linda awaited Saturday's dance class, where Martha Graham patiently encouraged her. By the time Linda was sixteen, she was taking three dance classes a week.

When Martha Graham inscribed a book to Lily and Bert years later, she wrote, "Deep gratitude for the gift of lovely Linda," and some years after that, in *The Notebooks of Martha Graham*, "With deep affection and eternal gratitude for Linda." My mother would say of Martha Graham, "She is the most important person in my life, and I can say that without any reservations."

Even though my father's childhood was troubled, his outlook on life inclined toward joy.

"Did you have a happy childhood?" I once asked Uncle Alfred.

"No." Alfred stole a glance at his older brother. The three of us were having breakfast at a neighborhood diner.

"Did *he* have a happy childhood?" I flicked a thumb at my father.

"Evidently, he did," my uncle said, the two of us laughing at my father's invincible optimism, his indomitable powers of denial.

"I did." My father beamed, missing the joke.

When the boys were young, the family moved to Miami Beach, where their father, Jack, opened a real estate business. When the marriage foundered, their mother, Kate, took her two young sons back to Brooklyn, and when a devastated seven-year-old Alfred announced that he didn't have a father anymore, his aunts and uncles told him, "Sure you have a father. He's 1400 miles away!" Stuart, on the other hand, accepted the circumstances, content with the explanation that his dad's hearing loss kept him in the warm southern climate.

Kate was a lover of the arts, a moral vegetarian, a sometime socialist, and a permissive parent. When one of her boys came home with a poor grade in math, she told him, "When you grow up, you'll buy an adding machine." When Alfred dared his older brother to pour ketchup on his head, then turned to their mother in outrage, she shrugged and said, "You dared him." Despite raising her boys during the Great Depression, she pressed them to forget about money and pursue what they loved.

At Brooklyn Tech high school, Stuart was a self-described "half nerd, half jock," the borough's champion backstroker, studying engineering and playing the violin. In a class picture he stands amid a cohort of scowling boys, the only face lit up with a show-biz smile. He'd just turned seventeen when the Japanese bombed Pearl Harbor, and after a semester at Brooklyn College he was thrilled to be drafted. In combat only a few months before the war ended, he flew seven missions in a B-17, dropping bombs on retreating German forces in Italy. Stuart loved being a pilot, "eighteen years old and heading into the unknown," as he put it. When he returned from a year in the army of occupation, a friend told him about the dancer Martha Graham, and in 1946, at the age of twenty-one, he signed up for his first class. A year later he left college to join the company. It was at the Graham studio that he met Linda Margolies.

"All my love on your beautiful day and for your wonderful life," Martha Graham wrote on my parents' wedding day in 1953, presenting them with a jade Chinese ornament, the symbol for double happiness. The newlyweds moved into a dark ground-floor apartment at 73 Saint Marks Place in the East Village. Stuart was twenty-eight, Linda twenty-one.

The critics called Stuart a magnificent dancer, but company members were paid only for performances, so he also had to work as a "chorus gypsy" on Broadway and beyond. "Wish I could buy you everything," he wrote to Linda when he was out of town, dancing in previews of the musical *Paint Your Wagon.* "Help me to get so good that we'll be everything together." In return, Linda drew two identical figures with the caption, "I'm beside myself," and finished the sentence inside the card: "with love."

My parents rehearsing on a hillside.
[Gertrude Shurr]

Linda joined the Graham Company too, and in 1954 they boarded the *Queen Elizabeth* for the company's European tour. Modern dance was still controversial, but audiences came around. Katharine Hepburn "can't do enough for us," Linda wrote to her parents, "tooting our horn all over town." In Amsterdam "there was a riot to get in," she boasted. "The police were called and the curtain held up almost an hour." They danced in Stockholm, Copenhagen, and Paris, then "opened with a terrific bang" in Zurich, audiences demanding "6 or 7 curtain calls for every number."

As cultural ambassadors for the State Department, the Graham Company soon brought Stuart and Linda to Asia, where Graham's insistence on dance as a universal language contributed to the tour's phenomenal success. The last stop was Israel, a special engagement paid for by company patron Bethsabée de Rothschild. Performances sold out, and Tel Aviv impressed Linda as a "white and pink sparkling city on the edge of an aqua sea." It was 1956. *Israel and I are not done with each other*, Linda thought.

Back in New York, Stuart danced in the Ziegfeld Follies and taught at the Martha Graham School of Contemporary Dance and at Juilliard, as well as in New Jersey and Philadelphia. "I miss you more and more each day," Linda wrote when Stuart was away on a job. When she signed off with "good night Darling Darling Darling Darling," she effused too about "your wonderful money order." On the road, Stuart wrote, "All that I can keep in my mind is the music and missing you and dinner, and you, and the show tonight and I love you."

After Catherine was born my parents left the decrepit East Village for more space in the midtown neighborhood of Murray Hill. Standing on a corner at the bottom of the hill, the "seedy" building offered "a rundown six-room apartment on the fifth floor," as my mother saw it, with "an ancient bathroom, rickety floors, bad wiring, and roaches." To pay the bills, my father danced at the Latin Quarter nightclub in Times Square, playing an army sergeant and a genie, and in a Broadway musical it was his "honor and pleasure," he would say, "to hold Carol Burnett in my arms for three seconds, eight times a week." The biggest allure of Broadway, though, was getting paid well just to dance.

After nearly twelve years with Martha Graham, it was time for my father to support his family with better-paying work in the dance world. Martha asked him to perform one last time, as the Husbandman in the film *Appalachian Spring*, and during the hour I was born my father was partnering with Martha herself, the two playing bride and groom to Aaron Copland's score. When my father told her the new baby's name, she said only, "*Martha* is a very dangerous name."

Within months, my mother accepted the invitation to tour Israel with the Graham company in a five-week run for the tenth anniversary of that nation's founding. Performing the major roles was thrilling: the Woman in White in *Diversion of Angels*, Eve in *Embattled Garden*, Cassandra in Graham's monumental *Clytemnestra*. The reviews were stupendous. My parents' marriage was faltering, but the letters my mother wrote from Israel were happy.

"I feel very grateful for what you've given Linda," my father wrote in a letter he drafted to Martha Graham while my mother was away. He then crossed out those words and substituted the more circumspect "For now I want you to know how grateful I am." He hoped Linda would bring her newfound happiness back home, but their lives had been "turned inside out," he confided. He crossed that out too, substituting, "After all, apart we have been together—together we are always somewhere apart." That he crossed out as well, finally simply thanking Martha "for what you have given Linda." All of that was followed by the admission, "I won't say there haven't been moments when one more wet diaper would have destroyed me."

Away from her husband and children, my mother flourished. If home and husband felt like prison, dancing was her jailbreak. Coming of age just after World War II, surrounded by idealized images of happy homemakers, she wondered if it was abnormal to spend her few extra dollars on a leotard instead of a cookbook. Yet my mother was not as abnormal as she was made to feel. Just before she got pregnant with Catherine, *Ladies' Home Journal* published "The Plight of the Young Mother," detailing the draining and isolated days and nights of women with young children. Soon *McCall's* published "The Mother Who Ran Away"—the policeman who picked her up called her "just another runaway wife." For the *Redbook* magazine feature "Why Young Mothers Feel Trapped," nearly fifty thousand readers wrote in to describe all manner of discontent: wishing to terminate a pregnancy, feeling like nothing without an artistic career, even disliking their own children. Other women shared my mother's unhappiness for sure, but my mother's decisions would have been unconventional in any era. ("Go and look again at the roses," said the fox to the little prince. "You will understand now that yours is unique in all the world.")

To help with the children when my mother was away, my father

Catherine and me in Central Park, New York City, 1960s.
[STUART HODES]

employed Mary Gallagher, a small woman of comfortable girth who spoke with an Irish brogue and had no family in the United States. Catherine and I loved Mary, who let us light candles inside Our Lady of the Scapular Chapel of the Sacred Hearts of Jesus and Mary a few blocks from home. She would share our care with my father for many years.

Soaking up the onstage elation, my mother kept touring with the Graham Company. She would go away, come home, and go away again. "I think my children are the most wonderful, the best looking, the smartest, and the most awe-inspiring children in the world," she would recall. "Yet it is as though they are not connected to me. They come to see the show at a matinee wearing lovely clothes that I swear I have never seen before. They meet the cast, charm everyone and are whisked home to do whatever it is they do there. I think about taking them to dinner between shows, but somehow never get around to asking if this is all right. All right with whom? I am afraid to answer my own questions."

While my mother was away on tour, my father met Elizabeth Wullen. It was 1963, and both were chorus dancers in a Broadway musical about vaudeville. My father and Liz were dance partners, and as rehearsals progressed, they began to fall for each other. In a cabaret scene, the chorus dancers mimed drinking and conversing, and one night Stuart mimed to Liz the words "I love you." She mimed back, "I love you too," but they left it at that. After all, my father was still a married man, even if his marriage had long been deteriorating.

The show flopped (the *New York Times* called it "a musical of shattering dullness," *Variety* "an elaborate dud"), but Stuart and Liz kept working together. When my father got a gig as a choreographer for the Santa Fe Opera, he invited Liz to dance as a soloist. Working back in New York as assistant choreographer for *To Broadway with Love* (the "Musical Show of the Century") at the 1964 World's Fair, he invited Liz to audition, and she got that part too. As deeply as my father had loved my mother, in Liz he'd found something more. "Truly Elizabeth, my own heart's love," he wrote to her, "I am happy to find that I can bring you a love I have never had for any other person," for everything that had come before was "preliminary to the love I feel for you."

Right around the same time, Martha Graham brought my mother to Israel again—and again with the assistance of patron Bethsabée de Rothschild. A member of the French banking dynasty, Bethsabée had left Paris as a young woman, just ahead of the 1940 Nazi invasion, and the new nation of Israel, she decided, needed a modern dance company of its own. For the first time, Martha Graham would allow another company to perform her choreography, and Bethsabée sought a dancer who could spend a few weeks in Israel teaching Graham's works. It was Graham herself who suggested Linda Hodes.

"Among the teachers and choreographers who arrived was one of Graham's most gifted dancers—Linda Hodes," a company historian later wrote. My mother was to teach *Diversion of Angels*, about the rapture and sorrow of first love; *Embattled Garden*, about the Garden of Eden; and *Cave of the Heart*, about the Greek figure Medea, who, as a program note explained, "destroyed her children and left Corinth in a chariot drawn by dragons." I was six years old, Catherine seven.

Landing in Israel this time, my mother, thirty-three years old, saw a panorama of sand and sea that promised freedom from the troubles at home. The jasmine-scented air felt soothing. The spare, clean apartment that had been arranged for her contrasted strikingly with the grime

and clutter at home. She was still jet-lagged when the handsome dancer
Ehud Ben-David struck up a conversation with her at a party. They kept
talking as they crossed the street to the Mediterranean, kicked off their
shoes, and walked to the water's edge. Back at her apartment, Ehud
kissed my mother on the cheek and asked what she was doing the next
day. Bethsabée was taking her to the beach in Netanya, my mother said,
up the coast from Tel Aviv. That was Ehud's hometown, and he quickly
devised a plan.

I am a million miles from New York, my mother told herself that night.
*Without a phone, radio, or television. In a country not my own. With a com-
pany not yet in existence.* She missed her children dreadfully, in a "visceral
way," but her life as a dancer was everything to her. On the Netanya
beach with Bethsabée the next day, Ehud suddenly appeared, and then
Bethsabée abruptly had to leave, and then Ehud said he would bring
Linda back to Tel Aviv. At dinner that evening, my mother told him
about her faltering marriage and her two little girls back in New York.
Within weeks, Ehud moved in. My mother had left one man for another,
but without the entrapment of children, she and Ehud could thrive
together in the exhilarating world of a young modern dance company
halfway around the world from home. Ehud was soon to become the
country's lead male dancer, and a *New York Times* critic would call him
"one of the finest modern dancers of our time."

Three weeks turned into five, then more. Bethsabée renamed herself
Batsheva, which was the name of the new company too, and my mother
wanted to be there when the Batsheva Dance Company premiered in
December 1964. It was "cutting into my heart," she remembered, "to be
such a neglectful mother." All too aware of her absence in our lives, even
when at home, she consoled herself by wondering whether Catherine
and I even missed her. Knowing that our father and Mary were entirely
devoted to us, it seemed plausible to her that we did not.

"School is fine," I wrote on a postcard. "How is the company? Catherine got goldfish for her birthday. Hope you are having fun."

Then, after a hugely successful premiere, Bethsabée de Rothschild
asked my mother to join the company permanently, as dancer, teacher,
and rehearsal director—in time she would serve as an artistic director

too. Bethsabée also assured my mother that Israel was a wonderful place to raise children.

"Linda has had an offer to stay there," my father wrote in a letter to Mary. "She hasn't yet decided what to do. Since I know that I cannot possibly get along without Catherine and Martha, if Linda decides to stay in Israel, the girls will stay with me. That is how it is, and there is no other alternative, unless Linda decides to stay here too." Linda, he explained to Mary, "loves the excitement of the world of dance even more than I do," since for him, home meant more "than dancing, or choreography, or all the excitement put together." Years later, he remembered my mother's response like this: "They could live with you if you get someone nice to marry you, and I can have them sometimes."

My mother flew to New York to sign the papers. In the semipoetic language of the law, the cause of my parents' formal separation was "disputes and unhappy differences." My father paid no alimony and had exclusive custody of his daughters, with visits to and from my mother permitted. Of returning to Israel, my mother said, "I cleaned up all of that mess, and then I went back."

All of this happened around me, but no one explained much of it to my sister and me. At twelve years old, sitting inside the airplane in the desert, mostly I knew that my parents were divorced and that my mother lived in Israel, and that's why Catherine and I were flying from Tel Aviv to New York on Sunday, September 6, 1970.

5

Did I wonder why my mother lived so far away that we only got to spend summers with her? Did I wonder why my family was unlike my friends' families?

On the plane Catherine and I were different from our fellow hostages. The group included Orthodox Jews and Jews who had rejected their Orthodox upbringing, religious Zionists and socialist Zionists, but the two of us may have been the most secular of all.

Both of my father's parents, born in New York City to immigrants from the Austro-Hungarian Empire, were, in the words of his brother, "world-class, non-practicing Jews." As for my mother's parents, both born to Eastern European immigrants, they strove for complete assimilation. My grandmother refashioned herself from Libbie Yetta to Lily Yvette, and as part of that transformation spoke with a British accent. "Oh, dahling," she would say, followed by a faux-English chuckle, "hoh hoh hoh." (Would she talk like she was born on the Lower East Side, my sister and I wondered, if we woke her up in the middle of the night?) Before my maternal grandparents moved to Israel, Catherine and I dined with them every Sunday, Lily preparing a ham by pressing whole cloves into the mound of *treyf* meat. She took us shopping for Easter hats at B. Altman on Fifth Avenue, and at Christmas I marveled at the miniature tree she decorated with tasteful blue and silver baubles. Neither of my parents attended Hebrew school as children, and no one had a bar mitzvah.

Our reason for traveling to Israel also made Catherine and me different from our fellow Jewish hostages: the only reason we were going to Israel was to visit our mother. The 1967 war marked the start of a decade of American Jews' intense loyalty and affection directed toward the emergent nation, with progressives viewing the victors as a model society, marveling that women joined the military. American Jews flocked to Israel in those years, including young people captivated by the counterculture, eager to experience life on a kibbutz, the young country's special brand of communal farms. Tourists thronged the territories wrested from Jordan in the war: the Old City of Jerusalem, including the Western Wall, and the holy sites of Hebron, Jericho, and Bethlehem on the West Bank. No one ever took Catherine and me to those sites, and where other American Jews who moved to Israel in the mid-1960s were making aliyah—the Hebrew word means "ascent" or "repatriation"—my mother's newfound love of country arose strictly from the opportunity to escape American domesticity. "Though of Jewish extraction," wrote a dance historian, Linda Hodes had "never been interested in Israel or Zionism."

The deep connection that Catherine and I felt to Israel came from the summers we spent there. If New York was home, Tel Aviv was a close second.

"I miss you a lot but I'm having A LOT of FUN so don't worry," Catherine wrote to our father one summer, in words that spoke for both of us.

*Our shared passport for our earliest trips to Israel. We never retrieved
the passport confiscated by the Popular Front commandos.*

[Author Photo]

"Not much more to say, except of course about all the swimming, movies, shopping, eating out, visiting new people, going with our friends, etc." Or as she wrote in another letter: "*I feel so free!*"

We had visited our mother for the first time, flying alone, when I was in first grade, Catherine in third. It was 1965, my parents were legally separated, and my father agreed that my mother could have us for six months, just this one time. For the nonstop flight we earned certificates from El Al, proclaiming our journey "one of the longest scheduled flights in the history of civil aviation."

My mother wanted us to get to know Ehud, so as soon as we arrived she sent the three of us out together. Catherine and I walked on either side of him, each holding a hand, astonished as he paid for something with Israeli bills that came in different colors. When he produced a pink ten-lira note, it was as if he had performed a magic trick. Ehud laughed warmly at our wonder. We liked him.

Our one-bedroom ground-floor flat at 19 Ben-Zion had no toaster or television, but the furniture was mod, with lots of bright Marimekko fabric. Catherine and I slept in the living room alcove, in beds that my mother had arranged head-to-head. Shutters opened onto the building's back garden, with pink, yellow, and white lantana that we threaded together to make necklaces and headbands. The shutters made it easy for neighborhood kids to come calling, and in the Hebrew we picked up quickly, we explained why we were there: "Mother—father—no love—mother in Israel—father in America." We made friends easily.

In Israel, my mother was happy. She made us French toast with a thick layer of sugar and cinnamon and invented a contest for the first one to reach a hundred mosquito bites. She showed us how to make miniature furniture out of matchboxes, taught us to crochet, and made us whole families of dolls out of colorful wool, ribbon, and buttons. We played her new record album, *Meet the Beatles*, thrilled that she and Ehud had really met the Beatles once, at a disco in London.

Tel Aviv in the late 1960s was a cosmopolitan city of four hundred thousand. With its broad boulevards designed to mirror a modern European city (it was founded in 1909 by Jewish newcomers to Palestine), guidebooks described it as bustling and booming, brash and noisy, "New

*My mother brushing
my hair in our Tel Aviv
apartment, 1960s. She
was happy in Israel.*
[EHUD BEN-DAVID]

York on the Mediterranean," Sodom compared to the holy city of Jerusalem. Ben-Zion, one of those boulevards, sloped upward with a central island of shade trees, and at the top stood Habima Garden, complete with a theater that hosted international dance companies.

To two kids from midtown Manhattan, Tel Aviv nonetheless felt old-fashioned, which we found appealing. Everything came to a halt from sundown on Friday to sundown on Saturday, even shops and city buses. On weekdays everything closed up between two and four in the afternoon, storefront blinds fastened tight against the Mediterranean sun. To our amazement, Sunday was a regular workday, and children went to school six days a week.

At the tiny grocery up the block, the owner would quaintly retrieve each item on our shopping list from the shelves behind the counter, and right next door stood an even more beguiling shop where Catherine and I picked out notebooks, pencils, hair clips, envelopes, and stamps. My mother called the grocer the Little Man and the general store proprietor the Little Lady. "It's not really that they're little," she would say, laughing. "It's just that their stores are." How much fun it was to share secret made-up names with my mother!

To finish out the school year, Catherine and I attended the English-speaking Tabeetha School, run by Scottish Christian missionaries in a

compound of Turkish Ottoman architecture amid the decaying buildings of nearby Jaffa. Teachers hit children's outstretched palms with rul-
ers (never us, for fear made us far too well-behaved), and we had to sit
through a class on the Scriptures ("Don't cringe at all this Jesus stuff,"
my mother joked in a letter to my father. "A little religion never hurt
anyone"). But school didn't last forever. Come summertime, we spent
weekdays at the Batsheva studio watching rehearsals and imitating the
moves on the Isamu Noguchi sets. The dancers adored us.

It never rained in Israel over the summer. On weekends we swam
in Bethsabée de Rothschild's pool, where Ehud would throw us off his
shoulders and perform outrageous dives that sent plumes of water onto
my mother and the other dancers bronzing their bikini-clad bodies.
Bethsabée, once married to Donald Bloomingdale of the department
store family (it was arranged, my mother explained to us years later, since
both were gay), lived in an ultramodern mansion filled with artwork by
the likes of Rembrandt and Kandinsky, but we rarely went inside, since
the pool deck had its own outdoor kitchen.

Other weekends we went to Netanya, where Ehud's parents lived in
an enchanting house at 53 Dizengoff, surrounded by fruit orchards. The
balcony, which Ehud's mother winsomely called the "veranda," looked
over a fish pond shaped like a fish, and horse-drawn carriages carrying
tourists would glide down the street, bells tinkling. Ehud's parents didn't
exactly approve of their son's romance with an older American divorcée
with two children, but they, along with our new aunt and uncle, treated
all of us with genuine love and kindness.

My mother rarely talked politics with Ehud, and none of the Ben-
Davids ever recounted their family history to Catherine and me: that
Ehud's father had attended the first Zionist Congress in Switzerland, in
1897, where Palestine was named the Jewish national homeland; that his
mother had lost her first sweetheart in the 1929 Palestinian uprising (a
history that could be told either as a morally indefensible massacre or a
morally justified rebellion against colonialism); that Ehud's parents both
joined the Haganah, the pre-1948 Zionist paramilitary organization that
fought Palestinians. We didn't know any of that.

Besides school, there were two other bad parts to our six-month stay in Israel. The first was that we missed our father terribly. Thinking about our return, I wrote to him, "We are so happy that we want to cry." The second was that my mother told us about their imminent divorce. Seated at the table in our narrow Tel Aviv kitchen, Catherine wept inconsolably while I remained silent, allowing her to emote for both of us. After we returned to New York, my father wondered, in a letter to my mother, if "things aren't completely clear to Martha yet." In fact, everything was clear. It was just that I preferred to entrust the display of feelings to my older sister.

That fall my mother came to New York for six weeks to dance in the Graham Company's 1965 season. Her portrayal of Cassandra in *Clytemnestra*, said the critics, was "eloquent," "remarkable," "brilliant." The whole season was a "wonderful triumph," with hundreds "turned away at every performance." On closing night, there were fourteen curtain calls and a seven-minute standing ovation. All of that represented the fulfillment of my mother's dedication and hard work since high school, maybe even since the day the fantastical Martha Graham had held the hand of nine-year-old Linda and told the little girl with an uncaring mother that her name meant *beautiful* in another language.

The divorce was finalized just before performances began, and as with the legal separation, the settlement gave custody to my father and visitation rights to my mother. Staying with her parents in Greenwich Village, my mother impressed upon my father that she wanted to see her daughters often. "I miss them very much," she confessed.

My father wanted so much to create a new family for Catherine and me. "Am I fooling myself," he asked Liz ("you, my darling Elizabeth"), or could there be a way to "create something out of what is normally a disaster to any child?" The day before the Graham season closed in New York, and a little more than two weeks after the divorce became official, he and Liz married. Liz wore a white satin minidress, and Catherine and I wore velvet flower-girl frocks. We liked Liz while she and my father were courting. She had a vibrant laugh and made a ritual of going out for hot fudge and butterscotch sundaes. But after she moved in, we objected to someone replacing our real mother. One day soon after the wedding, when Liz reprimanded us for playing too rowdily with our boy cousins, nine-year-old Catherine commanded, "Elizabeth Wullen, get the hell out of this house!"

When the Graham season ended and my mother got ready to return to Israel, I finally relented, joining Catherine in her grief. As my stepmother remembered the farewell scene, "You guys were howling."

After that first visit to Israel, Catherine and I went back every summer. Since there were no such things as video calls in those days, my mother didn't set eyes on her daughters for nearly a year at a time, finding us startlingly taller and more grown-up each successive June.

As we got older, Catherine and I stopped accompanying our mother to the dance studio. The days luxuriously stretching out before us, we'd order falafel at the stand down the hill, load up on candy from the kiosk at the top of the boulevard, then continue on to the serenity of Habima Garden to write poems together ("Let's do one about trees." "Okay, next let's do one about paths"). We'd stroll to Dizengoff Circle for ice cream or roam the streets carrying our stepfather's professional camera, focusing the viewfinder on a scruffy stray cat blinking in the sunlight or a withered old man dozing on a bench. We'd take the bus to the Gordon Pool, where we met boys who delighted in practicing their schoolroom English with us.

Our summertime best friend was Nurit, closer to Catherine's age, who lived on the top floor of our building. With her excellent English, she happily devised Hebrew lessons, correcting the vocabulary words I copied into a sky-blue notebook picked out at the Little Lady's. With the other kids, Catherine and I spoke a combination of English and Hebrew. One time we all had a big argument, "on account of all of us speaking different languages and not understanding each other," Catherine wrote to our father. "But now we are helping each other to learn the languages." With our friends, we sat every day on the set of white steps at 19 Ben-Zion, planning what to do next, while we played Israeli jacks. The game was called Five Stones, and the sharp corners of a new set of the golden cubes stung your palm, until by summer's end the points had worn down, smooth and rounded. Like everyone else, we napped in the afternoon in order to stay up late into the cooler nights, and on Fridays we went folk-dancing with our friends until midnight at Tel Aviv's *kikar*, the public square.

A special weekend destination was the hot-water beach, as my mother called it, where we'd perch atop a pile of rocks amid mysterious pipes discharging foamy warm water into the ocean (spewing from the city's electrical power plant, I'd learn later). When Ehud drove us to the prettier beaches in Netanya, Catherine and I played endless rounds of paddleball and leaped into gigantic waves. We built intricate sand castles and collected tiny shells to tape to the pages of the letters we wrote to our father. Sometimes we took longer weekend excursions as a family: to a Druze village in the mountains, where we gazed at the bright blue shutters painted to ward off evil, or to blissful Lake Tiberias; the whole day there, Catherine wrote to our father, was "glorious," as we "played on our big double raft in the water which was fresh, calm, and cool."

My mother and Ehud eventually married too, theirs a whim of a civil ceremony in London, while on tour. She was thirty-seven, he twenty-nine. One July day, on an early wedding anniversary, the four of us went to dinner in Jaffa. The city was sprucing up, especially down by the water. "We went to a beautiful place to eat," Catherine wrote to our father. "It overlooked the sea and we saw the sunset." With Magic Markers she drew a full-color replica, a table in front of a deep red half-dome sun dropping into inky ocean waters, then labeled each part of the drawing: *sunset, the sea, our table.*

My mother finally got a television set in 1969, just in time to watch that summer's moon landing, and a telephone in 1970, in time to call my father about their hijacked children.

Captive in the desert, I found that thoughts of home could bring solace as well as worry. When I envisioned myself at home, I saw the emerald-green drinking glasses in our New York kitchen. My mother had the same glasses in her Tel Aviv kitchen, only hers were aqua blue. When I arrived in Tel Aviv at the beginning of each summer, the blue ones looked so pretty. When I returned home, the green ones seemed more beautiful, and now I longed to see them again.

I missed our New York apartment, that ramshackle collection of rooms that embarrassed me in front of my friends, all except my best friend, Jody. (Once, when I asked my father what economic class we were, he said "artist class.") There were days I'd offer Catherine a dollar to turn on the kitchen light first, so I wouldn't have to contend with the stomach-heaving sight of skittering roaches. On the mornings my father got up early, I could hear him rhythmically thwacking away at the countertops. Still, I missed my tiny room, connected to Catherine's equally tiny room by a doorway with no door. I missed the wooden secretary that belonged to my mother when she was a child, where I completed my homework, then wrote stories and poems.

I visualized our apartment building, standing isolated on the corner, surrounded by a parking lot, and in my mind I wandered through the neighborhood. From my bedroom window I could see the north side of the side street, which shored up a line of tenements even more squalid than our six-story elevator building. If I looked the other way I could see across the avenue to the slip of a building where we picked up my father's pressed shirts every Friday afternoon, with its neatly painted sign, CHINESE LAUNDRY. Around the corner, the butcher Mr. Henry would present my father with packages of raw meat expertly wrapped in white paper. Down the block, Mr. Stern ran the drugstore, housed in the lobby of a single-room-occupancy hotel where drunken men sprawled on the balconies. I loved Mr. Stern's multiple miniature drawers of prescription medicine, from which he doled out our asthma pills. Back upstairs at the end of my imagined stroll, I'd drink from my father's green drinking glasses. ("I am always thinking that I am at home!" said the little prince.)

When thoughts of New York and my father brought too much long-ing, I summoned thoughts of Tel Aviv and my mother.

Our sixth summer in Israel had been a splendid one. "Oh there is so *much* to look forward to!" Catherine wrote to our mother from New York. "Sun and fun and mostly *all of you*." Both of us genuinely loved our summer visits, even as we coped with the permanent confusion of our family arrangement. Arriving in late June, walking up the steps to 19 Ben-Zion, it felt suddenly, welcomingly, like home. And then there was the new baby.

"Dearest Darling C & M," my mother had written to us over the winter. "I have some really great news for you. I'm going to have a baby." She would need us to help out when we came for the summer, she told us, adding, "I hope you are pleased. Let me know what you think."

"What news!" Catherine wrote back. "Unbelievable, fantastic and slightly shocking. I'm so excited." (Catherine soon wrote a letter to our grandmother, asking why our mother was having another baby, given that she hadn't stayed with her first two children, to which our grandmother wrote back, "What a smart girl you are.")

"Congratulations!" I wrote in purple and pink Magic Marker. Like Catherine, I admitted that it was "kind of a shock at first"—I too was surprised that my mother wanted another child after she had moved away from us—"but now I realize that it will be fun to have a baby sister or brother around. Actually I'm pretty excited!" If my mother had a baby girl, I could be Sarah Samantha in one of my favorite elementary school books, *The Middle Sister*. A timid eight-year-old on the Minnesota prairie, the girl finds her courage blossoming in the face of hardship. I drew pink swirls around the words I wrote to my mother.

When the contractions started on a mid-July day, Catherine and I helped time them into the night, then boarded a train to Haifa the next morning to stay with our grandparents in their elegant Kidron Street apartment. When my grandfather called the hospital that night, we could hear the shouting in Hebrew: *A girl! A girl!* Just as I'd hoped, I was now a middle sister.

Back in Tel Aviv, Catherine and I rushed inside, "our legs tingling & hearts pounding," I wrote in my diary. "Black hair, smooth skin, oh so sweet!!!" My mother and stepfather named their daughter Tal.

Both before and after Tal was born, the summer lived up to the sun and fun Catherine had predicted. We and Nurit left notes under each other's doors, suggesting activities for the day ahead ("Do you want to do a soap opera or a show?" I wrote, my stepfather's tape recorder at the ready. "I do. Come to our house now!"). We argued, then delivered makeup notes ("I think I was right telling you my feelings as friends always tell each other," Nurit wrote, "but please let's forget it"). Nurit's mother would take us all to the Savyon pool in an upscale suburb, or we'd take the bus by ourselves to the ultramodern Galei Gil Pool in Ramat Gan. In the movie theater down the block we saw *Mary Poppins*, and later that summer, *Airport*. "It was great," I wrote in my diary, summarizing the plot. "Suddenly one guy yells to a stewardess, 'He's got a bomb!'"

Catherine went to parties with Nurit's friends, where she met a boy who gave her a locket with his picture, inscribed with the words, "Be happy for ever." Most of those kids felt too old for me, so I spent time with a new girl in our building, Sonia, a Chilean Jew my own age who spoke English, Hebrew, Spanish, and Russian and brought steaming plates of meat and vegetables to the stray cats in our building's back garden. Sonia introduced me to her gang of friends on Mikhal Street a few blocks over, and their Friday night parties lasted until midnight or later. "All the kids welcomed me," I wrote in my diary. "They tried to speak English as best they could. I understood most of their Hebrew too."

That's where I met Gerry. Riding to the Gordon Pool on the back of his bicycle, I found myself interested in the sound of his breathing as he pumped up a hill. When Gerry gave me his picture at the end of the summer, I knew I would always treasure the black-and-white photograph of the smiling, handsome boy in a checkered shirt. On the back I wrote his name and the word "Israel" in the Hebrew letters Nurit had taught me.

As August drew to a close, Catherine and I paid our annual visit to

Catherine and me practicing our yoga poses on the beach.
This was our last day in Israel before the hijacking.

[EHUD BEN-DAVID]

Maskit, an emporium of beautiful objects (the Hebrew word *maskit* meant "ornament"), directed by our mother to select an end-of-summer present. Funded partly by Bethsabée de Rothschild, the enterprise employed immigrant women, Jewish and Palestinian, Bedouin and Druze, as designers and craftspeople. I chose a wooden box with an intricate inlaid geometric pattern, and Catherine chose a Jewish star on a gold chain.

On our last day in Israel, my stepfather took Catherine and me to Netanya while my mother stayed home with the baby. On the beach, we lazed on a raft, played paddleball, and posed for funny pictures with my stepfather and the British choreographer Norman Morrice. Back in Tel Aviv that evening, we packed our suitcases and got into bed early, since we had to wake before dawn for the flight home to New York.

In the desert, staving off fear with summer memories, I wished there was a way to get back to Tel Aviv or Netanya or Haifa—not very far away at all—back to my mother and stepfather, Nurit and Sonia, my baby sister, all the grandparents. Or that I could begin our journey all over again. Without the hijacking, Catherine and I would already be home in New York with my father, which is where we would be if our parents had never gotten divorced, or even if they just lived in the same country.

6

What was it like for my parents during the days and nights that Catherine and I sat confined inside the plane in the desert? When we got home, neither my father nor my mother answered that question. Their twin silences in turn nurtured my own unwillingness to think about the hijacking, marking it as an experience best ignored. Decades later, my mother's answer is vague, while my father's response has the expected ring of a narrative oft-repeated.

So many years later, with neither parent able to articulate the one week in their lives that both preferred to forget, I'm suddenly a historian again, setting out to investigate a poorly documented firsthand account of someone else's personally excruciating experience. To reconstruct that moment, I need to know what information flowed all around my parents, what they absorbed, and how they responded. I study the *Jerusalem Post* and the *New York Times*. I survey the television evening news that my father watched, ask other people what they remember about my parents that week, and unexpectedly come upon a revealing document preserved in an archive.

Mass Hijacking, read the front-page headline of the *Jerusalem Post* on Monday, September 7, describing the Popular Front's "spectacular and well-coordinated action." The *Post* and the BBC radio station were my mother's main sources of daily news, along with the English-language Broadcasting Service of the Hashemite Kingdom of Jordan. My stepfather translated the Hebrew newspapers and broadcasts, and my mother frequently called the American embassy, where someone would usually say—she believes these are the exact words—"We have no new information."

The news in Israel was dominated by the foiled El Al seizure. Amid those detailed accounts came a report that a TWA aircraft had made a "hazardous dusk landing on the open desert" at a "heavily guarded" makeshift airport. The *Jerusalem Post* reported too on stalemated negotiations and the "rapidly deteriorating situation," with the editors scoffing at the unprepared airlines and excoriating any possible surrender to Popular Front demands (that fall the *Post* advocated both "evacuation of the territories" and the destruction of "extremist organizations which reject any political solution"). My mother read that "the hostages spent another grueling day under the fierce sun." She read that the captives had "crossed the half-way mark of a 72-hour deadline, which Palestinian terrorists have set for their lives." She saw the words "the probable cost of the lives of the hostages," and she saw quotations from the *New York Times* about the hostages "facing the possibility of being cold-bloodedly murdered." She read a sentence, also quoted from the *Times*, that began "If these helpless people were to die tonight."

"It's a blur," my mother tells me so many decades later. ("Tell me that it is only a bad dream," said the aviator to the little prince.) "We heard all these horrible things. We heard they're going to blow up the planes. We heard that people had died. We heard that a woman had a heart attack, that someone shot someone." She was, she recalled, in "a highly emotional state," plus she had a seven-week-old baby. "There's a lot I don't remember," she admits. A dance teacher recalls the studio as "very tense" while "Linda Hodes's children were caught in the hijacking," but my mother has no recollection of contact with the dancers, no recollection even of contact with her parents in Haifa or her in-laws in Netanya. "We didn't know anything," she says. That's her most enduring memory.

In New York, meanwhile, the hijackings were the top television story. On the three national networks, news came on once in the morning and twice in the evening, first at six o'clock, then at eleven (it would take another decade for CNN to subject viewers to round-the-clock updates). Advanced technology, in the form of less cumbersome cameras, satellite communications, and videotape, had recently brought civil rights marches, the Vietnam War, the moon landing, and the assassinations of President John F. Kennedy and Dr. Martin Luther King Jr. right into American living rooms. Still, there was no running ticker at the bottom of the screen and few accompanying graphics; most common for stories about the hijacking was a line drawing of a Middle East map or the silhouette of an airplane or a gun.

"Good evening," intoned CBS anchorman Harry Reasoner that first Sunday night. "The Middle East conflict boiled over today with four Arab plane hijackings." After relating the story of the thwarted El Al operation, Reasoner moved on to our plane. "A TWA flight from Tel Aviv was hijacked shortly after takeoff from Frankfurt," he said; "and commando leaders say that it has landed at a revolutionary airport somewhere in Jordan." No other station added any further information. When my father got into bed that night, he kept both of his radios on his pillow, the two all-news stations playing into his earphones.

Suspended animation: that's how the days and nights felt, he tells me. Monday morning's *New York Times* carried a review of his company's performance at the Delacorte Theater ("Imaginative uses of media were made by Stuart Hodes's Ballet Team. Films, slides and even the songs of whales were incorporated"), but before he got to that, he saw the headline: 4 JETS HIJACKED; ONE, A 747, IS BLOWN UP. On a map, a dotted line from Frankfurt to Brussels reversed course, with the article noting that TWA "did not know the location of the 'forlorn desert airstrip'" where one of their planes had landed. A couple of pages in, another headline: US AIDES EXPRESS HELPLESS FEELING. On the next day's front page: "Unless the demands were met, the two planes would be destroyed . . . boxes of explosives inside the two planes . . . . deadline of 10pm Wednesday."

The day after that, the *Times* carried a photograph of the TWA and Swissair jets, surrounded by tanks, reporting the intensification of "uncertainty about the fate of the passengers." If my father made it to the editorial, "Ordeal in the Desert," he read that his daughters were being "held hostage in a burning desert, facing the possibility of being cold-bloodedly murdered," after which the editors speculated on world reactions "if these helpless people were to die tonight."

All week the hijackings remained the top TV news story. My stepmother remembers that the two of them watched all the stations on their black-and-white set, which meant that, with no remote control, they continually got up to flip channels on the dial. My father remembers that it seemed like the newscasters were enjoying themselves, repeating phrases like "blow up the planes with everybody in them," as if that was the fun part.

His memory is accurate. "They threatened to blow them up," said Walter Cronkite on CBS. "The Arabs now threaten to blow them up," said David Brinkley on NBC. "The commandos have stacked explosives aboard both planes," said Frank Reynolds on ABC, "and threatened to blow up the aircraft."

The station also displayed images of blaring newspaper headlines about the captured El Al hijacker, a woman named Leila Khaled: LEILA: "FREE HER OR PLANE HOSTAGES WILL DIE," and FREE LEILA OR 180 HOSTAGES DIE AT DAWN. In case viewers needed help imagining the scene, ABC rolled tape of the Pan Am aircraft that hijackers had blown up in Cairo. "Four explosions have been heard on board that plane," a reporter announced. "First gunshots, sporadic gun firing, and then four great explosions—the first one of them I saw, it came up like a huge great ball of fire." If my father glanced at any newsstand midweek, on any corner, he would have seen the *New York Post* headline in magnified lettering: HIJACKERS SET "FINAL" DEADLINE. ("Oh, no!" cried the aviator to the little prince. "No, no no! I don't believe anything.")

Even when the Popular Front temporarily rescinded or extended the deadline, even with "conflicting reports" about blowing up the passengers, even with hints of a less grisly course of action (a commando told a reporter that if they blew up the planes, the hostages would "probably" be moved), the television stations wrote scripts intended to keep viewers, if not the hostages' loved ones, tuned in through the commercials. Only after David Brinkley declared, "The Arabs said the TWA and Swissair planes would be blown up at ten o'clock tonight, eastern time, with the passengers aboard" did he add, "if their demands were not met." Then a moment later: "Now there are 298 people held hostage, and they are

These were the kinds of headlines my father saw on newsstands while his daughters were held hostage in the Jordan desert.
[USE OF THE NEW YORK POST COURTESY OF NYP HOLDINGS, INC. AND ASSOCIATED PRESS]

surrounded by Arabs who say they will kill them all if there is any attempt at rescue."

It turns out that my father had one chance to communicate with us. At the headquarters of the International Red Cross in Geneva, Switzerland, I comb through folders labeled "Hijacking of airplanes to Jordan, Zerka Airport, September 6, 1970." I create scans of the documents, translating the French here and there, reading reports sent by their delegates in Jordan: "Very serious situation . . . a tragedy. . . . possible failure." Amid the provisional lists of hostages and the reports about health conditions, I come upon a cache of telegrams: "Messages pour les otages transmis par la Croix-Rouge américaine" (Messages for the hostages sent by the American Red Cross). Family members were instructed to keep communications concise and warned that there was no guarantee of delivery. Unfurling a sheet of paper more than five feet long, I make my way through indecipherable numerical codes followed by messages in all lower-case type.

Some composed notes to their loved ones that resembled the most casual of postcard greetings, presumably as a way to mask forebodings: "Hope you are well." "Best wishes for a safe return."

Others conveyed practicalities: "Sister states will meet you upon arrival USA."

Some assured the hostages about those at home: "Parents fine." "Things all right at office."

A few changed the subject: "Mets in first place."

Some spoke in private code: "We are doing our thing."

A few expressed uncertainty: "Whole world trying to get you home."

Next to last, I come upon the one from my father. Decades later, he recalls how carefully he considered his wording. He wanted to write, "Keep your hearts and hopes up. We love you," but worried that even that hint of emotion might make us too sad. He considered joking—"Okay, enough of these side trips, it's time for you to come on home"—but someone at the Red Cross advised against that. He knew that Catherine and I would be worried about him, he knew we'd be worried about missing school, and he knew we'd be glad to think about our friends. In the end he wrapped his words in a breezy tone, speaking for himself and my stepmother. "Parents request children not be alarmed. Mom and Dad thinking of you. Rooms ready. Visited both schools. Great love from us and your friends."

In the archive in Switzerland, reading my father's cheery message (*Don't worry about me, I'm fine*), conveying his forced certainty of our imminent return (*Rooms ready*), I see that his crafted words were intended as much for himself as for his daughters. His resolve in the face of so much pain brings on waves of sadness.

We never received the message, and my father never told us that he'd written it until I asked him about it nearly fifty years later.

I know exactly where to find another piece of correspondence, one of the very few mementos I've saved from the hijacking, maybe the only one. It's inside the rose-colored Louis Sherry tin that holds assorted keepsakes from my childhood. The box also holds the photograph of Gerry and a tiny gift box from my mother on which she'd written on the cover, "Dear Martha, I miss you. Love, Mom."

The item I'm looking for is from my stepmother. A few days into the ordeal, she sat before a pad of plain white paper, fading black felt-tip pen in hand. "Dear Catherine & Martha," she wrote. "Sitting here thousands of miles away from you prompts me to write you a letter. I guess that's an odd thing to do when it would seem ridiculous for you to read it. Maybe it's to fill my own need of wanting to give you love and comfort in your hours of need." Wondering what it was like to live on a plane in the desert, she asked, as if we could send a letter in return, "Does one ever forget for a moment what the situation is? Do you eat, do you sleep? Do you talk to the new friends you're undoubtedly bound to through this crisis?"

She told us about life at home. "Dad and I have been living in a state of limbo," she wrote. When the news of the hijacking first came over the radio, they "couldn't really comprehend" it. They called the airline. They "cleaned, polished & shined" the apartment. "The radio has been on for 4 days," she wrote. "Dad goes to sleep with the ear phone in his ear." My stepmother listed all the relatives who were praying for us. Drawing on her faith as a Christian Scientist, she wrote, "We can only concentrate on your being truly in the arms of Love." In her letter she posed one more question: "What are you thinking & feeling?" It was a query that would go almost entirely unasked and unanswered when Catherine and I got home.

At home in New York the phone rang constantly: relatives, friends of my father and stepmother, friends of my mother, friends of mine, friends of Catherine, making sure it was true, asking my father to keep them informed. But my father didn't want to tie up the telephone line—in those days there was no way for someone else to get through if you were on the phone, no way even to leave a message. My father didn't want the airline or the State Department or the Red Cross or my mother to get a busy signal.

Toni, in between Catherine and me in age, was our shared best friend away from school, and she was in despair. Toni lived in the apartment adjacent to ours, where her mother, a labor and childcare activist, would pitch silverware down the hallway when we made too much noise. One of our preferred games with Toni was improvising scenes of families worse than our own. Toni might be a daughter who had to work as a prostitute to earn money, while Catherine was the mother who had to score heroin for a drug-addict sister. As the addict, I'd slump on the floor with a bottle of our spilled asthma pills. Before long someone would die, which was our collective cue to break up laughing.

Now Toni was sick with anxiety, plagued by fears that we might be wearing Star of David necklaces. The atheist daughter of a Catholic and a Jew, she made her way to Saint Patrick's Cathedral on Fifth Avenue to light a candle and pray. When Toni's mother encountered my father in our fifth-floor hallway, she found it impossible to interact with him. He was, she tells me so many years later, utterly unreachable.

Jody, my own best friend, had traveled to Europe for the first time that summer, and serendipitously we were going to arrive back in New York on the same day, just in time to start seventh grade together. Jody lived on the Upper West Side, in the kind of building I envied: on Riverside Drive, with a doorman (I had to step over the passed-out bodies of drunken men in my building's unguarded lobby). Jody's parents were divorced too, and after a Saturday-night sleepover, we'd have Sunday brunch with her father at his West End Avenue apartment, stopping first at Zabar's, the hole-in-the-wall deli where we'd take a number and stand in a snaking line for bagels and lox. On Sunday, September 6, Jody was in a taxi from Kennedy Airport when the driver mentioned the multiple hijackings, including the TWA plane that should have landed in New York. Jody didn't think I'd flown TWA, but she called my father when she got home, just to be sure. Brusquely, he informed her of my fate. Panic-stricken, she couldn't help feeling hurt that the usually warm and loving Stuart had hurried her off the phone.

On the first day of school at Hunter High, as the girls in my class circulated from homeroom to French, science, math, history, and art, each teacher called my name from the attendance roster. Although my father had notified the school as to why I was absent, no one seemed to have informed the teachers, and schools in 1970 offered no counseling to students whose classmates stood in harm's way. Instead, each time my name was called, Jody took it upon herself to speak up. "Martha isn't here because she's on one of the hijacked planes," she'd say. She couldn't say "She'll be back tomorrow" or "She'll be back next week," because she didn't know if I'd come back at all. The teachers were making seat assignments, and Jody knew that if I returned, I'd want to sit in the front row, since I was small. Making sure I had the right seat in each class helped Jody convince herself of my ultimate release. "I missed you so much," she remembers, "and was unbelievably distracted and worried."

Marsha, one of my other close friends from elementary school, had seen my name on the TWA passenger list in the *New York Times*, which was delivered to the front door of her apartment every day. The world was so filled with terrible news: the Vietnam War, Kennedy's assassination—which had happened right on Marsha's fifth birthday—the assassinations of Bobby Kennedy and Martin Luther King Jr. Now something else huge had happened, and it was on the front page of the *Times*, and her friend was there, part of world history. *Martha's sitting in the desert*, she kept thinking. *My friend Martha*. All the kids at school knew my father, and Marsha's next thought came fast: *Oh God, what's her father doing?*

My other friends from elementary school fretted too, one imagining me starving to death in a blazing desert, another worrying that my captors would confiscate all the letters she'd written to me that summer. Hunter girls who didn't know me yet were intrigued by a kid who traveled half a world away to visit her mother. There it was again: how strange my family was. Years and years later, Marsha confessed that my flying to Israel every summer to see my mother was exotic, already "a big deal even before this thing"—she meant the hijacking—"happened."

When I find my seventh-grade music teacher, she tells me, "I am absolutely shocked to learn that you and your sister were hijacked in 1970." Helen Finegold Friedman was "appalled," she says, "that I was not told about this when you were my student and thus could not offer you some special support." Was there, she wondered, "a notion which seems misguided today, that you would be better off if we did not know what had happened?" She also expressed dismay that Jody, one of her especially talented students, "had to suffer without the support of guidance counselors and faculty." She was amazed, she tells me a half century later, that "we seem to hold so much that is important in silence."

For my mother, the deadline set by our captors would come on Thursday morning, the same as for us. For my father, the deadline would come late Wednesday night. Even after that deadline passed, with the hostages still alive, their fears barely subsided.

On the cover of the *Jerusalem Post*'s Friday weekend magazine, my mother saw a photograph of the TWA captain, a bullhorn pressed to his lips, the caption bearing the words "hapless passengers" and "terrorist guards."

In New York, the Friday evening news described the situation as tense and dangerous. "Tonight the guerrillas were still threatening to blow up the three planes with the passengers in them," NBC anchor David Brinkley announced. "A Red Cross spokesman said that all the planes were wired up with dynamite and could be blown up at the touch of a button." On ABC, anchor Frank Reynolds sat before a crude graphic of a figure pointing a gun at a group of people, decorated with a row of question marks. "The hijackers have placed dynamite aboard the planes, and a Red Cross official said today the planes can now be blown up at the push of a button," Reynolds reported. On the screen my father saw the words reinforced in writing: PUSH OF A BUTTON.

On Saturday evening in New York, the television news commenced with the statement that "Arab guerrillas today blew up three hijacked airliners in the Jordanian desert," displaying images of armed commandos and a mangled plane. The next three words out of the mouth of Roger Mudd, the Washington correspondent for CBS News, were "all the passengers." That sentence ended, finally, with "had been taken off before the dynamiting, some at the last moment." Then my father heard the words: "It's still not clear what will happen to about two hundred and sixty hostages still in Amman."

That Sunday morning, one week after we said goodbye to our mother in Tel Aviv, the *Jerusalem Post* ran the front-page headline TERRORISTS BLOW UP THREE AIRLINERS. My mother had to make it to the next line to know that the hostages had been removed from the planes first. The subhead didn't exactly make everything clear either: SAY THEY'LL FREE ALL BUT 40 HOSTAGES. My mother remembers wondering, Would the commandos do what they said they were going to do? Were Catherine and I among those released or those detained? My stepfather listened to the news in Hebrew, read the Israeli papers, and told my mother it seemed likely the two of us had been taken out of the desert and brought to a hotel in Amman. *Well, now what happens?* my mother thought, still in retreat in the bedroom, with the baby. It wasn't as if everything was fine now, what with the war in Amman. *Now they're going to be in Jordan for the rest of their lives?*

Even though my father had already talked to us by telephone by the time he saw the Sunday *New York Times* headlines, the bold block letters must have momentarily unnerved him: ARABS BLOW UP 3 JETS IN DESERT read the top line, with the words AFTER TAKING OFF PASSENGERS only on the next. Paging through the paper, my father came upon words enshrined as the Quotation of the Day: "Now I am going to thank God and have a bath." The attribution read, "Catherine Hodes, a 13-year-old passenger from the hijacked TWA jet, in Jordan." He cut out the sliver of newsprint, then bought several more copies of the Sunday paper at the newsstand on Third Avenue. He cut out the Quotation of the Day in those issues too.

That evening, in front of the television, my father would have four seconds to fasten on an image of Catherine on NBC News, visible inside the first van arriving at the Intercontinental Hotel, then two more seconds in which she looked straight into the camera before she stood up, a wisp of a girl.

"They had spent six days and six nights as hostages in the desert, and now they were free, 121 women and children," reporter Douglas Kiker said, "all of them dirty and weary, youngsters traveling alone, pregnant women, mothers with infants in their arms, older women, nearly exhausted, and the airline stewardesses who had tried to take care of them all. They had spent six days and nights crowded inside three hijacked jets, held as hostages by fanatical terrorists who threatened to kill them."

After we spoke to our mother from the island of Cyprus, she reported to everyone—her parents, her in-laws, the dancers, the Little Man and the Little Lady—that we were free and on our way home. We would not see her again for seven months, when she came to New York for work.

Decades later, I ask my mother, "Did you ever think we were going to die?"

"I certainly must have had my concerns," she says. "They had threatened to blow up the planes, and they didn't say, 'Don't worry, we're going to take the passengers off.'"

I ask my father too: "Did you ever think we were going to die?"

"No," he says right away. "I always knew you were coming back." Not for a second did he think otherwise, he tells me, saying the words "never" and "totally unimaginable."

My stepmother remembers it differently, though. She describes my father during those days and nights as "a man on another planet," at once stoic, frozen, and devastated. "He would just stay on his positive course," she tells me, then adds, "Was he thinking of never getting you back? Well, yes. Killed and never coming back? Oh, yes."

Part Three

SEE, IT WASN'T THAT BAD

7

It's time to reconstruct the hijacking, starting from the beginning. Despite how much I'd forgotten, I always remembered the moment it began, the running and shouting up in the air, a moment before I or anyone around me knew what was happening, a moment none of the hostages would ever forget. But what happened after that, and before? I wanted to know what happened beyond my isolated image of those first startling minutes up in the air because I wanted to understand the fuller context of that enduring fragment of memory. What did other passengers do? What did they think was happening, and how did they feel? How did the cabin crew contend with their own fears, along with a planeload of terrified passengers for whom they were responsible? What did the flight-deck crew face, trapped inside the cockpit with an armed intruder, all of them surrounded by the instruments that controlled the aircraft? Could piecing together the experiences and emotions of everyone around me help to excavate my own unremembered state of mind?

I'd never forgotten the flight number. Now I studied the airline timetable. TWA 741, it turned out, was an around-the-world flight that began and ended in New York. Westbound, the plane stopped in San Francisco, Los Angeles, and Honolulu before crossing the international date line. It touched down in Guam, Japan, Taiwan, Hong Kong, Thailand, Sri Lanka, and India before landing in Tel Aviv to take Catherine and me, via Athens and Frankfurt, back to our father in New York.

The cockpit crew—the captain, copilot, and flight engineer—was working the entire trip, with Frankfurt to New York their last stretch. A new cabin crew, composed of five stewardesses, a purser, and a student purser, boarded in Frankfurt. I find the names of the stewardesses in newspaper articles, and when I reach out to June Haesler, she answers my query the same day, agreeing to meet at my apartment in New York on an October morning.

June is seventy-four years old, living on the Jersey shore, retired from TWA for fourteen years. In 1970 she had been a stewardess for four years, married for a year. June never thinks about the hijacking anymore, she tells me, unless she's asked, and now she speaks about it in a light-hearted manner. When she describes our week in the desert as "in prison in a tube, with a whole bunch of other people," she laughs. When I show her a picture of Catherine and me back then, she exclaims, "Oh, how cute!" June doesn't remember us—as it turns out, few of the hostages I contact will remember Catherine and me, perhaps for the same reasons that I remember so few of them. We were all preoccupied. So much time has passed. We wanted to forget after we came home. Even though the airline gave June time off, she wanted to get back to work sooner. She wanted to get back to normal.

Fifty years later, June explains to me the arrangement of our crew. Rosemarie Metzner was the most senior of the hostesses, assisted in first class by Bettie McCarthy. Tourist class passengers were served by June, Linda Jensen, and Vicki McVey—June and I both find ourselves saying *hostess* and *stewardess*, which feels right, since we're talking about 1970. Rudi Swinkels was the purser in charge of the cabin crew, and the night before, everyone had double-celebrated the student purser, Frank Allen, at a German wine festival: it was his very first trip, and he was getting married in California the next weekend.

I put June's memories together with information about our flight's stopover in West Germany. Along with the cabin crew, about forty new passengers boarded at Frankfurt, among them a woman named Miss Vásquez and a man named Mr. López. Since their passports were Honduran, the agent at TWA's Frankfurt ticket office was surprised that Mr. López couldn't converse in Spanish. Even though security in West Germany had intensified after Palestinians attacked El Al passengers at the Munich airport earlier that year, no one at either the ticket office or the

Frankfurt airport detected that the couple's passports were counterfeit. The single security guard who randomly searched hand luggage failed to uncover their concealed gun and grenades, and the metal detector seemed to be inoperative that day.

In seats near Catherine and me, Susie Hirsch, fourteen years old, was on her way home from Israel with her two younger brothers. Reboarding in Frankfurt, Susie was irked to find a man and a woman occupying their second-row seats in tourist class. Since their parents were flying home from Israel on a different flight, Susie was in charge of Howie and Rob, and they all needed to sit together. When the couple declined to move, Susie produced her boarding passes and summoned a stewardess. June Haesler apologized to everyone and directed the couple farther back—"I went up to them, and I said, 'I'm sorry, you have to move,'" June tells me. They were "very well-dressed," and she certainly didn't spy any weapons. The European-looking woman wore a chic outfit, and the man wore a suit. Politely, they complied. Later, when they ran up the aisle shouting, the Hirsch children recognized them as the passengers who had tried to commandeer their second-row seats.

At the back of tourist class, a passenger with a personal bottle of whiskey asked for Coke and ice, and as June readied his order, the man told her that someone in the aisle had a gun. "If you keep joking, I'll have to take away your Jack Daniel's," June told the passenger, smiling. She was working the front end of the liquor cart and didn't even turn around. Only when other passengers indicated that the man wasn't in fact joking did June push the cart back into the rear kitchen. She saw purser Rudi Swinkels "stumbling to the back galley" after his encounter with the two hijackers, pale and sweating, trying to convey to the stewardesses what had just happened up front.

Trans World Airlines no longer exists. The TWA archives, stored at the State Historical Society of Missouri, consist of nearly three hundred boxes, with a single box containing two folders about the 1970 hijacking. Inside I find a haphazard assortment of documents: newspaper clippings, flight maps, a letter from the airline president to a hostage's family. Best of all, I find detailed reports written by crew members, including June

Haesler, telling stories of things I'd known nothing about. What came to pass inside the cockpit. How air traffic controllers coped with the chaos. How the cabin crew managed everything.

The man entered the cockpit first, the woman behind him. Some forty-five minutes after takeoff from Frankfurt, Captain Carroll D. Woods, a fifty-one-year-old World War II air force vet from Prairie Village, Kansas, known to his friends as C. D., turned around to find himself "looking into a revolver." Copilot Jim Majer, a tall thirty-seven-year-old Marine Corps flier before his airline days, who made his home in Bermuda, saw "a man holding a grenade and pistol, and a woman holding an explosive device." Flight engineer Al Kiburis, a forty-five-year-old jokester with a ready smile, who lived in Paris, saw the snub-nosed, chrome-plated revolver and noticed agitation in the man's eyes. The woman, young and small, asserted that she was the new captain in charge of the flight. In a tense interlude, the man ordered the cockpit crew to remain still "and not try anything," and the crew assured the armed trespassers that they would comply. They knew there was no question, ever, of resisting. For one thing, if they tackled the woman, her grenade might explode. For another, if things didn't proceed as the hijackers wanted, the operation might turn into a suicide mission.

Captain Woods considered depressurizing the cabin, which would cause the hijackers, without oxygen masks, to pass out. Then again, passengers could pass out too, and the very young or very old could die. Right away, though, the man pulled down the cockpit's three masks, automatically depleting the air flow. The masks would have provided enough oxygen for the pilot to bring the plane rapidly to an altitude where people could breathe on their own, and the hijackers didn't want that to happen because they didn't want the plane to land in Europe.

When the woman, now occupying the jump seat behind the captain, ordered the plane turned around, Captain Woods had to convince her that he'd need clearance from air traffic control. The woman swiftly informed flight control that she was in command, instructing them that TWA 741 must henceforth be referred to as "Gaza Strip," after the ribbon of land that Israel had seized in the 1967 war. No one in the cockpit, she made clear, would respond to any other name. The woman also tried to contact another plane, Swissair 100, a DC-8 hijacked by accomplices while en route from Zurich to New York.

The woman, working from her own Jeppesen air navigation charts, possessed a rudimentary knowledge of aircraft communications and range capability. Unwilling to divulge the plane's destination, she gave directions for only one or two segments at a time: back over Frankfurt, then Munich, then Klagenfurt in Austria, Zagreb in Yugoslavia, Kumanovo in Macedonia, Thessaloniki and Rhodes in Greece. She soon relayed a political message to air traffic control, ending with words to the effect of "Down with Israel, down with Zionism, and down with imperialism." She still held the grenade in her left hand, her arm resting casually on the back of the captain's seat. The captain saw the woman's "middle finger through the loop in the grenade pin," less than a foot from his head. She would stay in that exact position for the remaining five or so hours of the flight.

The hijackers had by now announced their intentions to us, their hostages. Seated near the front of tourist class, Foozie Chesler watched people around her consulting the seat-back pocket maps, dubbing them "junior geographers." On her way home from Israel to start her junior year at Stern College for Women at Yeshiva University, she returned to the letter she'd stopped writing during the chaotic disruption. "Gee," she wrote, "we're being hijacked!"

David Raab thought it was exciting. Seventeen, blond and handsome, he knew all about the recent epidemic of Cuban hijackings. David was flying home to New Jersey with his mother, his three brothers, and his sister, Tikva. He was about to register for his freshman year at Yeshiva University, and now he thought, *Here I am, one of those making history being hijacked.*

With the takeover of the cockpit underway, Franz Zauner, a twenty-six-year-old Catholic farmer from Austria, heading to California to visit his sister, had a perfect view from his first-class seat. He asked himself if he were dreaming.

Learning some of the reactions of my fellow hostages, yet still unable to summon my own emotions, I consider my most vivid memory from that up-in-the-air span of time. Perhaps four hours after the hijacking began, one of the stewardesses moved Catherine and me into first class. It was then, right before I fell asleep—weary, and maybe exhausted from fear too—that I saw the copilot emerge from the cockpit with his hands up and a gun at his neck.

Or did I?

Vivid images of significant or traumatic moments, preserved with photographic authenticity, are called "flashbulb memories." For me, the gun at the copilot's neck was just such a memory. Across nearly fifty years, the fragment has remained sharp, the disembodied gun occupying its outermost edge. In my mind, I can see Jim Majer, his grown-up face cueing emotion to a bewildered twelve-year-old: eyes worried, lips pursed in silenced fear, hands up as if responding to a robber's command, the skin on the left side of his neck turning red as the nose of a silver revolver presses into it.

Trouble is, no one else who recorded anything about the hijacking, and no one else with whom I spoke about the hijacking, recalled a gun at the copilot's neck, not even when I asked about it directly. Scientists have long known that flashbulb memories are fickle. "I expected some deficiencies of memory, partly because the events I was writing of had occurred fifty or more years earlier," writes the neurologist Oliver Sacks, recounting his flashbulb memory of the thermite bomb that fell right behind his house in London during Germany's aerial campaign in 1940, when Sacks was seven years old. All those decades later, Sacks could still see the "jets of molten metal" that flew through the air, could hear the "vicious hissing and sputtering" of the water his brothers poured onto the flames. Yet almost a half century later Sacks learned that he hadn't even been at home when the bomb fell behind his house. He'd learned about it only later, in a letter, which induced his mind to fabricate a detailed personal memory. "Once such a story or memory is constructed," Sacks writes, "accompanied by vivid sensory imagery and strong emotion, there may be no inner psychological way of distinguishing true from false, nor any outer, neurological way," since brain imaging is "virtually identical whether the 'memory' is based on experience or not."

Unlike Sacks, though, I had in fact been there, in the plane, seated close to the flight deck. Was one of my most enduring memories nevertheless a fabricated trick of the mind? What about Jim Majer himself? What did he remember? In his crew report, he recorded that "a man, holding a grenade and pistol, and a woman, holding an explosive device, entered the cockpit." He noted that they "took command and ordered us to obey instructions and informed us that, if we did, no one would be hurt." He wrote too about the oxygen masks and the woman renaming the flight "Gaza Strip," but he said nothing about a gun at his neck, nothing even about leaving the cockpit the whole time the flight was in the air. Nor did any of the other crew members mention in their reports anything about a gun at the copilot's neck.

I spend two years wondering about that vivid memory while I query other TWA personnel and sift through social media, before finally locating Jim Majer. "Hello Martha," he writes from England. "Very pleased to learn you are alive and actively involved in teaching history." Jim, now in his late eighties, graciously answers my questions. He doesn't say so directly, but he doesn't remember Catherine and me. As to the gun at his neck: sometime after the plane reversed course, Jim tells me, he "felt a desperate need for the toilet," since his stomach had been unsettled since Bombay. The male hijacker, who "always had the gun in one hand," permitted Jim to enter the first-class lavatory directly adjacent to the cockpit. As Jim recalls, "I held my hands up en route."

This was the scene of which I'd caught a glimpse, one of the few passengers to glance up during the mere seconds it took the copilot to move from cockpit to lavatory, the expression on his face reflecting the discomfort of stomach pains as much as fear. A personal incident that did not merit inclusion in an official crew report appeared to an unwillingly alert twelve-year-old as the hijackers demonstrating their ability to kill anyone who did not obey their commands. The image had been too frightening to record in my diary.

When the second announcement came over the loudspeaker, I held on to the words "friendly country" and "friendly people." The word *friendly* was important to me because nice people would understand how much Catherine and I needed to get home to our father. As it turned out, many others recalled that word too, so incongruous after the shouting and the weapons, indicating as it did a promise of safety in the face of perilous danger.

I approach Catherine first. Almost fifty years later, when I ask for her memory of the second announcement, she writes it out this way: "This is your new pilot, who has taken command of this TWA flight. We are taking you to a friendly country with friendly people. For your safety, place your hands on your head."

Captain Woods paraphrased the second announcement this way in his crew report: the woman said that we "had a new captain and would be proceeding to a friendly country where we would be well treated."

Rudi Swinkels remembered the words, "This is your new pilot speaking. You are now going to a friendly country with friendly people."

Four of the stewardesses, who filed a joint report, agreed on this summary: "Female hijacker on PA announcing that she was the new captain, that no one would be hurt if they followed instructions, that the hijackers were with the Palestine Liberation Front, that we were going to a friendly country with friendly people, that we were wished a pleasant trip."

June Haesler, who filed her own report, had it like this: "She said she was the new captain, the plane was being hijacked for the PFLP. We would be taken to her country and the people there would be very friendly and not to be afraid."

Passengers repeated the word to the press when they got home, wrote it down in personal accounts, and recounted it in lawsuits against the airlines. Others recalled the word instantly, even nearly fifty years later. Over and over again: "We're going to a friendly country." "We're taking you to a friendly country." "We will take you to a friendly country with friendly people."

Paging through a *Life* magazine story so many decades later, I come upon the script that British authorities found in Leila Khaled's clothes when they arrested her in London, after the attempted El Al hijacking on the same day as ours. "Ladies and gentlemen, your attention please," she had intended to say to her hostages. "Kindly fasten your seatbelts. This is your new captain speaking." Passengers should remain calm, place their hands behind their heads, and "make no move which would endanger the lives of other passengers on the plane." She was to finish up with this reassurance: "Our destination is a friendly country, and friendly people will receive you."

Even as many of my fellow hostages held fast to that soothing word, many also felt suspicious. Just like the old lady sitting next to us, many were unable to reconcile Arabs with the idea of friendliness toward those with ties to Israel. *Who are these people?* Susie Hirsch thought. *What do they want from us? Will we survive?* In his diary, David Raab wrote, "In fact, we were quite terrified."

The cockpit crew asked the hijackers for a thirty-minute warning before touchdown, in order to decrease the cabin pressure. Jim Majer told the stewardesses to "prepare the cabin for a possible crash landing." As Jim explained to me years later, "The landing surface composition and its total length were complete mysteries to us." That meant the aircraft needed more weight forward of the landing gear, since the main gear might collapse if the plane touched down on soft ground. That's why the crew moved Catherine and me, along with a few others, up to first class. It was also important to have as many people as possible up front, in case everyone needed to evacuate upon landing, and with a good number of babies and elderly passengers on board, the crew chose the two of us: "Unaccompanied skinny teenagers can move fast," Jim recalled.

Memories of the landing elude me. Sitting next to Catherine in those first-class seats, what thoughts did I quell, then vanquish? Did I worry that the plane would crash? Was I confident that the captain could save us by working his dials and levers? Now I wanted to know: How safe or unsafe had we been at that moment?

Dusk made it difficult for Captain Woods to find the designated landing area, and the hijackers and flight-deck crew spent half an hour searching for it. Flying a commercial aircraft in 1970 required a pilot, a copilot, and a flight engineer (today a pilot can fly alone, and flight engineers are obsolete). Back then there was no flight management system (the equivalent of an extremely accurate GPS), and without digital maps, which visually situate an aircraft in its surroundings, pilots consulted paper maps and charts. There was no stream of weather data, landings were not automated, and even wing and engine design was less advanced and therefore less safe. In the rapidly falling darkness that Sunday evening, there was no technology to enhance visibility.

The cockpit crew told the hijackers that fuel would need to be dumped to bring the aircraft down to a safe landing weight. Captain Woods decided to "drag the field": fly over the area to make an evaluation. He worked the radar, began a gentle ascent, dumped fuel, and returned to the field, "avoiding our fuel dump spray." But the nose gear—the wheels that drop to steer the plane on the ground—didn't descend. The "unsafe" red light was glowing, and the hijackers thought the crew was trying to trick them.

What else, what the hell else, what in the world else, is going to happen to this particular flight? Captain Woods wondered.

After again trying to lower the stuck landing gear, the crew convinced the hijackers that emergency procedures were imperative. When the woman at last consented, flight engineer Al Kiburis saw that "her hands were still on her hand grenade, and she was passing the thing now, from hand to hand, and she was getting tired of holding it." Al mechanically locked the gear in the down position, then obtained permission from the hijackers to climb into the "lower 41," the equipment center under the cockpit, to check on the lock pin.

If we get this plane on the ground with him still holding that grenade, stewardess Bettie McCarthy thought, watching the male hijacker in the cabin, *we're going to feel like our worries are over.*

The landing was remarkable. Rudi Swinkels found it smoother than landing on a real airport runway, and Russell Morris, a TWA pilot flying as a passenger, called it "painted on the sand." With that, the two hijackers, still holding the gun and an unpinned grenade, ordered the captain to shut off the engine and open the doors at the front of the aircraft.

We had touched down on a strip of earth, marshland hardened into a natural runway by the desert's remorseless summer sun. The British called it Dawson's Field, after Sir Walter Dawson, a Royal Air Force officer who had once used the toughened land for military exercises with small aircraft. Known locally as Qā' Khannā, the spot was perhaps ten miles northeast of Zarqa, a city some twenty miles northeast of Amman. Reporters, diplomats, airline personnel, and the CIA would variously estimate our location as between fifteen and nearly eighty miles from the capital city. ("It is a little lonely in the desert," the little prince said to a snake.)

A geologist had assured the hijackers and their comrades that the mud-flat strip could support a commercial airliner, but they worried nonetheless. "We were afraid," remembered Abu-Samir, one of the Popular Front commandos stationed on the ground when the plane came in, sympathetic also to the hostages' fears about a desert landing. Dawson himself, sixty-eight years old in 1970, judged it a "dangerous place for these modern airliners to land," but a TWA executive believed that the 707's weight was well served by the strength and stability of the dry marsh bed.

One American passenger thought we had landed in a desert in Africa.

"You are in Jordan," commando Bassam Abu-Sharif enlightened him, "and we are Palestinian guerrillas."

"In Pakistan?" The man was confused.

"No. We are Palestinian. From Palestine," Abu-Sharif said. "You know, the country that is now occupied by Israel." Years later, he would recall his thoughts at that moment: *We will just have to go on hijacking until every American in the world has heard of it.* As another commando would later tell a reporter, "None of you foreigners had even known that there exists people called Palestinians." The Popular Front for the Liberation of Palestine called the strip of desert earth Revolution Airport.

From the start, one of the non-Jewish passengers saw that "the Jewish people were very worried," and right away our captors took particular notice of Israeli citizenship. One hostage heard the commandos criticize "the dual passport capability of American Jews," contrasting it with their own "inability to go home to Israel or Palestine." Another hostage, traveling home from a summer in Israel with her rabbi husband and their three young children, placed their passports at the bottom of an air-sickness bag with a soiled diaper on top, tossing the whole thing into the trash (soon, when a crew member asked for permission to investigate a blockage in the rear lavatory, he found fetid dual passports stopping up the toilets). The commandos also took a special interest in a nineteen-year-old American Jew named Sarah Malka, a student at Rutgers University in New Jersey—she was the one I remembered conversing in Arabic with our captors—whose passport indicated her birthplace as Sudan. When the commandos asked Sarah if she spoke Arabic, she demurred, until one of them held his gun to her head.

That same night, a Palestinian medical doctor consoled the planeload of fearful captives. David Raab wrote in his diary that the doctor "said not to worry, not to be concerned, not to be afraid—he didn't know too many words—so he said not to be angry, not to be confused." Al Kiburis heard the doctor say that we should not "fear for our lives," but Al nonetheless wouldn't let himself drift into sleep. He watched one of the commandos carry a wired device to the back of the aircraft and saw someone else place the same kind of device in the cockpit. Al reasoned that if our guards suddenly left the plane, that would be his cue, so he kept himself awake by devising the speediest evacuation plan. One of the stewardesses asked Al what the men were carrying.

"Forget about it," he told her. "Everybody's sleeping and don't tell anybody. I'll watch."

Bassam Abu-Sharif also wanted to comfort the frightened hostages that first night, not least to keep everyone calm. "Don't worry, it's only a hijack. Nobody will be hurt," he said, in what he considered his "best bedside manner." In an era when hijackings were mere inconveniences, his words might have sounded plausible, but by now the hostages understood that this one was going to be different.

"You expect us to be relaxed?" one man snapped. "Look at that guy! What the hell is he doing?"

"He's just laying a few explosive charges," Abu-Sharif said. Enigmatically, he added, "Not for you, though. Don't worry. It's just to blow up the plane in case anybody tries anything."

8

How did the world find out that our flight had veered off course? Even after I'd re-created the experiences of my parents and friends in New York and Tel Aviv as best I could, even after I'd reconstructed the moment of the hijacking up in the air, I wanted to comprehend more deeply that stunning day. The multiple September 1970 hijackings were far bigger than the plane that was taking my sister and me home from our summer visit with our mother. Maybe if I knew what the rest of the world knew, maybe if I studied the hijacking from a more expansive perspective, it would cease to feel as if none of it had ever happened to me. Again, the TWA archives proved accommodating, especially when I scrutinized those documents in tandem with telegrams to and from the State Department, along with other related US government communications.

On the ground, air traffic control knew something was wrong. In Frankfurt, shortly after noon, operators who saw an abrupt change of direction called Rome dispatchers with the suspicion of a hijacking. As the self-appointed new captain revealed the next segments to the flight-deck crew, supervisors in Rome monitored a frequency used for Middle East operations, and controllers across different cities tracked the plane's path, then contacted airports in Beirut, Damascus, and Amman. Soon the information became contradictory, with controllers unable to determine the plane's destination or whether it had already landed. Unable to get a response from the cockpit, a Rome dispatcher declared a possible emergency.

A radar code from our captain had come in at TWA's New Jersey facility, where every flight was tracked twenty-four hours a day: the code, 3100, indicated a hijacking, rendering spoken communication with the pilot unnecessary. Arriving at the airline's New York headquarters on Sunday morning, as the emergency was unfolding, TWA president Forwood C. Wiser contacted the US Department of State. The airline's public relations people would have to compile a list of passengers and contend with the media. In Amman, TWA's Middle East sales manager, a Palestinian named David Jenevizian, stood by to see where the plane would land.

No one at the State Department knew what was happening either. The American embassy in Paris telegraphed a staccato message to US secretary of state William Rogers: "TWA Flight 741 from Frankfurt to New York nonstop with full load passengers hijacked." The State Department cabled Amman that the plane was over Cyprus, "possibly planning on landing at Amman, Baghdad, Beirut, Cairo or Damascus." Should the plane land in Amman, the cable ordered, the Jordanian government should "arrange for immediate release of all passengers" and "seek to apprehend hijackers." Those actions would be in accord with the Tokyo Convention, a recent agreement that required authorities to assist everyone on an unlawfully seized flight "to continue their journey as soon as practicable."

The White House Situation Room was humming. National security advisor Henry Kissinger described the soundproof "Sit Room" as a cramped, windowless space with proximity to "the most advanced communications equipment." Known for composure under extreme pressure, Sit Room personnel transmitted up-to-the-minute intelligence to embassies all over the world, via teletype machines.

Information and misinformation poured into the White House, the State Department, and the Department of Defense—the TWA plane had landed in Yugoslavia, for example, or was about to land in the Gaza Strip. Along with the Swissair flight that the female hijacker had contacted, an El Al flight from Tel Aviv and a Pan American flight from Brussels were also flying off course. The hijacked planes would land in Syria, in Lebanon, in Jordan. The Popular Front for the Liberation of Palestine, a faction of the Palestinian resistance that favored hijackings, claimed responsibility. The Popular Front denied responsibility. The hijackings were coordinated. The hijackings were coincidental. By late afternoon on Sunday, the only landing the Pentagon could confirm was the El Al plane at London's Heathrow Airport, its hijackers defeated.

I'd known Alice Kessler-Harris, a professor of history at Columbia University, for years, but I'd never known that she was a passenger on El Al Flight 219 that same September morning. After another colleague informed me of our parallel experiences, I sent Alice a message. "I write simply to acknowledge something we did not know about each other across all these years," I told her, adding a version of the caveat I always appended when contacting fellow hostages: "I do not at all mean to intrude, and I completely understand if you do not wish to revisit any of this."

"I am blown away!" Alice wrote back. "Let's talk."

On a spring afternoon, we order coffee at Le Monde on upper Broadway, near Columbia. We are meeting to tell each other our stories, and each of us will be utterly aghast at what the other experienced. As Alice recounts her ordeal, her fingers play ceaselessly in the china bowl of sugar packets on the table. Her story, I readily find, dovetails with other sources that document the El Al hijacking.

The twenty-nine-year-old Alice and her six-year-old daughter were flying home after a visit with family in Israel. In the row just ahead sat a woman with such shiny black hair that the little girl wanted to ask if she could brush it for her. Soon after an Amsterdam stopover, the woman with the lustrous hair stood up, and so did the man sitting next to her. That startled the passenger occupying the window seat. The couple hadn't spoken a word the whole time, but their row mate was planning to inquire if they wanted to trade their English-language newspaper for hers. Now they jumped up, shouting.

The dark-haired woman was Leila Khaled, twenty-six years old, who had successfully led the hijacking of TWA Flight 840 a year earlier, diverting the Rome–to–Tel Aviv jet to Syria, where it was evacuated and partly blown up. Khaled's family had lost their home in Haifa during the

1948 war, making them refugees in Lebanon—she could remember the family driving away in a taxi when she was four years old, amid bombs and bloodshed. At the American University of Beirut, Khaled joined the Arab Nationalist Movement, with the 1967 war propelling her to devote her life to the Palestinian cause. Training as a commando with the Popular Front for the Liberation of Palestine, Khaled deployed her aptitude for physics and math to learn the workings of a Boeing 707. Gazing upon Haifa from the cockpit of Flight 840, she had taken in "the whole lovely coast of my country, occupied Palestine," she would say later. "Isn't it something awful that I could see my home town again only when I hijacked a plane?"

Since then, Khaled had undergone plastic surgery for the sake of disguise. Her accomplice in September 1970 was Patrick Joseph Arguello, the California-born son of an American mother and a Nicaraguan father, and a magna cum laude graduate of the University of California–Los Angeles. Like their comrades on TWA, Khaled and Arguello boarded with false Honduran passports. Revealing their grenades and a gun, the two demanded to enter the cockpit, but Captain Uri Bar-Lev refused to cooperate. Instead, he daringly steered his plane into negative-G mode, creating a petrifying midair plummet. Seat belts were still buckled, since the plane hadn't yet reached cruising altitude, so Bar-Lev knew his acrobatic dive would affect only the hijackers. As the plane dropped precipitously over the water, people screamed, and Alice groped for two life vests under the seats.

Khaled lost her balance, and the two grenades—she had pulled the pins when she stood up in her seat—slipped from her hands. Grenades explode within a few seconds of releasing the lever held in place by the pin, and Khaled would later admit that she had no idea why there was no detonation ("What amazed me is why neither of the bombs exploded"). The stumble allowed passengers to tackle her, tying her hands with neckties, scarves, and cables. Meanwhile, Arguello fired at the steward, after which an armed El Al guard ran from the back of the plane and shot Arguello. Amid the blasts, rolling hand grenades, screams, gushing blood, crashing dishware, and toppling luggage, Alice's six-year-old daughter said, "You mean I'm never going to see my daddy again?"

Captain Bar-Lev eventually straightened out his aircraft and landed at the nearest airport, London's Heathrow. When the press descended, someone thrust a microphone into the face of Alice's daughter, jockeying for a colorful story; when the little girl burst into tears, Alice swung her pocketbook hard, knocking the camera out of the newsman's hands.

The wounded steward would recover, but Arguello would be pronounced dead in the ambulance. With the bruised and battered Leila Khaled in police custody in West London, the press delighted in describing her. She was a "girl commando," "that girl-guerrilla," a "girl terrorist," and a "gal terrorist." The Associated Press called her a "black-eyed beauty," and Israeli prime minister Golda Meir referred to her contemptuously as "that Jordanian beauty." Meanwhile, *NBC Evening News* told American viewers that Khaled was "active in the Arab equivalent of something like women's liberation, since she says her two main causes in life are freedom for women and freedom for Palestine."

Up in the air during the El Al hijacking, Stanley and Miriam Hirsch held hands. Wondering if their plane was going to crash, they thanked God that their three children were flying home on a different flight. Once safely inside Heathrow, the two hurried to the TWA desk. Their children had spent the summer in Israel, Stanley and Miriam joining them in August for Howie's bar mitzvah. They had arranged for their own homeward-bound flight to arrive at Kennedy Airport just ahead of the children's. Now seriously delayed by the attempted hijacking, they asked TWA to contact relatives who could pick up the kids. Instead, the TWA agent came out from behind the counter, put his arms around the couple, and ushered them into a private hallway where he informed them that Susie, Howie, and Rob's flight home from Israel had been successfully hijacked.

El Al passengers later boarded the same plane, visible bloodstains and all, and arrived in New York twelve hours late. It was the middle of the night, and they were greeted by jubilant friends and relatives. For the Hirsch parents, though, there was no jubilation. *I have three children*, Miriam thought. *Maybe tomorrow I won't have any.*

Alice Kessler-Harris tells me something else that afternoon over coffee. Understanding just how traumatizing the hijacking was for her young daughter, Alice made two decisions. First, immediately afterward the two spoke frequently about the hijacking. Second, she put her daughter on a plane, alone, to visit her midwestern grandparents at Thanksgiving, assuring her that she was "hijack-proof," since no one could be hijacked twice. Alice tells me that her daughter's sense of accomplishment was caught in the photograph her grandparents snapped as the girl disembarked in Minnesota, smiling broadly, fully aware of her bravery (she would grow up to be a clinical psychologist).

My father did the same as Alice, putting Catherine and me on a plane again the next summer, back to Israel. He later told me that he protected himself with the same thought ("Lightning doesn't strike twice"), but he skipped a couple of steps. He didn't talk frequently with us about the hijacking, and he didn't share with us the improbability of another hijacking. When I flew to Israel the next summer, I didn't feel brave. I tried not to feel anything.

With the hijacking of a Pan Am flight in progress on Sunday, September 6, only "fragmentary information" was coming into the White House. Suspiciously, two men with Senegalese passports had paid cash for one-way tickets on El Al Flight 219, on the very day of the flight. Denied passage (they were meant to be accomplices of Khaled and Arguello), they instead caught Pan Am Flight 93, traveling from Brussels to New York. Before takeoff, the captain learned that the men had been turned away by El Al, yet a pat-down and an inspection of their briefcases missed the weapons inside their jockstraps.

"What's going to happen to this airplane?" John Ferruggio, the inflight director of Pan Am 93, asked a hijacker after the cockpit had been invaded.

"What do you care about this imperialistic airplane?" the man retorted.

"What about my imperialistic ass and my passengers?" Ferruggio shot back, forcing a chuckle from his adversary.

The 747 aircraft was too heavy to land safely at Dawson's Field, so the hijackers chose the Cairo airport instead.

Eight minutes: that's how long everyone had to get out before the timed bombs would detonate. It was 4:30 in the morning when the crew unfurled the emergency chutes, and the first explosion came within two minutes of evacuation. Reporters watching from the terminal saw the plane disintegrate in flames.

"Where was all your baggage?" a reporter asked a young man with long hair.

"Oh, all blown up," the man said, shaking his head, smiling. "It's complete ash, man. It's all ash. Very far out."

In the meantime, President Nixon read a memo that a Swissair plane had been "seized by Palestinians." Their hijackers, like ours, were a well-dressed man and woman in their twenties, carrying counterfeit passports and hand grenades (one passenger joked to his wife that women's lib was "really moving!"). The ordeal had begun shortly after takeoff from Zurich, and the woman informed air traffic control that they would respond only to the call sign "Haifa," a city lost to Israel in the 1948 war. Their announcement echoed the TWA script: "Our destination is a friendly country" with "friendly people."

Dim lights on the alleged runway showed a large obstacle below, but the darkness made it impossible for the captain to discern that it was another plane, and his aircraft landed hard, swaying violently and coming to a stop a mere 150 feet from us. Armed commandos boarded, the same as in our plane, distributing landing cards and confiscating passports. As in our plane too, the commandos apologized, explaining that they needed to bring the fate of their people to the world's attention.

With the sun gone nearly an hour in the Jordan desert, it was still afternoon in Washington, and US embassies around the world remained in the dark, real or metaphorical. "Israeli Air Force tells us they have info that TWA plane was heading for H–5, and may have landed there," the Tel Aviv embassy alerted the US State Department, using the code for a government air base in Jordan. The director of civil aviation in Jordan relayed that the TWA plane had landed safely in an area "under Iraqi and guerillas' control," while a telegram from Beirut informed Washington, "Situation still confused and we lack hard confirmation," noting only that the TWA plane had landed "somewhere in Jordan."

Foreign correspondents in Jordan made their headquarters at the Intercontinental Hotel in Amman, and that Sunday the telex machine clattered with news: of the midair shooting on El Al, of the Pan Am explosion in Cairo, of the TWA and Swissair planes flying the wrong way. Newsmen crowded around the spewing machine, prompting London television reporter Gerald Seymour to telephone a contact in the Popular Front.

"Yes," the man told Seymour, "we have taken the 707 and the DC-8. We are flying them to Jordan."

By early evening the White House had word from the Jordanian air force that two hijacked planes had landed "at a military dirt strip" in the Jordan desert. The US embassy noted the lack of "technical facilities for night landings," but cabled Secretary of State Rogers that the planes had arrived safely, adding in clipped language that "doors of both aircraft remain closed suggesting that Fedayeen still in control." That's what our captors called themselves: fedayeen, the plural of *fedayee*, "one who sacrifices himself."

Right away, the Jordanian government wanted to send troops to protect the hostages, but the Popular Front transmitted a message that they would (as Washington paraphrased it) "blow up themselves and the aircraft if any attempt was made to storm the aircraft or otherwise checkmate the hijacking effort." Instead, the army's tanks, armored cars, jeeps, trucks, and antiaircraft guns would surround the hijacked planes, forming a ring a couple of miles out, "powerless, or at least not prepared, to intervene with force," as a US official in Amman put it. Beyond the Jordanian troops were Iraqi and Syrian troops, siding with the Popular Front. Thus were we, the hostages, thrice surrounded: first by Popular Front commandos, then by the Jordanian army, then by allies of the commandos. A war was brewing.

The State Department needed to assemble a list of American hostages on TWA 741, which turned out to be no easy task. The American consulate in Frankfurt sent a provisional roster, and bits of information came from ticket records, mostly last names, some misspelled. "No info on passports possible," the consulate noted, since neither the airline nor German officials kept such records. The airline knew about sixty-four-year-old Rabbi Isaac Hutner, sitting in the row ahead of Catherine and me, dean of a rabbinical school in Brooklyn, "highly respected, elderly, ailing." Their incomplete list identified Lennett Cain of the US Army, a twenty-seven-year-old African American sergeant from Georgia, traveling with his wife, Mary, and their infant son; he had worked at the US embassy in Athens, and the family was flying home for his discharge. The State Department knew about the Hirsch children too, flying home from Israel unaccompanied, whose parents had endured the violently foiled hijacking of El Al 219. They likely also knew about the two men who destroyed their sensitive Defense Department documents up in the air. The Popular Front was compiling their own register, but the commandos declined to turn over the names, citing security reasons.

Catherine and I would soon appear on a list of passengers printed in the *New York Times*. It was our shared passport that prompted the pairing: "Hodes, Miss" and "Hodes (child)." Despite the fact that no one on the plane remembered us, there were our names, right before my eyes, proving our presence in the desert—yet rendered so oddly (as if Catherine wasn't a child too, as if she were perhaps my unmarried mother) that I could almost convince myself that the evidence was unconvincing.

None of the rosters solved the problem of who remained inside the planes. "According to reports from Jordan," the *Times* noted, "about 80 women, children and old people have been freed and some male passengers will be released later. Their names were not disclosed." Washington also needed to know what was going on out in the desert, not least to answer questions from relatives. "Request you send status report TWA 741," a State Department official cabled Amman on Monday. "We expect extremely heavy volume of inquiries from concerned parties." But no one at the embassy could get out to Dawson's Field. Indeed, for embassy diplomats there would never be any substantive contact with the Popular Front. ("You will see where my track begins, in the sand," said the little prince. "You have nothing to do but wait for me there.")

None of us hostages yet knew that we were part of the biggest hijacking operation the world had ever seen. One journalist called it "the most remarkable event in the history of aerial piracy." Another, headed to Amman to cover the story, felt "a frisson of excitement." This was going to be "a big story in an exotic place."

9

If I reconstructed our first day in the desert, could that be a way to reach the emotions that I must have felt at the beginning of our ordeal? Toward the end of that first day came the episode that forced me to break through my largely unfaltering attempts to bury fear. Now I wanted to throw myself back into the distressing events of Monday night, outside on the desert floor surrounded by armed commandos, but since my own scant documentation would leave me defeated, I would need to uncover the experiences and emotions of my fellow hostages. Like the running and shouting up in the air, Monday night was something no other hostage ever forgot. What was it like for them? How did they remember the sequence of events, and could their memories of details and emotions open up the feelings I had successfully submerged?

We were some 150 passengers and ten crew. Our Boeing 707 was a midsize narrow-body airliner, with the cabin a little over a hundred feet long, less than twelve feet wide, and less than eight feet high. Beyond a small lounge area and four first-class rows came twenty-three tourist-class rows meant to be divided between nonsmokers and smokers, the latter in the back. The plane, parked in the desert, pointed north-northeast, so the sun came up on the side where Catherine and I were sitting—the right side, if you were facing forward. Most of the activity outside took place on the other side, where the ladder was propped up against the aircraft's front exit, and where reporters would eventually arrive from Amman, which lay to the southwest.

It was time to reckon with my diary. Historians prize personal writings that date from the time and place under investigation, and I'd saved all of mine—bound volumes and saddle-stitched journals, spiral notebooks and loose-leaf binders—neatly stacked in several cartons. Occasionally I'd extricate one and peruse a stretch, but I'd never before returned to my childhood journals.

When I start out, I'm confident that my diary will be my trusted scaffolding: an in-the-moment account of what came to pass, along with my thoughts and feelings up in the air, in the desert, at release, and upon return. Inside, each day commands a full five-by-eight lined page, with the day of the week and the date printed at the top. At twelve years old, I'd already been keeping a diary for two years, and I loved to write on the crisp lined pages, composing entries about incidents and thoughts I deemed worthy of preservation. In 1970 I named my journal Claire, writing my entries in the form of letters. In that technique I copied Anne Frank, who began her diary entries with "Dear Kitty." Anne Frank and I both wanted to be writers, and her birthday was the same as mine. I was proud that I kept a diary so steadily, unlike most of my friends, who started and then inevitably quit.

On Monday morning, some twelve hours after landing in the desert, I picked up my journal for the first time since everything had happened.

Monday, September 7

Dear Claire,

Yes, I'm still sitting on the plane. It happened yesterday on the way from Frankfurt to N.Y. I was chatting with Catherine. Suddenly someone was running down the aisle shouting something I couldn't understand. The people's faces turned frightened and in awhile the hostesses told us that there were "some people" talking to the captain. It was a hijack! We didn't know where we were going to. Then a voice came over the speaker: "Good afternoon ladies & gentlemen. I am the new pilot who has taken command of your TWA flight." I began praying and praying. "Keep calm," she continued, with her accent. "Please cooperate and put your hands behind your head." We all obeyed & I could see the plane turning. The hostesses comforted a crying Catherine and calmed everyone. Finally, I slept. After a long time we landed in Jordan in the vast desert. We slept through the night. About 6 people (plus me & C.) were transferred to the 1st class section. I don't know why. It was good because the seats are wider. It might take 2 or 3 days but I continue to pray.

With a combination of ingenuousness and self-consciousness, I could be an observant twelve-year-old, but rereading my diary so many years later, it shortly becomes clear that during that week in September, I constrained my powers of observation. So much happened that I never recorded.

"I was chatting with Catherine," I wrote, as a setup to the commotion in the aisle, but soon I crossed out "chatting" and substituted "talking." When Anne Frank amended her diary for others to read, it may have been for the awkwardness of trying out a grown-up literary voice, and I likewise found myself almost instantly embarrassed by prose that feigned a literary ring. More than that, crafted prose indicated a too-keen consciousness, one that called for greater detail and reflection. Plainer sentences, on the other hand, could convey facts only.

"The hostesses comforted a crying Catherine and calmed everyone," I wrote that morning, but then I crossed out "a crying Catherine" to make the sentence read only that the hostesses comforted and calmed everyone. I'm certain that I made those cross-outs on the plane, or very soon afterward, since I reread the hijacking pages of my diary only once, when I transcribed them for a fellow hostage soon after I returned home.

That inked-over phrase, "a crying Catherine," unnerved me because my big sister, who was meant to protect me, might not be able to do so. When we flew from one parent to the other, Catherine was in charge, not only because she was older but also because she was far more outgoing than I. Teachers in elementary school described me as "serious" and "*oh so quiet,*" and (by sixth grade) "still rather shy." On the hijacked plane, Catherine would be my refuge from everything happening around me. "We leaned on each other," she would say when we got home. "But I guess Martha leaned on me a little more than I leaned on her." Catherine was brave and confident, but when things went wrong, she had no one to take care of her, and then how could she look out for me?

That dishonest early revision of my September 7 entry turns out to be a good indicator of just how deficient I was as a diarist. Those precious pages, I soon find, hold hardly any descriptions of genuine emotion. When my history students work with first-person historical documents— whether diaries or letters, travel accounts or courtroom testimony—I prompt them to ask, "Why did this person tell this story this way?"

Reading and rereading my diary, I see that the aspiring writer in me constructed not a full record but instead a tolerable story; not a truthful story but instead a bearable one; not an honest story but instead a story I could tell when I got home, most especially to my father. When I reached for my journal that first morning, I began the process of crafting that story, one that omitted the parts I didn't want to think about, one that excluded feelings that were too hard to describe and that I knew I wouldn't want to remember anyway. That narrative of omissions would comprise my version of the hijacking, and I would carry it with me for years and years afterward.

The information in my diary is complemented by a document I find, unexpectedly, in the American Jewish Archives in Cincinnati. There, in a room softly lit by Art Deco lamps on polished wooden tables, I am reading through the Sylvia R. Jacobson Papers. Sylvia was a fellow hostage, at the time a fifty-nine-year-old American professor returning from taking a summer course at Hebrew University in Jerusalem. I have no memory of her on the plane, but some weeks after we all came home, she interviewed Catherine and me—in my mind's eye, my father brings a tray of food into our living room as my sister and I speak with a small, serious woman. Sylvia, who died in 1994, was a sociologist, and an article would later arrive in the mail: "Individual and Group Responses to Confinement in a Skyjacked Plane," published in the *American Journal of Orthopsychiatry*.

I learn that Sylvia held a master's degree in social work from Columbia and taught at Florida State University. In one folder, I find a draft of an unpublished manuscript entitled "Children's Attitudinal and Behavioral Responses to Skyjack and Hostage Experiences." Leafing through, I come upon the notes from Sylvia's interview with Catherine and me. Everywhere she'd typed Catherine's name, she crossed it out and substituted the handwritten pseudonym Dora; for my name, she substituted Nancy. "They kept diaries," Sylvia wrote, and her notes include a transcript of my journal entries, ending with the pledge, "This is copied exactly from my diary."

Seeing those words, I remember typing up my diary entries and mailing the transcription to her. That was the only time I reread my diary after I got home, and comparing the transcript to the original so many years later, I see that my pledge was not entirely honest. I'd omitted the crossed-out words and phrases while transcribing ("The hostesses comforted and calmed everyone," I typed, again excluding those disconcerting words, "a crying Catherine"), along with a considerable number of exclamation points that by then struck me as juvenile.

Catherine kept a diary in the summer of 1970 too, but almost fifty years later she can't find it. She and I can both picture it: the tan cardboard of the spiral notebook, the back cover where she'd drawn a heart, curves not quite touching, an arrow shot through it, enclosing in raggedy script the name of the Israeli boy who'd given her the locket with his picture. But Catherine has moved from one apartment to another seven times in the past twenty-five years, and for all that packing and unpacking, she's never come upon the journal.

Then, in the hush of the American Jewish Archives, the other researchers turn their heads at my gasp. In Sylvia's notes I see the heading "Dora's Diary," and there, inside the folder, is a transcript of Catherine's long-lost journal. It ends with the same pledge, "This is copied exactly from my diary." It's a brief account that Catherine wrote after our release, likely just as soon as we got home, and there's no original against which to match the typescript. Still, there are two counts in Catherine's favor: she was unconcerned with the appearance of being a writer, and she was more honest with herself than I.

Thinking back to that first morning in the desert a week or so later, Catherine wrote down her own observations. "A man ran down the aisle shouting something," she recorded. "He had a gun. The purser came running after him. People's terrified faces were turning in all directions. People rose in their seats." Unsurprisingly, Catherine recounted the passengers' reactions, and her own, without compunction. "Women were crying as was I," she recorded. "Everyone was frightened at the thought of being hijacked for hours. We had no idea where we were headed for." Frankly acknowledging the limitations of the grown-ups in charge, she continued, "The hostesses comforted people as best they could." Describing the commandos she saw out the window upon landing, she wrote, "They were all members of the Popular Front for the Liberation of Palestine, and we were their hostages." In my own diary, I would write the word *hostages* only once, much later, and not in reference to myself.

Right away, Catherine acknowledged the fear she never got used to. When she found herself engulfed in hopelessness, she waited for the feelings to pass, and if that took too long, she would make a conscious effort to push them away. Sometimes Catherine felt alert and afraid, much of the time numb, withdrawn, and subdued.

Watching raw news footage in the Motion Picture Research Room of the National Archives, I find evidence that precipitates my most potent reaction yet. Searching the catalog for "Hijacking 1970" and "Hijacking Jordan," I locate three tapes preserved by the Central Intelligence Agency. They are labeled "Moving Images Relating to Intelligence and International Relations," and as the footage skips from one scene to another, I find the visual representation of fellow hostages unsettling.

I watch "people getting off vans and being interviewed," I jot down in my notes. These are the hostages that commandos permitted to leave the plane sometime during the day on Monday. From the TWA aircraft, our captors had chosen passengers of particular nationalities, including South Asians and Middle Easterners other than Israelis. From Swissair, they chose all the women and children, except for the stewardesses, along with five older men. On the tape, the travelers carry their luggage, some of the women carry children, and one little girl carries a doll. I can't find the woman in the sari whose impassive expression I'd studied so carefully, hoping soon to have the opportunity to emulate her, though later I will come upon a photograph of her in a newspaper. In tandem with a few other sources, I piece together the scene of release.

"You seem to be the first people out," a reporter says. "How was it out there, and how do you feel?"

"Oh, it was very wonderful," says a woman with a European accent. "The people and everybody helped us, and really were very polite, extremely polite." *Very wonderful?* Maybe the passengers had agreed among themselves not to speak ill of their captors for the sake of those still in the desert.

"They certainly were nice to us," says another woman, possibly telling the truth in this milder statement.

"They didn't want to hurt anybody, and they wanted to be friends," another says. "They just wanted us to know their position. They were very courteous."

Did she fear for the safety of those still inside the planes?

"Well, I'm concerned, naturally." The woman measures her words. "But I think they'll treat them well. I hope and pray."

"Could you tell us what happened out there on the plane all these hours?" the reporter asks another woman.

"No, not right now," the woman says, casting her gaze downward, unready to talk about it.

"How was the experience for you?" the newsman asks a woman in sunglasses.

"Well, it was pretty frightening." That must have seemed a neutral enough statement.

How were conditions in the desert?

"No light and no water," someone says.

"They brought water today," a teenage girl counters. "They brought us water and tea today, and they treated us fairly, considering"—she pauses—"everything." The girl was traveling unaccompanied but had made friends with another girl who remained captive. "I'm not sure what's happened to her because she's Jewish," she adds.

"Did you ever get hungry or thirsty?" a reporter asks a little girl.

"Yes, a little." The girl smiles. (As another clip reveals, once inside

Amman's Intercontinental Hotel, people chug water, glass after glass of water.)

"Did you ever get hot out there in the desert?"

"Yes!" The girl laughs.

"I got sick in the plane," a boy confesses, from the "rough landing."

Another boy, eleven years old, says it was "all pretty cool and groovy."

At the very moment that all of this was being captured on tape, Catherine and I sat imprisoned inside an airplane in the desert. In the National Archives, as the scenes play on the screen before my eyes, I'm racked by shivers.

Back in the desert, as afternoon turned to evening, anxiety escalated. My memory of the second night in the desert stops with Catherine and me standing in the darkness, huddled and surrounded by our armed captors.

What did other hostages remember of Monday night? Many recounted the anguish to reporters, or to lawyers when they sued the airline, and every time I meet a fellow hostage, the subject of that night comes up. Perhaps other people's experiences can fill in the blanks of my own disjointed images. If I can piece together what happened that night, could I also reach back to my own emotions? When we got home, Catherine insisted I was terrified. Was I, that night?

As people lined up in the aisle, crew members assisted to make sure everyone obeyed the commandos' orders and that everything remained orderly in the midst of increasing agitation and escalating fear.

Nancy Porter, a seventeen-year-old non-Jew from Long Island who had spent the summer with two Jewish friends working on a kibbutz, recalled that the commandos "asked each of us, 'Are you Jewish?'"

Arriving at the front of the plane, Sheila Warnock, a twenty-seven-year-old advertising stylist, answered that she was Catholic (people often assumed her Scots-Irish last name was Jewish), surprised that the commandos were asking about religion.

When a commando asked Foozie Chesler if she was Jewish, Foozie surmised that she could be released if she said no. Her last name didn't betray her, and she had already removed her *chai* necklace, the two

Hebrew letters forming the word for "life." When Foozie said yes, she didn't feel particularly brave. She just knew that she wasn't strong enough to live with a denial, either before her friends or, as an Orthodox Jew, before God. What's more, she had already taken responsibility for Connie Pittaro, a six-year-old flying all by herself, on her way home from a visit with her grandmother in West Germany ("Foozie just helped everybody," Catherine said later. "She was unbelievable"). Now Foozie looked at her young charge, blond and blue-eyed (a "poster child for the Aryan race," she would joke), and asked the little girl if she was Jewish (again, joking later: "Just because she looked like a Nazi doesn't mean she was one").

"Honey, are you Jewish?" Foozie asked gently.

"I don't know what that is," Connie said.

"Well, do you go to church on Sunday? Do you go to synagogue?"

"I don't know what that is," Connie repeated.

To the inquiring commando, Foozie said, "I am Jewish. She is not." But the girl flatly refused to leave Foozie's side, so Foozie's fate that evening would be Connie's too.

Next, all of us who lined up in the aisle followed orders to climb down the ladder and board the vans parked on the desert floor. Commandos apologized to us—Sylvia Jacobson remembered one of the men talking to the passengers through the window, saying that "he hoped that none of us had been personally inconvenienced," that "there was no enmity in the heart of his people towards any of us as individuals."

But then something changed. Outside the vans came shouting in Arabic, and suddenly the commandos ordered everyone to disembark, the sudden reversal bringing confusion and unease. ("And now I think I will go on my way," the little prince told a king on another planet. "No," the king said.) As everyone alighted, Sylvia saw her captors assisting women with babies who were juggling their carry-on bags.

Tikva Raab got scared as our guards "surrounded us with their guns," she would recall. A teenage girl too saw that "everyone was crying and we were surrounded by guns." Watching the armed commandos encircling the hostages, Sheila Warnock felt the chill of a cold sweat. *My God*, she thought, *I am going to be shot.*

One of the commandos began to read names from a list. If your name was called, you were to return to the vans, and a ten-year-old Jewish boy could tell that the names were all "non-Jewish." Susie Hirsch likewise realized that "those of us who were Jewish were detained, and most of the rest were sent onward." When Sheila's name was called, she understood that the list contained the information the hostages had supplied inside the plane, which included nationality and religion, and that those permitted to return to the vans were non-Jews only; indeed, back inside one of the vehicles, Sheila and her fellow passengers determined among themselves that none of them was Jewish.

For some of the Jewish hostages, the events of Monday night only reinforced the idea of Palestinians as an incarnation of Nazis. Especially after the 1967 war, Israelis likened Egyptian president Gamal Abdel Nasser and other Arab leaders to Hitler. For some in the Jordan desert on Monday night, it felt visceral. "That moment felt a little bit like a concentration camp," David Raab recorded, "because surrounding us were guerrillas with machine guns pointing down in our direction, and they were reading off names." With historical astuteness, though, David immediately clarified his initial sense of the scene. "Fortunately, it was nothing like a concentration camp, but what they were doing was taking all non-Jews to hotels; not one single Jew was taken to a hotel." David was correct when it came to the TWA hostages, but when he wrote those words, he didn't know that when the commandos released the women and children from the Swissair plane earlier that day, there had been Jewish passengers among them; as he would write in retrospect, "While this was happening on our TWA plane, the fedayeen took all the Swissair plane's women and children, including Jews, to Amman."

My most immediate awareness of concentration camps came from our pediatrician in New York, who made no effort to hide the series of numbers engraved on her inner arm just above her wrist, which, my father explained, meant that she had been imprisoned in a camp during World War II. In fact, she had done the work of a physician in Auschwitz, Bergen Belsen, and Buchenwald. I would steal glances at the blue-black tattoo and listen to her thick German accent with grave admiration, a feeling that intensified when Catherine and I came upon graffiti on our own block. Defacing the scaffolding where a public library was rising, someone had scrawled "Gas Jew Reds" and "Hitler was right." Catherine walked back home to get a black Magic Marker, then walked back to deface the graffiti. I followed her in both directions, but after her handiwork she stared straight ahead and wouldn't talk to me.

The last Nazi concentration camp had been liberated only twenty-five years earlier—less than a generation—and some of the hostages found it difficult to make historical distinctions when their captors read the names of Jews from lists and then detained them. *Why us and not them, why not us, why them and not us?* Those were the questions that ran through Foozie's mind. To her it felt like "selection": the separation of Jews from non-Jews. To a rabbi's daughter flying home to New York, it felt eerily familiar; she revealed to the commandos that she was Jewish, she said, "because all my life I had grown up in the shadow of the Holocaust, and I'd always thought that someday my turn was going to come," and now her captors were "dividing us up." A fifteen-year-old hostage found herself thinking, "This is going to be mass murder. Jews are going to be massacred again."

The commandos did not, after all, lift and point their guns that night. Instead, they ordered those of us still standing outside to climb back up the ladder. June Haesler, who had remained inside with the rest of the crew, knew only the bare outlines: women and children had left the plane to be taken to a hotel in Amman but "only about 20 were taken and the others were returned to the plane." Omitting much of what had happened outside, some of the commandos explained that it was because they "ran out of hotel space." Those of us ordered to reboard came "stumbling back," one young man recalled, some of the women in tears, the babies in their arms wailing. Another passenger who remained on board heard some of the children say that "as they started boarding the buses the commandos asked them if they were Jewish and, if they were, they were asked to get back on the plane."

In her diary, Catherine wrote about that frightening night only briefly, too much even for my forthright sister to document. "Oh—I forgot to say," she recorded, "that the second day we were all taken out and asked our names and religions, etc. All the non-Jews were taken on buses away."

When I wrote about that night in my diary, I began with the words, "The most frightening moment occurred like this." I'd already noted the food we'd eaten that day, my relief that Catherine and I had gotten cholera shots in Israel, and the names of fellow hostages we'd befriended. By the time I wrote the words "the most frightening moment occurred like this," I'd come to the end of the page, so I did what I always did: I wrote the words "loose paper" and continued my entry on a separate sheet. Since I wanted to be a writer, I treated all my work with care, placing drafts of stories and poems into manila envelopes and lining up the volumes of my diaries in chronological order. Each volume contained a collection of those loose papers for the days when my thoughts spilled beyond the allotted page, and I always tucked those sheets into the back cover, each one neatly folded and identified by date.

This one, though, the one for September 7, 1970, I treated differently. Carelessly, I allowed it to slip away, either on the plane or as soon as I got home. Whatever I wrote after "the most frightening moment occurred like this"—whether I wrote little more than Catherine or whether I wrote a detailed description—has not survived. If I'd recorded my worries in a rare moment of candor, that was the perfect reason to lose that piece of paper, the best way to destroy undeniable evidence of my own fear.

Yet again, then, my diary proves to be of little help—except for one oblique clue. The phrase I chose, "the most frightening moment" implies that there were other frightening moments. Perhaps I was referring only to the ordeal of Monday night, but I might also have been gesturing toward things that had frightened me before then: the commotion in the aisle, the gun at the copilot's neck, the hazardous landing, the glimpse of dynamite, the commandos with their weapons. I had, after all, recorded my own fear, even if I still couldn't retrieve that feeling so many decades later.

_____

10

What I called "the most frightening moment" was a harrowing experience that would remain fixed in the minds of every hostage ordered to line up in the aisle. Why had the commandos done what they had done? So much swirled around me on Monday night in the Jordan desert, some of which I understood at the time and some of which I did not. I wanted to sort out the turmoil of that night by connecting the experiences of the hostages to the strategies of our captors. As historian and memoirist alike, I needed to search for the larger context, since what happened that night would slant and sway the memories of so many of the hostages forever after.

When Catherine wrote in her diary, "All the non-Jews were taken on buses away," she was, I discovered, both right and wrong.

Inside one of the vans, Sheila Warnock sat across from Nancy Porter. The teenage Nancy was crying so hard that Sheila beckoned her to come sit next to her. Reading through State Department telegrams with random names of hostages, I see that Sheila's address is listed as just blocks from where I grew up, and blocks from where I now lived. Sheila writes back right away, amazed that we are neighbors. When she knocks on my door, she immediately asks for a hug before we take to the living room couch to pore over material she's saved for five decades. Among the items is an appointment book in which Sheila jotted down notes while in the air, in the desert, and in Amman. She tells me her own story of Monday night.

The crying girl, Nancy Porter, had been separated from the two Jewish friends with whom she'd spent the summer in Israel. Nancy told her story this way, soon after she got home: "They began reading out the names of all the Jews who they said should get back on the plane. . . . They singled out my two Jewish friends and when I asked why they were not coming, the commandos asked me, 'Are you Jewish?' When I said no, they said, 'Well, you can stay or go, but they are not going.'" All three girls wept, and Nancy boarded the van, still in tears. For one of Nancy's friends, sixteen-year-old Barbara Mensch, it was the first time she had cried since the hijacking began, and the first time in her life that she was treated differently "because I was Jewish," she would say later.

Catherine had watched the three girls—Barbara, Nancy, and a girl named Ann—aware that the commandos "released one of them, and they didn't release the other two." When we got home, she remembered seeing all of them "crying and crying," and figured out that "the one they had released was not Jewish." When I correspond with Nancy Porter, she agrees that she was one of the three girls Catherine saw crying on Monday, separated from her two friends.

After the fact, many of the hostages felt sure that no one who was released from the TWA plane that night was Jewish, and that was true. But it was not true that all the non-Jews on our plane were released. After the vans drove away, the TWA aircraft still held plenty of non-Jews. They included not only crew members but also the TWA pilot who was flying as a passenger, two US Army men, and two State Department officials. They included an Indian-born Hindu naturalized as a US citizen, who was a professor of electrical engineering; a Catholic spice importer of Italian descent who had boarded in Bombay; an economist with the Peace Corps; a street grader from Minnesota and his wife, returning from visiting relatives in West Germany; a couple heading home to New Mexico after an around-the-world tour; a couple flying home to North Carolina, also ending an around-the-world trip; newlyweds who were traveling to the groom's home in Mississippi; and an engineer on his way home to Ohio after conducting business in West Germany. (As well, some of the non-Jewish women who were offered release that night elected to remain in the desert with their husbands.)

Members of the Popular Front for the Liberation of Palestine fiercely maintained that they did not discriminate on the basis of religion. Only a few months earlier, the head of the Popular Front had told a Beirut newspaper that his movement was not "hostile to the Jews as Jews," and did not "aim at annihilating them or throwing them into the sea." The enemies, rather, were Zionism and imperialism; the goal, accordingly, was a democratic state in which all enjoyed full and equal rights of citizenship. (Although the umbrella term *Zionism* encompasses a spectrum of movements and ideas across history, including diverse opinions about both a Jewish state and a Palestinian state, the Popular Front invoked the term to mean those who defended the settling of Palestinian lands by Jews and those who defined Israel as a nation-state for the Jewish people.) The Front had likewise recently issued a statement: "We always make a distinction between Jews and Zionists; we harbour no hostility to the Jews but we shall fight the Zionists because they invaded and occupied our homeland."

Catherine and I heard our captors say that while they objected to Zionism, they had "nothing against the Jewish religion." Other hostages too absorbed the message that they "liked the Jews but they don't like the Zionists," that they "could live together with Jews as long as they were non-Zionist." (The American journalist Thomas Friedman, who reported from Beirut in the 1980s, found that members of the Palestinian resistance "knew I was Jewish and simply did not care," concluding that they "lived up to their claims to be 'anti-Zionist' and not 'anti-Jewish.'")

Despite such assertions, many Jews regarded the distinction between anti-Zionism and anti-Semitism with grave suspicion. Leila Khaled, the two-time Popular Front hijacker, illustrated their reasons for concern. Her mother's explanation that the family was forced to flee Haifa because "the Jews took Palestine" led to "a great hatred of the Jews" in her heart, Khaled said. "At first, I admired Hitler," she admitted of her early activist years, "because I thought he was the enemy of the Jews"; only when she discovered that Hitler also considered Arabs to be subhuman did her admiration cease. Later, while teaching in Lebanon, Khaled befriended an African American woman who convinced Khaled to differentiate between Zionists and all Jews. At the London hospital where she was treated after the thwarted El Al hijacking, someone warned Khaled that the doctor was Jewish, only to hear her say that she was "against Zionists, not Jews, and this doctor was British, not an Israeli."

The words *Jew* and *Israeli* were in fact a source of confusion. When members of the Popular Front spoke of Jews, they often meant Israelis: the terms *Jew* and *Arab* were commonly invoked in 1970, and some Palestinians eschewed the word *Israeli* for its legitimation of the state of Israel. As an American sympathetic to the Palestinian cause put it, "The Israeli is Jewish by his own definition, not by that of an Arab—it is simply that those who occupy Palestine are Jewish." Palestinian activists made a further distinction (one not always strictly honored in the spoken or written word) between *Jews* and *the Jews*. The former, *Yahud*, without an article, referred to individuals who were Jewish (as Sylvia Jacobson recalled one of the commandos saying that night, "there was no enmity in the heart of his people towards any of us as individuals"); the latter, with an article, *el-Yahud*, was synonymous with *Israelis*. To American Jews, such a conflation could be confusing, and confusion of language brought trouble. (The fox told the little prince, "Words are the source of misunderstanding.")

The commandos asked each of us our religion because they wanted to determine the connection of each hostage to the state of Israel, the same reason they asked whether each of us had been to Israel, and if so, why. Bassam Abu-Sharif knew that Israeli citizens "would naturally be more important than any of our other hostages" as the best "bargaining chips," since they could most readily be exchanged for Palestinian prisoners in Israel. Problem was, the aborted El Al hijacking meant there were far fewer Israeli hostages than the Front had counted on.

When Abu-Sharif told a British journalist that all the hostages, with a number of key exceptions, would be released in exchange for seven Palestinians in European prisons, the journalist recorded these hard-to-decipher words: "*except* (and this was not absolutely clear) the American/Jewish/Israeli passengers who enjoy dual citizenship," adding that "Jews of other nationalities would be freed like anyone else." Without a sufficient number of Israelis, it seemed the commandos were targeting Americans (as one Popular Front slogan put it, "Israel is America. America is Israel"), and in particular Americans with ties to Israel, most easily discerned in those who held dual citizenship. But to the hostages and to much of the world, invoking *Jewish* as a stand-in for *Israeli* appeared unmistakably like the intended separation of all Jews from all non-Jews.

In the press and among politicians, a streamlined story about Monday night prevailed. The *Washington Post* described the Popular Front's strategy as "to separate their victims into two groups, Jews and non-Jews," while an Israeli newspaper reported that "the Jews of the hijacked planes—women, children, and men—are being held inside the planes in the desert while the non-Jews were transferred to hotels in Amman." New York senator Charles Goodell spoke of Jews "particularly selected for this fate . . . simply because they are Jews," and Massachusetts congressman Thomas P. "Tip" O'Neill spoke of "the terrorists' separation of Jewish and non-Jewish passengers."

Statements like these were neither entirely true nor entirely untrue. In reality, the division was not strictly Jew versus non-Jew, since Popular Front commandos released Jews from the Swissair plane and detained non-Jews on the TWA plane. Since our plane had departed from Israel, perhaps the commandos assumed that all the Jewish passengers were Zionists, unlike the Jews on Swissair, which had no stop in Israel.

Yet our captors asked all of us to name our religion, asked whether or not we were Jewish, and divided the women and children into Jews and non-Jews, thereby reinforcing, as William Quandt of the National Security Council later articulated, a sense that the Popular Front was "somehow focused on people as Jews or non-Jews, rather than as Zionists and non-Zionists." The Front, Quandt said, claimed that "they were not anti-Semitic, that they were just anti-Zionist," but they "didn't go around and ask people about their political views, they simply asked them what their religion was," which was "not a very smart thing to do if you're trying to combat the common view" of anti-Semitic convictions. As Roy Innis, the African American leader and national director of the Congress for Racial Equality, put it, such actions subverted the claim that "their fight is against Zionism and not against the Jewish people."

As hostages' families absorbed the news out of Jordan, some made connections to the Holocaust. "My wife was four years in Auschwitz, and I was four years in a concentration camp in Hungary, and I lost four children by Hitler," said the father of a seventeen-year-old hostage, "and now I'm going through the same thing again." Elected officials and community leaders followed suit. "Prayers are being recited by many Americans who lost most of their families in the Nazi terror, and who now may lose the remaining few in the Arab terror," Senator Goodell said. The separation of Jews, said Congressman O'Neill, was "all too reminiscent of distinctions made another time in this century." Leaders of Jewish organizations in the United States invoked "Auschwitz in the desert," and an Israeli newspaper wrote of the terrorists setting up "an air field and a concentration camp."

Later, at a press conference held in the desert, the question came up. "Why are you keeping the Jewish women and children hostage?" a reporter asked.

"They are not kept because they are Jewish," Bassam Abu-Sharif answered. "They are kept just for interrogation for the reasons I mentioned, the dual citizenship." The *Los Angeles Times* headline would, unsurprisingly, miss the nuance: JEWS ON JETS HELD FOR 'INTERROGATION' ON DUAL CITIZENSHIP.

What happened to the hostages who left the plane on Monday afternoon (including the woman in the sari who walked so carefully up the aisle) and those who left on Monday night (after the ordeal on the desert floor)? Those of us who remained in the desert were pretty sure they had been taken to Amman, and so they had. As it turned out, when those hostages were transported from the desert to the Intercontinental Hotel, the Jordanian government thought they would be free to leave the country. The Popular Front at first concurred but then reversed itself. Soon it seemed that the released passengers were still hostages, since the commandos retained their passports, and in any case the city's airport remained mostly closed because of the unofficial war.

Anarchy engulfed Amman that first week of September. The fedayeen, intent on deposing Jordan's King Hussein, were taking over the city. Tanks rolled through the streets. Gunfire hit the US embassy. Government offices and schools shut down. Residents rushed to stock up as shopkeepers closed their doors. Commandos with megaphones urged residents to stay inside, even as many homes lay in rubble. "Amman is a battlefield," a group of journalists wrote in a pooled dispatch, with "exploding shells, mortar bombs, and machine gun fire." There was "no front line, no order of battle, just thousands of men with machine guns and mortars and rockets, shooting at anything that moved."

Even though the king claimed to support the resistance movement, the fedayeen were threatening his power. The Popular Front and their allies had steadily created a state within a state, establishing their own courts, schools, and hospitals (the Palestinian Red Crescent, who sent the kind doctor to our plane, went unrecognized by the International Red Cross). The Popular Front flew their own flag and patrolled the streets of Amman, carrying their own weapons and wearing their own uniforms. Most citizens, Jordanians and Palestinians alike, were unhappy with the violence—fedayeen had killed an American diplomat and had tried to kill the king himself.

The Intercontinental Hotel was contested ground in the undeclared war between Jordanian forces and Palestinian insurgents. Even before the September conflicts, reporters called the Intercontinental "the Middle East's most famous and most battle-seasoned hotel," and those released from the desert found themselves eyewitnesses. From the streets came the sound of heavy firing, along with the crash of exploding shells, each side vying for control of the hotel. Rounds of mortar landed in the driveway. Windows trembled and shattered—it might have been intentional, it might have been cross fire, and it wasn't always clear which side was shooting. People crawled on hands and knees to avoid the ammunition that lodged in the walls, taking refuge in interior corridors or hunkering down in stairwells, under beds or lobby furniture. Jordanian soldiers came straight inside, firing shots from the upper floors. Hotel staff went about their tasks, some silently sympathizing with the Palestinian resistance. Waiters served meals between bursts of machine-gun fire that sent guests to the bomb shelter, which was really the windowless basement nightclub. The Beirut bureau chief for *Time* magazine watched personnel "just sweep up the plaster and glass," then serve sandwiches.

"It's sort of all like a bad nightmare," a hostage told a reporter, smiling politely. "I thought I was safe after we left the plane, but now with the machine guns, it's a bad feeling. I'm very nervous." Another woman called the transfer from the desert "out of the frying pan into the fire," while a young teen pocketed a couple of bullets from his room. Feeling like pawns in someone else's war, some of those released indeed wondered whether they had been safer back at the desert airstrip, and US embassy personnel worried that the hostages could be turned into valuable assets in the fighting.

In between skirmishes, the commandos tried to persuade the hotel hostages of their cause, but Sheila Warnock declined to engage in political conversation for fear of causing harm to those still in the desert. When she finally gave an interview to ABC News, a commando stood by, then berated her for saying so much about the women and children who were ordered back to the plane. Other hostages listened to the commandos with interest. A seventeen-year-old girl released from Swissair reflected that before the hijacking, she "didn't know one thing about the issues, really, or the commandos." Where she lived at home, she said, "many of the people are Jewish, so my Jewish friends told me that side. The Palestinians told me something else entirely, so now I'd like to have time to form my own opinion, but only after I study and read up on it."

Through it all, reporters composed furiously on the manual typewriters they had lugged overseas, and sometimes they hounded the hotel hostages, cameramen in tow—once a photographer imitated the sound of a whizzing bomb just to get a shot of guests diving for cover. If the phone lines were working, the reporters shouted their dispatches into receivers. Other times, they hailed taxis to take them to the cable office to send out stories before the shooting started up again, and once a *New York Times* correspondent stepped outside to find that "boys pointed AK-47s in our faces." Pipes took a hit in the cross fire, water gushing through the telephone switchboard, and after a reporter watched a bullet crash through his window and land in the bedside lamp, he took to sleeping in his bathtub. Each day the journalists headed out to the planes in the desert and returned covered with dust.

Inside the plane that second night, after Catherine and I returned to our row, and after the vans drove away, shivering passengers seated near open exit doors traded places with those who welcomed the chilly air. Around eleven o'clock, stewardesses Bettie McCarthy and Vicki McVey were falling asleep when one of the commandos awakened them, requesting assistance in locating particular passengers. As my sister and I slept, a man armed with yet another list of names accompanied Bettie and Vicki as they searched for the individuals, one by one. All Bettie said to each male passenger was, "They'd like to see you up front," but she knew they were going to be taken away because the commandos instructed the stewardesses to make sure the men brought their coats and hand luggage with them. It seemed clear too that they weren't going to be driven to Amman to be released, and Vicki thought the passengers acted bravely as they gathered their belongings. Bettie wouldn't sleep for the rest of the night.

When Rivke Berkowitz heard a commando tell a stewardess that they were going to call the names of people they wanted to interview, she felt a tremor of foreboding just before she heard her husband's name. The couple was traveling with their two-year-old daughter, and Rivke was pregnant. "You better put on your shoes," Rivke told Jerry, a chemistry professor at Bronx Community College. "I think they are taking you off the plane."

When a commando mispronounced John Hollingsworth's name, he said, "That's me." He was a State Department diplomat flying home from Algeria.

Robert Schwartz and James Wood both worked for the US Department of Defense in Thailand. They were the men who had sliced up and disposed of sensitive classified documents while the hijacking was in progress, one of them swallowing some of the shredded pages. They were called as well.

"Sir, are you Mr. Raful?" a commando asked Abraham Harari-Raful, who affirmed his identity before the name of his brother Joseph was called too. Both were rabbis, and both were part of a close-knit Syrian Jewish community in Brooklyn. Both held dual US-Israeli citizenship, including Israeli passports.

As the selected men disembarked with their commando escorts, the women tried to reassure one another. Rachel Harari-Raful watched both of her sons disappear, while her daughter-in-law murmured "Don't worry" and "They'll be back." Some of the wives swallowed tranquilizers. "We sat all night," Rivke Berkowitz remembered, "and we waited for them to come back, and they didn't come back."

Press reports about the removal of those six men on Monday night were incorrect. The headline from the Jewish Telegraphic Agency read CORRESPONDENT CONFIRMS GUERRILLAS REMOVED JEWISH PASSENGERS FROM HIJACKED PLANES, which made it sound as if all the men identified on Monday night were Jews, when only half of them were. It was clear why the commandos had chosen five of the men. The two rabbis held dual Israeli and American passports, and three—Hollingsworth, Wood, and Schwartz (the last a practicing Catholic, with a Jewish father)— weren't Jewish, but they worked for the US government. It was less clear why they had chosen Jerry Berkowitz—he wondered if it was because his captors thought he looked Israeli. In any case, all six of them could prove valuable if negotiations for the hostages inside the planes faltered.

After the frightening events of Monday night, the commandos stopped making distinctions between Jews and non-Jews. Even though her captors knew she was Jewish, one woman said, they treated her "very well all the same"—they "just didn't talk politics." Other Jewish hostages felt they were treated "no different from the non-Jewish passengers," "like all the others," not "singled out in any way." Later, to a jumble of questions about Jewish hostages, flight engineer Al Kiburis told reporters, "There's no differentiation, they're not segregated, and they're being treated nice."

The next day I wrote in my diary, under the heading "News": "Several names of men were read off from a list (6) & these men were taken off the plane." Catherine and I quickly absorbed from the talk around us that the men called up in the middle of the night had not been taken to the same place as the hostages who had earlier left the plane; they had been taken, Catherine wrote in her diary, to "God-knows-where." No one knew what was going to happen to the rest of us either. A writer for the London *Observer* called the whole ordeal in Jordan "a tightly focused life-and-death drama, with the whole world watching."

11

With the whole world watching, what did our captors tell the world they wanted? Was it different from what they told us, their hostages in the desert? I knew from the start that our captivity was related to Palestinian prisoners, but almost certainly I didn't permit myself to think about what would happen if the commandos didn't get what they wanted.

Now I set out to discover the contours of their demands and negotiations. What was going on while all of us sat there, confined inside the airplane? Because my parents' experiences of the hijacking ultimately shaped my own so profoundly, learning what they had faced about those demands and negotiations becomes central to my quest. Perhaps understandably, neither my father nor my mother ever recounted to Catherine and me their own knowledge of—or reactions to—our captors' ultimatums. After so many decades I find their memories too deeply buried to excavate, which means that our conversations can go only so far. That means I have to search a different way, by looking to the archives of September 1970. Returning with this new focus to the newspapers my parents read and the television broadcasts they watched during the days and nights of their daughters' captivity will, I suspect, be one of the more haunting parts of my investigation.

Again in the Motion Picture Research Room of the National Archives, I watch the old-fashioned countdown leader at the start of the tape, just like the ones I saw when my elementary school classes watched films. This time it feels eerily like a countdown to a fatal deadline.

"A room with PFLP pics on wall," I write in my notes. Scrutinizing the images, I identify Lenin and Che Guevara, along with photographs of Palestinian dead and wounded. In the room, three men sit behind a table. One, wearing a striped button-down shirt, will be named as Comrade Bassam. This is Bassam Abu-Sharif, the commando who apologized to us upon landing and the one who would tell a reporter that the Popular Front sought to identify Israeli citizens, not Jews. Even though he'd spent considerable time on our plane, he doesn't look familiar. Seated next to Abu-Sharif is a man who will be identified only as Comrade Ibrahim. He's wearing sunglasses that he never removes. A third man, sitting behind the same table, is never identified.

I see that I'm watching a press conference. Earlier on Monday, a television crew quartered at the Intercontinental Hotel had ventured out to the desert. Approaching the airstrip, they saw the planes, "tiny as plastic toys," but when they got nearer, commandos shouted and pointed their guns, then confiscated their equipment and exposed their film. But late that afternoon, members of the Popular Front agreed to speak with journalists inside a whitewashed house on a hillside near Amman's center—the Front's temporary headquarters since their proper headquarters inside the Wahdat refugee camp had been shelled by the Jordanian army. Abu-Sharif, who could communicate in Arabic, English, and French, assumed the role of spokesman.

Again I find the visual representation unsettling, bringing on that same queasy sensation of time travel, knowing that while these people were conversing back and forth, Catherine and I were inside the plane in the desert. Again I use various sources to piece together the dialogue.

"Can you tell me what is being done for the passengers out there in the desert?" a reporter asks.

"They are in very good health, and they are treated very well by our fighters," Comrade Ibrahim answers.

"Has there been any violence on the plane? Any attempt by the passengers to—"

"Not a single one." Abu-Sharif shakes his head. "Actually, in the beginning they were terrified. Then they were calmed down."

Eavesdropping so many years later, I consider that Abu-Sharif used the same word that Catherine used when we got home: *terrified*. In my diary I recorded that, up in the air, "people's faces turned frightened," removing my own feelings from the scene. Only an admission to my diary that "I began praying and praying" aligned my feelings, if indirectly, with Abu-Sharif's description, and Catherine's.

"When are these people going to be released?" a reporter asks. "You said today, but the media—"

Abu-Sharif evades the question, taking the opportunity to proclaim the Popular Front's larger goals of creating a socialist state in Palestine and fighting worldwide imperialism.

"When will the women and children be released, can you tell us that?" a reporter demands.

"Today," Comrade Ibrahim says, though that would be only partly true, since many of us would be ordered back onto the aircraft.

"When is the seventy-two hours over? When did that period start?"

There's a jumble of conversation before Comrade Ibrahim says, "Now, twelve hours." He means that twelve hours have passed since the start of the deadline.

"Help me a little bit," says the baffled reporter.

"After sixty hours," Comrade Ibrahim says, laughing mockingly at the reporter's apparent lack of elementary subtraction skills.

The reporter persists, asking the men to "pick a day and an hour."

"Sixty hours," Comrade Ibrahim repeats, smirking.

"And what will you do if the Israelis don't meet your demands, or if the other people don't meet your demands?" Listening in, I brace for the answer, but Comrade Ibrahim's words are evasive.

"They can do nothing," he says. "I told you, we will get the answer." In my notes, I write, "Men being asked about their demands, not answering directly or at all."

Reporters want to know what the spokesmen make of the ways their actions are inflaming negative world opinion.

"Where was world opinion when a million of our people were hijacked out of Palestine by the Israelis?" Abu-Sharif retorts before softening his tone and explaining more patiently. "We are Marxist-Leninists fighting a people's war against Zionism, American imperialism, and all the reactionary Arab regimes—such as Jordan's," he says, smiling disarmingly. Elbows on the table, cigarette propped between the fingers of his clasped hands, Abu-Sharif calls the hijackings a chance to "convince the whole world."

A document in the archives of the Richard Nixon Presidential Library in California quotes the spokesman as saying the Popular Front has brought explosives on board, ready to "destroy the planes along with their prisoners," should anyone approach the planes or should the demands of the Popular Front not be met before the deadline. I study the document with care to be sure I understand everything correctly: the spokesman "hedged when asked if the passengers would be permitted to get off first but guerrilla sources said the plan was apparently to blow up the hostages also." As Abu-Sharif would later recall, "My PFLP colleagues went around wiring detonators to large lumps of plastic explosive placed under the seats."

Watching the tape and reading the documents that corroborate it, I understand that this pronouncement to the reporters is different from what Bassam Abu-Sharif told us when we landed in the desert ("Don't worry, it's only a hijack. Nobody will be hurt"), and when he tried to calm passengers who spied the dynamite ("Not for you, though. Don't worry"—to which he added, disconcertingly, "It's just to blow up the plane in case anybody tries anything").

Listening in all these years later, I understand that our captors intentionally kept us, their hostages, off balance. I understand that the frightening pronouncements at the press conference are entirely different from the message I've preserved in my memory: copilot Jim Majer relaying to the passengers that our captors promised "no bodily harm." True, I'd never been able to erase the impression of the men laying dynamite that first night, but I always placed the memory of the copilot's words ahead of that tenacious image.

On the tape, the reporters leave the press conference, exasperated.

Within days, the Popular Front added a major bargaining chip to their side of the negotiations.

"Speedbird, this is Revolution Airport GCA calling," our copilot Jim

Majer said, using the call sign for BOAC (British Overseas Airways Corporation, the predecessor of British Airways), and referring to ground-controlled approach. "Steer 043° off the Amman Beacon, and proceed about 11 miles. Look for a TWA 707 and a Swissair DC-8. Please land after these two aircraft. There should be about 24,000 feet remaining of runway available."

The trouble had started on BOAC 775 soon after takeoff from Bahrain, an island in the Persian Gulf, en route from Bombay to London.

"What is that chap up to?" the steward in first class asked a stewardess serving coffee. Next thing, the suspicious passenger was pointing a gun, telling the passengers to "sit down and not move" or the hijackers would blow everyone up with a bomb in a briefcase.

"Sit down and have a talk about it and tell us what you want us to do," Captain Cyril Goulborn told the man who burst into the cockpit, finger on the trigger. Since the hijacker spoke Arabic in his radio communications, the flight-deck crew didn't know where they were going.

Captain Goulborn announced over the intercom that the flight had been taken over by the Popular Front for the Liberation of Palestine and apologized to his passengers, but the hijacker grabbed the instrument and contradicted him—one boy remembered the man saying "he wasn't sorry and that they were fighting for their rights."

With the fuel supply diminishing, the flight would have to stop at the Beirut airport, and just before landing, an accomplice entered the cockpit with a briefcase full of explosives, announcing, "I hope I don't have to use these, but if anything happens I will blow up the airplane with us in it." With takeoff from Beirut, it seemed obvious they would be, as the copilot joked, "joining the party in the desert." Soon enough, the scene appeared below: two airplanes on some sort of improvised runway. Swissair captain Fritz Schreiber joined our captain in the TWA cockpit to assist Goulborn with the desert landing.

Counting the nearly 150 new arrivals, Revolution Airport was now home to almost 300 hostages (the commandos quickly identified Arab and South Asian passengers and drove them to Amman). The BOAC crew was pretty sure the commandos immediately wired their cockpit with explosives, and one of the passengers later glimpsed stacked blocks of orange TNT. Soon the International Red Cross representative in the desert ordered nine hundred more meals, marking his telegram to the Geneva offices URGENT! Everyone on our plane felt bad for the new arrivals, but as David Raab reasoned, since "we were up for some type of trade," the more people to trade, "the better our chances of getting out."

The three hijacked planes in the Jordan desert. Our plane is in the middle, in between BOAC and Swissair.

[ROLLS PRESS/POPPERFOTO VIA GETTY IMAGES]

The hijacking of BOAC 775 wasn't part of the Popular Front's original scheme but rather the spontaneous work of a Palestinian sympathizer. The new plane would give the Front more than fifty British hostages to exchange for Leila Khaled, still in police custody in London for the attempted El Al seizure.

Along with the hostages in the desert, the world wondered: How had hijackers taken down another plane within three days of four spectacular hijackings? Just the day before, BOAC had tightened its operations, searching pockets and carry-on bags and advising travelers to arrive at airports more than an hour early. In Bahrain, security forces had diligently implemented enhanced search procedures, but that went only for baggage, not bodies, which is where the BOAC hijackers hid their weapons and explosives. Still, it was perplexing. "To conceal a six inch gun is not difficult," mused the British copilot, "but to conceal a large container which had explosives—how that got through security I do not know."

Airport security in the United States was in its infancy in 1970. It wasn't just that nobody thought of Cuban hijackings as dangerous, it was also that individual airports and airlines were responsible for their own procedures. In some places, ramps and runways might as well have been public recreation areas. ("Do you have the guns?" my father called out to the dancers as his company boarded a plane in the late 1960s, making sure the wooden props hadn't been left behind. No one reacted.) The Federal Aviation Administration recommended—but did not require—simultaneous metal detection (crude machines in those days) and psychological profiling, which pertained largely to hijackers setting their sights on Cuba.

Then, immediately after September 6, 1970, airports all over the world stepped up security. Passengers had to produce identification to buy a ticket. Holders of passports from Arab nations underwent "special checks," and certain passengers departing Israel were ushered into hastily constructed booths. The US scrambled too, but procedures remained unsophisticated and uneven, with searches sometimes conducted only by airline ticket agents. Even as Washington was adamant about new measures, the industry fretted over alienating passengers. "The airlines have really bitched about that," Secretary of Defense Melvin Laird told Henry Kissinger the day before the BOAC hijacking, to which Kissinger replied, "We are going to ram it down their throats."

Nothing was foolproof, of course, since, as one skeptic pointed out, nothing could stop "a pair of hands choking a stewardess." After September 6, President Nixon planned to place armed guards, disguised as civilians, on select US flights, which prompted visions of on-board shoot-outs—just like the one on El Al—or fatally wounded hijackers detonating bombs in their last living moments. While one citizen wrote to the White House to suggest that crew members overpower hijackers with spray cans of oven cleaner, the security director of a US airline called the whole thing a "monumental task."

The press conference on Monday night left the demands of our captors both clear and unclear. Sifting through communications preserved in the

Nixon Library (some marked "Top Secret"), in the State Department
Archives in Washington, in the Swiss Federal Archives, and in the British
National Archives, I set out to make sense of the negotiations for our
release, or its opposite.

At the State Department, the Bureau of Near Eastern Affairs swiftly
formed a working group headed by national security advisor Henry
Kissinger, and at six o'clock on Monday morning—noon for us in the
Jordan desert—they marked the status of the hostages as "unclear." The
Popular Front was, as the Amman embassy cabled to Washington, "in
total control of area surrounding planes," and the Front announced that
the planes at Dawson's Field were, as United Press International put it,
"loaded with explosives wired for quick detonation in the event any attempt was made to approach them." King Hussein of Jordan knew it
would be impossible for his forces to act in any way without endangering
our lives. The hostages, Hussein said, were "a gun at our heads."

Now I sort out the terms. The Popular Front wanted to exchange their
Swiss hostages for three Palestinian prisoners in Switzerland, all serving
twelve-year sentences for a machine-gun attack on an El Al plane in February 1969 at the Zurich airport. They wanted to exchange their German
hostages for three Palestinian prisoners in West Germany, awaiting trial
for a February 1970 guns-and-grenades attack on an El Al bus at the
Munich airport, in which one among the wounded had died. After
the British plane landed, they added to their roster the exchange of
the British hostages for the El Al hijacker Leila Khaled. Only when the
various governments met all of those demands would the Front release
their American hostages. Finally, and most important, the Popular Front
wanted to exchange Israeli hostages for an as-yet unspecified number of
Palestinians held in Israeli prisons.

Countdown began on Monday at 6:00 a.m., just as Comrade Ibrahim
had told reporters, and if those demands were not met within seventy-
two hours, the planes, "including remaining hostages," said a Front spokesman, as recorded in a telegram sent to the State Department from the US
embassy in Amman, "will be blown up." The commandos' ultimatum
was repeated in another telegram: "Time period for meeting all of the
demands . . . is 72 hours starting from six a.m. local time. If demands are

not met within this time, planes with all passengers will be blown up." Kissinger reiterated the ultimatum to Nixon. Television news announced the deadline on Monday evening, and newspapers carried it the next morning. A Swiss official (described by a colleague as "level-headed and not given to emotional talk") noted the serious possibility of a "blood-bath" in the desert.

Right away my father sent a telegram to Nixon. As he recalled decades later, it said something to the effect of "For God's sake, pay whatever they want, and get those kids back." I never found that document, but my father's plea joined those of other relatives, some of which I find filed away in the Nixon Library archives.

"As parents we beg you have our daughter released," Foozie's parents implored the president.

"My Daddy is in the hijacked TWA plane in Jordan," the eight-year-old daughter of a hostage wrote. "Please help my daddy come back safe. I love him more than anything else in the world."

Nixon had a lot on his mind in September 1970: the continuing war in Vietnam, recently expanded with the invasion of Cambodia months earlier, along with upcoming midterm elections, college campus unrest that he planned to condemn during the midterm campaign, and a European tour planned for the end of the month. With the hijacking, Nixon was eager to "develop some dramatic Administration action," take some "tough shocking steps," as White House chief of staff H. R. Haldeman recorded. Kissinger, on the other hand, wanted the president to skip the drama and release nothing more than terse statements conveying that he remained "closely informed." Nixon, recalled one diplomat, was known for impulsively "suggesting strong actions" (when he later talked of bombing Dawson's Field, Secretary of Defense Melvin Laird knew the results would be disastrous, and invoked the weather as an excuse to nix the plan).

Nixon and Kissinger had to coordinate with the other nations involved. Representatives from the United States, Switzerland, West Germany, and Great Britain met in the Swiss capital of Bern, calling themselves the Bern Group, to be led by the Swiss foreign minister. Switzerland and West Germany were ready to release their Palestinian prisoners, while

Great Britain was still deliberating. Israel, not initially invited, and consistently refusing to submit to air piracy and extortion, would be a more shadowy presence in the group.

Very soon the International Committee of the Red Cross called an emergency meeting in Geneva to create a special mission to augment their permanent Jordan delegation (which normally supplied relief to refugees and prisoners). The organization opposed hostage-taking and retribution directed at civilians, both of which violated the 1949 Fourth Geneva Convention, and the principal aim of their new mission was "purely humanitarian": to bring relief to those of us held in the desert. Their second objective was to get everyone released. The Popular Front agreed that the International Red Cross could serve as a neutral intermediary, acting as "a channel of communication" so that "the captors and the governments understand each other." The delegates departed Geneva for Amman on Monday night.

Leading the delegation was André Rochat, an Arabic speaker in his mid-forties with experience in the Middle East. Tall, attired in khaki clothing and desert boots, he wore a signature white hat to shield him from the sun. The British ambassador to Jordan found him "prickly" and "difficult," suffering from "an inflated idea of his own indispensability." One reporter described him as "a flamboyant figure"; another called him a "latter-day Lawrence of Arabia." Camaraderie with the Palestinian commandos was Rochat's preferred method, even as he struck some of them as imperious. Not two months earlier, he had intervened when Palestinian commandos took over an Olympic Airways plane in Athens and threatened to blow it up with everyone on board. Those hijackers demanded the release of seven comrades, imprisoned in Greece, who had participated in three air-travel related attacks, including one in the El Al terminal, in which a child was killed. Rochat had boarded the Olympic plane at the airport and negotiated the release of hostages and prisoners alike.

The trickiest part of the September 1970 negotiations would be to figure out how to free the hostages without submitting to blackmail. The terms of release would be entirely up to the parties involved, with a single imperative from the Red Cross: all hostages must be released *sans discrimination*, with no divisions by nationality or religion. That meant that Switzerland or West Germany or Great Britain could not exchange Palestinian prisoners respectively for the Swiss or West German or British hostages. Should any separate negotiations with the Popular Front come to pass, the Red Cross would withdraw and depart. In the plane carrying him to Jordan, André Rochat contemplated the crisis ahead with "a great uneasiness."

The airline also had a stake in our rescue, and on Monday night a task force from TWA arrived in Amman too. Richard Wilson, assistant to airline president Forwood C. Wiser and a Middle East expert, led the group. Joining Wilson were Farid Alonzo, who worked in the Beirut office and spoke Arabic; Art Zuger, manager of international flight operations and a maintenance executive, who could ready the plane for takeoff; Claude Girard, director of international flight operations, who was capable of flying the plane out of the desert; and Thomas Bell, in charge of international public relations. Right away, Wilson and his men felt "extreme tension everywhere," amid "the volleys of sniper fire" in Amman. They wanted to head out to the desert, board the aircraft, evaluate the plane's airworthiness, and talk with the hostages, but that would prove impossible. As they soon found, we hostages "might as well have been on the moon."

Circumstances would be tough for all negotiators. Telephone, cable, telegram, and telex were the modes of international communication in 1970. If a phone line was busy, you just had to wait, or call someone else to relay the message. If you couldn't get through by telephone, you could send a telex via Western Union—in Geneva, operators at the International Red Cross read the dots and dashes of Morse code. In Amman, negotiators would meet with commandos "at all hours of the day and night," as an embassy official put it. If neither a face-to-face meeting nor a telephone call was possible, the parties sent messages back and forth via taxi drivers or pedestrians. Sometimes Red Cross delegates found themselves blockaded in the streets, other times Popular Front members neglected negotiations in favor of combat.

Israel's intransigence further complicated everything, with foreign minister Abba Eban asserting in his stentorian British-accented English that the exchange of prisoners for hostages only "encourages the terrorists." *Haaretz*, Israel's independent daily, which advocated withdrawal from the 1967-occupied territories, editorialized that "haste in accepting the exchange deal would only increase the terrorists' daring and award a prize for their audacity." Israel did not want the other nations to negotiate either (as one diplomat said, that would leave the Israelis and presumably other Jews "to broil in the airliners"), which exasperated the others, eager to get their citizens home.

Over time, Rochat would come to believe that no one would get out unless Israel agreed to talk. A top Middle East negotiator in the State Department figured that when Israeli politicians faced the "sentencing to death" of their own citizens, they would quit being so stubborn. Blowing up the planes with the hostages on board: for all the diplomats, that was the most anxiety-provoking possibility.

So many decades later, wanting to know what our captors told the rest of the world they were going to do with us, I turn the pages of the *Congressional Record* and the *Central Intelligence Bulletin*. I immerse myself in heaps of telegrams between the US embassy in Amman and the State Department. I scrutinize the Nixon administration's "situation reports" about the 1970 crisis in Jordan. All of these documents contradict the copilot's assurance of "no bodily harm" and Bassam Abu-Sharif's reassurance that no one would be hurt because it was "only a hijack." Because there was so much I didn't know at the time, these documents feel remote from whatever fear may have come over me in the desert. But as I imagine my parents taking in any of this information while Catherine and I sat inside the plane, a surge of emotion engulfs me, an emotion that feels oddly familiar and distant at the same time. ("Were you so sad, then?" the aviator asked the little prince.)

On Monday morning, Secretary of State William Rogers felt "a sense of tremendous urgency," facing the reality of hundreds of people trapped on airplanes "wired to be blown up," a deadline looming.

On Tuesday, the State Department wanted the Jordanian government to alert the Popular Front that none of their members would survive if they were to "carry out their threat to destroy the aircraft and passengers."

On Wednesday, Rochat thought the situation had become "extremely serious," warning that "we may face a tragedy." He predicted "one chance in two we will get everyone out." The Washington Special Actions Group was keeping open the possibility of rescuing the hostages, but Popular Front reps told Rochat that any such action would mean "the three planes will blow up immediately with all occupants." Any rescue attempt, Kissinger relayed to Nixon, would come to pass only with "conclusive evidence that the hostages would otherwise be killed." Top-secret minutes had Nixon considering an attack on Jordan if "the planes and passengers are destroyed." When television anchorman Walter Cronkite announced that the commandos had indefinitely extended the deadline, he added, "There is still great concern tonight about the fate of some three hundred passengers and crew aboard those three hijacked planes," while White House correspondent Dan Rather reported that US military intervention was unlikely, save for "some disaster out there in the desert."

On Thursday, the CIA made clear that despite the temporary rescinding of the deadline, "the lives of the hostages are still in danger." New York senator Charles Goodell spoke that day of "human cargo" sitting inside "mined and fused airplanes." He said the words "possible death," and he said the words "Today could be their last."

When the hijackers first uttered the words "Popular Front for the Liberation of Palestine," stewardess June Haesler heard a passenger say, "Palestine? Oh, that's Israel." That equation was the root of the trouble. On the plane in the desert, I found the history lessons imparted by my captors unfamiliar.

My sister and I felt a deep attachment to Israel, as the place where our mother lived and where we got to live with her, that place of "sun and fun," the place that became our home between school years. At twelve years old, even as I pushed away my own feelings, I grasped that my captors and fellow captives alike were fully human, all part of complicated histories that evoked genuine emotions. Now I wanted to leave behind reductive dichotomies, to draw instead upon the nuance and empathy that historians prize. I wanted to understand, on a human scale, the conflicting convictions that rippled around me in the desert.

Six summers in Israel, and Catherine and I knew nothing about the people who lived on the land when the nation was founded in 1948. Back then, I knew that Jews moved to Palestine in the late nineteenth century to escape oppression, but I didn't know that conflicts with Arabs intensified as Jewish emigration from Russia and Poland continued into the early twentieth century, or that Britain and France carved up the Ottoman Empire at the end of World War I, handing Palestine to the British. I'd never learned of Britain's 1917 Balfour Declaration, calling for Palestine to be "a national home for the Jewish people," and I didn't know that in the 1930s a British diplomat had predicted an "irrepressible conflict" between two peoples with "no common ground" and "national aspirations" that were "incompatible."

By the time my parents toured Israel with the Martha Graham Dance Company in the mid-1950s, Israeli and Palestinian perspectives had already hardened into virtually irreconcilable narratives. With the end of World War II and the British withdrawal from Palestine, the United Nations proposed a partition, which Palestinians rejected, indignant that they, who had nothing to do with the Christian, European genocide of Jews during the Holocaust, should bear such a disproportionate burden. A British scholar of Lebanese descent felt "deeply and personally" the "suffering of the Jews," he said in 1946, yet "guilt for creating that problem," he protested, "does not rest upon the shoulders of the Arabs, but on those of Europe."

On the other side, for Holocaust survivors living in displaced persons camps, their homes destroyed or overtaken, their relatives murdered, a Jewish homeland in Palestine seemed the only possible sanctuary. Even when diplomats said, "You realize there are Arabs in Palestine and you must get along with them," or "Do you think it is democratic to impose a new majority on an Arab majority already there?" the survivors pointed to Europeans as their exterminators and wondered if one day the United States or Great Britain too might expel Jews. Displaced persons, observed a British politician, saw Palestine as the "one hope of escape from Hell," even if it meant they would have to "fight the Arabs." When a Holocaust survivor returned to his family's home in Lithuania, a neighbor said to him: "Are you still alive? We hate you, go away!"

At twelve years old, I knew that Jews who escaped Nazi Germany arrived in the new nation of Israel, but I didn't know that the postwar United States had barred most Jewish refugees from entry or how much the Holocaust bolstered the Zionist idea of a Jewish homeland all over the world. With the declaration of Israel's nationhood in 1948 came war, in which the victorious Israelis acquired even more land than proposed in the United Nations partition plan—Leila Khaled would later praise the "co-ordination and brilliant military strategy" of her enemies, compared to the poorly trained and ill-equipped Arab states.

When my mother returned to Israel soon after my birth in 1958, the

Zionist story of the founding of Israel reigned: Arabs had started the war, then left their homes either voluntarily or on order from their own leaders. For the sake of national survival, Israel could not permit the nearly 750,000 refugees, their hostile foes, to return. Moreover, the new state of Israel had not displaced a legitimate nation, which meant the inhabitants of Palestine possessed no rights. Rather, as generic Arabs they were the responsibility of the vanquished Arab nations, where there was plenty of room for resettlement. In any case, the worldwide persecution of Jews justified the liberation of their ancient homeland.

I knew the part about the Holocaust and the founding of Israel but not the part about displaced Palestinians.

Our captors in the desert told a different story, one I'd never heard before. Theirs was a narrative of a centuries-long homeland wrenched away by Zionists and the state of Israel, of Palestinians expelled, often violently, of villages destroyed, of homes and property appropriated for and by Jewish immigrants.

The family of Bassam Abu-Sharif, who was born two years before the 1948 war, lived near Jerusalem for hundreds of years. In 1948 his mother's family lost their land and house ("an Israeli family we shall never meet now lives in it," he explained), along with the hotel and shops they owned. In 1967, with defeat, occupation, and increasing numbers of Palestinian refugees, came the loss of his native Jerusalem home. "I could have sat down on the spot and wept until death," he wrote. When the Popular Front for the Liberation of Palestine was founded later that year, their goals aligned with his: to fight relentlessly for return. Almost twenty years later, Israeli scholars would consult newly opened archives that shored up the information our captors tried to impress upon us, but in 1970 that history was largely unknown to American Jews.

I didn't know that Haifa, where my grandparents had recently moved from Greenwich Village, had once been the home of Palestinians. (The house from which Leila Khaled's family fled stood a few miles from my grandparents' apartment.) I didn't know that Jaffa, where Catherine and I attended school, and where we watched that memorable sunset by the sea, was once a city of Palestinians. I didn't know that nearly half the population of Tiberias, where Catherine and I had floated blissfully on the lake, had once been Palestinian. When my mother and stepfather took us to visit friends in the artist's colony of Ein Hod, I had no idea that the hundreds of Palestinians there in 1948 had been exiled to refugee camps, the village soon resettled by Israeli artists. ("Painters, printers, and sculptors live there in quaint little Arab style houses," Catherine wrote in a letter to our father, enraptured, and also entirely unaware of the history she was describing. "Everywhere are beautiful mountain views and flowers.")

Palestinians referred to 1948 as the Nakba, "the catastrophe," but I had no idea that Palestinians had once lived in Israel, because most Americans in 1970 had no idea either. The writer Sandy Tolan confessed that "like many Americans, I grew up with one part of the history, as told through the heroic birth of Israel out of the Holocaust." Tolan "knew of Israel as a safe haven for the Jews," but "knew nothing about the Arab side." Or as an American Jew recalled of her Hebrew school education, "the whole story about Israel was told as if Arabs didn't exist at all," making her wonder whether she had even known there were Palestinians in Palestine. Nor did the Israeli kids we played with have anything to teach us on this count. Israeli writer Ari Shavit, around my age (his great-grandfather emigrated to Palestine in the late nineteenth century), noted that his grandparents and parents proceeded with their lives as if Palestinians "never existed." Omer Bartov, whose elders had made their way from Eastern Europe to Palestine, "lived next to 'abandoned' Palestinian villages" but as a child "never once" considered the origins of those ruins.

In the same spirit, a typical 1960s guidebook counseled visitors to Jaffa that "the most ardent tourist need not worry about remains of the past, but can simply relax and enjoy the cosmopolitan human scenery of the present," explaining that in 1948, "the empty houses rapidly filled up with assorted Jewish immigrants from all over the world." Right around the time that Catherine and I sat imprisoned in the desert, the Israeli journalist Amos Elon noted that the settlers "came to a country which, in their eyes, was empty, or almost empty—a common optical illusion among Europeans in the late nineteenth century." Zionists, Elon wrote, exhibited "a combination of blind spots and naivete, of wishful thinking, paternalistic benevolence, and . . . ignorance."

A tiny minority of Jewish settlers in Palestine saw things differently.

When a Holocaust survivor came upon the toys that belonged to the Palestinian children who had inhabited her Jaffa home, those objects summoned what the Nazis had done to her own family. When Polish Holocaust survivors found a set table in their new home, they returned the key to the Israeli government, remembering "how we had to leave the house and everything behind when the Germans arrived." Even Israeli prime minister Golda Meir, who resolutely disallowed the return of Palestinian refugees, recorded finding houses in Haifa "where the coffee and pita bread were left on the table," bringing to mind "many Jewish towns" during World War II. And in an autobiographical novel published in 1949, an Israeli soldier gave voice to his own horror while following orders to violently evacuate a Palestinian village. "We came, we shot, we burned; we blew up, expelled, drove out, and sent into exile," Yizhar Smilansky writes, in the voice of his protagonist. "What in God's name were we doing in this place!" As the character reflects, "What indifference there was in us, as if we had never been anything but peddlers of exile, and our hearts had coarsened in the process."

I was turning nine years old in 1967 when Israel claimed victory in a war that lasted only six days. Many American Jews had shivered in fear when Egypt's president Nasser spoke of the destruction of Israel that spring, even as US intelligence remained confident of Israel's ability to defeat all Arab armies combined. When my sister and I arrived in Israel at the end of June that year, my mother's windows were still taped in a crisscross design, and Nurit showed us our building's bomb shelter. We joined our friends singing "Jerusalem of Gold," the hit song that quickly became the country's unofficial military and religious anthem. But there were anxieties too: one of my mother's fellow dancers said that "no good would come from the results of the war." I had no idea that Israel's occupation of more territories meant yet more Palestinian refugees, or that refugees who had resettled on the West Bank of the Jordan River after 1948 had now been displaced for a second time.

The late 1960s was a time of burgeoning political awareness for me. I was in fifth grade when the election returns came in for Richard Nixon in 1968. Even though it was a school night, Catherine and I went up to the roof with our two boy cousins, who lived two floors below, and threw paper airplanes off the roof, shouting to passersby to pick them up. Inside the folded pages we'd written, "Nixon is a fuck." In sixth grade the Vietnam War and civil rights movement loomed large. At school on Moratorium Day my friends and I wore black armbands and peace buttons and sang "We Shall Overcome." One day a "really neat Negro guy" came to our school assembly, I told my diary, to sing freedom songs. That winter I wrote to my mother about another assembly where "Shirley Chisholm (the first Negro Congresswoman) came and gave a wonderful, meaningful speech!" When the Ohio National Guard killed four college students protesting Nixon's invasion of Cambodia, Catherine and I collected donations for the antiwar Student Mobilization Committee to End the War in Vietnam.

I knew about the Black Power movement, and I knew about the Black Panthers, but I didn't know that the Panthers supported the cause of our captors. By the late 1960s the Popular Front was in fact part of a global movement against imperialism, colonialism, and capitalism. Just that summer, Panthers and representatives from other militant organizations had traveled to North Korea, North Vietnam, and China, and while we sat inside the plane that Labor Day weekend, the city of Philadelphia hosted the Revolutionary People's Constitutional Convention, with thousands attending, including supporters of women's liberation and gay liberation, chanting "Power to the People." Even though I knew so little about the history of Israel and Palestine, Catherine and I sometimes argued with our Israeli friends. "I could NEVER live in such a segregated place as Israel, where only Jews live," I wrote in my diary after one such heated discussion, my words unwittingly erasing the Palestinian minority who remained within Israeli borders.

Few of my fellow hostages had heard of the Popular Front for the Liberation of Palestine, and some found themselves suddenly yearning for a better grasp of the history and politics that had brought us all to the Jordan desert.

The Palestine Liberation Organization, founded in 1964, served as the umbrella organization for an array of diverse resistance groups, and with disillusion in the aftermath of the 1967 defeat came a new generation of young people who wanted to strike out, not as oppressed refugees but as revolutionaries. Among them was Bassam Abu-Sharif, who had graduated from the American University of Beirut just as the 1967 war was starting. It was there that he met George Habash, forty-four years old in 1970. Born to a Greek Orthodox family in the Palestinian city of Lydda—now the Israeli city of Lod, home to the airport where Catherine and I said goodbye to our mother each fall—Habash had been studying medicine in 1948, when the war forced his family to flee.

As a university student, Habash led the Arab Nationalist Movement, which attracted other young intellectuals. He put his medical degree to use in refugee-camp clinics before founding the Popular Front for the Liberation of Palestine six months after the 1967 war. Though a Christian among Muslims, Habash was "fast becoming the voice of the new Arab revolution," reported the *New York Times*. As the "fastest-growing Palestinian commando organization," the Popular Front was more militant than Fatah, the largest of the resistance groups, headed by Yasir Arafat (who also served as chairman of the PLO). The *Times* also characterized the Front as "the most extreme of the guerrilla groups."

Return to the Palestinian homeland: that was the goal of the Popular Front, including "every piece of land, every rock and stone." Members harbored childhood or young adult memories of the two wars that made refugees of their families, but Zionism was not the only enemy; so too, as Bassam Abu-Sharif explained to the assembled reporters on Monday afternoon, were anti-Arab imperialism and reactionary Arab governments. Objectives included nothing less than a radical transformation of the Arab world—in the summer of 1970, Habash spoke of a secular, democratic state encompassing the entire Arab Middle East—with a zeal for modernization, including women's liberation.

Armed resistance: that was the strategy, which meant (in the words of the Popular Front) "guerrilla warfare" and "striking at the enemy everywhere possible, with the greatest degree of violence possible." Diplomacy and negotiation were unacceptable, since, as Habash made clear, his organization was "totally against any peaceful solution that leaves behind an Israel." It was in the Front that George Habash met Wadi Haddad, a fellow doctor and Christian Palestinian who would become the "mastermind" of the September 1970 hijackings.

Bassam Abu-Sharif described Popular Front members as belonging to the educated middle and upper classes ("We had traveled more extensively and often knew several languages," he said, and one of our stewardesses indeed noticed that the commandos spoke "excellent English, even some French"). As Marxist-Leninists, they extolled peasants and the working classes, even if their leadership came from the ranks of doctors, lawyers, and intellectuals (one American journalist noted that most "could get excellent jobs anywhere in the world"). If the Western press mocked the Popular Front as "bourgeois intellectual revolutionaries," Habash insisted that sympathy for the masses mattered more than one's own class status, and the refugee camps of Jordan, Lebanon, and Syria provided fertile ground for his organization's growing membership.

By September 1970 the Popular Front had become an influential militant minority within the Palestinian resistance movement. Members thought of themselves as freedom fighters, even as much of the world called them terrorists (a term most often defined as those who deliberately target—and often kill—civilians for political aims). For George Habash, terrorism was "what made of us refugees—what drove our people to the camps." Though notably absent in the desert, presumably traveling in North Korea, maybe China and North Vietnam too, Habash would declare within ten days of the hijackings that the Front could "accept a third world war if that were the only possibility to annihilate Israel, Zionism, and Arab reactionaries." Peace was not his objective until there was "a socialist Palestine," he said. These early years would turn out to be the Front's most successful.

Most expansively that autumn, the Popular Front wanted to call attention to the plight and cause of Palestinian refugees. Much later, Bassam Abu-Sharif would call the whole hijacking plot a "media operation," intended to become the top story in every newspaper and on every television and radio station in the West. George Habash put it like this: "We said that the world does not understand or know about the Palestinian problem. This is how the idea of hijacking planes came about." Even

*A door of our plane wrapped in a Popular Front flag, with a
ladder reaching the sand for entering and exiting.*

[NIK WHEELER/CORBIS HISTORICAL VIA GETTY IMAGES]

Palestinians who condemned the hijackings noticed that, in the words
of one, "Suddenly, everyone was talking about the Palestinians, a subject
long deemed buried in obscurity."

The idea for multiple hijackings had developed as a protest against
that summer's ceasefire between Israel and Egypt, negotiated by US
secretary of state William Rogers, who was pursuing a version of the
land-for-peace deal spelled out in United Nations Resolution 242. That
resolution, passed soon after Israel's victory in 1967, called on Israel to
withdraw from newly occupied territories in exchange for official recognition, but ignored the loss of Palestinian land in 1948. In 1969 Israel
and Egypt both refused the plan, but in the summer of 1970 Rogers
proposed a more limited three-month ceasefire, and both countries accepted. Egypt's President Nasser supported the Palestinian resistance, but
he also endorsed diplomacy. That was anathema to the Popular Front,
which condemned any diplomatic recognition of Israel. Besides, any
exchange of land for peace—and this one, in particular, which left the
fate of Palestinian refugees unresolved—would foil the Front's goal of a
secular, democratic state for Jews, Muslims, and Christians. The Pan Am

hijackers chose Cairo for the destruction of the aircraft precisely because Egypt had agreed to the Rogers plan.

Sitting inside the plane, I didn't know why our hijackers had taken us to the Jordan desert. As it turned out, the Popular Front chose Dawson's Field because in 1970 Jordan stood at the center of Palestinian resistance. Since the defeat of Arab armies in the 1967 war, the resistance was keen to fight Israel on their own, apart from the Jordanian army, and Jordan's borders provided a perfect venue from which to launch attacks. King Hussein, thirty-four years old that autumn, navigated an uneasy relationship with the resistance: Jordan and Israel were enemies of each other, yet both were allies of the United States.

When Jordan annexed the West Bank following the 1948 war, it accepted Palestinian refugees, and many readily assimilated. After 1967, though, many identified more with the resistance than with the Jordanian government. Hussein advocated for Jordanian-Palestinian unity, but his citizens neither divided neatly nor united easily. "Anyone trying to divide Jordan into Palestinians on one side and Jordanians on the other," a US diplomat would say, "just did not understand the reality and dynamics of that country." Accordingly, Hussein voiced support for the resistance, while distancing himself from the commandos, for fear of Israeli retaliation.

The problem for us, the hostages, was Jordan's precarious status as both an enemy of Israel and an ally of the United States. With tensions escalating between Hussein and the Palestinian resistance, Henry Kissinger worried that US military support for Jordan would prompt the Soviets to intervene. Nor did Kissinger wish to divert resources from his other, bigger fight against Communism: the Vietnam War.

At twelve years old, I was just beginning to make sense of a world shaped by Vietnam and superpower politics. When it came to the Middle East, Rogers and his State Department disagreed with Kissinger and his National Security Council. Nixon tended to side with Kissinger, and both tended to understand the Middle East as a conflict between Israel and the Arab nations, with little room for the grievances of Palestinians. Kissinger worried about the desert hostages, but he also worried about the future of Jordan and the possibility of a world war. Kissinger's world-view in fact subsumed everything into the Cold War rivalry between the Soviet Union and the American crusade against Communism. "Nixon and Kissinger automatically viewed all Middle East crises through a 'cold war' prism, even when it made no sense," recalled a CIA official in Amman.

While we sat in the desert, CBS aired a television special called *The Hijack Conspiracy*. The commandos had "thrust back into the world's attention a problem diplomats have tended to shunt aside in hesitant steps toward Middle East peace," Walter Cronkite narrated. The "problem of the Arabs, displaced by the creation of the state of Israel twenty-two years ago," was one "demanding solution if there is to be peace." Still, the hijacking of airplanes to the Jordan desert had "triggered a shock wave of indignation and concern throughout the world."

King Hussein of Jordan called our captors "non-rational people" and the hijackings "the shame of the Arab world." Writing in telegram shorthand, Secretary of State Rogers echoed the idea of "harm done overall Arab image by current detention hundreds of innocent travellers." Rogers knew that the Arab nations were not responsible for the hijackings, and that the Popular Front would be "minimally influenced" by Arab governments, but he nonetheless made a personal appeal to ten Arab ambassadors. Could any of them convince the Popular Front to release the hostages right away? Kuwaiti ambassador Talat Al-Ghoussein, the group's spokesman, condemned the crime from "a humanitarian point of view," while making clear that Palestinians had "lived 23 years in desperation."

Indeed, in an era of radical student uprisings and anticolonial movements across the globe, the Popular Front gathered some tempered sympathy. Burmese diplomat U Thant, secretary general of the United Nations, called Popular Front tactics "savage and inhuman," operating by the "law of the jungle," yet conceded legitimate grievances. Support for the cause, together with disapproval of the tactics, characterized the opinions of the *Guardian* in Great Britain and *Le Monde* in France. Egypt and Lebanon likewise warned that hijacking and hostage-taking harmed the Palestinian cause, while *Pravda*, the official newspaper of the Soviet Union, along with the voices of other Communist regimes, made the same point: support for the mission, not the method. Newspapers in

Algeria and Tunisia were more forgiving of the tactics, focusing on the plight of Palestinian refugees.

American politicians and the press had mostly harsh words for our captors. Secretary of State Rogers called the commandos "fanatical," a favorite description leveled by US statesmen. The commandos were "fanatics" in "the Jordanian wasteland," whose leader, George Habash, was "a fanatic Maoist." The hijackers were "madmen" and "wild men." Jacob Javits, the progressive Republican senator from New York (the only Republican my father ever voted for), interjected a word about "the tragedy of the Palestinian-Arab refugees," even as he branded our captors as uncivilized. One *New York Times* reporter characterized them as "shuffling to and fro on a patch of desert, like caged animals"; another called them practitioners of "unspeakable barbarity." A *Washington Post* editor put it differently: "To dismiss their cause merely because some criminals and moral savages among them act in a self-destructive way" was "an injustice to the Palestinians." Meanwhile an alternative paper out of Berkeley, California, endorsed the hijackings, calling the commandos "beautiful barbarians."

The Popular Front remained unimpressed by condemnations and equivocating support alike. Although Habash and other leaders wanted the world to see Palestinians as modern and civilized, they cared little that the act of hijacking provoked images of savagery. As Comrade Ibrahim put it to the reporters, what mattered most was that the world ask "Why?"

If our captors hoped to impress their history upon us, many of my fellow Jewish hostages felt secure in the history they already knew, and each side excluded and demonized the other. Two asymmetries further complicated the intertwined, if willfully disconnected, histories. Palestinians focused on the far greater power held by Israelis after the 1948 and 1967 wars. Jews focused on the Holocaust as far more monstrous than the Nakba—a point ironically best articulated by a Palestinian scholar and activist: "Our opponents are the greatest victims of racism in history," wrote Edward Said.

Catherine and I were aware that our captors wanted us to sympathize with them, and we were interested in the stories they told. *This is how we live every day. This is all we have to eat. We can't feed our children. We have no homes.* Listening to their history, Catherine's first thought was *How is it my fault?* followed by, *What can I do to help?*

"They kept impressing upon us about how their people have to live, so intense, without anything," she said after we got home. "They wanted to give us a taste of it."

"To show us," I added. ("And once again," said the aviator in *The Little Prince*, "without understanding why, I had a queer sense of sorrow.")

The two of us puzzled out the question: Could Israelis and Palestinians live on the same land? Maybe it had once been possible, we thought. But there was so much anger now, so much hatred, that it didn't seem possible anymore. We couldn't think of a solution.

13

What was it like to live on the plane? This was the part of the ordeal I'd most thoroughly forgotten, the part I couldn't recall no matter how hard I concentrated. It was also what everyone wanted to know when I got home—*What did you eat? How hot was the desert? Did the toilets flush?* It was what I barely recorded in my diary, what I didn't much want to talk about, and what I succeeded in blocking out very soon afterward. Could reconstructing other people's experiences become the means to transport me back in time? Could researching and documenting the sights, smells, and sounds of my surroundings begin to dispel that oddly persistent sense that I'd never really been there?

Catherine wrote in her diary that everyone was "very hot and uncomfortable." Reporters called the planes "sweatboxes" and "sun-scorched airliners," and Red Cross officials recorded that daytime temperatures reached between 95 and 120 degrees Fahrenheit, with a high of 131. Early on, the Amman airport sent a generator intended to supply air-conditioning, but it ran only for infrequent ten-minute intervals. Opening the aircraft doors increased ventilation but also drew in the ferociously hot air and the rays of the blinding sun.

Water rations mattered, and plastic cups became prized possessions, some fished out of garbage bins. Once, when student purser Frank Allen was filling and refilling the water bottles eventually supplied by the Red Cross, he took to the megaphone, vexed at those demanding more, retorting, "What the hell you think we got up here? A waterfall?" Still, copilot Jim Majer made it his business to encourage the children to drink, invoking the New York Mets pitcher hero from the 1969 World Series as a model water guzzler ("Jerry Koosman drinks water and you do too!"). When at one point the only available water came sterilized with chlorine tablets, which tasted worse than a swimming pool, Sara Raab had to bribe her six-year-old to take a sip, with the promise of a new toy tractor. ("I had scarcely enough drinking water to last a week," said the aviator in *The Little Prince*. His predicament in the desert was "extremely serious," for there was "so little drinking-water left" that he "had to fear the worst.")

Food was in short supply too. At first the stewardesses distributed leftover dinner rolls, and the commandos provided hot sweetened tea, hard-boiled eggs, cheese, tinned English biscuits, bananas, grapes, watermelon, jam, and pita. Parents relied on Red Cross deliveries for baby food, condensed and evaporated milk, and infant formula, while our captors supplied a burner to boil water and sterilize bottles. "In the first two days, we did not have a problem with food," recalled the commando Abu-Samir. Soon, though, the numbers of hostages meant that "we could not just give them falafel that we ate ourselves." Nevertheless that's exactly what the commandos did. Catherine and I both noticed that when rations ran low, they shared their own meager supplies. As I later recalled, "They really gave us all their food."

Hoarding was pointless, since everything spoiled so quickly in the heat, and rotten food only added to the rank cabin air. Some felt justified in stashing away provisions, though, since no one knew whether there would be more, or how long we'd remain in the desert, and crew members did their best to discourage what flight engineer Al Kiburis called "the 'me first' attitudes shown by many." More inventively, the Raab children created snacks out of watermelon seeds, using the packets of salt from Red Cross meals and baking the seeds on the airplane's sunny wing.

Those who kept kosher had to decide what to do. The commissary at the Frankfurt airport had loaded our flight with forty-three kosher and three strict-kosher meals, all of which were soon consumed. Some passengers who accepted nonkosher food looked askance at those who obeyed religious dietary laws under such trying circumstances, and the crew likewise expressed frustration with those who chose hunger, and especially those who deprived their children. Some of the kosher hostages turned to Rabbi Isaac Hutner, sitting in the row ahead of us, but he brushed off requests for guidance. "Don't ask me questions," he said, "because if you do, the terrorists will look at me as someone important." (When the rabbi implored Captain Woods to ask the commandos to supply kosher meals, the captain pointed out that our captors were mostly sharing their own food.) Kosher and nonkosher passengers soon enough worked out exchanges.

Reading the menu in my seat-back pocket, pretending to make my selections (New York sirloin, French fries, Kona Koffee Parfait) could transport me to an imaginary normal airplane trip, flying swiftly toward home. When I find that very menu in the TWA archives—stylishly printed on round pages, including an embossed map displaying TWA 741's original flight path—this private diversion comes back to me. No doubt I thought longingly then about the Israeli food I'd devoured all summer: the delicious deep-fried chickpea falafel patties, the large-granule sugar that my mother sprinkled in a thick layer over egg-soaked French toast. If I flipped back the pages of my diary, I could read about the chunky fruit stewed in sugar and spices prepared by my stepfather's mother, or the rich, sweet cake she served us for breakfast. In real life, in the desert, we could augment airline leftovers and the food supplied by our captors only with fare from our carry-on bags. People passed around boxes of candy, and grown-ups rationed swigs of duty-free booze.

Sanitation inside the plane worsened steadily, beginning with the problem of garbage. The crew continually walked the aisles reminding passengers, "Pick up your trash, pick up your trash," and did the best they could to discard everything in trucks parked outside. But there was always more garbage, much of it accumulating under the seats, then edging into the aisles. The accumulation meant little to those who believed they would soon be released, and even less to those wondering if their lives might end within days or hours. People threw all kinds of items into the toilets too—soda cans, baby-food jars, ripped-up Israeli passports. One reproving hostage called the plane a pigpen, another found the adults to be inconsiderate slobs.

Bodies smelled too. There were just too many people in too small a space, with no real way to wash. The crew diluted commando-supplied rubbing alcohol with water and passed around the bottles so we could wipe our hands, while the commandos brought in jerry cans of water from one of the trucks. "We hardly had the privilege of perspiring individually," as Sylvia Jacobson put it, while a teenager noticed, "It's true what they taught us in psychology. You can smell other people's sweat before you can smell your own."

With seven infants on board, the supply of diapers rapidly dwindled, even though the Palestinian doctor supplied sheets of cotton to cut up with nail scissors. When Susie Hirsch's period came, she rolled up a sanitary napkin and placed it inside her purse, but a male commando guarding the lavatory made her surrender the bag, which meant she had to take out the napkin in front of him. Her minidress, her stained underwear, and a sense of "the prying eyes of the terrorists" added considerably to her distress.

Worst of all were the bathrooms. Even though the water rations amounted to just enough "not to drop dead from dehydration," as one hostage put it, it was tempting to drink as little as possible to avoid the sickening toilets. Sunlight on the very first morning found purser Rudi Swinkels cleaning the lavatories, which already smelled. With the exception of the reserves in the first-class faucets, there was no more running water—if you turned on a tap in a tourist-class bathroom, nothing came out. Because the toilets in the five tiny lavatories required both water and electricity to flush, the result was, as the Red Cross reported, "the piling of excrement."

The flight-deck crew worked alongside the cabin crew, and the commandos joined in too, using clothes hangers from first class to shove waste farther down, to little effect. Already by the second day the odor was intensely pungent. The bathrooms were, according to one hostage, "nauseatingly dirty"—not only the smell but also the sight, with the toilets "clogged up to the top practically." Without electricity, it was also pitch-dark when you closed the door, which made it worse, not knowing what you might touch. When the generator first arrived, crew members locked themselves inside, lights and air-conditioning running, to scour everything, but the machine only recirculated the soon-renewed odor throughout the cabin, and passengers eventually begged the crew to turn it off for good.

Once hostages realized that the aircraft might remain our home for quite a while, some committed themselves to tidying up, organizing sanitation details to help the crew collect garbage and to remind passengers entering the bathrooms to be as neat and clean as possible. Everyone, including the children, had to take turns on the toilet brigade, pumping a stick up and down to chop and plunge the waste. When it was her turn, a woman who had survived the concentration camps passed out from the smell. To another woman who gingerly declined to participate, Sara Raab, traveling with her five children, snapped, "If you don't shove, you don't shit!"

After a few days crew members spied three drain handles under the jet—normally the toilets would be evacuated with hoses on the ground—and had an idea. With permission from the commandos, they dug a ditch under the plane, after which Captain Woods pulled one of the "lav dump" handles. Nothing happened, so Jim Majer tried next, again with no result. When Al Kiburis took his turn, balancing on a box since he was shorter than the other two, "a huge flood of feces poured out into the ditch and a teetering Al almost fell," according to Jim. After that, a miasma of sewage emanated from the toilet pits under the plane, but at least it was marginally better inside.

When the commandos invited representatives from the International Red Cross to board the planes, the reps found conditions on TWA becoming "quickly unbearable" (*rapidement insupportables*). By comparison the Swissair plane, with far fewer hostages—with the women (except for the stewardesses) and children gone, they were only about fifty— "looked like paradise." Red Cross staff in Switzerland drew up long lists of essential supplies, and personnel scrambled to assemble toilet paper, rubbing alcohol, disinfectant, talcum powder, tampons and sanitary napkins, diapers, washcloths, deodorant, five hundred garbage bags, gallons of cologne, even portable latrines. Swiss pharmacists and shopkeepers answered middle-of-the-night calls, while staffers contacted doctors and nurses from their emergency rosters. Weighing hostages' nerves against stale cabin air, the Red Cross added cartons of cigarettes to the list. Among the requested equipment that never arrived were the latrines.

Hostages suffered everything from sand-fly bites to pneumonia. People developed hives, rashes, swollen feet and ankles, backaches and stiff necks, bruised legs from climbing up and down the ladder, diarrhea, constipation, colds, and intestinal infections. They fainted in the heat and ran fevers, and the dry, dusty air brought on coughs, hoarseness, and laryngitis. Preexisting maladies flared up too: sclerosis and heart conditions, asthma and allergies, hypertension, nephritis, arthritis, and migraines. One passenger got infected eyelids from contact lenses, another suffered a worsening impacted wisdom tooth.

Dr. Ahmed Kamal, the Popular Front commando with a medical degree and sparkling dark eyes, set up a mobile clinic in a tent on the sand. We all found him to be a kind man who offered everyone, Catherine said, all the "medicine or comfort they needed." Rudi Swinkels judged him "a very understanding and good person," and Sylvia Jacobson found his "superb medical care" heartening. When Tikva Raab burned her foot on cigarette ash, Dr. Kamal told her, "A girl with such beautiful eyes should not cry." She thought he was "the best of all of them."

Two doctors from the Red Cross came on board too, bearing, as one of the stewardesses said, "every type of medication that we could possibly need." When my father informed TWA of his daughters' allergies (that was the telegram I tracked down in the National Archives that contained our names), the airline in turn informed the State Department, which cabled the US embassy in Amman, which informed the Red Cross. Soon one of the doctors supplied us with Tedral for our asthma, the prescription pills Catherine and I were used to swallowing when we felt the familiar tightening that made it difficult to draw breath.

The Red Cross, the crew, journalists, and politicians all singled out women and children as particularly fragile (as our captain told a reporter, "Our main problem is the women and children"). Placing women in the same category as children appealed to the idea of natural female frailty, but it might also work as a strategy to reduce the number of people living on the planes. André Rochat very much wanted all the women and children out of the desert, and President Nixon, as his chief of staff reported, "wants some action regarding women." As a Democratic legislator declared, "Kidnapping women and children" and "holding them hostage at gunpoint in hostile surroundings" was "disgusting," and only brought the commandos' "entire cause into disrepute."

Convictions about natural female fragility would have been shattered, had anyone thought about it, by what appeared to be an extraordinary event. "For your info," a Red Cross representative reported to Geneva headquarters, "a young American woman gave birth today in TWA plane." The Red Cross president composed a congratulatory letter and attempted to send a bouquet out to the desert, noting that the flowers represented admiration for women the world over who gave birth under inhumane conditions: in prisons, in concentration camps, in refugee camps. Word spread quickly.

"Number of persons involved in hijacking upped by one when TWA passenger gave birth last night," the embassy in Amman cabled Washington, and the baby quickly became the top story on CBS News, with anchorman Walter Cronkite crowing about "a happy moment in the agonizing hours." Communication troubles precluded transmission of the mother's name, or the baby's, but both were "doing quite well," Cronkite told the nation.

The news was disseminated far and wide—but alas, none of it was true. "One of modern history's most talked-about wept-about babies does not exist," the Reuters news agency eventually conceded. Soon the Red Cross issued a correction, and journalists and network anchors retracted their heartwarming stories. A semiexplanation came from the Red Cross, which called it a "bad joke" that even their senior officials had fallen for.

Some of the younger children, especially those traveling alone, were indeed vulnerable. When six-year-old Connie Pittaro developed tonsillitis and a high fever, she didn't always cooperate, and sometimes a crew member had to stay up through the night "to hold, comfort and spoon feed her the necessary medications," Jim Majer recalled. "*Everybody* looked after her," June Haesler remembered, and when Jim took his turn, holding Connie in his arms, she willingly swallowed her dosage. That was probably because he told her, his genuine warmth readily evident, "I love you, Connie." I liked to watch Jim comfort the smaller children. He was "sort of like a father to the unaccompanied kids," I'd say later. He was "so fantastic." No doubt he reminded me of my own faraway father.

Even when I immerse myself in other people's memories of the climate, I can't recall the daytime heat or the nighttime cold. Nor do stories of our meager provisions call up recollections of thirst or hunger. Reacquainting myself with the facts of the terrible sanitation, I can't resurrect any memory of the plane's stench. A line in my diary—"without my cholera shot I'd probably get the disease from the water"—points to anxiety about getting sick, but that feeling too remains unfamiliar.

Then there was the fear all around me. After his first visit to the hijacked planes, André Rochat departed filled with anguish. It wasn't just the deteriorating conditions on TWA, or that he groped for words to describe the whole "strange spectacle," including our captors, "calm and armed to the teeth," many of them surprisingly young. It was also that Captain C. D. Woods had handed Rochat a piece of paper that bore a list of names: these were the men the commandos had removed from the plane late Monday night.

"If you can bring me these six passengers," our captain said, "we would all be very happy."

All around me, radiating from Catherine to the rabbi in the row ahead, to Mark Shain and Mimi Beeber sitting behind us, to the Hirsch siblings and the Raab family seated nearby, from the whole cabin up to the cockpit and back, people felt afraid, yet nothing of that feeling has come back to me either. There is still more to reconstruct to see if I can get there.

14

___

On Sunday, just after takeoff from Frankfurt, I wrote in my diary: "We've stopped in Athens already, and from Frankfurt it's another 8 hours. *So* long!!!!" Even though those eight hours till home turned into days and nights, and more days and nights, I can envision only a static image of myself, confined to my seat, head bent to look at my hands, idle in my lap.

Calling up that image, trying to picture the aircraft's interior, I find no recollection of the colors of the seats, drapes, or carpets. No one at the TWA Museum in Kansas City or the TWA Hotel and Museum at Kennedy Airport has a conclusive answer for Boeing 707s in 1970, and when I post an inquiry on a social media group for former TWA employees, responses range from orange, yellow, and gold to blue and green. When I ask fellow hostages what the inside of our aircraft looked like, many, just like me, are unable to recall the colors, and among those who produce an impression, some see orange and gold, others red and gray. What should be a simple detail proves impossible to determine.

Leaving aside the physical space, I look instead to the element of time. What did we do all day, stranded inside an airplane grounded in the desert? When we got home, everyone wanted to know about that too; it's the question my stepmother asked in the letter she wrote to Catherine and me, a letter she didn't know if we'd ever read ("Do you eat, do you sleep? Do you talk to the new friends you're undoubtedly bound to through this crisis?")

In between the images that involuntarily remained with me—the gun at the copilot's neck, Monday night huddled on the desert floor, the woman commando pointing her gun at me—stretched the undramatic passage of time. Again my diary is of little help, and so I turn to the records of other people's experiences. Historians commonly employ this technique: if the person whose life you're researching left only scant records, you turn to the accounts of others in the same place at the same time. Now that I have a better sense of the conditions of our makeshift home in the desert, I consider the day-to-day lives of the hostages, hoping that the combination of conditions and activities will help me reach more deeply into both memories and feelings.

The only hostages who never suffered boredom were the crew, playing their roles as service providers whose obligations wouldn't end until all passengers arrived safely at their final destinations. There was, Captain Woods said, always "something to do from early in the morning until late at night."

Instead of simply preparing and distributing food and drink, the crew of a hijacked plane had to procure food and drink from their own captors. Instead of contending with a few airsick passengers, they had to tend to a planeload of hostages with physical and psychological ailments—Bettie McCarthy found the passengers "had a million little problems," most of which could be resolved "if you talked to them for a while." Instead of reassuring passengers about turbulence, they had to soothe fears of destruction and death. At times sleeping no more than three hours at a stretch, the crew remained attuned to one another as well. "Everybody sort of knew when someone else's energy was down and they would just take over," June Haesler said. Rosemarie Metzner took refuge inside her mind, conjuring a world of her own, with "beautiful thoughts about beautiful things." She loved piano music, and it was the Beethoven bicentennial that year, so she thought about Beethoven.

Time rarely moves more slowly than for a child with nothing to do. Years later, when I ask Catherine what we did all day, she thinks for a moment, shakes her head, and says, "I have no idea."

Others couldn't remember either. "I've tried to recall exactly how we spent our time," Sylvia Jacobson would say later. "I can't recall anything in particular."

No wonder it was hard to remember. "We did nothing the whole day," Foozie recorded. Then: "The next day we did nothing." And after that: "We again did nothing." One man observed a fellow hostage, whose wife and baby had been driven away on Monday night, sitting "still as a statue, his hands folded, staring straight ahead"—maybe the image in my mind's eye of myself sitting motionless was accurate after all.

Conversation helped relieve the tedium. You could join others in a row with an empty place, or just stand in the aisle by someone else's row. People talked about travel, recommended hotels or restaurants, exchanged opinions about literature and art, discussed current events, and swapped jokes, sometimes with a dash of gallows humor. Smoking the fresh supply of cigarettes from the Red Cross became sociable, so nonsmokers smoked too. "We got some cigarettes," seventeen-year-old David Raab wrote in his diary, "and had a good time smoking. You know, we never smoked before."

The heat made us fidgety, but we soon realized that it was least uncomfortable just to sit still. People read whatever they had packed in their carry-on bags, along with outdated newspapers and magazines found on board, some turning eagerly to the pages of crossword puzzles or word games. Barbara Mensch had a study guide for her college entrance exams, along with a copy of *Coffee, Tea or Me*, the best-selling, if fabricated, "uninhibited memoirs of two airline stewardesses" (Catherine and I had read our mother's copy that summer). One teenager was reading the more highbrow bestseller *Manchild in the Promised Land*, Claude Browne's autobiographical novel about climbing upward from a Harlem childhood (it was on my father's bookshelf at home), which got her in trouble with the commandos, who thought they discerned Zionism in the title.

Games occupied children and grown-ups alike, including cards, chess, checkers, and guessing games, and when some of the kids played backgammon, the Palestinian doctor showed them strategic moves.

Birthdays arrived with no regard for captivity, and when a passenger turned twenty-eight, the crew fashioned a card from the TWA menu and produced a bottle of German wine purchased at the Frankfurt airport, doled out by tablespoons, while fellow hostages improvised presents: a scarf from India, an extra bottle of water.

Singing helped too, whether standards like "Yankee Doodle Dandy" or popular tunes like "I'll Never Fall in Love Again" and "Sealed with a Kiss." More pointedly, we sang the jazz classic "Show Me the Way to Go Home" and the airline jingle "Up, Up, and Away with TWA." We changed the lyrics of Bob Dylan's "Blowin' in the Wind" to "How many days must we stay on the plane/Before we are left to go free?" We changed the lyrics of the Beatles' "Yellow Submarine" to "We all live on a white TWA," and we sang "Five Hundred Miles" as "One hundred hours/In these clothes." My favorite, though, remained Peter, Paul and Mary's "Leaving on a Jet Plane," changed to "Living on a Jet Plane." Laughing at the line "Don't know when I'll be back again" was a way to tame the worry of never getting home into an impossibility. One little boy later told a reporter that the hostages had so much fun singing songs that "you wouldn't have known it was a hijacked plane."

Even though Catherine and I wanted to think of the hostages as one happy family, we also heard the grown-ups around us snarling and bickering; as Catherine put it, there was "so much pent-up emotion." Some passengers resented those who stashed away food, poured too much water, or appointed themselves to head committees. Elderly hostages criticized younger ones, Europeans blamed Americans for the whole ordeal, and Holocaust survivors scoffed at anyone who complained about living inside an airplane. Hostilities flared between non-Jews and Jews too. A West German hostage told one of the commandos that he shouldn't be detained, and another non-Jew told a Jew, "I really don't know what will happen to you. I have my own problems." As the days passed, fear and anxiety simmered, strife boiled.

Nighttime brought peace to some. Catherine thought the desert darkness beautiful, with all the stars visible, and Foozie found the beauty almost unreal, the sky, stars, and moon so calm and silent. Foozie knew that all kinds of writers described such landscapes in soaring literary terms, but all she could think was, *What a place to be with the boy of your dreams.*

Small children slept the most soundly, "twisted like acrobats" in their seats, as one grown-up observed. For others, nighttime was harder than daytime. Crying children, pacing guards, and snoring passengers broke the silence, as did the coughing brought on by desert dust. Anxiety accompanied intrusive thoughts about the next day's water rations or the steadily worsening bathrooms, whether we would ever leave the desert, whether we would live or die. Tova Kahn, divorced, cried quietly, imagining her arrival home with no one to greet her. With the early morning glare of the sun, I understood what Foozie meant when she called the desert a "prison with no walls."

Night or day, religious rituals offered comfort and took up time. Susie Hirsch found solace in a small souvenir prayer book, focusing on the Shema, the daily prayer of observant Jews. David Raab selected Psalm 27, fastening on the words "Though a host should encamp against me, my heart shall not fear; if a war should be waged upon me, in God's succor I put my faith." *Now, you can't really ask for a better verse than that*, he reasoned. Even though Rabbi Hutner wished to be left alone, he noted a prayer intended for one of four circumstances, each one a perfect fit: "When you are in the desert, when your life is in danger, when you are making a long voyage, or when you have been taken prisoner." Meanwhile, a Christian hostage took in "the magnificence of the stars," seeking comfort in the thought that his fate lay in the hands of God.

Asking God to save us was a tricky endeavor for me. Since Catherine and I never went to Hebrew school, we learned most of what we knew about Jewish holidays from reading and rereading our treasured copies of *All-of-a-Kind Family*, a series of children's books about five sisters growing up on the Lower East Side. To be sure, we sometimes lit a menorah for Hanukkah, and some years we attended a Passover seder at Central Synagogue in midtown Manhattan, but like many of my Jewish friends in New York, my family celebrated Christmas. It was a pagan holiday, my father told us, where you brought a tree inside and illuminated it during the shortest days of the winter solstice, no praying involved. When I asked my father about God, he told me that a part of God existed in all human beings. When I asked my mother, she told me that a long time ago, when people didn't understand science, they made up God. I considered both alternatives, and though I admired my mother's brazen answer, I sided with my father.

Up in the air, when the armed hijackers ran through the aisle shouting, I prayed. That first night in the desert, I prayed. "I've continued to pray to God and I have faith in Him," I wrote in my diary one day, but soon I crossed out that sentence. When the commandos took men off the plane, I wrote, "I'll pray," then crossed that out too. If I tried to make time pass by communing with God, the exercise didn't last long.

Sifting through the TWA archives so many years afterward, I come upon two items that feel strangely familiar, as if a faraway bell were tolling ever so faintly. The first is the September 1970 issue of the airline's *Ambassador* magazine, which must have provided hours' worth of absorption on the plane. The lined face of an elderly Native American woman graces the cover. Inside, the story opens with a "young Navajo shepherdess" on an Arizona reservation, "a remorseless land of scrub and sand and canyons." Turning the pages, I read now—as I did then—about the fashion craze of peasant-style clothing and the waterways of Zurich (where "Wagner, Lenin, Mussolini, Joyce and Einstein sought solace"). Good for flights of fancy too must have been the feature about the chef at the Athens Hilton, including a recipe of feta cheese, butter, oil, tomatoes, onions, and brandy. I remember that fellow hostages savored the single page of puzzles and brain teasers, and on the TWA route map in the back, we could trace our stalled progress or imagine the passage home.

The second item in the TWA archives that feels familiar is the mail-order catalog. Glossy pages in the booklet entitled *TWA Flight Shop: Gifts, Souvenirs & Travel Accessories* had merited repeated visits. Emblazoned with the airline's logo are bright red flight bags, playing cards, and drinking glasses (to "remind you of pleasant journeys and convivial friends"). There are atlases, globes, and charm-bracelet tokens to mark one's travels: for Albuquerque a tepee, for Atlanta a cotton bale, for Bombay a snake charmer.

And there they are: my friends, the international dolls ("for little girls, and big girls too"), in their "authentic, colorful native costumes." Lonely at moments, hungering for something beyond my immediate surroundings, I'd visited these pages often. The Hawaiian doll wears a grass skirt and a lei. The Irish doll wears a hoop skirt decorated with shamrocks. The North African doll is dark brown with an orange-flowered skirt. The

The dolls from the TWA in-flight catalog, my friends during my week in the desert.

[COURTESY OF THE STATE HISTORICAL SOCIETY OF MISSOURI]

Hong Kong doll is clad in blue silk pajamas. Each one costs two dollars, or you could choose five for $7.95, or collect all thirty for the princely sum of $39.95. I remember arranging them in groupings of five, assembling and reassembling which ones I would choose for the discounted price. I remember pretending to be a teacher, calling on the different dolls as if they had raised their hands in my classroom. There in the TWA archives, it's as if they have waited patiently for me to come back, to resume our lessons.

In my reconstruction of daily life on the planes, two memories prompt feelings more vivid than any that have come to me before. The triggers are different, but the feeling is the same, and it isn't fear. First, paging through the catalog, studying the dolls, the emotion that comes over me is sadness. (Speaking to his own echo, the little prince pleaded with the reverberating voices: "Be my friends. I am all alone." When a fox appeared, he pleaded with the fox, "Come and play with me.") Then, all these years later, listening to the gentle guitar strums and background vocals of Peter Yarrow and Paul Stookey accompanying the honeyed voice of Mary Travers, the melody and the lyrics ignite feelings I'd walled off in the desert. Listening now to the words "leaving on a jet plane" and "don't know when I'll be back again," I weep for the girl who laughed that day under the wing of the airplane, desperate to preserve a happy moment for her father.

Reporters and their cameramen, our only contact with the outside world, served as an interruption to the tedium. Over the days, they made their way out to the planes, hiring drivers who ferried them past "mile upon mile of squalid refugee shelters," including "ragged tents, hideous one-room concrete block huts and corrugated tin shanties," in the words of a *New York Times* writer. Sometimes the reporters had to get past barricades and roadblocks, manned by commandos or Iraqi soldiers. British journalist Gerald Seymour traveled with another newsman, "bumping along a dirt road, seeing absolutely nothing," until a Land Rover veered into view.

"Excuse me, sir, have you seen any airplanes?" Seymour asked.

"Yes, over there," the man said, pointing.

After Seymour and his companion crested a rim, we came into view: three airplanes in the middle of nowhere. Drawing closer, he saw a Palestinian flag flying amid a tableau of jeeps, tents, and weapons, and a van with the sliver-of-moon Red Crescent symbol, before commandos forbade the men to advance any closer.

To a reporter flying over the airstrip, the three planes appeared as "three dots on a domino." Another day, on the ground, the Beirut bureau chief for *Time* magazine saw "a fantastic sight" of "three jets shimmering against a backdrop of endless sand," and a *New York Times* reporter wrote of "a glassy mirage," upon which "gleamed the trinity of airplanes." In a "surreal" experience, a United Press International correspondent saw the planes over the top of a dune, as if "on a tarmac waiting for take-off." Members of the press who got closer, and those who could read Arabic, saw "Popular Front for the Liberation of Palestine" spray-painted on the airliners, along with, in English, "Down with imperialism, Zionism & Israel." *They are never going to blow up the planes, at least not with the passengers aboard,* one reporter thought, before it occurred to him that if the Jordanian army moved in to wipe out the guerrillas, that could *seal the hostages' fate.*

One day, as journalists kept arriving, the commandos approved a press conference with the TWA crew and selected passengers. Since the gathering took place outside the western flank of the plane and Catherine and I were seated on the other side, we had no view of the goings-on.

Watching tapes of the footage nearly five decades later, I see a group of hostages hovering close to the aircraft, with reporters and cameramen keeping a certain distance, as dictated by the commandos. The visitors stand in a ragged line, the men's white button-down shirts gleaming in the bright sunshine. C. D. Woods, Al Kiburis, and June Haesler look familiar. Lennett Cain, the African American US Army soldier, stands with his arms crossed, wearing much-envied sunglasses. Sarah Malka stands with her arms folded too, also looking familiar. In between the press and the hostages, Bassam Abu-Sharif directs the proceedings.

"We demand that everybody should be seated," he begins, speaking into the TWA megaphone, "including our guests."

"Excuse me," a newsman calls out. "We want the captain and the stewardess to tell us about the sanitary condition on the TWA plane."

"Would you like to smell?" Abu-Sharif calls back.

The newsman retorts that he would.

"What do you think?" Abu-Sharif interrupts him. "They don't have water. What do you mean, asking such a question?" Abu-Sharif means that there isn't enough water for washing.

"The American girl here, can she tell us how the passengers are?" A newsman points to June, who would later tell me that as she began to speak into the megaphone, Al whispered to her, "Tell them we've run out of jokes."

"We are very crowded," June calls back, "and I think the women and especially the children are very restless." Her blond hair is pulled back, her bare feet tucked underneath her. She will later admit to me

A press conference on the sand with crew members and passengers. Captain C. D. Woods, stewardess June Haesler, and flight engineer Al Kiburis are on the left.

[© ZUMAPRESS.com/Keystone Pictures USA/agefotostock]

that she'd kicked off her shoes in the desert heat because her feet were hurting.

"How old is the youngest child you have on board?" a British reporter calls out.

June calls back that there are two infants who are three months old, both in good health.

An Orthodox passenger I don't recognize stands up and speaks into the megaphone. "We've been given food and water and whatever else was possible to be given that we requested," he says. "We're all waiting anxiously for a settlement to be made, so we can go home."

A reporter wants the captain to address the press, and he obliges. C. D. wears the dark pants and white epauleted shirt of his uniform, his tie and hat in place. The sanitary conditions, he says, speaking in his deliberate midwestern intonation, pausing to choose just the right words, are "deteriorating."

"How long can they hold out in there, Captain?"

"Well, that's a kind of a difficult question," C. D. concedes. "If we can flush out the toilets, why we can go for quite some time."

"What about morale inside the cabin, Captain. How are the passengers?"

"Well, actually, it's been quite good considering the number of people involved." Of course there were problems with "almost a full airplane and a small space," but "really, it's been real good."

Bassam Abu-Sharif permits Al Kiburis to step right up to the reporters, face-to-face.

"Can you take this airplane out of here?" one of them asks.

Puffing on a cigar, Al smiles. "Absolutely," he says. "If given a chance, I'll take it out of here before you get in your cars." There's laughter all around.

"Are there any group activities, such as singing or anything?"

"Oh, yeah. We're about out of jokes, if you know any new ones . . ." Al flashes his winning smile, and the reporters laugh again.

"How long can you hold out, do you think?"

Al's smile is more tentative now. "As long as a human being can hold out, I guess we can hold out." Just before the journalists disperse, he adds, "They're being very humane, seriously" (later he would explain that the crew's strategy was to portray the Popular Front as benign, "in order to keep everyone alive").

Abu-Sharif gives the cameramen five minutes to take pictures "of the plane only."

"Can we also shoot the passengers?" a reporter calls out, his careless wording unnerving hostages within earshot.

"You can shoot only the two planes," Abu-Sharif says. Anyone "directing his camera anywhere else, his camera will be confiscated."

A reporter asks directly if the commandos plan to blow up the planes, and Abu-Sharif says only, "You will know later."

Surely the hostages at the impromptu press conference filled in the rest of us when they returned to the plane, but I have no memory of listening to, or overhearing, any such conversations. If I heard anyone repeat Abu-Sharif's cryptic answer, I omitted it from my diary.

When the visitors headed back to Amman to file their stories, Gerald Seymour found himself feeling "disgust and shame" as he returned to his air-conditioned hotel, "leaving people behind, who are in a bad and unpleasant and frightening situation." He also thought the whole show bizarre, captors and captives alike assuring everyone of their well-being, while the reporters understood "the dangers under which these hostages were living."

One day the commandos sent TWA passenger Tova Kahn and her two children outside to speak with a Dutch television reporter. Tova felt sure it was because she held an Israeli passport; the commandos, she believed, wanted to prove that they were treating her the same as everyone else. Right away she said, "My name is Tova Lev Kahn, and I'm an Israeli citizen." Another time, when a cameraman pointed his instrument at Rob Hirsch, standing in one of the airplane exits, the ten-year-old made sure to smile a big smile, in case his parents saw him on TV.

Reporters asked lots of questions, and the hostages had plenty of questions for the reporters too. Why wasn't anyone getting us home? Was the American government trying to get us out? Didn't the airlines care? Had everyone forgotten the hostages? Did people even know about us? One day Al Kiburis asked a reporter what was going on in the outside world, explaining, "We're on a news blackout."

"You *are* the news," the reporter said. "You are the *only* news."

Mostly the commandos didn't allow reporters or cameramen inside the hijacked aircrafts, but I unexpectedly come upon an Associated Press report that includes a ten-second, black-and-white segment shot from the interior of our tourist-class cabin. It shows little more than a male crew member walking the aisle to collect trash in an open shopping bag, and another man, maybe a commando, walking behind him, then moving quietly ahead of him. The soundtrack is only a din of indecipherable voices. There are many faces I don't recognize as the cameraman pans from one side of the aisle to the other, but I identify David Raab and the Hirsch siblings, along with Mitch Meltzer, a young man I remember as taking a special interest in looking out for the children.

At the left-hand edge of the screen I alight on an image that's visible, if out of focus, for just a few seconds. In a row with two occupants, only eyes and foreheads are visible. Both faces turn to look at the camera, and it seems to be Catherine and me, even if I have no memory of anyone filming from inside the plane. The arrangement makes sense: I'm in the window seat, with Catherine right next to me, even though she could have taken the empty aisle seat to give each of us more room. But it's so partial and so blurry that I can't be sure, or I don't want to be sure.

15

Absorbing the uncertainty over whether our captors intended to blow up the planes with all of us inside, I need to reckon with the emotion of fear. Fear is integral to any experience of hijacking and hostage-taking, and fear is the abiding memory of many of my fellow hostages, including my sister. Even though I remember the commandos as mostly friendly, it seems impossible that I never felt afraid. Yet even though Catherine insisted, when we got home, that she'd observed my feelings of terror, fear isn't the emotion that returns to me when I think about the hijacking all these years later, and even the most meticulous reconstruction—mining archival documents, newspaper articles, television broadcasts—hasn't impelled that feeling to resurface. If I could find out what my fellow captives felt—again, the historian's trick of parallel accounts seems the logical pathway—could I hope to reach the fear I felt back then?

Amicability between captors and captives was partly a product of strategy on both sides. Al Kiburis worked on the assumption that "If they're thinking about blowing up my brains, I'm going to try to win them over to our side, and be cordial." For their part, our captors at times assured us we'd be safe, and the crew, also wishing to keep passengers calm, echoed those encouragements. The commandos wanted to release at least some hostages who would tell the world that they had been treated well, but Leila Khaled gave another partial explanation for kindness: they needed to put us at ease, since "frightened people can do foolish things."

Some of the hostages couldn't help but admire the phenomenal organization that had gone into September 6, 1970, agreeing with a dip-lomat's assessment that the Popular Front had demonstrated "remarkable powers of planning and execution." Many were also surprised to find our captors even a little amiable. Where they expected crazy fanatics, they found polite men and women. One man felt the commandos treated us as "brothers and sisters," sharing food and water and talking about their lives. Abu-Fadi, the guard in charge of the Swissair plane, had studied at Ohio State University and spoke excellent English. One evening he took a group for a sunset walk, impressing them as "a kindhearted, soft-spoken, surprisingly pleasant fellow."

On our plane, Hallah Joseph made an equally positive impression. She had a married sister in Cincinnati, she said, and because of her own membership in the Popular Front, her parents, brothers, and other sisters were imprisoned in Israel. One hostage found her "a beautiful personal-ity," "strong-willed," yet with "kindness in her face." *Do I hate the Arabs?* Foozie asked herself as she sat in the desert. She disagreed with their ide-ology and methods, but she didn't think she hated them—after all, they were part of God's creation. Did she actually like Hallah? There was "such pain in her eyes and face," Foozie observed, feeling as if she trusted her. She couldn't be sure, but either way, she found herself wishing her captor "life and peace," aware that she would "probably get neither."

All the commandos treated with care the youngsters who played in the aisles, prompting one hostage to admire the "tough soldiers with ma-chine guns" who were "marvelous with the children." Children found the guards friendly too, and some of the younger boys thought their guns were cool. When a kid fashioned a game of cat's cradle out of a piece of string, a commando communicated via sign language that his own children played the same game. "Every time a child cried for milk," one woman said, "they would run, give them milk." When a reporter pressed Daniel Kahn, eight years old, for thoughts about his captors, Daniel brightened a bit. "They're pretty nice," the boy said. "They're friendly."

Meanwhile, up in the first-class lounge, captors and crew relaxed and conversed together (some passengers disapproved of the fraternizing). Al Kiburis's wife was a stewardess, and when a commando joked that he could hijack another plane so she could join her husband in the desert,

Al offered his warm smile and a quick "No thanks." Joking aside, it was clear to June Haesler that while the commandos were friendly, they were also "in complete control." Catherine put it another way. While we passengers looked to the airline crew to serve as our leaders, the crew didn't serve as "leaders to the guerrillas," she said, since "the guerrillas were *the* leaders."

Like Catherine and me, some of our fellow hostages found themselves interested in the political cause of our captors, and Catherine observed others growing sensitive to their experiences. One hostage, who identified as a Zionist, gained a measure of empathy for the conditions under which the Palestinians lived as refugees. One of the stewardesses, who became "very sympathetic to the Palestinians" during her week in the desert, pinned a Popular Front button to her uniform.

One day Bassam Abu-Sharif took an empty seat next to one of the rabbis. "Naturally, he was very much against the idea of taking innocent third parties to advance our cause," Abu-Sharif recalled. "We ended our talk without reaching any common ground," he admitted, yet the two continued to converse, and Abu-Sharif "enjoyed matching wits with him," finding himself "looking forward to our daily exchange of views." When the rabbi said that in the Popular Front's place, he would have done the same, Abu-Sharif understood that any hostage might have said something similar, but he was nonetheless impressed that the rabbi said that at all. As Al Kiburis saw it, the commandos wanted both "a fair hearing of their grievances" and "favorable propaganda for their cause."

Inside the Swissair plane, when a young commando named Louma explained in fluent English, "I am a soldier because I want to fight for my lost fatherland," a hostage challenged her, asking, "Do you believe that you can reach your goal by violence?" Louma had lost her parents, brothers, and sisters and spent two years in an Israeli prison. "I was humiliated and beaten," she said, emphasizing that Palestinians were driven out of their homes "by force" and would return "by force." Her listener had two thoughts: *They have staked their lives on a kind of game as only fanatics, desperadoes can do*, followed by, *For us westerners who live in comfort, such an act is not comprehensible.* Over on BOAC, a teenage girl found herself angry and disgusted, but she also knew that only something "*very* serious" could cause someone to do what her captors had done. *What can it be like to be made to leave your home and country?* she wondered. *They're refugees. They're homeless. They're men with a cause.* Sometimes she thought they were brave.

"Stockholm syndrome" didn't exist in 1970. The phrase would be coined several years later, after a Swedish bank robbery in which some of the hostages identified with their kidnapper. The "syndrome" was invented during a television interview, and no professionally endorsed symptoms or diagnosis ever followed. "Why is it so hard to believe," a Yale University psychiatrist has asked, "that persons who are exposed to views they would not have chosen to hear can discover in themselves some sympathy for those views?" Why, he asked, "assume that conditions of captivity automatically cancel out the capacity for logic, judgment, belief?" Applying Stockholm syndrome retroactively to hostages in the Jordan desert in 1970 is problematic too, because the "syndrome" includes rejection of the opportunity to escape, and hostility toward one's rescuers, neither of which pertained to any of us.

Instead, as I discover so much later, currents of hostility between captives and captors ran alongside the geniality, manifestations of far deeper antagonisms. From the start, the commandos engaged their hostages in conversation, but since the crew cautioned the passengers against talking politics, people mostly listened. We listened as they justified the hijackings as a way to bring attention to the expulsion of Palestinians from their homes and their subsequent twenty-two years as refugees, and we listened as they spoke of the thousands of Arabs held and sometimes tortured in Israeli prisons. Sometimes hostages warned one another not to anger the commandos, not to say the wrong thing within earshot ("No, no, shh, don't say that").

To some, the commandos who initiated conversation were merely running indoctrination sessions. One night Catherine and I heard one of the women guards talking to a group of hostages, who were nodding and murmuring, "Yes, yes, you're right." After the woman walked away, Sara Raab burst out, "Why do you always defend them? They're wrong!"— only to be met with fearful admonitions of "Don't say that!" and "Shut up!" revealing that at least some of the assent was calculated. Occasionally an unguarded child would cross our captors. When commandos on TWA asked a boy if he thought it was right that the Palestinians had been kicked out of their homes, the ten-year-old answered that he didn't think it was right that Jews had been kicked out of their homes either, listing nations and dates of expulsion. When the men walked away, some of the hostages cheered softly.

The occasional hostile exchange between the commandos and Rabbi Hutner, sitting in front of us, made Catherine and me uneasy. When the rabbi asked the commandos questions like, "What have I done to deserve this?" the crew or other hostages would politely ask him to desist ("Please be quiet, sir, please"), and sometimes Catherine just wanted to tell the old man to shut up. Other times, when commandos paused at his row, staring and laughing, we felt sorry for him.

The commandos also paid special attention to Sarah Malka, the Arabic-speaking college student, whom I remembered observing with admiration as she engaged in dialogue with our captors. When Jim Majer puts me in touch with her—the two of them remained in touch— she confirms my memory over the course of a long phone call. (Sarah doesn't remember Catherine and me either, though she does recall that someone's mother was a dancer.) As it turns out, the commandos hoped to mobilize Sarah to explain their cause to the rest of us, and so they frequently engaged her in discussions of political philosophy. Sarah took up the challenge, arguing about Marxism, revolution, and democracy, making it her mission to gather information to relay to her fellow hostages. She also made it her mission to dissuade our captors from causing harm. "You can win a revolution without blood on your hands," she told them over and over again. "You do not want blood on your hands."

Nice guards could all of a sudden turn mean as they combed through our luggage, searching for evidence of connections to Israel, which might help them target particular hostages to exchange for Palestinian prisoners.

For most American Jews in 1970, the Israeli flag stood for courageous victory, whereas for our captors it signified the occupation of their homeland. Damning evidence might also include paperwork proving time spent on a kibbutz or a photograph of an Israeli soldier. Even Israeli hotel bills and car-wash coupons could provoke them. On the sly, Al Kiburis managed to dispose of various items, ranging from an Israeli address book to an Israeli army uniform (which he simply handed over to the commandos) to Six-Day War service ribbons. Jim Majer saw that mementos from the 1967 war especially angered our captors. Images of General Moshe Dayan or an Israeli shell casing became grounds for "a severe grilling," in which Hallah Joseph became, as Jim put it, "uncharacteristically irate." In fact, the usually kind and helpful woman seemed to change personalities upon discovering souvenir shells from the Six-Day War, asking, "How many did this kill?" Jim soon learned that the war had taken the life of her fiancé.

Around Catherine and me, the crew served as go-betweens, coaxing hostages to cooperate with the confiscations, then comforting those who became distraught. One day Hallah Joseph explained that everything from Israel "except religious articles" would be collected, and the crew saw "quite a mountain of things" piling up on the sand. Foozie surrendered her made-in-Israel army jacket but refused to give up her knapsack. Although it too was Israeli-made, she told the commandos she'd bought it in Brooklyn.

"Don't lie to us," one of the men warned her.

"I'm not lying," Foozie lied, naming an army-navy store on Coney Island Avenue.

Our captors soon turned to our checked luggage. "We had to list items in our suitcases from Israel," I wrote in my diary, as the commandos ordered the cargo hold opened and laid bags out on the desert floor, calling hostages one by one. As the crew collected our lists, they advised us not to omit anything, since that would only cause more trouble. Brusquely, the commandos questioned a teenage girl about photographs of Israeli soldiers, Israeli bus tickets, and a tape she'd made at a concert, accusing her of being an Israeli soldier herself, or married to one. One commando, who became especially aggrieved over souvenir Israeli bullets, kept showing a raw head wound to another hostage, saying, "See? That's an Israeli bullet."

Despite Hallah Joseph's insistence that religious items would be spared, Susie Hirsch lost her Israeli prayer book (she continued reciting the prayers, by heart), and the Raab family lost prayer books too, along with some of the children's toys (the commandos let one of the younger boys keep a model El Al airplane because it was made in Japan). Tova Kahn lost jewelry, Howie Hirsch lost his bar mitzvah presents, and Mitch Meltzer lost a statue of Moses. One couple lost their movie camera with all the film from their travels, even though they had boarded the flight in Frankfurt; the husband wondered if his curly dark hair and tanned complexion made the commandos suspicious.

In her diary, Catherine wrote, "Our suitcases were emptied and confiscated of all things made in Israel." By "our," she meant our fellow hostages, since the commandos took nothing from either of us and never called our names for questioning, maybe because we were young girls traveling without parents, maybe because we made ourselves inconspicuous, or maybe because our carry-on bags included no victory souvenirs from 1967—my mother and stepfather owned no such collectibles. I got to keep my blue-and-white-striped barrette from the Little Lady, the golden cubes of our Five Stones game, and the inlaid box I'd picked out at Maskit at summer's end.

All that—along with the return of Gerry's picture by a sympathetic commando—would serve as proof for the story I could tell myself and everyone else whenever I got home: our captors were nice to us. When I recorded the ordeal of Gerry's photograph in my diary, I wrote, "I cried like crazy to get it back," crafting the entry as if my tears were a strategic performance rather than an expression of genuine sadness or helplessness or fear—sadness most of all, I suspect. I wanted to keep Gerry's picture forever because he lived in the same faraway place where my mother lived. ("It is such a secret place, the land of tears," said the aviator in *The Little Prince*.) When I placed Gerry's photograph in my rose-colored Louis Sherry tin at home, I intended it as a memento not of the hijacking but rather of my summer sweetheart.

Some of the hostages in the desert never feared for their lives. Foozie didn't believe that our lives were in danger, and Barbara Mensch wasn't scared for her life either. Some found ways to forbid such thoughts. Susie Hirsch mixed faith and denial with "fantasies of being magically saved," soothing herself by singing lullabies to the babies, comforting herself through comforting others. The Hindu engineering professor turned to yoga to find "a state of mind when you refuse to think of certain things"—he conjured Nehru and Gandhi sleeping peacefully while incarcerated. Others, though, wrestled with visions of murder. One woman wondered which would be less traumatic for her daughter: to be shot in front of her mother, or to see her mother shot first.

Fear hovered everywhere. It had to. When a Red Cross rep came on board one day to assure the hostages that "the entire world knows what is going on here" and that everyone was working on "a solution," he candidly added, "We don't know if we will succeed."

In a report I later unearth in the International Red Cross archives in Switzerland, Dr. Claude Frascani describes the hostages as "collectively terrorized," reacting in varied ways. "Some wept, some were petrified, others were silent or courageous, fatalistic, defiant, ironic, cynical, gay, apparently exhausted or normal." Just as some assumed that women and children were physically fragile, Frascani assumed that women and children were psychologically fragile, "terrified," he said, to the point of "a psychosis problem." True, since only men had been removed from the plane, it was mostly women—wives and mothers—who displayed the greatest alarm, but men were afraid too, even if some were adept at hiding their feelings. A US Army colonel among the hostages said that anyone who wasn't scared "didn't understand these fellows, the guerrillas." A psychiatrist among us described the hostages as living in "a state of controlled fear and uncontrolled anxiety."

Holocaust survivors faced their own demons, with confinement and weaponry stirring up unbidden memories, only intensified by the troublesome construction of Arabs as Nazis incarnate (as an Israeli journalist observed right around the same time, the "lingering memory of the holocaust makes Arab threats of annihilation sound plausible"). One woman, thirty-eight years old and born in Czechoslovakia, was traveling from Israel back to Brooklyn with her two young sons. Her father had been murdered in Buchenwald, and ten aunts and uncles died in Auschwitz, while she had gone to Bergen-Belsen in a cattle car. Her captivity inside the plane "brought me," she would say later, in her broken English, "all the memories again back from concentration camp," which was a "very big nightmare." (When Holocaust survivors afterward told one of the hostages, "I know what you went through," the hostage felt stunned. "Whatever we dealt with, there was no comparison," he said, "but in their minds, there was.")

The one person I admitted fearing was Palestina, one of the women commandos assigned to our plane, maybe because everyone else did too, maybe because it was impossible to react any other way to a gun pointed right at me. One hostage thought she was "the angriest and the bitterest," with "no pity or softness," and another described her as "this one lady commando who constantly came in with a gun" and "looked like she was going to shoot everyone down."

I didn't mind knowing that other people were scared, except for Catherine. Although my sister never hid her tears or feelings from me, I never again wrote in my diary about her forebodings, after that first day when I crossed out the words "a crying Catherine." Nor, despite its importance to me, did I ever record Jim Majer's assurance of "no bodily harm." As comforting as his words might have seemed, their slightly menacing ring—leaving open the possibility that other kinds of harm might come to us, or that we might never get home—dissuaded me from preserving them, which was also a way not to preserve my own fear.

16

How convincing, over time, was Jim Majer's assurance, seared into my mind from the night we landed? Was I really so sure that our captors would not harm us? Even though feelings of fear remain stubbornly elusive so many decades later, I must have been at least partly aware of the backdraft of antipathy suffusing the plane. I must have known that the same friendly commandos were also party to the negotiations and the deadlines, and negotiations and deadlines pointed to the prospect of death, a possibility that slithered quietly through each hot day, each pitch-dark night, every early gleam of sunlight. Catherine understood that, and I had to have known.

For one thing, there was the stream of weapons-laden visitors who filed up and down the narrow aircraft aisle, a "constant parade," as Catherine would recall, "of guerrillas and officials." We would all quiet down and tense up, sensing that our captors wanted to make us afraid. Some people tried to fabricate a dignified demeanor, others just pretended to be asleep. Sometimes the visitors smiled to one another, shook hands, or slapped one another on the back. Some pointed to the hostages and laughed, others acted like tourists taking in the sights. Susie felt like a "freak in the circus," and Foozie joked that we were "the main attraction at the Jordanian branch of the Bronx Zoo." Other times we felt like inmates, or like the goods for barter that the Popular Front hoped we were. "You don't feel exactly human," Catherine reflected after we got home, and given how filthy we all were, "we didn't even look human." After days of this, Captain Woods requested a stop to the parades, and the commandos desisted. Even when the processions of armed sightseers stopped, though, weapons still filled the inside of the aircraft, including the Kalashnikov AK-47 machine guns swinging from the shoulders of the commandos stationed by the exits.

Some of the grown-ups told us that the commandos wouldn't harm the hostages because that would turn world opinion against them. "But when people are walking up and down with guns, you don't think of the practical side," Catherine allowed. Even the nice commandos carried guns, as did the young ones (one hostage didn't "trust any child of fifteen or sixteen with a rifle"). June Haesler didn't think the commandos would harm anyone on purpose, but she worried anyway—"People shoot each other on hunting expeditions," she said. One time, a commando holding a hand grenade unsettled stewardess Vicki McVey by feigning a tossing motion, with a playful "Here, catch." Within sight too were tanks and heavy artillery. A reporter described "manned anti-aircraft and anti-tank guns in trenches dug round the three aircraft and a big detachment of guerrillas armed with submachine guns and hand grenades," standing "on the alert." We were surrounded in turn by Jordanian army troops, signaling our position in a war.

Besides the guns and grenades and armaments all around us, there was the dynamite and the shifting deadline. ("From time to time you will condemn him to death," a king instructed the little prince, speaking of the single animal on his planet. "But you will pardon him on each occasion; for he must be treated thriftily. He is the only one we have.")

"We're glad to see you here," a Red Cross official told the TWA hostages one day.

"Thanks a lot, man!" someone called out. What the man meant, since he knew the plane was wired, was *It's good that you're still alive.*

"Explosives," the British ambassador to Jordan reported early in the week, had been placed "inside the aircraft cockpits and under the fuel tanks and wired for remote detonation." One diplomat thought the commandos' "reputation for irrationality" worked in their favor, since it made it more believable that they would follow through, no matter the negative repercussions to their cause.

I'd watched my captors wire the plane that first night, even if I purposefully omitted that observation from my diary. Other children knew about the explosives too. One of them was Tikva Raab, whom I'd placed first on my list of friends.

I reunite with Tikva after finding a notice in her temple's online news-letter, "celebrating the 48th anniversary of Tikva and family's safe release from being hijacked." Over lunch at a restaurant near her home in New Jersey, we compare memories, share stories, and try to make sense of our feelings as two girls about the same age back then. She tells me how kind the Palestinian doctor was to her, and she tells me how frightened she felt on Monday night when the commandos ordered all of us off the vans. In the desert, she'd heard the commandos say that the plane was wrapped in dynamite, that if they didn't get what they wanted, they would blow us up—but she and I never talked about that on the plane.

When I show Tikva the places in my diary where I wrote about her, she marvels that I spelled her name correctly, without an *h*. "We must have been friends," she says. Even though I remember her, she doesn't re-member me, at least not specifically. She tells me, though, that she never let her own children fly alone when they were young, because of her keen memories of the unaccompanied children on our flight—because of little Connie, she says, and "because of you."

Adults certainly knew about the dynamite. For one thing, Sarah Malka heard our captors speaking in Arabic about making the planes explosion-ready. For another, some of the commandos warned their hostages with words like "We cannot wait forever, and you will all go to a fiery death if this thing isn't settled soon." June Haesler, trying to lighten the mood, would joke, "Don't come up here and trip over any wires!" I didn't un-derstand that the commandos also assured us that we were safe and out of harm's way precisely because, in Leila Khaled's words, "frightened people can do foolish things."

"What you think about the most," Catherine later recalled of the lengthening hours and unbounded days, "is your life."

Some interactions between captors and captives were frankly combative and intimidating. These interrogations took place at night, in the com-mandos' quarters in the first-class lounge, yet despite my home near the front of tourist class, I have no memory of being aware of them. Maybe I remained fast asleep, or maybe, if I knew anything about them, I success-fully scrubbed that knowledge from my mind.

The commandos singled out certain passengers for this intensive questioning, with the aim of exposing an Israeli citizen, an Israeli soldier, or an Israeli spy, all for leverage in their negotiations. Since she spoke Arabic, Sarah Malka came in for follow-ups to the spirited daytime back-and-forth I overheard. The commandos were determined to expose Sarah as a secret agent, and another hostage recalled that at least once she emerged from the first-class compartment shaking with fear, eyes red-rimmed.

Another disturbing incident comes to me from Tova Kahn, who was traveling with her two children. I don't remember Tova, but when I contact another of the dancers in my father's company to ask for any memories of the September 6 performance in Central Park, he says that, coincidentally, a neighbor in his West Fifty-Sixth Street apartment building—the older woman directly across the hall—had been on a hijacked plane too, which turns out to be TWA 741. Even though she doesn't remember Catherine and me either, when ninety-one-year-old Tova answers the door, she embraces me right away, overcome.

Tova lays out slices of cake from the neighborhood Persian bakery next to the blueberries and strawberries I've brought, but when we say goodbye hours later, all of it remains untouched. "We were supposed to have coffee, but we got lost," Tova says. Then spying the fruit: "Oh, the berries! We really got lost."

Tova tells me that when the commandos took her up front (she was the one who announced to a reporter, "I'm an Israeli citizen"), she would ask nearby hostages to watch her two children, in case she never returned. Tova's ten-year-old daughter must have suspected the danger, since one time she ran up the aisle after her mother, calling out, "I want to die with you!" The story touches me deeply because it reveals that children traveling with parents suffered in a special way, fearful that their mother or father might be killed right there on the plane.

One night the commandos questioned Sara Raab, the lounge lit only by a lantern in the galley. Aware of her agitation, not least from leaving her five children in the cabin, the man eventually offered Sara a cigarette, which she accepted even though she'd long ago quit smoking.

Searching Sara's wallet, a commando came upon her membership cards for Hadassah, the American women's Zionist organization. It was an organization, Sara explained, that raised money "to support hospitals and outpatient clinics for Jews and Arabs in Israel," where "Jewish people and Arabs sit side-by-side being treated equally." When her interrogator asked if she was a Zionist, Sara said no, which wasn't true, adding, "I am a humanitarian." When Sara returned to her seat, her younger children were crying. When the commandos called her again the next night, the little children cried again, and Sara instructed the older ones to care for their siblings if she didn't come back. This time a woman served as the interrogator. When asked her husband's profession, Sara said "teacher" instead of "rabbi." When pressed, she said he taught language.

"What kind of language?"

"Hebrew."

Did she have an Israeli passport? Sara answered truthfully that she was born in New Jersey, that she and her husband and children were all American citizens. This time she didn't dispute her Zionist identity, saying, "I feel that all people should have a homeland, their own country. All people." Afterward she accepted a cigarette from a fellow hostage.

While Catherine and I slept, the commandos also brought Mimi Beeber, who sat behind us, up to the lounge.

I remember Mimi as tall and willowy with honey-blond hair. In the intervening years, she has become a professor of anthropology at a university out west, and when Mimi and I connect via a video call, I ask her if my memory is accurate. Yes, she tells me, she's tall and her hair was bleached from the Mediterranean sun that summer. I'd listed her among our adult friends, but she doesn't remember Catherine and me.

Mimi had spent the summer of 1970 working on a kibbutz and boarded the plane with an Israeli army shirt and a photo of an Israeli soldier (even for counterculture Americans who protested the Vietnam War, handsome Israeli men in army uniforms were cool). Years after her release, she remembered the commandos' words as, "We know you are in the Israeli army, and we are going to kill you unless you tell us more information." Just as her interrogators did not believe her denials, she convinced herself that she did not believe their threats. She was interrogated twice, she tells me, both times "very intense."

Unaware of these frightening exchanges, focusing on the nice commandos who played with the children, grateful for the ever-attentive crew, for our prized Foozie, and for Mark and Mimi watching over us, Catherine and I wanted so much for our father to know that we were all right. One day the commandos passed out postcards and ordered all of us to write to our governments, but Catherine and I wrote home instead. Demanding that everyone compose pleasant messages indicating our good treatment, the guards read each one to make sure everyone obeyed. Nearly fifty years later, in the folder my father labeled "Hijack," I find the note Catherine and I sent:

> *We are both okay and looking forward to being home. Many people are watching out for us so please don't worry.*

Each of us signed our names, with the designation "Americans" underneath, but my father would have seen right away that the message was in someone else's handwriting. Gazing at it so many years later, the penmanship is instantly familiar. We had dictated it to Foozie, who no doubt helped us choose the words. Those words, all of us knew, would serve

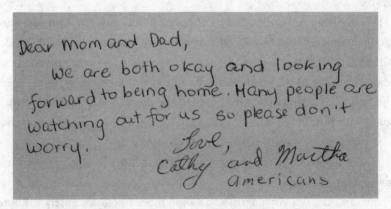

The postcard, in Foozie's handwriting, that Catherine and I wrote to our father and stepmother. It would arrive in the mail weeks after we returned.

[AUTHOR PHOTO]

two purposes: they would placate our captors and they would soothe my father. The parallel with my father's telegram to us is striking. In our message, my sister and I instructed him not to fret (*please don't worry*). My father gave us the same instructions (*Parents request children not be alarmed*).

Reading through the Sylvia Jacobson Papers at the American Jewish Archives, I study the notes Sylvia took when she interviewed Catherine and me shortly after our return home. Our accounts, she observed, were filled with discussions of "fear and efforts at its management." Sylvia invoked Catherine and me as proxies, unaccompanied children "with their expressions characteristic of the feelings and responses of others." She listed "the ordeals of capture, flight into the unknown . . . captivity, physical hardships and deprivations . . . haunting threats of disease and death."

At first these words strike me as so overblown that I actually laugh. Soon, though, I begin to wonder why I find Sylvia's narrative so absurd. The fact is, as a sociologist she was keen to discover feelings that I was keen to censor in my diary as a way to obliterate them from memory. Maybe I laugh all these years later because I can't absorb the fact that some—or much—of what Sylvia described was true. Decades later, it's still impossible to conjure my twelve-year-old self as a prisoner fearful of death.

While Catherine worried about her life, I built a fortress around that fatal possibility. Nearly a half century later, I scale the walls to look inside. Turning the pages of Sylvia Jacobson's notes, sifting through stacks of State Department telegrams and White House reports, trying to re-create the feeling of sitting inside the plane in the desert, I can summon only a space with nothing in it, bare and clean. It is the inside of the fortress that I constructed all those years ago, and now it is empty.

The weapons and the dynamite and the deadline: "I didn't really think about that," I would say when I got home. Singing "Leaving on a Jet Plane" and the brawny guerrilla jumping rope: I held resolutely to those scenes, crafting them into my own version of the hijacking. *See, it wasn't that bad. We had fun.*

Part Four

———————————

IT COULD HAVE GONE A THOUSAND WAYS

17

After Monday night ("the most frightening moment"), the only other time I preserved a record of my fear was on Friday, although this time in far more coded language. When I woke up that morning, more men and boys were missing, and my friend Tikva was crying hard. Ever willing to record the emotions of others—beyond Catherine and me—I wrote in my diary, "She was hysterical." What had happened? Something scary, I knew.

It was around 2:30 in the morning when Jim Majer stopped by a row occupied by the Raab family.

"David, they want you up front," Jim said, "for questioning."

Waking to the stench of the toilets, squinting in the harsh beam of a flashlight, David could see Jim's sympathetic, unshaven face. Instructed by a commando to put on his socks, shoes, and shirt, David knew he would not be returning to his seat. His mother understood that too. "Though this was probably the saddest moment of our lives, we shed no tears," David later recalled. "Crying would only make us feel worse." Silently the two exchanged a message: *Thank you for being so close to me for seventeen years, be brave, do the best you can, and try to survive. Hopefully, we'll be together again.*

As David proceeded up the aisle, Sara walked behind him. When her boy's body began to shake, another of the summoned hostages put an arm around him. Up front David obeyed the order to sign a sheet of paper, unable to stop his hand from shaking too. Still holding back tears, he climbed down the ladder into the darkness. His overwhelming feeling was of loneliness. Back in her seat, Sara Raab could only recite prayers. No one knew where the commandos had taken any of the removed men and boys or whether they would ever return. When morning came and Tikva awoke to a missing brother, Sara told her daughter that she had to stop crying or she would make her leave the plane.

Friday morning brought an atrocious sandstorm, and when the desert returned to its unbroken featureless form, arriving vans materialized out our windows. Were we—about 270 of us—going to be taken somewhere else? Were we being released? Whatever was happening, our guards seemed on edge: abrupt and preoccupied, including the kind Palestinian doctor, who no longer seemed kind.

First the commandos halted a caravan of International Red Cross trucks carrying food and relief supplies, just a few miles from the airstrip. Next they ordered the Red Cross doctor, Claude Frascani, to leave. The reasons weren't completely clear, but purser Rudi Swinkels thought the commandos no longer believed the Red Cross fairly represented their interests. Before long, the commandos instructed all of us to bring our belongings, in an orderly fashion, to the front of the plane. We were then to return to our seats, while they once again inspected our carry-on luggage ("Guards threw everything outside the plane on the desert floor," Rudi would write in his crew report).

Swissair hostages noticed the tension too. *Something must have happened last night*, one man thought, *or something decisive is just about to happen.* An agitated Abu-Fadi ordered everyone to remain quiet, then announced that negotiations had broken down and that the hostages would pay the price. On BOAC, the Popular Front released notes written by the hostages, possibly dictated by their captors. From the steward, "The plane is already loaded with explosives. In God's name release the Palestinians." From a stewardess, "Please don't play games with our lives," and from the flight engineer, "These are desperate men. Our lives are on a razor's edge." Some of the passengers used airline stationery to pen a message to the US embassy: "Conditions getting worse. Commandos serious in their threat. Please do not gamble with our lives. Release their prisoners immediately. Help us now."

I didn't notice, or I didn't pay attention, or I noticed then forgot, but on all three planes the commandos upped the installation of dynamite.

Ever hoping to impress their cause upon their captives, the commandos distributed envelopes of written material that day—what some of the grown-ups around me called propaganda. I always remembered the apology, words I imagined spoken directly to me in the voice of the kind Palestinian doctor, but I recalled nothing else about the handouts. Able to envision the typed-up pages, along with an image of myself reading with great concentration, I wondered if holding and absorbing those pages once again could bring back whatever feelings I'd felt in the desert, at least at that moment.

On a winter day at the National Archives in Washington, I pore over a stack of telegrams to and from the State Department. Eight thick folders, preserved for some reason in boxes labeled "Aircraft and Aeronautical Equipment," contain communications from September 1970. Everything is in haphazard order, all shoved away a long time ago. I wade through ceaseless sentences without verbs, punctuated by strings of acronyms intelligible only to intended readers (DCM: deputy chief of mission; GOJ: government of Jordan). Weary, I nevertheless do what historians are wont to do and pick up the next folder, dated October 1. Since everything was over by the end of September, this would be a cursory leaf-through. As soon as I open the folder, though, I see it, right on top: a thick packet of papers, yellowed and crumbling. The first words are "Ladies and gentlemen." And there's the apology, the words I'd never forgotten: "I feel that it is my duty to explain to you why we did what we did. Of course, from a liberal point of view thinking, I feel sorry for what happened, and I am sorry that we caused you some trouble during the last 2 or 3 days."

I feel myself slipping back into the narrow seat of a cramped airplane stranded in a desert. All this time, reading through documents about the hijacking, whatever emotions I'd felt sitting inside the plane have remained almost completely inaccessible. Not this time. Without casting my eyes beyond the familiar opening lines, I photograph all twenty-five pages. Nearly two and a half years pass before I can bring myself to read the document. When I decide to do so, I take the pages with me to the top floor of a summer-empty college library where I search out a carrel next to a window with an expansive view of a sloping green hillside. Reading and transcribing, I push through waves of claustrophobia and loneliness.

The apology, and everything that follows, turns out to be a speech, not originally intended for us, the hostages in the desert. Rather, it was a presentation delivered by the Popular Front's founder, George Habash, earlier that summer. In the desert, had I noticed that the material was dated June 12, 1970, my twelfth birthday? That June, while Catherine and I were finishing up eighth grade and sixth grade, respectively, the city of Amman was hosting the worst fighting yet, with the Popular Front gaining advantage. ("The old dream of Palestinian nationalism is suddenly alive," wrote *Life* magazine, explaining to American readers that refugees from the 1948 and 1967 wars were "scattered over the face of the earth, as once were the Jews, longing for a homeland controlled by the enemy.")

When Habash apologized, he had been speaking at the Intercontinental Hotel in Amman. Demanding that the Jordanian army quit shelling refugee camps, the Front had seized two hotels and was holding Western reporters and guests hostage. (While Habash denounced King Hussein of Jordan, Yasir Arafat denounced Habash's imperative to unseat the king and the Front's strategy of hostage-taking.) Fighting had gone on for days, with casualties in the hundreds, ending in victory for the Palestinian resistance, which prompted Hussein to remove two Jordanian army officers hostile to the Palestinian cause. "Believe me—and I am not joking," Habash said afterward, "we were determined to blow up the hotels with the hostages in them."

Three months after Habash delivered his speech to the hotel hostages, his words served just as well for us, the desert hostages. Imprisoned in my airplane seat, I kept reading. Fifty years later, I keep reading too.

"I hope that you will understand, or at least try to understand, why we did what we did," Habash said. Palestinians had been "living in camps and tents" for twenty-two years, "driven out of our country, our houses, our homes, and our lands." Imploring his listeners—and now us, the desert hostages—to "try to understand," Habash noted that his people did not wake up each morning to a cup of coffee or to thinking about vacation itineraries. "We cannot be calm as you can. We cannot think as you think."

Inside the plane, I'm sure I paused at those words. I loved to take time to be calm and to think, and summers in Israel were especially conducive to that pursuit. Sometimes Catherine and I did that together, when we went to Habima Garden up the street and rested on a bench, sheltered from the city's noise. Or at bedtime, in our makeshift Tel Aviv bedroom, I liked to lie with my hands folded, no book, no snacks, just—as I put it to myself—*thinking*. I felt sad that Palestinian people couldn't do that, and that their children couldn't do what I liked so much to do.

"Anything that protects our revolution would be right," Habash went on, which seemed like it could refer to the hijackings, especially when he added that "in the plan was you—what happened here." Habash's tone then turned from plaintive to belligerent. His people were "really determined." They were "not joking." If their enemies attacked the Palestinian refugee camps, the Popular Front would blow up the Intercontinental Hotel. That threat seemed to apply to us as well, and now the face of the kind Palestinian doctor I'd visualized turned frightening, as I sat trapped in the aircraft amid weeping adults, armed soldiers, and at-the-ready dynamite.

"I know that some of you will be saying at present 'What have I to do with these conditions? This is very unfair and very unjust and rude and selfish,'" Habash continued, seeming again to speak directly to me (listening to the commandos describe their impoverished lives, Catherine had wondered, *How is it my fault?*). Resuming a sympathetic tone, Habash said he hoped the hostages would be treated well. "From the personal side, let me say, I apologise to you," he repeated. "I am sorry about your troubles for three or four days. But from a revolutionary point of view, we feel, we will continue to feel, that we have the very, very full right to do what we did" (Catherine's next thought had been *What can I do to help?*). He ended politely, with the words "Thank you very much."

The envelope also contained an essay entitled "Road to Surrender," with the subtitle "From the Security Council Resolution . . . to the Rogers Plan: A Study Presented by the PFLP." This was longer, the anonymous

writer expounding on "the swamp of American filth" and "the Imperialist Zionist strategy," on growing resistance among the Arab masses and
on "a new revolutionary stage that will threaten imperialist interests and
its major supporter in the Arab land—Israel." Anything but revolution,
then, spelled the "road to surrender." Even though I liked to try my hand
at reading books from my parents' bookshelves, I'm sure there was little
in these pages that I understood. Nor did I ask Catherine to explain any
of it to me.

Held hostage in the desert, Catherine and I were children, in distress.
Some of our fellow hostages had been children during the Holocaust,
and some of our captors had been children during the 1948 war. All of
those traumas—our own, those of Holocaust survivors, and those who
survived the Nakba—differed mightily from one another, in duration, in
scope, in intensity, though in one way or another we were all thinking of
home. ("I stopped in my tracks, my heart torn asunder; but still I did not
understand," said the aviator in *The Little Prince*.) As Catherine reflected
years later, "It's hard to look back on a personally terrifying event at a
young age from an adult perspective of having a political context." That
made for "an uncomfortable, tense place—trying to hold nuances in a
life and death moment." There in the desert, Catherine and I just felt
sorry for everyone.

A woman whose husband was taken away on Monday night turned
the propaganda into drawing paper for her five-year-old, but some of
the hostages packed the pages in their carry-on bags, hoping it would
become a memento in the not-too-distant future. June Haesler brought
the pages home with her, and after she and I reunited in New York, she
sent me her copy, mine to keep. Holding those pages meant something
else too, something unexpected. The pages, and the memory of sadness,
felt like another possible modicum of proof that I had really been on that
hijacked plane.

Friday evening felt more menacing than usual. After the crew served food
to the passengers, the commandos served dinner to the crew. *What the
hell*, June Haesler thought. It was then that our captors announced the
removal of all male hostages. When the announcement came, I wrote in

my diary: "*all* the men PLUS the crew members (that were men) were to be OFF the plane." I was especially stricken by the old rabbi in the row ahead of us. "My God! The rabbi!" I wrote. "It was the 1st time in his life that he broke the Sabbath! Poor man!" That was my coded language, shrouding my own fear in sadness and pity.

One by one, the men climbed down the ladder. Many found it ironic: the crew had been asking for days that the women and children be released, and now the men, along with some older boys, were the ones departing. In her diary, Catherine wrote that "every remaining man including the pilot were taken away."

As Captain Woods descended, he asked June to toss him the bottle of liquor he'd stashed away. "See you!" he called up to her, bottle in hand.

"Good luck!" she called back.

A couple returning from their honeymoon were to be separated. "Don't worry honey," the recent groom told his bride. "Everything will be all right. You just take care of yourself." Another man, who felt sure the commandos were going to drive him farther out into the desert and kill him, felt sad for his wife.

On the desert floor, the commandos told the men to locate their suitcases—it was already dark, and the bags were covered with dust from the sandstorm that morning. Then the men were crowded into vans, a commando taking the wheel of each vehicle. Against religious law, Rabbi Hutner and the other Orthodox Jews traveled by car on the Sabbath.

On Swissair, a rumor circulated that the Israelis were going to attack the desert airstrip, prompting crew and commandos to agree on preparations for a rapid evacuation. Stewardesses instructed the passengers that, when signaled, they would have twelve seconds to slide down the emergency chutes and run from the plane. One hostage remembered the captain's words like this: "My friends, I am sorry to tell you, the news is bad. The plane is loaded with bombs. They expect to be attacked, and if such an attack comes they will blow it up—whether with us or without us, we don't know. All I can tell you is, in case you get a signal, rush out of the plane as fast as you can." A Christian hostage turned to God for comfort, wondering, *Will I be ripped into pieces or will I burn?*

Louma, the woman commando on Swissair, was crying. One of the young male commandos, sitting by an exit, head in hands, looked up to promise the hostages that he would not shoot anyone who attempted to escape. He would cut off his own hands first, he said.

Day and night on our plane, the hostages had imagined departure. Susie Hirsch imagined her pilot-cousin coming to the rescue from his home in the Negev, flying his boss's private jet. David Raab envisioned the Israeli Air Force swooping in. Every night, I imagined flying home the next morning.

Both our prison and our means of escape, the Boeing 707 remained airworthy. When the cockpit crew dumped fuel to land safely in the desert, they had saved just enough for a one-hour flight, "enough to take us anywhere we wanted to go," Al Kiburis said, with a mere half-hour preparation necessary for departure. Early along, the crew had tied blankets over the four engines to protect against sand.

But now Al was gone. Captain Woods was gone. Russell Morris, the TWA pilot traveling as a passenger, was gone. Jim Majer, copilot and surrogate father, was gone, and I hadn't even had a chance to say goodbye to him. This was when, for the first time, I wrote the word *hostages* in my diary. "These men are being held as hostages," I recorded, as if the term didn't apply to all of us held in the desert since Sunday, as if it didn't apply to Catherine and me. That was also the last time I wrote the word in my diary.

Catherine and Foozie had been preparing a Shabbat program for Friday night, but now it was called off. Others had been planning a talent show, and that was scrapped too, much to my chagrin, since I felt sure Catherine would have won a prize. I must have kept my mind as blank as possible, barricading panic in a faraway corner, while imagining running into my father's arms at Kennedy airport. If anything feels familiar now, it is that blankness of mind I so expertly honed.

Darkness enveloping the aircraft, I heard the women around me talking softly about rape, then tried to cast that conversation into something less real, a play or a movie that would soon be over. A group of hostages, including Sylvia Jacobson and Sara Raab, appointed themselves to sentry duty. Sylvia found it reassuring that the three women commandos on our plane appeared to be in charge. Tova Kahn uneasily watched some of the young male commandos "kind of flirting" with teenage girls. "You know," Tova told Hallah Joseph, "we are all women here."

"Don't worry," Hallah said, touching Tova's hand, much to her relief.

When a passenger told Vicki McVey that one of the male commandos had started "touching" her, Vicki told him to get away, then reported the incident to Hallah, who promised to accompany any male commando who walked down the aisle from then on. Hallah next turned on the offender. "Get off this plane or I'll shoot you like dogs!" she said, pointing her gun at him. The usually unkind Palestina took our side too, berating her male comrade in Arabic—translated by Sarah Malka—warning him that he better stay away if he didn't want to get shot. Hallah spoke up again, warning the man, "If you go near those girls, I'm going to kill you with my bare hands." The women were our allies, and in the Popular Front, women held power.

Vicki overheard something else: a commando telling some of the hostages that we would leave the desert the next day. Rumors circulated among the stewardesses, and Vicki checked with Hallah, then warned anyone listening that no one knew for sure what would happen. June stayed awake most of the night, much of it talking with Hallah, the two women avoiding the looming question, instead playing games like guessing the ages of different passengers. Late that night, one of the women guards whispered to some of the passengers, allowing Sylvia to hear the words: "Good-bye, good-bye, darling. Tomorrow you fly home." Another woman heard the words, "Don't worry, darling. Tomorrow you'll be free." In her ever-fearful state of mind, she wondered if that meant: *They're going to kill us tomorrow.*

What was happening beyond the desert on Friday, while we hostages sat on the plane, afraid? Our captors had asked the Palestinian Red Crescent to organize a convoy to take the desert hostages into Amman, while the negotiating parties contemplated an updated proposal from the Popular Front: release the six Palestinian prisoners in Switzerland and West Germany, Leila Khaled in Great Britain, and the body of her accomplice, and they would release all women and children, plus anyone who was ill, from all three planes. The remaining hostages would then be exchanged for specific Palestinian prisoners in Israel, including women and girls, those suffering physical or mental hardships, and "particularly important or heroic fedayeen." One US diplomat thought the proposal "a clever PFLP stratagem," holding "a certain amount of public appeal."

But the Israeli government remained uninterested in exchange. They had in fact compromised, they believed, simply by not objecting to the possibility of releasing Palestinians in European jails, all of whom, they pointed out, had "committed crimes aimed against Israel." Instead, the Israeli government advocated a firm stand on the part of the other four nations, along with Arab governments and the International Red Cross, to press for the release of all hostages, with appropriate consequences for the hijackers. That would make a strong statement against air piracy, and it would also, Israel believed, force the Popular Front to back down. Meanwhile, the Rabbinic Council of America, an organization of Orthodox rabbis, convened an urgent meeting. "In Jewish law, saving a life takes precedence," they wrote to Israeli prime minister Golda Meir. "If there is no choice, the State of Israel must comply with the terrorists' demand to save the hostages' lives."

The Red Cross had its own objections to the new proposal, since it violated their imperative to make no distinctions whatsoever among the hostages. Although the Red Cross would later come around—citing the Fourth Geneva Convention as rationale for the immediate release of women and children as a humanitarian measure—Switzerland, West Germany, Great Britain, and the United States turned down the proposal too, precisely for its "discriminative nature." The Bern Group would agree to release the seven Palestinians in European prisons only in exchange for all the hostages, without exception.

In Amman, André Rochat found the mood at the Popular Front headquarters to be one of "fantastic tension." Lamenting his team's "failed humanitarian action," he clung to "the mad hope that I could still do something," all the while wondering whether "the worst could happen now, at Revolution Airport."

Tension inside our plane also reflected increasing strains between the Palestine Liberation Organization and the radical Popular Front. While every faction of the PLO opposed the Jordanian regime and its allies, the PLO's Central Committee asserted that "everyone except the PFLP was against hijacking," and that "it was wrong for the PFLP to involve the rest of the movement—and the whole country—in an affair like this." The PLO leadership now offered its own proposal: in exchange for the seven Palestinian prisoners in Europe, the Popular Front should release all the hostages, men, women, and children, with the exception of Israelis of military status, then exchange those Israelis for certain Palestinians locked up in Israel.

Another complication was brewing, stoking Popular Front anger: a report about the possibility of foreign military intervention. The BBC had broadcast a story about American fighter planes arriving at US bases in Turkey, which turned out to be why the commandos halted the Red Cross relief convoy and ordered Dr. Frascani out of Revolution Airport. Indeed, the United States had flown military planes to Turkey, ready to evacuate the hostages, if possible or necessary. The Reuters news service reported a rumor that "the U.S. Sixth Fleet was steaming eastwards through the Mediterranean to back up an operation to snatch the hostages out of the guerrillas' hands."

By urgent telegram and radio messages, the concerned governments scrambled to assure our captors that no such interference was forthcoming. Secretary of State Rogers (who admitted, "It's so confusing from here") insisted that the planes had no military purpose; their presence was "purely humanitarian," standing by for the delivery of medical supplies or in case evacuation proved necessary. Rochat met with Popular Front reps, making every effort to "calm their angry mood and persuade them to trust the Red Cross and not believe rumours." Chaos reigned, with Rochat worrying that if the Popular Front thought military intervention imminent, they would massacre the hostages in the desert.

After midnight, the Red Cross got word of a new decision made by the PLO, to which the Popular Front would need to agree. It conformed to the Front's plan: everyone except Israelis of military status would be released when the three European governments and Great Britain released their Palestinian prisoners. Israelis of military status would then be exchanged for a certain number of Palestinian prisoners in Israel. But when the Bern Group met, into the early hours of Saturday, "in a state of major international crisis," they got nowhere with the PLO's proposal. They wanted to know what military status meant, and they wanted to know how many and which imprisoned Palestinians were needed for exchange.

Frantic at the news coming from Jordan, hostages' relatives placed international calls to the Geneva headquarters of the Red Cross, forcing staff members to balance expressions of sympathy with the imperative to save their phone lines for negotiations.

Worries in Washington escalated as everyone confronted, yet again, a plausible deadline to blow up the planes with everyone on board. Somewhere along the line, Henry Kissinger was informed that "the Palestinians were threatening to kill the remaining hostages," and he now believed that the United States had "considered every possible military step for rescuing the hostages and concluded that nothing would work." Negotiations had "reached a critical stage," he reported to President Nixon, and that evening the two argued over making threats to the Popular Front, with Kissinger interjecting, "No! No, only if any passengers are harmed."

"Dead or alive," Nixon said, referring to the commandos, after the murder of every last hostage, "we would have a terrible thing on our hands, I guess."

Bettie McCarthy had thought plenty about what it would be like to find out that everyone was going to be released. The odd thing was that when it finally happened, on Friday night, it wasn't at all the way she'd imagined. She was nearly asleep when another stewardess told her that we were all probably going to leave in the morning. The plane was completely quiet, and Bettie fell asleep.

When morning came, either the commandos or the crew told the hostages we would be leaving the plane. I have no memory of that moment, but I do remember that it wasn't entirely clear to Catherine and me whether we were being released or taken somewhere else, still to be held hostage.

18

———

How little I knew about everything swirling around me! At the time, I had no idea why the commandos let us leave the desert, and in all the years of studiously not thinking about the hijacking, I'd never felt any curiosity about the decision to evacuate the planes. Once our departure was underway, it felt inevitable. Of course I would see my father again.

Together, the Jordanian army and the Popular Front oversaw our transfer out of the desert, with the vans escorted by Fatah, the largest of the Palestinian commando organizations. One last time, some of the commandos quizzed a few of the hostages about their cause.

"Do you believe that people should fight for their country?" one of the men asked a ten-year-old boy, the same boy who had listed the places that expelled Jews across the centuries.

"Yes," the boy said, "if it is their country."

That presented a disagreement that couldn't be resolved in a matter of minutes, if ever, and so the commandos helped us descend the ladder, assisted with our luggage, and moved everyone toward the line of vans parked on the sand. The Swissair and BOAC hostages were boarding too. Outside the aircraft, some of the hostages glimpsed plastic explosives in the wheel bays; one watched as commandos added "all kinds of dynamite" to the jets.

As Sylvia Jacobson retrieved her coat, pocketbook, and carry-on bag, scattered on the desert floor, a commando confiscated a few last items: articles of clothing he thought were made in Israel, despite Sylvia's protests, along with books in Hebrew and figurines. One of the commandos asked Sara Raab to open her bags. "How many times are you going to go through my luggage?" she asked, starting to lecture the man—they weren't "the only country in the world suffering," and "if we had any sympathy for your people, for your cause, it is vanishing." When a commando asked how she felt about leaving the desert, she snapped again. "How can I feel? You are making Jews ride on the Sabbath for the first time in their lives. You have taken away my son. How can I feel?"—until another passenger cautioned her, for David's sake, "Go easy."

Stationed at a TWA exit to help passengers disembark, June Haesler saw that no one else was lined up, even though a few women and teenage girls remained on board. She started down the aisle to inquire, but a woman commando with a gun stopped her, telling June to gather her own belongings and leave the plane, assuring her that those remaining would follow. Soon, confusingly, commandos shepherded the remaining women and girls from TWA into the Swissair jet, along with a small group of BOAC hostages. Eventually they called out names, sorting everyone into the last vans. All three jets were empty now, and the commandos moved quickly away from the hulking creatures on the sand.

Our van, at the head of the convoy, had already gained distance when Catherine and I heard the enormous booms that made us duck. If you were at Dawson's Field, the first thing you saw was an explosion near the nose of the BOAC, followed by an orange-yellow ball of flames obscuring its tail before turning into dark smoke. With two deafening blasts, you would have seen shards of metal catapult through the air. Within seconds smoke engulfed the TWA aircraft, in between the other two, creating a panorama of plumes, white, gray, and black, until all three planes disintegrated behind a painting of orange, gold, and dark gray. Midnight-black billows soon expanded across the two-tone expanse of tan sand and blue sky, the jetliners smoldering, orange and yellow blazes shooting from the shells of metal. Three streams of smoke poured upward, meeting high in the atmosphere. The whole time, television cameraman Hassan Dalal stood just three hundred yards away. Popular Front leaders wanted the eruptions captured on film, and they had given permission only to Dalal. As soon as he saw the commandos sprinting, he started rolling his

*The hijacked planes blowing up, as the hostages were driven from
the Jordan desert into Amman. All three planes soon exploded.*
[BETTMANN VIA GETTY IMAGES]

sixteen-millimeter Bolex. When the smoke finally cleared, there emerged
a tableau of twisted wreckage with fires burning here and there.

The last hostages to board the vans saw and heard everything. Their
drivers had ferried them a short way, then turned around and parked
perhaps five hundred or a thousand feet from the planes. In one of the
vans, a commando told everyone to open their mouths and hold their
fingers in their ears, to prevent their eardrums from rupturing. Sarah
Malka found it "an extraordinary sight," and the BOAC captain called
it "quite spectacular." The vans swayed violently, and Barbara Mensch
thought "pieces of metal were going to come right at us." As a Swissair hostage watched each plane explode, two thoughts occurred to him:
Damned fanatics, idiots, followed by *For more than 22 years, more than a
million Palestinians have lived in refugee camps.* Mimi Beeber watched the
commandos cheering "like school kids."

Watching the flashes and billowing smoke, TWA stewardess Rosemarie Metzner felt sorry to see the airliner ("a beautiful thing") destroyed
(even though "it was so filthy it would have taken a year to clean"), and
some of the hostages found themselves unexpectedly sad that their "home
for a week" had blown up.

All the negotiators were caught off guard. Popular Front leaders, along with Yasir Arafat, head of the Palestine Liberation Organization, had been meeting with Red Cross delegates in Amman. While Arafat enumerated demands, someone from the Popular Front arrived to say that the commandos out at the airstrip had blown up all three airplanes. Arafat was displeased, since the PLO had wanted the Front to return the planes to the airlines. Fatah denounced the destruction, criticizing the desert commandos for "exposing the safety and security of the revolution to dangers" (the PLO Central Committee would briefly expel the Popular Front).

No one was sure why the commandos at the airstrip blew up the planes. Maybe it was to intimidate the more moderate PLO, or maybe it was out of frustration with their leaders, or to provoke panic by demonstrating unpredictability. One Red Cross official called the explosions "an expression of rage" (*un geste de rage*), but in fact the Popular Front was employing a strategy intended to foster continued negotiations, since they still held a substantial number of hostages in locations unknown to their adversaries. Accordingly, the Popular Front issued a statement about inflicting loss in return for "unjustifiable provocations" and "imperialist maneuvers." According to Bassam Abu-Sharif, the rejection of the Front's proposal for exchange demonstrated an "utter lack of respect" for the "ability to carry out its threat," thereby displaying "an arrogant colonialist mentality." The Popular Front blew up the planes "to ensure" that the "colonialist powers submit to the Front's just demands."

Even though he knew that the hostages were off the jets, Henry Kissinger was still worried. "They have blown up the planes but without the passengers," he told President Nixon that afternoon. "That removes some of the danger," he reckoned, since if the commandos wanted to kill the remaining hostages, they would have to "kill them individually." As CBS News put it on Saturday, "Although the giant jetliners were rubble, the hostages were not hurt. And, not out of danger."

While Catherine pondered whether our captors were taking us to a hotel or a prison, other departing hostages contended with fears of their own. Sara Raab imagined an internment camp. A teenager watched the armed commando in the passenger seat of her van and wondered whether she would live through the journey out of the desert. Another hostage thought everyone might be "shot right there."

Catherine felt relieved that none of the Jordanian soldiers along the way approached our van, but army tanks swiftly moved in to surround the last two vehicles in the caravan. Here was the war between the Jordanian army and the Palestinian resistance, up close. In response, Popular Front commandos jumped out of the vehicles, opened up the back doors, unlocked their loaded weapons, and aimed them straight at the hostages. In her van, Sarah Malka translated the Arabic exchanges for her fellow passengers. The Jordanian troops wanted the Palestinians to hand over the captives, and the Palestinians warned that if the Jordanian soldiers fired a single shot, they would kill all the hostages immediately. Another passenger heard the commandos say, in English, that if the Jordanians did not retreat, the hostages would die.

Weapons pointed, the two sides argued. Time slowed. People prayed. Some felt faint, and the twenty-one-year-old steward from the BOAC plane nearly "lost contact with reality." Finally the Palestinian doctor spoke up, in Arabic, somehow turning the mood. The commandos lowered their weapons. The Jordanians climbed into their vehicles, turned around, and drove away.

As the convoy proceeded, our van still in the lead, refugee camps came into view. On the outskirts of Amman now, I saw tents and clotheslines and whole families, including children, behind fences. (After traveling "for a long time through sand," and finally reaching a road, the little prince was "overcome with sadness.") I couldn't tell if the smiling boy in the crowd was happy about our week-long detention or about our possible release, precisely because the agitated crowd that surrounded us harbored a mixture of sentiments. Some hoped our release from the desert would ease the unofficial war in Jordan. Some yelled "Imperialists!" and "Zionists!" (NBC News missed the nuance and enmity alike, reporting that the hostages were "greeted warmly by Palestinians and Jordanians along the way.") Surveying the refugee camps, Sylvia Jacobson found the sight "indescribably horrible," far worse than the slums of New York City in the 1960s.

Departure from the desert had been "indescribable confusion," according to the Red Cross. Our evacuation was so chaotic that no one possessed an accurate record of released hostages or an exact count of how many might still be missing. Over the phone, TWA gave names to the Red Cross, but spellings were incorrect and some listings denoted only "and wife" or "and child"; a few indicated the absent ("without son," "without husband").

I find the list in the International Red Cross archives in Geneva, and Catherine and I are there, in the typed document entitled "List received from TWA Zurich at 5:30 p.m. by telephone and forwarded to the American Red Cross at 7:00 p.m." We're listed in all capital letters as MISS HODES AND CHILD, again as if Catherine were my unmarried mother. Again I feel a pinprick of surprise at the certitude of our presence. Still, the end of the page bears the notation, THIS LIST IS UNOFFICIAL AND HAS NOT YET BEEN CONFIRMED BY OUR DELEGATION IN AMMAN. Illogically that sentence prompts me to think that maybe we weren't there after all.

Catherine and I were in fact among some 120 hostages driven away from the three planes on Saturday. It was proving impossible for the Front to break the solidarity of the negotiating parties, and by detaining a smaller group, with a certain number of hostages from each country, the commandos hoped to exert pressure on each government separately. The Front had also acquiesced to the PLO's demands to get us out of the desert for the sake of humanitarian treatment—the difficulty of caring for their captives was increasing exponentially—but the commandos also removed us as a way to prevent a foreign military attack at Revolution Airport.

The PLO and King Hussein had worried too about fatal violence erupting in the desert, and as Kissinger saw it, getting the hostages off the planes was a way to loosen the grip of the Popular Front. Cautiously Secretary of State Rogers concurred that in Amman "the threat to their lives is lessened." It would now be "almost unthinkable," reflected a British reporter, for the Front to "blow them up or do the equivalent," by which he meant, to kill the hostages once we were off the desert-stranded planes and in the city of Amman.

No one knew whether we were free to fly home. Just the day before, the commandos had returned passports to hostages released from the desert back on Monday night. Jordanian police escorted a group to the airport—those permitted to depart hailed from Indonesia, India, and Ceylon, and some were Jews from the Swissair plane.

The aim of the US government was to get us, the newly released, out of Jordan as quickly as possible, but the commandos still held our passports. A Red Cross official thought the hostages had been "transferred," not "released," and the CIA wondered if the Jordanian government had the authority to fly us out or, alternatively, if the PLO had the authority to detain us. The Jordanian ambassador to the United States assured Washington that his government was doing everything it could to get us safely out of Amman, and to protect us while we were there. The problem was that the Popular Front tended to act independently of other Palestinian organizations. After some of the commandos heard a BBC report that Leila Khaled would not be freed, they issued threats about the hostages taken to Amman: that we might be "retaken by force and possibly even killed." A CBS News television special on Saturday reported that another 260 were "free from their captors, but not from danger," since the city of Amman provided "more anarchy than safety." Our fate remained "as uncertain as the political balance there," and as for leaving the country, "extremists control many of the roads to the airport."

Seven hills ascend from the center of Amman. In 1970 the city of a few hundred thousand presented a landscape of rectangular white limestone buildings bearing the signature level rooftops of a Mediterranean climate, punctuated by a mosque's dome or minaret here and there. The Intercontinental Hotel opened in 1963, a single white building surrounded by brown hillsides. Part of the city's expanding business and tourist trade, it was Jordan's first five-star hotel, boasting a swimming pool, four bars, and a nightclub. The coffee shop served "American style" food, and the whole place was air-conditioned. Enormous, with more than a hundred rooms, it instantly became the venue for banquets, galas, and fashion shows, as well as the temporary home of diplomats, royalty, and world leaders.

Taking in the pack of reporters awaiting our arrival, June Haesler thought, *Lights! Camera! Action!* as if we were all movie stars.

Arriving hostages could see the hotel facade marred by mortar shells and bullets. Susie Hirsch couldn't believe how shot-up the building was.

On a summer day nearly fifty years later, I watch more unedited news footage in the Motion Picture Research Room of the National Archives. The scenes appear in haphazard order, mixing our desert departure with what came afterward, and later a graduate student in Middle Eastern studies will translate for me the words of the commandos in the army vehicle riding ahead of our van, singing in Arabic through a megaphone: "We have brought the planes down. They are ours. May the Palestine revolution live forever."

Though the three planes had sat only about thirty miles from Amman, the trip out of the desert took a couple of hours, and it was early afternoon in the capital city when we arrived. Watching the tapes, I see some of what I remember. The building stands against the hilly terrain beyond the city's downtown, palm trees reaching to the top of the ground floor. The letter *J* in the sign for *Hotel Jordan Intercontinental* sports a 1960s-style curlicue. Soldiers direct our vehicle. A commando holds a megaphone. Horns honk. People speak in Arabic. Men in khaki uniforms wear red hats. Some men wear kaffiyehs. A man runs alongside us, then waves on the driver. Cameramen run beside our vehicle. Thirteen minutes in, the tape switches to the inside of a van, passengers displaying expressionless caution—a photographer has thrust his camera straight into one of the open windows.

And there we are. I sit impassively, hand to cheek. Shielding me, partly obscuring me, Catherine looks straight into the lens, serious, responsible, afraid. She twists around to look out the windows, scanning the commotion, planning what to do, thinking, *How can I keep us from being separated? How can I keep Martha safe?* Tentatively, then, I look around too. Large cameras and microphones completely surround us, shooting pictures, rapid-fire ("Reporters, TV cameras, other cameras, microphones, EVERYTHING!," I would soon write in my diary). Another reporter's hands, holding a camera, come in through the window, snapping one photo after another ("This one guy took around 25 pictures of me in a row").

Right there, on the screen before my eyes, is the twelve-year-old girl I've been trying to conjure. But there's that feeling again: despite all the documents, despite all the people I've talked to—many of whom, after

Catherine looks into the camera (center), with me visible immediately behind her, upon our arrival at the Intercontinental Hotel in Amman.

[KEYSTONE PRESS/KEYSTONE PICTURES USA/E0YM2C/ALAMY]

all, don't remember Catherine and me—the hijacking must have happened to someone else. Studying the moving image of that girl makes me feel more than anything else like a historian coming upon a visual representation of her long-researched subject for the first time. Watching the tape all these years later, I write down, "I can't believe I was there."

From an assortment of sources—the CIA tapes, television news footage, reporters' interviews—I piece together the chaotic scene that came next.

"Here they come! They're here!" someone hollers from inside the hotel lobby, prompting a surge of people to join the throngs outside.

"C'mon," a man in a white shirt calls out, waving his arm at our driver. The armed commando in the passenger seat opens the door and stands up, even though the van is still moving.

When our driver puts on the brakes, he looks around, trying to figure out what to do. A man leans into an open window, talking to a gray-haired passenger in a red-striped dress who nods, then rises. Catherine looks out the windows on both sides, and I turn around, one hand hesitantly at my lips, before we both stand up, looking confused. The man with the long gun stands up too and says "Yallah," Arabic slang for "Let's go" or "Okay." The word is the same in Hebrew, so Catherine and I would have understood. A woman in the last row speaks into a microphone that a reporter has pushed through the window. A little boy wearing shorts and suspenders frowns, then looks for his mother, seated somewhere behind him. A man shouts in Arabic, "We urge all the passengers to exit," then directs someone else to tell the passengers what he just said. Red-striped-dress alights, and others begin to follow.

On the tape, the next van pulls up.

"TWA," a Jordanian man in a suit announces.

"How are you?" a reporter calls to the passengers. "You all right? Are you all right?"

"Oh, couldn't be better." Our stewardess Linda Jensen flashes a huge smile. "Had a great time." Since everyone knew that some of our fellow hostages were still being detained, perhaps the crew agreed on the kinds of things they would say to reporters, or maybe the elation of freedom momentarily distorted everything that had come before.

"TWA! TWA!" the man in the suit calls out.

"Wait a sec, hold on," someone says in Arabic, trying in vain to tame the bedlam.

"How is everybody? You all all right?" the reporter repeats.

"Everybody is fine," says Bettie McCarthy. A uniformed man wearing a beret graciously assists her in stepping down from the van.

"How about the women and kids, are they all right?"

"They are fine," Bettie says. "Everyone was very well treated."

Not everyone is as composed as Linda and Bettie, though. One woman is shaking, another breaks down crying. Spectators see that we're covered with sand, "caked with dust," as a reporter will say—one woman's white dress has turned light brown. A separate vehicle has transported our luggage out of the desert, and on the tape I watch Jordanian soldiers unload the equally sand-washed suitcases, as clothing threatens to spill from one bag's broken zipper. Hotel porters carry the bags inside. The entrance is jammed: hotel staff, airline personnel, Red Cross workers, armed soldiers, the mob of newsmen. One of the reporters will describe a scene of "wild confusion."

When we got home, Catherine described our arrival at the Intercontinental, recalling a man materializing to guide the two of us through a sea of people as she gripped my hand so we wouldn't lose each other. I have no such memory, but fifty years later David Raab gives me footage from the BBC that contains an eight-second snippet of Catherine and me, grainy in the few frames, our long-sleeved white blouses and colorful bell-bottoms a blur. I clutch my tote bag. On one side of me, a man in a suit has clamped a hand on my shoulder, propelling us inside, just as Catherine narrated.

There I am again—there we are, in Amman. Catherine is taller, my protector, holding me tightly, the two of us small amid the crowd on either side. The cameraman must have been walking backward, facing us, but the tape is too blurry to make out the expressions on our faces. Then, in a close-up of my profile—the cameraman has shifted position—my eyes are closed and my head cast down. It's as if the man whose hand is on my shoulder is about to spin me around for a game of blindman's bluff. It's as if the film is documenting my resolution not to remember any of this.

As Catherine recalls, "I wanted to grab your hand and run, but there was chaos and a crush of people."

19

*The Jordan Intercontinental in 1970. This was our view from the
van as we drove into Amman upon release from the desert.*

[AP PHOTO]

The fear that I so rarely acknowledged, that remained so elusive to
me so many years later, must have begun to subside.

"Go inside there and have food and drink, anything you
want," a man with an Arabic accent said. "Just tell them that you are a
TWA passenger."

"We're with TWA, come this way," said another official, the airline
eager to identify its customers. As the reps helped locate suitcases, our
faithful stewardesses stayed close, unceasingly on duty to inform, arrange, reassure.

"I'm Richard Wilson, special assistant to the president of TWA," another man said. "I'm in charge of you now," and soon another man uttered the confirmation I'd been hoping for. "You're our responsibility,
you're safe now."

No less chaos or crush met us inside the Intercontinental, but I thought the lobby was beautiful. Watching the unedited footage of our arrival, I see emotional scenes of those released earlier in the week reuniting with the just-released men from Swissair and BOAC. People cry out, or just cry, running into each other's arms, smiling and sobbing at the same time.

"It was a rough day," one of the men says. He is grinning but shaking his head. "They blew up the planes," he explains, then tells how his van was stopped, pantomiming the machine guns aimed at him. "It was really something." He shakes his head. "Wow."

"Well, you're here," a woman says, and repeats, "You're here."

Watching those reunions at the time, Sheila Warnock, who had been driven out of the desert on Monday night, found herself near tears, then found it nearly unbearable to watch the women who couldn't find their men among the fresh arrivals. TWA's Richard Wilson noticed Sara Raab looking distraught. "My son," she told him, "he was taken away from me." A few women and girls were missing too. One of Nancy Porter's friends from the plane had appeared, but Nancy couldn't find the other member of their trio, Barbara Mensch.

On the tapes, a man calls out over the din, "If you haven't registered, please register." People take turns sitting at makeshift tables, answering questions, reciting names and children's ages.

"Your husband is . . . ?" an official asks a woman cautiously, not knowing whether her spouse is among the released or the missing.

Someone directs little Connie Pittaro to a desk, where she stands by herself. Blond hair swept into a high ponytail, she clutches a doll while she gives her name to a man shuffling untidy sheaves of paper next to an ashtray brimming with snuffed-out cigarette butts. Foozie is nowhere to be found, so Connie is on her own.

For Tova Kahn, the most important thing was the glass of water someone placed in her hands. She would remember the taste of that water until the end of her life, some fifty years later. Tikva Raab saw long tables filled with food, most of which she still couldn't eat because it wasn't kosher. When a teenage girl briefly blacked out, an Arab man put a glass of water in her hands too.

Between the unofficial war and the cholera epidemic, tourists were scarce at the hotel that autumn, while reporters and cameramen from all over the world made the Intercontinental their headquarters during the Jordan crisis. Now they swarmed, clamoring for interviews, each in search of the most gripping, the most harrowing, the most heartbreaking story, with "hot lights and stupid questions," as one hostage put it. *What were the sanitary conditions like? Were you frightened?* "They all poured down on top of us when we got to the hotel," Catherine said, at some point uttering the words everyone in my family would always remember: "Now I am going to thank God and have a bath."

QUOTATION OF THE DAY: "Now I am going to thank God and have a bath."—Catherine Hodes, a 13-year-old passenger from the hijacked T.W.A. jet, in Jordan. [1:6.]

My father bought and saved multiple copies of Catherine's Quotation of the Day in the New York Times, *Sunday, September 13, 1970.*

Susie Hirsch, hoping her parents would see or hear their children on the news, headed straight for the reporters. "They did certain things to frighten us, and then they reassured us, and frightened us and reassured us," she said.

One released hostage answered questions—*How are you? Are you all right?*—with a perfunctory "Tired and hot. Not bad." Another just said her children were hungry.

Tova Kahn said the commandos "did everything they could for us," even though the plane felt like "a big cage" (the *Jerusalem Post* wrote the headline, FREED HOSTAGES CAREFUL TO EMPHASIZE "GOOD TREATMENT").

Not everyone put on a brave face, though. "I am on the verge of a nervous breakdown," one woman confessed, prompting people around her to instruct one another in Arabic, "Help her, step back, give her space."

"There have never been this many Jews in Amman before," an Arab bystander observed.

"I am happy to see these people," said the hotel manager. "They are our guests."

"Miss McCarthy," said NBC's Douglas Kiker, "for six days and nights, how was it out there for you? What did you do? How did you arrange your time?" Tall and thin, with ears that stuck out, Kiker was known for his caustic reporting. He'd been in the Dallas motorcade when President John F. Kennedy was assassinated, and he would later win an award for his coverage of Jordan in 1970. Bettie smiled a charming smile, her dark hair falling loose, sunglasses atop her head, before turning serious.

"We learned as each day went by," she said, describing how the passengers plunged the toilets and everyone helped out with the young children.

"People who started out as strangers ended up as close friends?" Kiker asked.

"Oh, my heavens!" Bettie exclaimed. That very morning on the plane it had felt like "the last day of school."

"Were you ever uncomfortable?" Kiker asked.

"No, never." Bettie turned solemn for a moment. Afternoon heat was the hardest, she allowed, but "after about four hours, evening comes and it's quite cool out there."

"People able to sleep all right in their seats?"

"I hate to admit this," Bettie laughed, "but sometimes I slept eight hours!"

"You'll be happy to get home, I suppose?"

"Yes," Bettie said, "but I'm also very glad to have been here. It was an absolutely unmatchable experience. And it gave me a great chance to see something that I'd never really thought about before."

June Haesler's stomach was cramping, and she was racing to find a bathroom when a reporter blocked her path to ask what it was like to live on an airplane for a week. Desperate to get to a toilet, she gave a sarcastic retort: "Everyone went around in stocking feet. It was a six-day pajama party." When *Time* magazine printed the quotation, the sarcasm didn't come through.

How much to say? There was still reason to be careful. Even Sara Raab told a far more favorable tale than her experiences warranted. "At first we were frightened," she said. "But later we relaxed as the commandos, who treated us well, brought food and medicine. They really showed interest in our well-being." It was harder to prevaricate when it came to her eldest son. All she could say about David was, "I don't know where he is" and "I have been assured that he is safe and that I shouldn't worry" (the *Jerusalem Post* wrote that those with relatives still detained "had especially good words for the terrorists"). It wasn't only that some of the hostages were missing, it was also that we were not yet home—the *Los Angeles Times* noted the reluctance of many to say "anything that might be considered offensive by the commandos," since they "clearly wanted to get out of the Middle East as soon as possible."

Rivke Berkowitz, whose husband, Jerry, was one of the six men removed by the commandos on Monday night, spoke with caution as she tended to her two-year-old daughter. Rivke wore the same colorful sleeveless dress she'd sat in all week, her short brown hair mostly in place. When a reporter asked where her husband was, she said, "I don't know."

"How were the six days and nights?"

"They were fine." Rivke remained composed.

"What about your husband?"

"He left Monday night from the plane," she said, as if he had gone of his own accord.

"So you are all alone?"

"Yes." Someone picked up the pacifier the baby had dropped, and Rivke flashed a smile.

"Tell me," the reporter continued, "when were you told that you were going to be freed—"

But Rivke thought better of her previous answer. "We weren't alone," she corrected herself. "We were quite together. All of us."

"And how were you treated aboard by the captors?" the reporter barreled on.

"We were treated very nicely."

What would be her "one prevailing memory"?

"It would be," Rivke said, "wanting to be home again with my family." As to the absent hostages, the commandos "assured us they'd be fine and we believed them, because everything was fine and we feel we can trust their word." Perhaps that seemed the safest story to tell, as long as Jerry was missing.

Elsewhere in the lobby, a couple and their crying daughter gave Douglas Kiker a less sanguine story. "It was rough," the man said. "That's about all I can say. Right now I'm a little too shaky to say anything else."

"Did you see the planes explode?" Kiker liked to go for unsettling questions.

"Yes, we saw them. We were only two hundred yards away from them." The man's voice wavered.

"Were you ever afraid that you wouldn't make it?"

"Yes, all the time I was there," he said. "We saw the men putting charges into the planes four or five days ago. We thought they were going to blow them up with us any day."

A BOAC stewardess spoke plainly of the possibility of destruction too. "We've seen the stuff they've put on the plane," she said, speaking in present tense, even though she was out of the desert and the planes had already blown up. "It's loaded with dynamite. There's dynamite in the cockpit, they've put it in the undercarriage, and everything." She added that the commandos were "really nice to us," then added another thought. "They're desperate men," she said. "They feel they've been done a wrong, and to get their ends, they will do what they say."

Captives and captors mingled in the hotel lobby, both sides answering reporters' questions, and members of the Palestinian resistance had their own stories to tell. Kiker chose a clean-shaven man with short light-brown hair, wearing a long-sleeved black T-shirt. The man was relaxing on a barstool, and Kiker inquired if he was one of the hijackers.

"Not these ones," the man said in accented English. "We took the one off Athens." That was the Olympic Airways flight that Palestinians had threatened to blow up in July, with everyone on board, unless the Greek government freed seven of their prisoners. The man had been imprisoned, then released.

"How do you hijack a plane?" Kiker asked. "How do you *feel* when you're hijacking a plane?"

"What nationality are you?" the man asked Kiker.

"I'm an American," Kiker said.

"You have fought wars before," the man said. "How did you feel when you did something to your country? Or you have believed to a cause, to something you believe in?"

"In other words, it's an act of patriotism for you?"

"Yes."

Kiker pressed. "You weren't a bit frightened when you hijacked your plane?"

"Never," the man said. "Never will be frightened."

"What about the men and women who pulled these four hijackings? You don't think they were afraid?"

"I don't think so," the man said. "Because when you believe in something, you do it without fear."

As another commando would put it to another reporter, "You only worry when American and Jewish women and children are threatened"—*Jewish* standing in for *Israeli*—"never when Palestinians are killed."

Meanwhile, elsewhere in the hotel lobby, a waiter politely asked a group of the just-released, enjoying drinks on the balcony, to move into the dining room. His explanation: "You must eat now because the shooting starts in one hour."

On another tape, I watch Douglas Kiker do three takes facing the camera, each time repeating the same words: "The big question now is what happens to the men. They've been taken off the planes, but they're still being held prisoner somewhere in the desert, and their lives are still in danger, perhaps an even greater danger now that the women and children are all safe." That evening in New York, CBS News would call the missing a "major haunting problem," explaining, "No one knows where they are, whether they are well, how to get them out."

The press hadn't yet figured out that the missing included some of the women and older girls. I didn't record in my diary—and neither did Catherine—that Foozie never arrived at the Intercontinental. It was too awful for either of us to write down.

When the Popular Front announced, finally, that Saturday's released hostages were "free to leave Jordan," the State Department and the Red

Cross wanted all of us to depart right away. A truncated telegram from an official at the Amman embassy relayed that "PFLP hostages—even if all located at hotel—could find selves in danger from civil disturbances and fedayeen terrorism." The prime minister of Jordan added that he couldn't guarantee our security beyond eight o'clock on Sunday morning, but Red Cross officials thought it unsafe to transport everyone to the airport after dark, given the possibility of a showdown (*épreuve de force*) in the vicinity of the hotels. A nighttime convoy, they worried, would present "great danger." We had to stay in Amman until the next day.

Crowded with journalists and hostages, the Intercontinental didn't have enough space for everyone—Catherine had made her way to the front desk, trying to book a room for us. Some went to the Philadelphia Hotel, near the restored Roman amphitheater, a drive that took them through roads packed with soldiers and military vehicles, punctuated by bursts of gunfire. From her van, Sara Raab saw "panic in the streets," the man at the wheel "driving like a maniac" to beat sunset. To her questions, the driver would say only, "Very bad trouble. Terrible trouble." That hotel was crowded too, so Susie Hirsch's two younger brothers—someone had separated them from Susie—had to bed down in an outdoor area where they could hear the war in the distance. Staff members told the boys they had grown up in Palestine and hoped one day to return.

Someone drove Catherine and me to the Shepherd Hotel, on a backstreet a few minutes away. "C. & I & Rina & Sue & another woman Patsy are in a room together," I told my diary. Patsy Ridenhour, twenty-eight, was the woman who kept to herself; the commandos had removed her husband from the plane the night before. Along with Susie, the other girl with whom we sang songs and "conversed about boys and family" was Rina Bedar, the same age as Catherine. Her mother had died less than a year earlier, she told us, which I felt was far worse than my own mother living in a different country. Among the messages that hostages' relatives sent via the Red Cross, I would find one addressed to Rina: "Father requests message. All miss you. We are anxious for your return."

What did Catherine and I tell our roommates when we talked about our families that evening? What did we say about our mother living in Israel while we lived in America with our father? Likely we spoke matter-of-factly, and if Susie or Rina thought that was odd or sad, they didn't say so. ("If you love a flower that lives on a star, it is sweet to look at the sky at night," said the little prince.)

Where my diary entries for Saturday were exuberant, Catherine's were guarded.

I wrote, "We were going to Amman, to a hotel. Then maybe to New York tomorrow! Thank God! Thank God! We all left in groups in little trucks. Our truck was the first to drive up to the hotel!" By contrast Catherine wrote, "We drove to the hotel with a machine gun truck ahead."

Where I wrote, "When we got inside, Catherine & I were interviewed by *Time* magazine & later by the *New York Times*!!!!" Catherine wrote, "We were interviewed and pictured."

At the Shepherd Hotel, where I made no mention of the sounds of gunfire, Catherine wrote, "In the middle of the night shooting was heard." Even she needed to distance us from that frightening experience, writing in the passive voice.

Where I wrote about our "boys and family" conversation, Catherine recorded a more nuanced scene. "It was still tense not knowing where our men were," she wrote, attuned to Susie's worries about her brothers and Patsy's silent anxieties about her husband, identifying with them in her choice of the first-person plural (*our men*). "Many women were without a husband, father or son," she explained to her journal.

That evening I threw away my red-and-gold bell-bottoms. I remember dropping them into a wastebasket, part of my plot to forget.

Only when the telephone call came the next morning, informing us that we would be leaving Amman, did Catherine lower her guard. As she recalled in her diary, "We were all jubilant!" Reading that entry now, I can almost conjure that happiness. Maybe that's because it was a feeling I knew I could relay to my father. We were out of the hands of our captors, and whatever lingering fear suffused our stay in war-torn Amman must have begun to evaporate. The jubilation that Catherine documented was, for me, a powerful current, capable of dissolving every obstacle of memory in its path.

20

On my way home, I would launch a voyage of my own making, into the land of forgetting.

Catherine and I were among some 350 hostages to depart Amman on Sunday, September 13, but not everyone shared our jubilation. For those whose loved ones were unaccounted for, the decision to return home was difficult. State Department officials urged Sara Raab to return to New Jersey, since no one could say when David would be released. Terribly distraught (in "complete hysteria," she later recalled), she swallowed a tranquilizer and yielded to the assistance of other women in an effort to board the airport bus.

"Come on now, smile!" a news photographer called out to Catherine and me, as we hauled our suitcases up the mobile stairway to the plane. "You've just been rescued. You're going home! Look happy!"

"Move apart a little so we can shoot you better!" another shouted, annoyed that the two of us were standing too close together to get a good photo, with no sense of how those directions sounded after a week surrounded by weapons. We laughed at the man's unthinking words, even as we remained unwilling, just yet, to stand even a few inches apart.

We flew on a Swiss plane chartered by TWA and the International Red Cross, flown by a Red Cross pilot. On board, the front page of the September 9 edition of the *International Herald Tribune* caught the attention of the Hirsch children, just reunited after their night apart in Amman. A FAMILY FLIES SEPARATELY—STILL IS HIJACK VICTIM, read a small headline with the dateline New Rochelle, their hometown. "Mr.

and Mrs. Stanley Hirsch were home safe from Israel today," the article began, reporting that while the couple had survived the attempted El Al hijacking, "their three children were hijacked to Jordan." It was the first Susie, Howie, and Rob knew of their parents' ordeal, and everyone was astounded. I felt genuinely sorry for Susie and her brothers, even as their family's plight became another story I could tell my father: an incredible twist of fate with an especially happy ending.

Two hours later we landed at the stylish state-of-the-art terminal at Nicosia International Airport in Cyprus. The US ambassador was there, and the media was there too, flinging their questions as usual. "I am a Jew," Catherine told a reporter. The commandos did "not believe in a one-religion, one-nation state," she explained. "They gave us a lot of things to read. A lot of it sounded like propaganda, but some of it was true." I'm sure that I marveled at my sister's grasp of the politics I found so bewildering. The reporter meanwhile described me as a twelve-year-old "schoolgirl from New York" who "said she was going to write a composition about her experiences in the desert." I'm sure too that I was more interested in portraying myself as a writer than in actually offering any teacher an account of the hijacking. In fact, although just such an opportunity would arise, it is one I would decline.

The bus ride from the airport took us to the Regina Palace Hotel, inside the sixteenth-century Venetian ramparts of Nicosia's old city. Today it's boarded up, but back then the hotel's deluxe classification meant an elevator and air-conditioning. As we ascended the curving staircase a uniformed bellman handed us a carton of cigarettes. "Catherine & Sue & I share a great room," I wrote in my diary. "Wooden floor, soft beds. Neat! The food here is good too!" Upstairs we tried out the cigarettes, the vapors all too familiar from the aircraft interior of the past week.

Cyprus telephone lines linked directly to both Israel and the United States, and from the Regina Palace, in a room filled with switchboards and human operators, Catherine and I spoke to our father and our mother, in a pair of conversations that none of us would remember, except for my mother's recollection that Catherine said she had to go because a reporter wanted to interview her.

How could all of us have forgotten those moments—the feelings, if not the words—children and parents hearing one another's voices for the first time after such an ordeal? With so many people phoning relatives at the hotel, and with overseas calls so rare in those days, I imagine we were allotted little more than a minute or two per conversation, just enough to say "We're fine," and for my father to say "I'll be at the airport." For him, the memory of that brief connection would be overtaken by our real reunion.

If we said "We're fine" to our mother, what did she say to us? That there was no time for her to fly to Cyprus to see us, since we were flying out so soon? Or that she couldn't anyway, because of the new baby? In the rare times we talked about the hijacking in all the years following, she would always, with a smile, tell the story about Catherine hurrying off the phone to be interviewed. Was that to cover over the emptiness of knowing, after everything that had happened, that she wouldn't see her daughters again for months and months? Were I to ask, I knew she would tell me that she didn't remember anything else about that phone call, and I knew she would be telling the truth. As for the two of us, Catherine likely did the talking, making it one more burdensome task in the urgent, if self-imposed, imperative to take care of everything for both of us. Nor did I record these conversations in my diary, unwilling to preserve the onrush of emotion that must have accompanied hearing my parents' voices. After all, we were not yet home.

On the flight to New York, the little kids were everywhere underfoot, and the older kids went a little wild too. Tikva Raab and her brothers—minus David—were so glad not to be confined to their seats that they were "hanging from the rafters," Tikva recalled, their mother likely too preoccupied with her eldest son's absence to keep the others in check. Grown-ups drank and smoked. The stewardesses from TWA 741, at long last not on call, guzzled champagne.

During the Rome stopover, newsmen and their cameras once again streamed toward us.

"My husband is still there," one woman said, "and several of our husbands are being held. And some of the sons."

"There has been one story that the guerrillas have threatened to start shooting the hostages one by one until their demands are met," a reporter said. "Do you think they'd do that?"

The woman paused to give an almost imperceptible shake of her head at the man's utter callousness. All she said was that the commandos had guns, that "they were all around us, day and night. And if one shot were fired, you don't know what might happen."

Vicki McVey, who had applied mascara and a thick stripe of eyeliner that morning, got the same question. "I can't say that they wouldn't do it," she allowed, adding, "They would have to feel pushed extremely far, so I feel they would like to avoid that sort of thing at all costs."

Rivke Berkowitz was determined to inject a note of optimism, either out of caution for the still-missing or for her own peace of mind. "I believe them, and I trust them when they say that they won't be harmed," she told the newsmen.

That evening, NBC News would report, "All said they'd been well-treated by the guerrillas, even the Jewish passengers."

We were up in the air again, for the last stretch of our prolonged journey home.

The TWA Flight Center at Kennedy International Airport was famously futuristic, designed by Finnish-American architect Eero Saarinen, with its glass exterior and swooping staircases intended to summon the marvels of the Space Age and the exhilaration of flying. Inside, everything was planned for optimal efficiency, from the flow of passengers to the retrieval of luggage, even as the rapid introduction of jet aircraft made the whole building obsolete almost as soon as it opened in the early 1960s. With the moon one night away from full on September 14, the white interior seemed to glow in the dark. The airline had called to give my father our arrival time and flight number, and he and my stepmother arrived two hours early, to be directed to a special area. It was a madhouse.

Touchdown was at 8:30 p.m., and decades later I watch a tape of the press conference Catherine and I glimpsed as we disembarked and made our way through the sealed-off passageway.

"Can you tell us what your first experience was with the guerrillas? Did you have an opportunity to talk to them?" a reporter asks a young boy in a red turtleneck, speaking into multiple microphones at the front of the room.

"They were real nice," the boy says.

"Why do you say that?" The reporter sounds doubtful.

"I talked to one of them," the boy explains.

"Did they express an interest in your thoughts about what they were doing?"

"They said that that was their life, what they were doing, fighting—"

Another reporter cuts the boy off. "Did you feel menaced by all the weapons around you, or not?"

"No," the boy says emphatically, and smiles.

"Were you frightened at any time during this experience?"

"No." Again emphatic, again a smile.

"Did you find it exciting?"

"Yeah." Only then does the boy back off a little, adding, "I had a good time, I guess."

"Would you like to do it again?"

"I don't know," he says. "I'll probably miss too much school."

Across the years, I'm unable to find any fellow hostage who can identify the boy, but listening now, the child's impulses feel familiar: assuring the grown-ups that everything was fine, then hedging with an innocent reason for wanting never to repeat the experience.

Inside the terminal building after we disembarked, I saw little Connie with her big stuffed animal. There was Tova Kahn, who had cried at night in the desert, wondering if anyone would be there to greet her if she came home, and now she found an enormous welcoming party from her hometown.

About our landing at Kennedy Airport, I wrote in my diary, "It was so great," finally free to preserve a feeling with complete candor, because it was a truly happy one. The moment my father saw Catherine and me running toward him: from that moment forward he could believe that he never doubted we were coming back. Just the same as my own feeling of inevitability, once I was finally on my way home (*Of course I would see my father again*), he too wanted to forget.

Our first recounting of the hijacking came as we drove through the neighborhoods of Queens, along the Van Wyck Expressway. Catherine and I told our father and stepmother how hot it was in the desert, about the food we ate, how we couldn't wash even our hands and faces, and about the stopped-up toilets. We told them about some of our fellow hostages, and we said it was scary not to know what was going to happen next. Catherine did most of the talking.

The Queens Midtown Tunnel emerged from the East River into Manhattan just blocks from home, my father steering us south on the avenue, past the furniture showrooms to the corner liquor store and the corner bar, then to the telephone booth right in front of our building, standing desolate as always. Crepe-paper streamers and homemade welcome signs brightened the drab lobby, the handiwork of Toni and her two brothers. Upstairs they had decorated the dirty, mustard-colored fifth-floor hallway too. "The whole family was waiting with a huge strawberry cake!" I wrote in my diary. In her diary Toni wrote, "They are free now, but I thought they might get killed and they might have."

The moment Catherine entered her room, she caught sight of her spiderwort plant, its trailing green, purple, and silver vines thriving in the indirect sunlight of her north-facing windowsill. That's when the plant's common name slid into her mind—*Wandering Jew*—and then she thought about wandering Palestinians too.

We needed to call our mother. With no direct-dial to Israel, the task required operator assistance, and three minutes would cost the equivalent of more than $100 in twenty-first-century money. None of us would remember that conversation either. No doubt we told her we were fine. Might I have heard her voice waver? ("Goodbye," the little prince said to the flower. "The flower coughed. But it was not because she had a cold.")

On Catherine's bed, we found a letter from our stepmother. "Dear Catherine & Martha," we read, "Sitting here thousands of miles away from you prompts me to write you a letter. I guess that's an odd thing to do when it would seem ridiculous for you to read it." But now we were reading it, my father right there, unwilling to leave our sides.

"We couldn't really comprehend the news," my stepmother had written. As the "nightmare continued into its 2nd day," she and my father "lived with the hope that you had been taken to the Intercontinental Hotel," as they cleaned the apartment for our return. "Linda called," she recorded, "and felt that things would be handled quickly." When the news came that "Jewish women & children were returned to the plane," she and my father "received many loving phone calls, filled with encouraging prayers." Reading the letter meant that we were home now, which is why I could save it. It meant that everything was over and everything was fine.

Catherine and I must have been utterly exhausted. There I was, in my own sliver of a room, connected to Catherine's equally tiny room by the doorway with no door, and there was my own iron-frame bed, no more than one step away from my beloved wooden secretary. In my diary, ever cheerful, I wrote, "I'm so glad to be home!"

From my bed that week, I wrote a letter to Nurit. "I'm finally home!" I told her. "It's great to be here. How are you? How is Tibi?"—that was her dog. I didn't elaborate on the circumstances of "finally" arriving home, as if our flight had been delayed by severe weather or a mechanical failure. "My school began on September 8th and I still haven't gone, because I was sick," I wrote, as if I had a bad cold. "I put Gerry's picture in a frame on my desk where I can always see it," I continued, omitting the part about its near confiscation by my captors. I closed the aerogram with the promise to "write you a much longer letter next week when more things have happened," as if nothing much had come to pass since we said goodbye in Tel Aviv.

Although Catherine wanted to forge ahead too, she made room for the hijacking in her first letter to Nurit. "All is well now with Martha and me," she wrote. "We were quite sick for awhile after getting home from our ordeal. But all is fine now, and thank God we are safe!" Our friend Toni, she told Nurit, "said she never realized how much we meant to her until she realized she might never see us again!" Catherine stopped there, with the reassuring words, "But it's all over now," even though she was going to be the one who understood, better than anyone else, that everything was neither "fine now" nor "all over."

The first weekend after we got home, we visited my stepmother's family in New Jersey. Out on the patio in Upper Saddle River, Catherine and I ate hamburgers and hot dogs while we answered a stream of questions.

We talked about the friends we made, especially Foozie. We talked about the crew. Jim was so great, Al was so funny, and Linda and Bettie and June and Vicki and Rosemarie were so nice. There were eleven unaccompanied children, we explained, and six-year-old Connie was flying all by herself and got sick. Mothers made diapers out of cloth napkins, a nice commando jumped rope with the kids, and—unbelievably!—Susie and Howie and Rob's parents were on one of the other hijacked planes. It must have felt good to talk about the good parts and to make it into an adventure story. In my diary that day, I wrote nothing about recounting the hijacking, and neither Catherine nor I can recall this conversation.

"These children look like they just came out of a concentration camp!" Dr. Rosemarie Meldola told my father when he took us for a checkup. Dr. Meldola would have known, of course, because of the numbers engraved on her inner arm. With that, we began a regimen of five meals a day, with refreshments in between. My favorite snack that autumn was Ritz crackers with an inch-thick topping of cream cheese. "Good news!" I would write to my mother later that fall. "I have gained 10 pounds!" I double-underlined the number, before admitting, "Actually I don't look it, but the scale says so!" As for Catherine, it took her more than a month to gain back five pounds. "I'm plugging away at gaining more so I'll look half-normal," she told our grandparents in Israel. That's what we all wanted: for the two of us to be—or at least to look—normal. Months later, Catherine would brag about weighing eighty-eight pounds and "pushing for more!" Our talk of weight gain was the single continuing reference we made to the hijacking, without naming it.

In my diary, I stayed the course. When I went with my father to Hunter High School to see my friends and get my class schedule—I was still too weak to start back—I wrote, "It was great. Our homeroom & English teacher is Mr. McNeil. Everyone says that he's great! I'm DYING TO START SCHOOL!" At home I assembled my new loose-leaf notebook, lovingly filling it with fresh lined paper. Back in the classroom two weeks late, I too loved the flamboyant Mr. McNeil. I loved Mr. Moy, the shy math teacher. I loved Miss Finegold, the vivacious music teacher. I loved my earnest science teacher and my peculiar drama teacher.

Since I didn't bring it up myself, the girls who knew me from elementary school tentatively asked about the hijacking, inquiring about the weather and the food. I said it was hot and that we ate a lot of hard-boiled eggs. I said the bathrooms were horrible, the crew and other passengers were nice, and that it was scary when all the men were taken away. All in all, my friends found me completely unchanged: "No harm done, no lasting effect," one would tell me years later. In my diary that first week back, I wrote, "I love school! Everything's great!" exclamation points once again standing guard.

Catherine had been so excited to begin ninth grade at the High School of Performing Arts ("I'll have 3 acting classes a day!!" she'd written to our mother), but now she felt fragile. For her first day back, she wore a blue-and-green-striped jumper, hoping to appear a little less scrawny. Then she too stepped willingly into the whirl, loving her all-morning theater classes. "Martha and I are fine now," she wrote to our grandparents in Israel, repeating the phrase she'd written to Nurit. "We've both been in school for a week and all is well." She felt two ways. It all seemed "like a dream," she reflected—the feeling that would persist for me across a half century—yet at the same time Catherine knew she would "never forget the whole thing." The difference between us was that Catherine understood the impossibility of forgetting.

"Thank God for our safety and return," Catherine wrote in her diary, then added an appeal. "Please let those who are still prisoners be safe and also return soon!" Before long the *New York Times* published a list of those "not known to have been released." I remember worrying too—about Foozie, about Jim and Al, Mark and Mimi, Sarah Malka, Barbara Mensch, and David Raab—even if I didn't record those feelings in my diary. Indeed, the plight of the remaining hostages was the sole intrusion into my zest for pretending that nothing bad, or nothing at all, had happened to me.

Perusing the stack of the *New York Times* that had piled up in the dining room each day that Catherine and I hadn't come home, I was amazed to read that a baby was born on our plane. That single erroneous story provided exactly what I needed to speed along my voyage into forgetting. The *Times* had accurately reported what Popular Front spokesmen told the world about threats to the lives of the hostages, but because I wanted so much to believe that our lives had never been in danger, I seized on the mistaken story of the baby as an efficient means to dismiss the entirety of the *Times* coverage as disgracefully sensationalistic, then extended that dismissal to all news coverage, none of which I wanted to believe.

Life, the popular American magazine known for its top-notch photography, arrived in the mail weekly, and in one issue I recognized some of my fellow hostages sitting on the sand. "The guerrillas threatened to blow up the planes, with the passengers inside," I read. "Palestinian guerillas strike savagely at the big jets and their helpless passengers," one subheadline announced. The article also contained the phrase "lives in jeopardy." Absurd exaggeration, I told myself, calling up the comforting words of Jim Majer as evidence: "no bodily harm." That our captors strategically told one story to their captives and another to the world was something I didn't understand.

On the mid-September day when Jordan installed a military government and declared war on the Palestinian resistance, I wrote in my diary about four stray cats that my stepmother hoped to rescue, recording the names she had given each one: Tai Chi, Nimbus, Gandolph, Limbo. Outside, I'm sure I averted my eyes from the cover of *Time* magazine, prominently displayed on every corner newsstand, with a photograph of our own aircraft on the cover. A ladder reached from the front exit to the back of a truck—the very ladder I'd climbed down, then up, several times—with the words Pirates in the Sky plastered below. Inside, the story I didn't read was headlined Drama on the Desert: The Week of the Hostages. The cover of *Newsweek*, displayed right next to *Time*, blared The Hijack War, an image of the Swissair jet underneath, with the burning planes above. I'm sure I averted my eyes from that too.

Rereading my stepmother's letter nearly fifty years later, my eyes alight on a question near the top of the second page, the one that would go unanswered, for me, for so long: "What are you thinking & feeling?" she had wondered. It was a question that, despite my historian's handiwork in reconstructing the experience of the hijacking, remained unanswered.

21

Catherine and I were home, but our beloved Foozie was still held hostage, which meant that I couldn't yet banish everything from my thoughts.

We had come to love Foozie just as soon as we met her on the plane, but when she didn't show up in Amman, I tried to stop thinking about her, since it felt too scary and too sad. All these years later, I want to know what came to pass for the missing hostages: the six men removed from the plane on Monday night, those taken away on Thursday and Friday, and the others who never showed up at the Intercontinental Hotel on Saturday. That last group included the daughter of Rabbi Isaac Hutner (he too was unaccounted for), along with sixteen-year-old Barbara Mensch and three college students: Sarah Malka, Mimi Beeber, and Fran Chesler—our Foozie. Altogether, from all three planes, fifty-six people were missing, including six Swiss, six Germans, and six Brits.

"How are you doing?" eight-year-old Mike Majer wrote to President Nixon. "My Father, James Majer is being held as a hostage in Jordan. He was the copilot from the hijacked TWA 707. Would you please do something to get him back?"

In Washington, President Nixon consulted with his national security advisor. "Hi, Henry, anything new?" he asked Kissinger by telephone.

When Kissinger informed Nixon of the missing hostages, the president said he wanted the United States "to go in" and "support the king."

"It would strap us militarily," Kissinger countered. "Use all our available military reserve." He was thinking of the Vietnam War.

The Popular Front was proposing by now familiar terms of exchange between Palestinian prisoners and the hostages, but Israel remained adamant, with foreign minister Abba Eban denouncing even the release of the Palestinians in European jails since, he said, "these people have tried and will try to kill Israelis," with Prime Minister Meir once again in agreement. Then the Popular Front rejected all further negotiations, because, a spokesman said, "our stand is simply the release of the fedayeen" in exchange for the remaining hostages.

A lot was going wrong. Negotiations were stalled, and some feared that the European governments would agree to unilateral deals. André Rochat was causing discontent, there was growing ill will between the Red Cross and the Popular Front, and the Red Cross was wavering in its role as intermediary. Even worse, during the weekend of our release Israel had arrested 450 Palestinians, residents of the occupied West Bank and Gaza Strip, including businessmen, lawyers, doctors, and teachers; eighty were women, and the authorities rounded up entire families. All, Israel claimed, were suspected members or sympathizers of the Front. Authorities called the operation a "security check" unrelated to the hijackings—even as an Israeli official told an Arab West Bank mayor, "We're collecting counterhostages." The Israeli government warned the Front that should any harm come to the remaining hostages, their new prisoners would suffer death sentences; moreover, relatives would be arrested, property confiscated, and homes blown up. Now it was the Front's turn to call their enemy "barbaric," to promise "unimaginable" retaliation, "with complete ruthlessness." After interrogation, seventy-five of the Palestinians were released, and within a week, all were free.

Much later, my mother would explain the release of all the hostages, including Catherine and me, this way: "The Popular Front told Israel, 'If you don't release our prisoners, we're going to kill all these hostages,' and Israel said, 'If you touch one of those hostages, we're going to kill all our Palestinian prisoners.'" I see now that in her fog of anguish, in her inability to absorb the news, she compressed everything into one weekend's high-profile spectacle.

Listening to Israelis around her, my mother heard a mix of opinions. Many had long wanted King Hussein to take on the Palestinian resistance, and some saw Israel's hard line as a sign of strength. Others understood that the Palestinian cause was not going away. Israelis knew, wrote a British journalist in Jerusalem, that "the victims have been the same Palestinians who were originally the losers from Israel's own establishment," and "arguments that their plight was of the Arabs' own making" had little effect on feelings of "responsibility, even of guilt." Problem was, the reporter admitted, "peace talks cannot make much progress without the extremists among the Palestinians, and the extremists will not agree to the peace talks."

Views among Arabs varied too. When King Hussein installed a military government in Jordan, then sent in the Jordanian army, some believed that a victory for Hussein—getting the Palestinian resistance out of Jordan—could bring peace with Israel, while others denounced the king and worried about the despotism of a military government. Still others worried that a fedayeen victory would leave no room for peace and security, that the Popular Front was too radical to aid the cause of ending the occupation. Meanwhile, the US ambassador to Jordan called the king's imposition of a military government "a very courageous act" (Henry Kissinger agreed), while Palestinians in Jerusalem and the West Bank called the king's actions a massacre (Leila Khaled agreed).

With war officially declared, the parts of Amman that Catherine and I had traversed grew ever more dangerous. Some of the worst fighting took place around the Intercontinental Hotel—itself a pawn in the battle—where a hundred or so journalists remained (with no water, the hotel had become "dilapidated and dangerous," just like the planes in the desert). Outside, the sounds of warfare mixed with cries of the wounded, while the dead lay "black and bloated in the sun." David Jenevizian, the Palestinian TWA employee, was trapped in his Amman apartment with his wife, bodies piling up outside. "How many dead? In my city? In my home?" he asked. The whole country, reported the *New York Times*, was "running with rivers of blood."

"Where are the hostages?" Nixon asked, once again on the phone with Henry Kissinger.

"We don't know," Kissinger said. "So they are in danger."

The Bern Group worried they might never be found.

Riding out of the desert as part of the Saturday morning convoy, Foozie had noticed that "all the buses went to the right while ours went straight ahead." Others also noticed their vans traveling in a different direction.

Stopping first at the Popular Front headquarters in Amman, the commandos informed the captives that they were now political prisoners, held because their governments had not met the Front's demands. *Oh, my God I'm going to be here forever,* Barbara Mensch thought. *This is never going to end.* At a press conference, Bassam Abu-Sharif repeated the phrase "prisoners of war," and that day the Popular Front announced that they had taken their now-prisoners to a "more cozy place," with conditions superior to those on the planes in the desert, promising to "treat them very kindly." TWA purser Rudi Swinkels would be released after a few days on account of his Dutch citizenship (a Dutch citizen from BOAC was also released early). Gazing out the window on the flight home, he caught sight of the wreckage of the three planes in the desert below.

Over the next two weeks, the Popular Front scattered their prisoners among undisclosed locations to discourage rescue missions, then moved them around: there was a small house in Irbid; two rooms in Zarqa; an apartment in the Ashrafiyeh neighborhood; the Wahdat refugee camp. Conditions varied. On her first night as a prisoner, Barbara Mensch ate the freshest pita and best falafel she'd ever had, while Walter Ridenhour ate canned food from China, Russia, and Bulgaria. Ever handy, Al Kiburis mixed lard with the oil in sardine cans to assemble lamps with burlap wicks. To pass time, the prisoners crafted a chess set from cardboard boxes and a Scrabble board from memory. They sang songs (Foozie sang Frank Sinatra lyrics in an angelic voice that Jim Majer would remember as a soothing tonic) and played cards with their guards, especially poker, assuring their captors that it was "a good Marxist game which redistributes the wealth." Lennett Cain fabricated poker money he called "dings" and "lings," prompting his fellow prisoners to elect him president of the Ding-a-Ling Republic.

Some of the guards brought in books: Nathaniel Hawthorne's *The Scarlet Letter*, Franz Kafka's short stories. If a birthday came around, the hostages celebrated. Captain C. D. Woods turned fifty-two, Sarah Malka turned twenty. With plenty of time for spirited conversation, Al Kiburis defended atheism, while David Raab found comfort in the thought that if the hostages died, they would be sacrificing their lives for Israel. Foozie, the Orthodox Jew from Brooklyn, nurtured an unlikely friendship with an army sergeant from Alabama.

Relations with the guards could be cordial. One man characterized his captors as "very proper gentlemen," and even Rabbi Abraham Harari-Raful observed that "we ate whatever they ate" and "drank whatever they drank." Some of the Jewish hostages were afraid of being singled out, but Mark Shain saw that "we were all treated alike." One of the non-Jews agreed that the commandos "treated us all alike, even the Jews" (he observed his captors accommodating Rabbi Hutner, who was "very demanding of special food and iced Pepsi Colas"). One Jewish college student felt himself becoming "a little more sympathetic toward their cause," and Mimi Beeber's fears were eased by the sense that her captors were "just trying to get us to understand what their life was like." Another hostage came to believe that "the situation in the Middle East is something the whole world must take care of." Later he would tell a reporter, speaking of his captors, "I learned they also are human beings." (The little prince told the fox in the desert that he himself still had "a great many things to understand.")

There was antagonism too. Abu-Fadi, the guard from the Swissair plane, was now in charge of some of the prisoners, and Foozie thought he was a bastard. When the prisoners wrote letters home, he looked over their shoulders with a smirk, censoring their words. "You know that we're related," Foozie told him one day. "Abraham had two sons. We're first cousins. You know that Father Abraham is turning in his grave because of what you did." Abu-Fadi walked away.

If the prisoners kept up their spirits, they also found it hard to dispel fear. Mark was pretty sure his captors understood that "if anything happened to us it would be the end of them as far as world opinion is concerned," but there were also moments when Mark thought he'd never get home. Another man believed that, despite all the camaraderie, if they "had to," the commandos would not hesitate to kill them. For her part,

Sarah Malka served as mediator, "bringing back to us tidbits of information," David Raab recalled. Still under suspicion for her Arabic language skills, Sarah had it the worst, enduring hours-long interrogations.

The remaining hostage-prisoners were also surrounded by warfare. Jim Majer was heartened that their captors went outside "under fire to get water for us," even as three daily meals became two, then one, and distant gunfire gave way to nearby battles: a hundred yards away, then fifty, then twenty, with the smell of dead bodies drifting inside. Someone told Barbara Mensch, "If you don't hear the shell land, it's because you're dead."

I always remembered that Barbara was among those who didn't show up at the Intercontinental Hotel. I hoped to find her, and our reunion was hastened by a coincidence: when my sister Tal mentioned the 1970 hijacking at a gathering of friends, it turned out that someone knew Barbara, and knew that she had been on the same plane.

When Barbara and I meet, she looks entirely familiar, but when I show her a photograph of Catherine and me right after we came home, she still can't remember us. So far, no one has, which kindles that feeling: *Were we really there?*

In the quiet of my office at the Cullman Center for Scholars and Writers at the New York Public Library, Barbara and I spill out our respective stories, marveling over how little we each remember ("I don't remember what went on that week," she says. "I don't remember what we did"). One of her distinct recollections, though, concerns the shelling, after she left the desert. Each time it began, she would dive into a corner, the others piling on top of her, even as she told herself, "I'm sixteen years old, I'm not going to die."

Others weren't so sure. One night, as the pounding came close, some thirty hostage-prisoners lay on the floor of a twelve-by-sixteen-foot room, *waiting for the shell that will kill us,* Foozie thought. Mimi Beeber felt "so close to dying so many times."

Despite early successes, the Palestinian fighters were ultimately ill-prepared to face the Jordanian army, and soon King Hussein ordered his forces to search for the hostages. On September 25, Jordanian soldiers found sixteen Brits, Swiss, and West Germans locked inside a house inside a refugee camp, their captors having deserted. That was a Friday; at home Jody had invited seven girls from our class to her family's house in Amagansett for the weekend, where her mother, thrillingly, took us to the beach after dark, in our pajamas. The next day the Popular Front announced the release of the remaining hostages, acting in concert with the PLO, claiming food and water shortages. In fact, the resistance was losing the war. If Jody's mother read the news that weekend, she kept it from me.

"All well," read the telegram Foozie transmitted to her parents in Brooklyn, two weeks after Catherine and I had arrived in New York. "We're with Red Cross. I am coming home."

"Oh God, I am fine and in a Red Cross hospital," Mark Shain wrote to his family in Milwaukee. "See you tomorrow. I love you."

"Dearest Roz," Jim Majer wrote to his beloved wife, "The Jordanian holiday is rapidly coming to a close." Speaking in their own code, he added, "Don't half love you."

"Honey, safe and OK," Frank Allen wrote to his fiancée in California. He had missed their September 12 wedding, and on the flight home everyone would sing him a chorus of "Get Me to the Church on Time."

Met by reporters in Cyprus, Lennett Cain praised the commandos for taking "the best possible care for us under the circumstances."

"You weren't singled out for, uh"—the white reporter stumbled, starting to ask Cain about being Black, then changed his mind—"any special treatment because you're an American? They didn't separate the nationalities?"

Cain picked up the reporter's drift. "No, I was not singled out," he said, "in the sense that I stayed with the group at all times. But some of the commandos did individually express sympathy for me and expressed their support for the cause of Black men in America."

At least one of the hostages, who declined to give his name, told a different story. "I suppose we're saying just what they wanted us to say—what great guys they are and how they've got a real point," when the fact was, he surmised, the hostages were "worth more alive to them than dead."

"It was exciting to be part of this whole, fantastic thing," David Raab told a reporter. "We had a great time." Momentarily he reconsidered. "Well, not really a great time, but under the circumstances we did all right."

Half a century later, in his late sixties and living in Israel, David would allow that "the hijacking affected me tremendously." He would recall three weeks of "constant fear of imminent death," including watching commandos wire the plane with dynamite, being surrounded by guns on Monday night, being separated from his family on Thursday night, and worrying through the war in Jordan. David's conflicting assessments across time feel familiar to me. As a seventeen-year-old boy, his sense of adventure paralleled my own studied cheeriness in the pages of my diary. In our own ways, it would take each of us decades to reckon with the hijacking.

Before he flew home to Paris, Al Kiburis left a note for Jim Majer in the room they shared at the Cyprus Hilton, signing it "F.A.I.T.H.," their invented acronym for Forsaken Americans in the Holy Land. His message: "Lots of luck Jim baby—couldn't have done it without you."

Those continuing on to New York had a stopover in Rome, where they were greeted at the airport by Nixon, on his long-planned European tour.

"Nice to see you," Foozie called out. "We were missing you for three weeks." (When she relayed her hometown, Nixon replied, "Oh yes, we've always got one from Brooklyn," a possible slip of his well-documented anti-Semitism.)

"Have you all signed up for speaking tours?" the president joked.

"No comment," someone answered.

Later Nixon described the meeting as "very moving," while White House chief of staff Bob Haldeman wrote in his diary, "Gave us a big news story."

Landing at Kennedy Airport, Foozie found herself greeted by the Foozie Fan Club from Stern College, along with the press, once more warming their targets with television lights. As to the whole experience, Captain C. D. Woods put it diplomatically: "I wouldn't recommend it more than once in a lifetime."

On the day Foozie came home, I filled my diary with details of math-class antics. Mr. Moy had arrived late, after the second bell. Since he was so young, he felt like a big brother to us twelve-year-olds, so we told him he had to go to the principal's office to get a late pass, and then some of us put on a skit for him. It was called "Kill a Chicken"—some of the girls had learned it at summer camp—and when Mr. Moy said, "I better see a dead chicken after this," we thought it was hilarious. I must have been relieved that all of this filled twenty of the twenty-six lines of my diary's page for September 28. That meant that if I wanted to note Foozie's return, I'd need to go to the trouble of continuing my entry on a separate sheet of paper. I still began every entry with "Dear Claire," and I wanted Claire to forget all about the hijacking too.

22

J ust as I didn't know why the commandos let us leave the desert, I had no idea, at the time, of the ultimate resolution of the September 1970 hijackings. My refusal to read or watch the news after I got home satisfied my unwillingness to think about everything, and so I maintained my lack of awareness for many years.

The last six hostages came home at the end of September. They were the first six men the commandos had taken off our plane three weeks earlier, on that frightening Monday night, when Catherine recorded in her diary that they'd been taken to "God-knows-where." Now, in late September, I didn't write about their return, at least not directly.

"I didn't feel so good today so I decided to stay home," I told my diary. That afternoon I suffered such an acute asthma attack that I had to go to the emergency room for an adrenaline shot. That evening another attack came on, this time so bad that a doctor made a house call to administer another shot. I remained sick for days afterward. ("I have come on a long journey, and I have had no sleep," the little prince said to a king on another planet.)

The Western governments kept their promise to release the seven Palestinian prisoners, in an effort to prevent another incident, in which hostages might really die. Soon Leila Khaled boarded a Royal Air Force plane from London, stopping to pick up the six Palestinians released from Swiss and German jails. The heart attack and death of President Nasser of Egypt had just stunned the world, and the seven former prisoners arrived in Cairo in time to place a wreath on his grave (Nasser was a controversial figure for Palestinian insurgents; as Khaled put it, she was "distressed over the death of someone I had denounced the day before"). Israel's grudging contribution amounted to the release of two detained Algerians and ten Lebanese prisoners. The now-defunct Bern Group spoke of the "rule of law" yielding to the "imperative necessity of saving lives," but the United States had achieved its goals. All the hostages were home, King Hussein remained in power, the Palestinian resistance was losing ground, and there had been no Israeli, Soviet, or American intervention.

As for the hijackers, they would never be prosecuted. In a Federal Aviation Administration report issued more than a decade later, I find the man and woman from our flight listed by the assumed Honduran names in their counterfeit passports, marked as "aliases," with the notation: "Fugitives. No positive identification." No other documents shed any light on the well-dressed couple who disrupted TWA 741 on September 6, 1970. They had disappeared into the waiting crowd of commandos that Sunday evening in the Jordan desert, and no one knew what had become of them after that.

The question arose again: Had the Popular Front singled out Jews when they detained the last fifty-plus hostages? Many of the detained were indeed Jews, among them Foozie Chesler, Mark Shain, Mimi Beeber, David Raab, Sarah Malka, Rabbi Hutner, Rivke Berkowitz's husband, Jerry, and Barbara Mensch, whose non-Jewish friend Nancy Porter had been released that first Monday night. ("I know them all," Catherine said when we got home.)

Of the fifty-four hostages held longer, nearly two-thirds were not Jewish. The crew members were not Jewish. Neither was Russell Morris, the TWA pilot flying as a passenger, nor Walter Ridenhour, husband of Patsy, the quiet woman who shared our room at the Shepherd Hotel in Amman. Neither was Bob Palagonia, a spice importer returning from Bombay (true, as a collector of passport stamps, he had acquired an Israeli stamp during the flight's Tel Aviv stopover), nor Lennett Cain, the African American army sergeant from Georgia, nor Derrell Suttles, a white army man from Alabama. Prasad Kadaba, the Kentucky engineering professor, was Hindu. Most, perhaps all, of the detained crew and passengers from Swissair and BOAC were not Jewish.

Reports at the time were mixed, some speculating, others definitively declaring the separation of Jews from non-Jews. Soon Walter Cronkite of CBS News correctly reported on the remaining American hostages, "not all of whom are Jewish."

Yet the idea of the Popular Front detaining only Jews would persist across decades. A documentary produced more than thirty years later asserted that "Barbara Mensch and 54 other Jewish passengers and all the male crew members were separated from the rest," and a Wikipedia article on the "Dawson's Field Hijackings" asserted that "the PFLP segregated the flight crews and Jewish passengers, keeping the 56 Jewish hostages in custody, while releasing the non-Jews." In 2020, on the fiftieth anniversary of the hijackings, the *Jerusalem Post* wrote that "the 56 passengers thought to be Jewish were segregated and held hostage." None of that was correct.

By some measures, the Popular Front gained support after September 1970. "No longer can the plight of the Palestine refugees be swept under the rug," said the Reverend Theodore Hesburgh, president of the University of Notre Dame. "The State of Israel was created in large measure to respond to the anguish and the hopes of Jewish refugees. Need we be less imaginative and compassionate now in responding to the anguish and the hopes of Palestinian refugees?" The *London Times* wrote about "a gain in public awareness of the Palestinian case," pointing out that "even Israeli organizations, both Zionist and anti-Zionist, while condemning the hijack technique, cautiously acknowledge that the Arabs may have scored some propaganda points." Opinion was far from entirely favorable, though, especially in the United States. Politicians and journalists continued to call the hijackers and their comrades fanatics, barbarians, and animals.

Many believed that the Popular Front's extremism harmed the Palestinian cause. After September 1970, members of the Front disagreed about the roots of their failures. Some blamed the too-moderate PLO, while Arafat continued to consider hijacking and hostage-taking a strategic error. Some pointed to Jordan as the wrong home base; others lamented an inability to convince the masses, both Jordanian and Palestinian, that the cause belonged to them too. George Habash remained militant, telling a newspaper that autumn that "killing one Jew off the battlefield is more effective than killing 100 Jews on the battlefield," since it would gain "more attention" (if Habash invoked *Jews* to mean *Israelis*, that nuance would be lost on most of his listeners), and the Popular Front continued to defend airline hijacking, pointing out that the lives of their own imprisoned people were "not one particle less valuable than the safety or life of any Westerner."

Then, less than two years after the spectacular show of air piracy, Habash explained the Popular Front's decision to stop hijackings in deference to their many allies who did not endorse the strategy. Leila Khaled would later renounce the strategy too, though without regret for September 1970, adding, "I can apologize for making the people traumatized." That same year, Bassam Abu-Sharif opened a package that turned out to be a bomb from Israel's secret service, intended to kill him. Badly maimed instead, Abu-Sharif went farther, renouncing violence (when he went public some years later, the Popular Front expelled him). Nearly twenty years after the 1970 hijackings, Abu-Sharif endorsed peace talks for a two-state solution, an idea anathema to the Popular Front's original aims. As the decades passed, the Front fragmented, marginalized revolutionaries eventually burdened by poor leadership and corruption. A half century after all the hostages came home, a noted scholar and activist of Palestinian descent would condemn the 1970 hijackings as part of the resistance's "pattern of recklessly provoking its enemies."

The old irreconcilable narratives held firm over the years too. Where Israel's supporters saw generosity rejected in negotiations, supporters of Palestinian rights saw the most meager of unjust compromises.

After all the hostages came home, politicians and journalists debated, in retrospect, whether our lives had been in danger. Commandos told a British reporter that they "never had any intention of killing or illtreating any of the passengers." The *Washington Post* found that observers in Amman, asked about the possibility that the commandos would have blown up the planes with hostages aboard, believed it "unlikely that they would carry out such a threat." Looking back, journalist Gerald Seymour thought the commandos were not about to "press home the initial attacks on the airplanes by killing people," since they simply "did not have that ruthlessness." A few had worried less about deliberate murder and more that a commando, or even a hostage, would, as a British diplomat said, "break down under the strain," causing an "unpremeditated shot" to be fired, or that the hostages would be "caught in the crossfire between the fedayeen and the army" (exactly what almost happened to the last two vans out of the desert). All in all, the diplomat thought it very lucky that "no hostages lost their lives."

But it was also possible to look back with a greater sense of doom. David Jenevizian, the Palestinian who worked for TWA in the Middle East, had occasion in 1970 to listen to a phone call between a Popular Front commando and the Front's Beirut headquarters. When Jenevizian asked the commando point-blank if the Front was serious about blowing up the planes with the passengers on board, the man said—in light of the murder of Palestinians, with no sympathy from anyone—"Why not?" Thinking back years later, Jenevizian said, "Yes, they were serious." That was the sense of some of the hostages too. When a reporter asked Al Kiburis if he'd ever felt the lives of the hostages out in the desert endangered, he gave a sober, "Oh, many times. Many times."

Afterward, it was impossible to know what alternative scenarios might have come to pass. Years later, Bassam Abu-Sharif claimed that one of the Popular Front's conditions, at least internally, was "not to hurt any civilian hostages, but to keep them only for exchange," exactly what copilot Jim Majer had conveyed to his passengers in the assurance I remembered as "no bodily harm." George Habash concurred, also many years later, recalling that his comrade Wadi Haddad, the mastermind of the 1970 operations, always told his hijackers "not to hurt anyone in any way."

Speaking fifty years on, a student activist made an eloquent case for Palestinian rights, punctuated with a troublesome point about the 1970 hijackings: "Many of the people who were on the planes that day were interviewed later on, and they said that they didn't feel fear. I even watched an interview of a little boy where he said it was cool and he had fun." That was likely the boy in the red turtleneck speaking at the press conference that Catherine and I bypassed at Kennedy Airport. The speaker was correct that the smiling boy had said he wasn't afraid and that he had fun.

But young children, especially young boys in 1970, were the ones least likely to perceive danger. As Tova Kahn's son, Daniel, eight years old at the time, explained to me, he'd focused on the life rafts and the orange soda, and he thought the guns were "kind of cool." As another hostage, a twelve-year-old boy, recalled decades later, "I wasn't afraid. I was a kid."

All of those children had been traveling with a parent, and like them I had someone to shield and protect me: Catherine. That allowed me to focus on the fun parts too, like singing "Leaving on a Jet Plane" and watching the commandos jump rope. Catherine, though, like the grown-ups traveling with children, had no one, and so she was left with a responsibility that made fear impossible to dismiss. Indeed, Catherine's feelings matched those of most of the adults on the hijacked planes. Recall the assessment of the Red Cross doctor: the hostages were "collectively terrorized"; or the remark of the US Army colonel: those who weren't afraid "didn't understand these fellows, the guerrillas"; or the psychiatrist hostage: people were in "a state of controlled fear and uncontrolled anxiety."

Threats of violence and death are necessary to attempt a hijacking—hence Leila Khaled's threat to "explode the plane." In September 1970 the strategy of the Popular Front included two contradictory strands: assuring us, the hostages, that we would not be harmed, and at the same time threatening death. That's why the hijackers announced that we would be landing in a friendly country with friendly people, then wired the planes with dynamite before our eyes. That's why the commandos in the desert instructed copilot Jim Majer to assure us that we would suffer no bodily harm, then threatened death to those they interrogated ("We are going to kill you unless you tell us more information") and sometimes to everyone ("You will all go to a fiery death if this thing isn't settled soon").

One journalist put it this way, decades later: "None of the hostages on flights seized by Palestinian guerrillas in September 1970 died, and some would later report that under the circumstances, they had been treated reasonably well. But fear and violence are integral parts of any hijacking, and at times in their ordeal, many of the hostages must have wondered if they would ever see their homes or families again."

After unearthing and studying so many experiences from so many different points of view, I find it fully plausible that the commandos never intended to make good on their threats to blow up the planes with the hostages inside. Yet that logical conclusion sits uncomfortably next to so much of what I learned in the course of reconstructing the experience: the early decree by Bassam Abu-Sharif that the Popular Front was ready to "destroy the planes along with their prisoners," the apprehension emanating from diplomatic correspondence, the mentions of murdered hostages by Nixon and Kissinger, the pronouncements about deadlines and dynamite on the evening television news. Even fully understanding the strategic nature of such assertions, I learned of other ways we might have been harmed or lost our lives: there was Leila Khaled's point that "frightened people can do foolish things"; there was the British diplomat's worry that someone—anyone—might grab a weapon and fire a shot inside the aircraft; there was the averted shoot-out between our captors and Jordanian soldiers on our way out of the desert.

As a historian, I teach my students about contingency, and especially, as a historian of the American Civil War, about contingency on the battlefield. Perhaps our fates in the desert were, above all, contingent and unpredictable. Thinking back on the whole ordeal fifty years later, a fellow hostage put it this way: "It could have gone a thousand ways."

Part Five

A MATTER OF SO MUCH IMPORTANCE

23

"None of us will soon forget those incredible days of anxiety," wrote the president of TWA in a letter sent to each of the hostages, expressing "personal sorrow for the emotional suffering you experienced." September 6, 1970, had been an awakening, Forwood C. Wiser reflected, and "indeed, we should not be permitted to forget." His ultimate point: "We must remember, to ensure that it will never again happen."

Of course the airline president was thinking about lapses of security, but the media coverage offered a different message. "They had spent six days and nights crowded inside three hijacked jets, held as hostages by fanatical terrorists who threatened to kill them," NBC News reported the day Catherine and I flew from Amman to Nicosia. "And now their nightmare was over." Even for those held two more weeks, amid a war, reporters spoke of their homecoming as the finish line. "Just this minute, thirty-three Americans released by the Palestinian guerrillas are completing a homeward journey that began three weeks ago," *ABC Evening News* told the nation at the end of September. "Now it's all over: the fear, the anxiety, the hardship." One of the teenagers, ABC News reported, could return to high school with "nothing to worry about but his course of studies."

Was the airline president correct that "we should not be permitted to forget"? Or was everything "all over" with "nothing to worry about"? My father and I chose the second path. In opposition to both of us, Catherine tried the first. It was a battle I wish she had won but that she did not.

Writing in my diary in the desert, I didn't entirely exclude what distressed me. I noted when food became scarce and the pita bread grew stale, and when I wrote that we were subsisting on bread and water, I added a heartfelt "Oh dear!" When I wrote that the hostages had to make lists of all Israeli items in our possession, I ended the sentence with "ANYTHING!"—appointing capital letters and punctuation to convey feelings I couldn't articulate. I recorded that our captors took certain hostages off the plane, to unknown destinations, and I wrote that Tikva Raab cried hard when she awoke one morning to find her brother David gone. When the commandos removed all remaining men from the plane on Friday night, capital letters and underlining became my deputies of dismay ("*all* the men PLUS the crew members that were men were to be OFF the plane"). That same night, I recorded my feelings for the old rabbi seated in the row ahead of us ("Poor man!"). My final acknowledgment of a troubled emotion came with the information that the commandos had blown up the three planes: "Gosh!"

For the most part, though, I saved the reporting of emotions for the happy ending: talking and singing at the Shepherd Hotel ("It was really nice"), our room at the Regina Palace in Cyprus ("Neat!"), touchdown at Kennedy Airport ("It was so great"), seeing my father ("Oh Glory!"), and being home ("I love school!").

Excluding fear from the pages of my diary followed logically from omitting so much of what had come to pass before my eyes. I never wrote about the gun I saw at Jim Majer's neck, or the commandos I saw wiring our plane with dynamite. As for Monday night, when it felt as if we hostages might be shot to death, I conveniently misplaced the piece of paper on which I'd recorded some version of that experience. I never wrote about the frightening conversations I heard between Sarah Malka and the commandos, or about Mark Shain's brooding face when he feared the results of his luggage being searched. I never wrote about the commando who pointed her gun at me, or the women around me whispering about rape on Friday night. I never wrote that we saw and heard the war from our room in the Shepherd Hotel. I never wrote about those things because I didn't want them to have to be part of the story I'd tell when I got home. It was all too much, and besides, I had Catherine right next to me the whole time, to figure everything out. To make sure we'd never be separated. To make sure we'd survive. To make sure we'd get home.

Soon after her return from Jordan, Foozie came to visit us. We were so happy to introduce her, sweet and ebullient as ever, to my father and stepmother. We talked about her extra two weeks of captivity and, continuing the conversation we'd begun that long-ago Friday evening in the desert, we talked about God. Catherine asked Foozie if she really believed that God had written the Bible, and Foozie said she did.

"Literally?" Catherine pressed.

"Yes," Foozie said. "He took a Bic pen and he wrote the Bible."

We were happy to imbibe her humor again, happy to laugh again with our Foozie.

Still, in keeping with my studied erasure, I didn't record our reunion in my diary, and I didn't write anything when Foozie sent Catherine a present for her birthday that winter. The last time I named Foozie in my diary had been in Cyprus, when I wrote, "the only thing I want is that the men return & Foozie & the 4 other girls." I didn't write about her release or her visit or the present because I didn't want to stir up memories of the hijacking.

The only other fellow hostage we saw after we got home was Sylvia Jacobson. Later that fall she came to our apartment to interview us for an article she was writing for a professional sociology journal, and that would be the last time we told the story of the hijacking with any proximity to the event. "Curiously," Sylvia wrote in her notes, "in talking with the Hodes children a number of facts came to light which are less optimistic than the diaries." But it was Catherine, not I, who waded into that "less optimistic" territory. When Sylvia asked what we considered to be the most difficult part of the whole experience, Catherine named the night we stood outside the planes, surrounded by armed commandos. Calling up that terrible fear, she told Sylvia that she had "expected the ring of women and children to be shot," that she had "waited to die." Yet according to Sylvia's notes from follow-up telephone interviews with Catherine and me, after a while we "no longer thought too much about what had happened," unless someone asked, or another hijacking appeared in the news; occasionally the "sound of a low-flying plane" would provoke a memory.

Sometime during the fall of our return too, the mail brought the post-card that Catherine and I had written to our father and stepmother from the desert. "Due to the turbulent conditions in the Middle East, attendant to the recent hijackings," wrote a TWA customer relations rep, "the attached note has just arrived at our Corporate Headquarters in New York City. We thought you would like to have it, notwithstanding the unavoidable delay." Had it arrived before we came home—or if we had never come home—my father would have seen unfamiliar handwriting. Now we explained that Foozie had written out the message for us ("We are both okay and looking forward to being home. Many people are watching out for us so please don't worry"). My father slipped the square of paper into the manila file folder he'd labeled "Hijack," which already held multiple copies of Catherine's *New York Times* Quotation of the Day, newspaper articles from the day of our release (none from before that), and the Popular Front slogan cards we'd brought home.

Other released hostages and their families saved memorabilia too: collections of newspaper clippings, tickets, boarding passes, the issue of *Ambassador* magazine from the seat-back pocket, the pages of the speech by George Habash, the slogan cards. I threw away my red-and-gold bell-bottoms, but Tova Kahn kept the pink dress that her ten-year-old daughter had worn all week on the plane. Now and again my father would add an item to his folder: a request to participate in a lawsuit against the airlines, along with a copy of his refusal; a plea from someone writing a dissertation who hoped Catherine and I would fill out a ques-tionnaire, which he never showed us; Sylvia Jacobson's published article, mailed to us with a note of gratitude. Collecting mementos was a way to impound the experience, to tame the memories. As for me, I had no desire to preserve my brush with history, no desire to create a record after the fact. The fewer memories I had to organize, the easier to move on.

Some of the hostages looked back on a meaningful experience, consid-ering themselves witnesses to history. Some felt invigorated, telling and retelling the story. Within days of her return, Sylvia Jacobson spoke at her synagogue about the hijacking, and all that fall she spoke at temples and churches, to college students and school guidance counselors, and eventually at scholarly conferences, as both sociologist and participant-observer. Another hostage found an "emotional high" speaking to community groups from memories so vivid that he never prepared notes. That fall one of the Swissair hostages delivered a speech to his alumni association, opening with humor ("a sunny vacation" where "everything is free—except yourself"), recalling his fellow hostages with warmth, and offering his audience an uplifting takeaway. "It was a great human experience" that gave him "new faith in life and in human beings."

Some families refused to forget. "Inside our house, we were always encouraged to talk about it," one of the Raab children recalled, "and that was our therapy." But other families, like mine, aimed to move on swiftly, and my father was hardly the only parent who wished to evade talk of the hijacking. Indeed, Sylvia Jacobson found that often it was the parents who tried hardest to maintain silence. Some asked principals and teachers not to draw attention to a returning child; one banned all print and broadcast news about the missing hostages.

Susie Hirsch took it upon herself to face her feelings just as soon as she returned, in a short story called "Hijacked!" that she wrote for one of her tenth-grade classes—the protagonist wasn't exactly herself, but the character reflected her "state of mind at the time." Where I could have done the same, I declined. When I was still too sick to return to school, Jody relayed our first English assignment to me: to write an essay about an important experience or, alternatively, to review a book or a movie. I'd told the reporter in Cyprus that I was going to write a school composition about my experiences in the desert, but I changed my mind. Instead, I wrote a review of the Beatles documentary *Let It Be*, the title a perfect reflection of my determination. "I'm very pleased with it," I told my diary. I didn't discuss my school assignments with my father, but I knew he would have been pleased too.

Repercussions kept their own timetable, and some of the hostages faced mean demons: apathy, dread, anxiety, depression, rage. Parents lived in fear for their children, and children felt afraid to be alone. Extroverts became introverts, and some just felt numb for a long time. Some who at first felt emotionally stable later developed serious symptoms, sometimes years later. In my multilayered telephone conversation with Sarah Malka, she reflected that all of us "came home to an environment and time when very few understood post-traumatic stress." Or as Mimi Beeber put it, "We didn't have words for trauma then." As for Susie, she would later write a paper for her master's degree in social work, called "Resilience and Coping in the Face of Trauma: A Retrospective Account Thirty Years after a Skyjacking." Susie wrote that paper so long afterward because her family had been "very into the denial of just how traumatic the experience was." As she wrote in the paper, "We went back to our lives as usual," she and her two brothers returning to the "routine of school, homework and social activities." As her brother Howie put it later, "We didn't really have any deep discussions about our experience."

Erasing and forgetting remained my best defense, and my father's. Hoping to prevent us from suffering more than we already had, my father quelled conversations about the hijacking, and I stayed silent, following a pattern of traumatized children who do not wish to upset their parents. Post-traumatic stress disorder, or PTSD, would not be named until ten years after our return, but when it was, "being taken hostage" counted as a possible cause. Like the majority of children who experience a traumatic event, Catherine and I did not suffer from PTSD, whose symptoms include months or years of insomnia, nightmares, flashbacks, fear, anger, disinterest, and self-destructiveness. Our autumn nightmares were short-term symptoms ("acute stress disorder," which could be a reaction to "threatened death"), as was lying in bed feeling like I was in an airplane (an "altered sense of the reality of one's surroundings").

One of my few long-term symptoms harkened back to our arrival at Kennedy Airport. I'd loved that moment, when the wheels touched the ground in New York and all the passengers broke into applause, but that was the last time such a scene brought me comfort. Forever after, if passengers clapped upon landing—if there had been a delay, say, or turbulent weather—the sound would agitate me, tears springing to my eyes as I hunched in my seat amid happy travelers. If I was flying with my husband, Bruce, he would warn me, taking my hand and saying gently, "People might applaud at touchdown." Taxiing to the terminal at Kennedy Airport on September 14, 1970, passengers must have shed tears of joy and relief. As for me, I held back, the same as I'd done all week. I was going to see my father, and I didn't want him to think that anything bad had happened to us. ("The companions who met me on my return were well content to see me alive," said the aviator in *The Little Prince*. "I was sad, but I told them: 'I am tired.'")

I can't ask Sylvia Jacobson what she recalls about the two girls she interviewed in the autumn of 1970, because she died some twenty years before I began to think about the hijacking again. I very much hoped to find Mark Shain, thinking he might remember the two sisters sitting in the row in front of him, and a promising lead has me writing to a school board member in a Wisconsin town. But this Mark Shain writes back, "No, that was not me on that TWA flight. At that time, I was taking care of a herd of Angus cattle on a farm in southwest Ohio." Soon after that, I unearth a 2008 obituary, where everything matches up.

I'm unable to talk to others whose memories might also prove valuable. I can find no trace of Rina, the girl who shared our room at the Shepherd Hotel in Amman, and Patsy Ridenhour, our other roommate that night, is no longer alive. Others among the hostages have died too: Captain C. D. Woods and flight engineer Al Kiburis (Al died in a swimming accident twenty-five years after the hijacking); and Rivke Berkowitz, whose husband the commandos removed from the plane early in the week. Sylvia would have remembered Catherine and me, of course, but there was no guarantee that any of the others would—not even Mark or Rina or Patsy. What memories might Connie Pittaro, the six-year-old flying all by herself, have? Although everyone remembers her, I can find no trace of her either.

In April we saw my mother for the first time since the hijacking, when she came to New York to work with the Martha Graham Dance Company. It had been seven months since our release, and she was in town for five days. In my diary, I wrote that she bought us maxiskirts at Alexander's Department Store, I wrote out the plot of the movie we saw (*Love Story*), and I enumerated the dishes we ordered in Chinatown. When my mother wrote a letter to her parents back in Israel, she offered the standard proxy reference to the hijacking: the girls "look well and have both gained weight." Now imagining myself as too grown-up to feel sad when we said goodbye, I didn't even record her departure in my diary.

In seventh grade, seated at the tiny wooden secretary in my room—the desk that had belonged to my mother when she was a neglected child—I began to write what I called an autobiography, though it was more a glorified daily log. On my manual typewriter I filled the blank backs of the pages of my father's Ballet Team stationery with single-spaced prose. "Occasionally giving the ball a bounce, I made my way up the avenue," I began, describing a recent turn through our Murray Hill neighborhood. "It was a nice walk to take if one wanted to think awhile." At the end of that Saturday-morning stroll, I turned into our run-down lobby, its dull gray paint slapped over cracked plaster, gateway to the upstairs hallways filled with paper bags swollen with tenants' garbage that attracted the vermin I never got used to.

"The lobby was beautiful," I wrote, "if one cared to look hard enough." I recorded the delight of playing handball as spring approached, pounding the pink Spalding against the cement wall down the street. I wrote about leaning against the sunny slope of our roof, Catherine reading *Anne of Green Gables* aloud while we ate chocolate-covered marshmallow cookies, about riding the carousel in Central Park followed by lunch at the decrepit snack bar bordering the grimy lake.

I wanted to explain to my imagined reader about my family configuration of parents and stepparents, but whatever I attempted, I soon crossed out, first in a coiled spring of black ink, then with a slathering of black crayon. Much later, a friend from seventh grade reveals to me her impression of those circumstances: "Everything was fine. It was great that your mother lived in Israel. Your stepfather was great. Your baby sister was great. Everything was great." Later too, another seventh-grade friend admits to me that as our high school years progressed—we were classmates all the way through twelfth grade—she would wonder sometimes if she'd imagined the whole hijacking thing.

24

———

atherine and I flew to Israel the next summer, our first flight since the hijacking. I have no memory of any conversation with my father about getting on a plane again, and if my sister felt any trepidation, the two of us didn't discuss it. By that time I'd successfully made the passage from earnest twelve-year-old to blasé thirteen-year-old, exchanging the model of Anne Frank's literary sensibility—albeit minus her forthrightness—for the scoffing voice of Holden Caulfield in J. D. Salinger's *Catcher in the Rye*. In place of exclamation points, Holden-style deprecation would serve as my newfound shield.

"Boarded 747 6:30pm," I wrote in my diary. "Shit ride. Change TWA at Rome, stop in Greece, on to Tel Aviv." If the Eero Saarinen terminal at Kennedy Airport, or flying on a TWA aircraft, or listening to the captain's announcements precipitated any sort of flashbacks, I kept no record of those feelings. If Nurit or the other kids in the neighborhood, or their parents, or the Little Man or the Little Lady, or the Batsheva dancers mentioned the hijacking, I left that unrecorded too. Moodier that summer, I was also lonely. Catherine hung out with Nurit's friends, but Sonia had moved away, and so had Gerry. I'd moved on from that twelve-year-old's crush. Anyway, feeling lonely made me feel older, more mature.

The night before our return flight, my stepfather took us to the ice cream place "where we had gone the year before on our last night," I typed on my typewriter when I got home, describing the chocolate and vanilla sundaes topped with nuts, cherries, chocolate sauce, and whipped cream, omitting what had come to pass "the year before," right after "our last night" in Tel Aviv. In my best Holden Caulfield imitation, I wrote that everything fit into my suitcase "except for this one goddamn shoe." Only when I wrote about Lod Airport did an unfiltered scrap intrude. "There were these steps with a big 'Bon Voyage' sign hanging over them," I wrote, admitting, "How I hated those steps!" while neglecting to explain that this was the place where my mother always put on her sunglasses when she had to say goodbye to us. ("Flowers are so inconsistent!" said the little prince. "But I was too young to know how to love her.") My next sentence mixed honesty with distance: "There were tears and hugs and kisses, while the stewardess who was taking charge of us just stood there patiently waiting." The description is elusive, and rereading it so many years later, I have no memory of Catherine or me ever crying when we said goodbye to our mother. I ended my entry this way: "And finally we went up those fucking stairs."

Our first flight, this time on British European Airways, took us from Tel Aviv to London. Feigning the bored, experienced traveler, I noted "the usual announcements" of flying altitude and local temperatures, apparently successfully fending off memories of the more fateful announcement from last summer's trip home. And then, at last, I explained to my imagined reader, "I despise plane trips, especially since last September Catherine and I had been hijacked to the Jordan desert where we had stayed for a week as hostages." Right after that, I described the game of rummy that Catherine and I played on the way to London. I won with three sixes and four sevens.

At our Heathrow gate during the stopover, I observed two men holding "weird-looking things," including an object "with two metal tongs sticking out." The men would glide the instrument across the surface of each carry-on bag, and "it would squeak in a funny noise." This was, I explained, "a metal detector to see if anyone was carrying guns," even as I made no mention of the gun that had gone undetected on last summer's flight home. Instead, I immersed myself in observing and describing the people around me, one wearing red corduroy pants, another with droopy jeans and long hair, filling my page with the conversations I overheard. ("What's that for?" "Some kind of detector." "Not for drugs, I hope.")

"Did they treat you especially well, or just OK?" my mother asked in the first letter she wrote to us in the fall of 1971.

"No," I wrote back, "they didn't treat us *especially* well, but I doubt they even knew we were hijacked." That comprised the extent of our mutual acknowledgment.

On September 6, 1971, a year to the day of the hijacking, I dreamed that Catherine and I were running away from a crowd of people. I often interpreted my dreams in the notebook I kept beside my bed, but this time I drew a question mark, unwilling to think back to the crowd in which Catherine and I stood on the desert floor in the dark, surrounded by armed commandos.

That same year, in eighth grade, I wrote an essay entitled "So Far Away," naming it after a favorite Carole King song. "I live two lives," I wrote, "my life in New York and my life in Israel, where I go every summer." I tried to explain that Israel was "my home too," but Mrs. Schiff asked, in red pen, "In what way?" since I didn't explain that my mother lived there. "Try to concentrate more on the effect of the experience," she commented. "Your feelings need to be defined more clearly." She gave me a B+, a dismal grade for me in English class. My teacher was right, but I only felt misunderstood.

Summer 1971 turned out to be our last summer in Israel. The following year, at fourteen and fifteen years old, Catherine and I wanted to work as camp counselors, like our friends. Two years to the day of the hijacking, on September 6, 1972, I wrote in my diary: "Well, 2 years ago today was the hijacking—heh heh." That was the same day the *New York Times* blared the headlines about the Munich Olympics. The newspaper would have been laid out on our dining room table, as it was every day: 9 ISRAELIS ON OLYMPIC TEAM KILLED WITH 4 ARAB CAPTORS AS POLICE FIGHT BAND THAT DISRUPTED MUNICH GAMES (the final toll would be eleven Israelis). It would have been impossible to miss, but I made no record of the news. I remember the Soviet gymnast Olga Korbut winning a gold medal, and the American swimmer Mark Spitz winning seven gold medals, but I have no memory of reacting to the massacre at the Munich Olympics at the start of ninth grade, no memory even that Palestinian commandos were involved.

For my father, our reunion at Kennedy Airport crowded out almost everything else. "I can't really remember the drive home," he admits forty-seven years later, the "final chapter of a grueling experience," the "conclusion of an ordeal."

Oh, Dad! We were so worried about you!: Catherine's words at the airport became one among a handful of stories that my father would tell about the hijacking over the years, if prompted to think about the week during which newscasters had announced his daughters' potential death each evening. He liked to recount Catherine's words because it fostered the sense that his children hadn't suffered so much. Another of his favored stories concerned performing at the Delacorte Theater without telling the dancers that his daughters were on one of that morning's hijacked planes. A third story concerned the meeting he attended at my school while the two of us were held hostage in the desert. In the auditorium he listened patiently—parents were miffed about the color of the classroom walls—then sought out an administrator to say that I would be late for the start of the academic year.

"Why is that?"

"She is being delayed by the hijacking."

The woman's eyes widened. "And you had to listen to those parents complaining about the color of the walls!"

Just like my father, I selected stories that I didn't mind telling. If my father cast himself as stoic, I cast myself as a kid having fun. Singing "Leaving on a Jet Plane" and the brawny guerrilla jumping rope were my favorites, of course. Another was Catherine's *New York Times* Quotation of the Day, about thanking God and taking a bath. My aim was the same as my father's: to craft stories we could live with. In the rare instances that I told those stories, I made sure to convey everything in an offhand manner. That was the best way to prove to everyone, and to myself, that none of it held any significance for me.

Other hostages crafted their own stories in the weeks, months, and years afterward. As time passed, the story Sylvia Jacobson told became one of greater distress. Immediately upon return, Sylvia had recorded that she offered a flashlight to a commando, whereas later she wrote that her flashlight had been "commandeered." Where at first she said that the female guards "seemed determined that no harm should come to the women and children and none did," her 1994 obituary (no doubt reflecting the narratives she related across the years) averred that "she and others kept watch for terrorists entering the plane at night in order to alert other witnesses to prevent molestations and rapes." Were Sylvia's fresher memories more reliable because they were closer to the event, or less reliable because she told a more sanguine story while others were still missing? In her own scholarly explorations, she observed that hostages' negative memories often surfaced later ("Curiously, in talking with the Hodes children a number of facts came to light which are less optimistic than the diaries"), yet her own earliest story about the female guards protecting the hostages turned out to be the version that was true.

Some of the hostages brought lawsuits against the airlines, and their testimony disclosed especially disturbing memories of the commandos confiscating items for which the plaintiffs were seeking compensation: throwing belongings into the dirt and trampling on them, tearing up papers and spitting on them. No such actions appear in the reports of the cockpit crew who supervised the desert confiscations, but it's hard to know what really came to pass. Did the plaintiffs recall their experiences as more emotionally damaging at the prodding of legal counsel? Were the crew reports more accurate because they were written immediately upon return, or less accurate because they wanted to protect TWA from liability, or just because crew members unwittingly wished to present the entire experience as less devastating than it was?

For two reasons, my father declined to participate in the lawsuits: he believed that the airline had acted honorably, and he did not want Catherine and me to be forced to dwell on the worst parts of the ordeal. The suits dragged on for years, with courts disagreeing over definitions of mental anguish, years during which none of us—neither Catherine nor I, nor my father and stepmother, nor my mother and stepfather—talked about the hijacking anymore.

The world's memories faded too, making it easier to sustain my own erasure. Television coverage was crude in 1970, but just two years later viewers all over the world watched graphic footage of the Munich Olympics, and in 1976 events at the airport in Entebbe, Uganda, quickly became synonymous with the Popular Front. The hijacked Air France flight departing from Tel Aviv landed at the Entebbe airport, with the Front setting a one-week deadline for the release of Palestinian prisoners. (As in September 1970, Entebbe is often erroneously recalled for the singling out of Jews. "There was no selection of Jews versus non-Jews," said one of the Israeli hostages, who had assumed the role of leader, and "many of the freed hostages were Jewish.") With about a hundred hostages ultimately detained in an unused terminal building, the Israel Defense Forces executed a daring rescue mission that resulted in the death of all the hijackers, along with four of the hostages. I'd just graduated high school, and that summer I read the *New York Times* every day. In my diary I wrote about presidential running mates, the Mets, and Russell Baker's pleasing columns, but I had nothing at all to say about Entebbe.

I reach out to my high school boyfriend, now a Hollywood producer. Back in twelfth grade, did he know that I'd been on a hijacked plane? If so, what had I told him?

"Hey!! Of course I remember," Ed writes back, surprising me with his immediate memory. An image of the three planes stranded in the desert was, "at the time we were together," he tells me, "already seared into my mind." But, he reflects, "I don't think I ever strongly associated your relating the experience with a sense of great trauma." Maybe that was his own "teenage obliviousness," but he remembers too that I spoke of the hijacking with enough nonchalance that he could do no more than put it in the same category as other things he thought were "cool and sophisticated" about me, like that my father was a dancer and that I had a "groovy" older sister.

As it turned out, among my future classmates at Bowdoin College would be Forwood C. (Duke) Wiser III, son of the man who was president of TWA while Catherine and I sat imprisoned in the Jordan desert. Some twenty-five years after we lost touch, I meet Duke near his home in New Jersey, at Small World Coffee on Witherspoon Street in Princeton.

"Did you know I was on a hijacked plane?" I ask. I'm pretty sure I never told Duke, even though we were friends in college and close friends for a stretch after college. I remembered that his father was president of

Pan American Airlines, but I'm not sure I even knew in college that his father was president of TWA in 1970.

"Yes, you told me lots of stories about it," Duke says, readily recalling a few anecdotes and even reciting the quotation that Catherine gave to the *New York Times*. Again I'm perplexed at my complete blanking out of these conversations, until Duke explains, echoing Ed, that I always mentioned the hijacking with such casualness—"just something that happened"—that any listener would have dismissed the possibility that the experience caused any degree of trauma.

Exchanges with other good friends forge a pattern. "I thought you were not making a big deal of it," remembers my best friend from college, "which was surprising to me, as we had not held back on our emotional lives with each other." My college roommate, also a dear and close friend then, offers a similar assessment. "What is significant to me," she says, "is that, with all we shared, you wouldn't have related that experience in great detail." Other close college friends agree. "I was more than a little blown away," another tells me, "and struck by your relatively calm demeanor when you told me." Two more intimate friends can barely muster any recollection at all. "There is a vague memory of *something* about it that I can feel but not quite connect to," one reflects, "something important you mentioned but didn't really share." The other notes "only the vaguest recollection of that episode in your life which I would not have been able to summon at all if you had not mentioned it now."

As more time passed, I talked about the hijacking less and less, and if I broached the subject at all, it was in such a way as to make those conversations unmemorable to myself and, I hoped, to others. My after-college boyfriend, when I lived in Oregon, puts it this way: "You told it as a funny story. Your sister said something funny." My closest friend from the years I studied for a master's degree in comparative religion at Harvard remembers that "you had been involved in a hijacking, but I don't remember much more than that." One Cambridge summer I worked as an editor of the *Let's Go* student travel guide for Israel, Egypt, and Jordan, never divulging the hijacking to anyone. "Is it possible we didn't discuss such a momentous event in your life?" a fellow editor and once-intimate friend asks when I query him.

My housemate and close friend from graduate school at Princeton, where I was working toward a PhD in history, paraphrases my attitude this way: "By the way, we were hijacked and it wasn't that bad." A graduate school boyfriend recalls Catherine's *New York Times* quotation too, and even though I'd mentioned the weapons and the army tanks, he realizes on thinking back that I was "de-emphasizing fear," talking about it "with an air of detachment," omitting "how you felt." The only thing another dear friend from grad school recalls is that our captors were kind to us. My closest friend in Santa Cruz, California, where I took my first job after grad school, recalls my mentions of the hijacking as "very casual," with "no details."

It was in Santa Cruz that I met Bruce, whom I would eventually marry. I first told him about the hijacking on a misty Saturday in October, as we hiked in Big Basin Redwoods State Park. Our romance was progressing, and as we ascended and descended the ten-mile Berry Creek Falls trail, surrounded by soaring old-growth trees, I haltingly explained, as we stopped first at Silver Falls, then at Cascades, then at Golden Falls, that my sister and I had spent that summer in Israel because my mother lived there when we were children. Bruce could tell right away that I didn't like to talk about the hijacking. He also noticed that I seemed even more unsettled telling him about my mother's departure from the family.

Maybe I staved off conversations about the hijacking because I didn't want to have to explain why I was on that plane. Maybe it was that confluence of circumstances that fortified my many and steady evasions across the years.

From Santa Cruz in the early 1990s, I gave a telephone interview to a writer who was researching a book about terrorism, in which I comfortably insisted on the lack of lasting effects. "I don't like to fly, but I don't connect it to the hijacking," I told Jeffrey Simon.

"It's an experience that you go through that you never forget," Simon suggested.

"I guess," I equivocated, laughing. "I don't know, it's not—" I didn't finish that sentence, instead talking about those who looked out for us, "a lot of very friendly and concerned grown-ups."

Simon describes me in his book as a former hostage who recalled "trying to see the bright side of things." But Simon also interviewed Catherine, and she told him a different story. "I would say there were a couple of months of adjustment in terms of school and gaining weight back and feeling secure again," she said. "We had similar dreams, of running through mazes inside planes."

The bright picture I painted for our interviewer twenty years after we came home was the same bright picture I'd wanted to paint for my father. It was the vision that, by then, pervaded my own memories. When I found Catherine's words in Simon's book another decade later, I drew a question mark in the margin, her answers unrecognizable to me. My sister hadn't forgotten the anxiety, but I found myself entirely unable to call up any such recollection.

25

The brittle issue of the newspaper that I find in my father's filing cabinet nearly fifty years later is dated October 6, 1970. The front page of the *Boston Phoenix*, an alternative weekly, offers a teaser: "Inside: Hijacked to the Desert." Flipping through, I see that an image of a smiling Catherine graces half the page. On another half page Catherine and I stand side by side, staring solemnly into the camera, two wraiths in turtlenecks. A byline indicates that the interviewer was an older cousin, Jeremy Cole, my father's nephew. Catherine clearly did most of the talking—her words form solid blocks of print, broken by my occasional interjections.

"Amazing!" my father exclaims when I show him the newspaper. "Stuff about the hijacking I never knew." What he means is *stuff about the hijacking I don't remember ever knowing*.

"Wow, I haven't thought about that piece for decades," Jeremy tells me. Now a filmmaker, back then he was a twenty-two-year-old aspiring journalist who thought it would be cool to interview his two young cousins, just home from the most famous incident of air piracy in world history. Jeremy's college roommate, a freelance photographer, had a connection at the *Phoenix*, and the other byline, A. J. Sullivan, is his. As to the original tape, "I hope I didn't throw anything out," Jeremy cautions. "I get into these cleaning fits every so often and dispose of the past." When Jeremy locates the originals, the date on the label shows that we spoke with him less than a week after our return. It would hold memories that Catherine and I had summoned singularly close in time to our desert sojourn.

The old reel-to-reel tape has sat neglected in an uninsulated New England attic for forty-seven cold winters and forty-seven hot summers. Even if it hasn't deteriorated, the interview was recorded on an obsolete half-track machine so that on a standard machine everything is garbled, mixed up with a department store training on the other half of the tape's width. Jeremy's half-track player is broken, and replacement parts are hard to find, so he has to rent a deck from a media preservation company. When he threads the slim brown ribbon from supply reel to take-up reel and presses play, there it is, seventy-five minutes' worth of conversation. Jeremy digitizes the whole thing and sends me the file.

From the contact sheets of photographs that A. J. Sullivan sends me, I see that Catherine and I sat next to each other on the flowered settee in our living room, facing our friendly inquisitors. Volumes of *Collier's Encyclopedia* stand at attention on a bookcase next to the couch, as if we might look up the answer to a hard question. Trinkets from my parents' world tours with the Martha Graham Dance Company surround us: an ornate glass candy jar, a statue of a Hindu god. My father has pulled out the piano bench to join the circle, and everything is set to record.

Hearing our voices from so many years ago—Catherine and me as children, my father not yet an old man—is both familiar and startling. On the brink of plunging ahead, I'm filled with curiosity and apprehension in equal parts, wondering what this in-the-moment testimony will reveal.

The first voice is my father's. "You're on," he says. "Have a ball."

"Where do you want us to begin?" That's me.

"Anywhere you'd like," Jeremy says.

"You go, kid," I say to Catherine. Although she will talk far more than I, if she senses that I want to contribute, she will encourage me ("Go ahead, say something" or "Go ahead, you tell"). I look out for her too. When I hear a rasping breath, I tell her to inhale from the vaporizer in her bedroom. Another time I say quietly, "Your lips are white. Just relax."

Listening so many decades later, rewinding and transcribing, I'm confounded by how much I knew back then, so much more than I have any memory of knowing. Repeatedly I jot down, "No memory of this."

"How did it all start?" Jeremy asks.

"They ran down the aisle," I say.

"About half an hour after we left Frankfurt," Catherine says.

"I think they had a gun in the copilot's neck," I say, recalling the image of Jim Majer with his hands up. Catherine doesn't contradict me, and I realize then that she too had witnessed this scene.

My other few vivid memories are here as well: the frightening Palestina, Mark Shain's amusing "Dear Bastard" message to Nixon, the confusing, cheering crowds we passed on the drive from the desert to Amman, the swarm of cameras awaiting us at the Intercontinental Hotel. Shreds of memories drift back as I listen in: orange marmalade inside our pita bread, the commandos bringing their own children onto the plane.

Sometimes we speak as if we're still in the desert: "You wake up, five o'clock, it gets light. They start moving at five o'clock." Or, "When you close the bathroom door, there's no electricity." Or, "When you look outside the window, you can see miles of nothing."

I find myself surprised too at how much Catherine absorbed: she knew how many miles we sat from Amman, the number of men our captors removed each day, that our captors had turned away the Red Cross. I'm floored to hear myself say, "They kept accusing everybody of being Israeli, and of double nationality." In my notes I write, "I knew all this?"

A few times the interview is interrupted by phone calls coming in on our household's single line. One time I hear my father say, "My kids are being interviewed right now. You know about my kids, don't you? Right. They were there six days in the desert." When our conversation is interrupted by a phone call from Foozie's mother, I find myself overcome. On the tape, my father tells us, "Well, Foozie's still all right, but she's still a hostage." A feeling comes over me, a disconcerting brew of what I must have felt that day, at the moment our voices were recorded: overjoyed to be home with my father, yet so terribly worried about Foozie. In my notes I write, "crying as transcribing."

I learn also, to my utter astonishment, that Catherine and I saved the speeches our captors distributed to us on Friday afternoon. ("Oh, you'll have to show some of the propaganda you brought back," my father says on the tape.) In all the intervening decades, neither of us has ever come upon those pages. Perhaps one of us eventually threw them away, or perhaps I might still find them, buried somewhere in my father's apartment.

Jeremy is interested in what we think of our captors' cause.

"I was very naïve about the political aspect," Catherine says. "I learned more, a lot more than I knew before." Their purpose was to "get back their homes," and "the plea of any peoples to get back their home," she says, is "a valid plea." On the other side, she considered, "Jews have been kicked out of so many places."

I start to say something, then stop.

"Go ahead," Catherine says.

Even after listening to the commandos, even after reading the materials they distributed, I still don't understand everything as well as Catherine does, and I feel embarrassed about that. Timidly, I say, "What I don't understand is who was actually in Palestine first."

"*They* were," Catherine says, disagreeing with Jews who look back to the biblical Promised Land.

"The Arabs?" I ask.

"Palestinians," she corrects me. "And then they were kicked out."

"Then it's obvious," I say. "I don't know the whole story, but it seems then that maybe—"

"They belong there, but—" Catherine isn't sure either. "Is it right or wrong?" she asks. "Who doesn't want their own home back?"

Could Arabs and Jews live together? "It might have been possible before," Catherine reflects, "but I don't know how possible it's going to be now, because so much hate has been built up. Mistakes were made when these people were kicked out in the first place."

"Yeah," I say.

"They are being listened to," Catherine goes on, talking about our captors. "But I don't think things are working out exactly as they want them to, because a lot of world opinion is turning against them, even more than it was, and now there's fighting with the Jordanians."

That brings us to a vexing question. "I think their whole general plea of wanting their home back is right," Catherine says. "But I couldn't see

Israel being wiped off the map," which is what the Popular Front wanted to happen. "On all the maps in Amman," Catherine tells Jeremy, "Israel is called—"

"Occupied Palestine," I fill in. I remember that Catherine and I had puzzled over those maps, hanging on a wall at the occupied Intercontinental Hotel.

"And in a way it was shocking, but in a way it's true," Catherine says. Terrible oppression, and then the Holocaust, had prompted the desire of Jews for "a country of their own," she says, but now Jews, in turn, were practicing discrimination. She thinks there is "no solution right now."

Soon my father interjects a question: "What are your feelings toward the guerrillas now?"

"The Palestinians," Catherine says again. "No anger. No resentment."

"They have some type of point, which I didn't know before," I offer.

"Sometimes sympathy, some understanding," Catherine says.

"They have something they are really trying to say, and they need to say it, and the only way they can say it is by hijacking planes," I continue. "It's pretty sad."

"I have more understanding now than I did for them before," Catherine says.

"They even told us, 'We're sorry to cause you trouble, but we hope you understand our point,'" I add. I was thinking of the apologies offered by the commandos, and I was paraphrasing the speech by George Habash ("I am sorry that we caused you some trouble during the last 2 or 3 days. Maybe it will be difficult for you to understand our point of view"). I never forgot when grown-ups apologized.

Children trying to make sense of global politics in human terms, Catherine and I knew that our sympathies were at odds with those of most of our fellow Jewish hostages. We had traveled to Israel, lived in Israel, and felt an attachment to Israel for reasons different from theirs. As best we could, we stirred the new history we had learned into the history we already knew, then stirred the pain of our captors into our own fear and the fears of our fellow hostages. In Israel, our friends' parents had taken refuge from the Holocaust, witnessed the death of family and the loss of homes in Europe, escaping the destruction of the Jewish people.

*Catherine and me in our living room, posing for a photograph after our
interview with Cousin Jeremy less than a week after our return.*

[A. J. SULLIVAN]

Our captors, who bore no responsibility for the Holocaust, had in turn
lost their homes in Palestine, many of them raised in refugee camps.
Everything was intertwined. History was the key, yet each side told completely different histories.

From the beginning, up in the air, I'd let Catherine do the hard work, the
same as when my mother told us about the impending divorce, at our
kitchen table in Tel Aviv. That day, I'd remained silent, sealed up, while
Catherine cried a torrent of tears. During our Jordan sojourn, Catherine
took charge too, from answering the commandos' frightening inquiries
on Monday night to responding to the barrage of questions from reporters amid the chaos of arrival in Amman. Because Catherine felt responsible for both of us, she had to think about what to do if things got any
more dangerous—if anyone tried to separate us, or if our lives became
more imminently threatened—which meant she had no choice but to
face her own fears. My sister's assumption of responsibility made it easier
to govern my own dread, but her distress frightened me enough that I
crossed out the single mention of her tears in my diary.

Back home, I never unpacked the fears I must have kept so tightly
boxed up all during the week in the desert: of never seeing my father
again, or my mother or my new baby sister, of being held prisoner forever,

of dying. When I did talk about the hijacking, I conveyed most of all that I believed—no, I *knew*—that we would not be harmed. I knew this not only because our captors were nice to Catherine and me, but also because copilot Jim Majer conveyed that message from the commandos just as soon as our plane landed in the darkening desert.

But listening to the conversation with my cousin Jeremy so many decades later, I find startling proof of an inaccurate memory. I always remembered Jim telling us, on the night we landed, that our captors promised "no bodily harm." In my memory, that's the story I told myself every day and night thereafter: Since Jim told us right away that our captors wouldn't harm us, I wasn't scared. But listening to the tape I find that my timing is all wrong.

"They made an announcement around the fourth day," I tell Jeremy. The copilot said, repeating to the passengers "what the guerrillas had said," that "the most they can do is keep us here as hostages, but there will be no bodily damage." I'd gotten the gist of the key words right, but over the years or, I suspect, soon after my return, I shifted the copilot's comforting words backward in time, in my memory, from the end of the week to within hours of landing. That shift was part of my determination to craft a story I could tolerate, one in which I knew, from the beginning of the ordeal, that no harm would come to Catherine and me.

Playing the tape, I listen too as Catherine and I argue about Monday night, "the most frightening moment" whose full record was missing from my diary. When I tell Jeremy that we were standing outside the plane among women and children only, Catherine contradicts me.

"Not women and children," Catherine says. "Everybody!"

"No," I counter.

"Everybody they took off the plane!" Catherine repeats.

"Not the men," I insist.

"Yes, Martha, even the men!"

"Well anyway, they took them off and started putting them in buses," I say.

"To go to Amman," Catherine says.

"And then they took everybody off again, and we were standing all together in a circle," I say.

"Except the non-Jews!" Catherine interjects. "You should say that, it's very important."

"Then they put them back on, stupid," I say, riled up enough to call my sister names. Momentarily reverting to present tense, I say, "We're all standing in a big circle with the Arabs, with their guns down at their sides," before confessing, "and it was very scary."

"See because they let all the non-Jews off—" Catherine interjects.

"Then they called names of several people," I go on, "and they were all non-Jews, and they brought those to Amman."

"The non-Jews left to Amman, while all the men and women—we were all Jewish—in a little knot," Catherine says. Then, backing up in time, she explains, "They put some of us in buses, and they said you're going to Amman. Or we thought we were going to Amman. Then they took us all off again, and—"

"Only the non-Jews," I add this time.

"They put only the non-Jews on the buses and the buses left," Catherine says. "So all of us Jews, we were mostly Jews, I think we were all Jews except a couple of young children"—maybe she was thinking of little Connie, who refused to leave Foozie's side—"we were standing in a little knot, and there was a circle of Arabs around us, and they had their guns. They weren't cocking them, but they had their guns. And I thought for sure they were going to fire, and I was so scared."

In that jumble of conversation, we got some of it right and some of it wrong, but Catherine and I argued about what happened that night in the desert because it was confusing and because it was terrifying. Surely I'd already lost the loose page from my diary where I described what had happened.

Listening to the tape, I also hear my own denials of fear.

"Martha, did you ever think you were going to be blown up?" Jeremy asks.

"No, I didn't really think about that," I say.

Jeremy presses me, asking whether the commandos talked to the hostages about blowing up the planes. After all, their threatening pronouncements had been all over the news.

"I think there was dynamite in the cockpit all the time," I say. Then I hedge, probably because my father is in the room, and I'm still concerned not to distress him. ("Children should always show great forbearance toward grown-up people," said the aviator in *The Little Prince*.)

I concede this much: "We thought maybe they'd take out all the passengers and blow up the planes."

26

S oon the conversation with our cousin Jeremy reveals another in-
ducement to forgetting.

"What did you do to pass the time?" he asks.

"Dozed," Catherine says. "We were drugged with tranquilizers." As
long as "we had a tranquilizer," she says, "we could just go to sleep."

I knew that the Red Cross and Red Crescent doctors had doled out
pills, but I didn't remember that Catherine and I had accepted them.

Another clue lies in the interview Catherine gave to the writer Jeffrey
Simon twenty years after our return. She remembered "a lot of bewilderment and fear," she told Simon, but also "a certain amount of just
shutting down," explaining, "It was so intense that I think you really do
shut down, emotionally shut down when it's just so overwhelming and
so unknown." There were "a lot of guns around" and "from time to time
somebody would say something about dying or being killed," either a
hostage or a commando. In the face of that, both of us "withdrew," she
said. We "slept a lot."

The hostages slept during the day because it was hot, because it was
exhausting to do nothing, and because it was a way to escape fear. But we
also slept because both the Red Cross and Red Crescent doctors plied us
with soporifics. Dr. Claude Frascani of the International Red Cross documented that a "liberal distribution of tranquilizers" delivered "the de-
sired result, a little peace for everybody," and thus became "the medicine
consumed in greatest quantity." Dr. Ahmed Kamal of the Red Crescent
dispensed pills too, to anyone who asked. Children were not exempt,

but women were the favored recipients, and Sara Raab noticed some of them in an "almost comatose state." One female hostage lost count of the white and pink tablets she consumed during the day, and at night her teenage daughter saw her mother fall into "a queer sort of sleep." Over on Swissair, the steward so freely distributed the doctors' tranquilizers that he earned the nickname Sleeping Pill Mike.

All these decades later, my memories are so dim because so many years have passed, because I was a child at the time, and because human memory is capable of blocking traumatic events. But my memory loss, and Catherine's too, were also—at the time—drug-induced. Now I understand why Catherine and I, seated near the front of tourist class, were never awakened by hostages walking up the aisle toward the first-class lounge during the night, never heard any of the frightening interrogations that took place there, and were never awakened by hostages returning to their seats in states of emotional distress.

There's no way to know for sure which medications our doctors supplied, or what dosages we ingested, but 1970 was the age of diazepam, the anxiety-easing pill best known as Valium. That year, doctors across the Western world wrote more prescriptions for Valium than for any other medication. Without sedation, Valium alleviated anxiety and panic, with a side effect of anterograde amnesia, meaning that whatever happened while under the drug's influence could be permanently lost to memory. Likely the doctors combined that with a sleep-inducing tranquilizer. Catherine and I had also taken asthma pills that week, which contained both a stimulant and a drowsiness-inducing depressant, whose side effects included diminished alertness. Our capacity for making memories had been reduced from nearly our first day in the desert. It's remarkable that we remembered as much as we did when we got home.

Memories are imprinted by the telling and retelling of stories, both to oneself and to others. Along with the passage of time, my young age, the trauma, and the drugs, I also remembered so little because Catherine and I never talked to a counselor or a therapist for the purpose of "clarifying the facts" or "encouraging feeling expression," as mental health professionals would come to recommend for traumatized children, on the theory that talking with adults helps children make sense of troubling experiences. Even when I did talk about the hijacking, there was so much I didn't tell my father, so much I refused to tell Jody and the other girls at school. There was so much that I had purposefully omitted from my diary, the volume I'd named Claire—meaning *clear*, as if to fool myself that I wrote my entries with any transparency.

The only exception, I now discovered, came when Jeremy posed questions to the two of us with his signature sensitivity. Five days after we got home, in our living room in New York, I tried to articulate my fears, even as I simultaneously resisted doing so—after all, my father was in the room with us. It was when Catherine described her feelings with complete candor that everything escalated.

Listening again to the part of our taped dialogue that so palpably captures the tension between my sister and me, I find that the tone and volume of our voices, the pauses and interruptions, the particular words each of us chose—all of these expose just how intent I was on telling an unalarming story about the hijacking, one that would remain my agreeable companion for the next half century.

"The first three days, I was terrified," Catherine says, "and then I felt hopeless, and then I was terrified, and I was hysterical, and then—"

My father interrupts. "Were you that bad?"

"I was," Catherine affirms.

Quietly I interject: "She wasn't."

With Jeremy present, serving as a buffer between the two of us and my father, Catherine had decided to tell the truth, and that proved too much for me. I often let her take the lead in conversations, but this time I felt compelled to contradict her.

My whispered refutation gives my father the evidence he needs.

"You never gave me the impression you were *that* scared, dear," he says to Catherine.

He's referring to the stories she told on the way home from the airport, and the stories she told to our stepmother's family in New Jersey. When she first saw our father at Kennedy Airport, Catherine had reassured him with the words, "Oh, Dad! We were so worried about you!" but now Jeremy offered an opening, now someone was asking her to tell a fuller story, and she was ready. The same was not true for me. Between siding with Catherine or with my father, I chose to join my father in the land of denial.

"She wasn't," I repeat on the tape, louder this time.

If my father couldn't bear to imagine his daughters afraid and alone in the desert, I couldn't bear to think of my father knowing that we were afraid and alone in the desert. Nor could I bear the thought of Catherine's fear, since she was my protector, the one I'd counted on to make sure everything was going to be okay. Even though we were home now, all of this still felt urgent. My room felt like an airplane. We talked about the hijacking in the present tense. None of it was really over yet, and the stories we told when we got home would define what the hijacking meant to us for the rest of our lives. And I didn't want it to mean anything.

"I was!" Catherine insists, determined to disrupt the adventure stories, the demonstrations of resilience.

Unready to follow, I echo my father. "You weren't that bad," I say.

Catherine perseveres. "I was terrified the first few days, and so was everybody else on the plane." This is exactly how Bassam Abu-Sharif had described the state of the hostages to reporters at Monday's press conference in Amman ("Actually, in the beginning they were terrified").

"Was it something that you kept under the surface?" Jeremy asks gently.

"Everybody wasn't flying around in hysteria," I interrupt, contempt in my voice.

"I didn't say everyone was flying around hysterical!" Catherine is shouting now.

"That's what it sounds like." Contempt again, from me.

"Did I say everyone? I said me!"—actually she had said *everybody*, but now she retracted that. "And I wasn't flying around!"

"Wait, wait, okay," my father says, coming around a bit but also eager to lessen the tension. "However you felt, you were there—"

"When I say hysterical, I simply mean that I was scared!" Catherine says.

"You just didn't give me the impression that you were that scared," my father repeats. "But if you were, you were."

"I said I was terrified, and I've said that before," Catherine declares, still angry. Apparently when she mentioned those feelings before, neither my father nor I had listened.

"Well, yeah," my father says. He turns to me. "Were you terrified, Martha?"

Very softly, as if I hope Catherine won't hear, because I know it isn't true, I say, "I was fine."

"No you weren't." Catherine turns on me again. "That's a lie!"

"I wasn't terrified!"

"Yes you were!"

"What emotion did you feel?" That's Jeremy, speaking to me, attentive to the conflicts around him.

"I was scared, but I wasn't—I knew—" I don't know how to finish the sentence.

"*Terrified* is simply a stronger word, that's all," Catherine says, more subdued now.

"I knew that they couldn't do anything to us because all around was the Jordanian army," I say, reaching for rationality.

Catherine, making peace with her little sister, ever my ally, takes that as a cue to explain how we could see the tanks on the horizon, but she isn't quite done with the battle in our living room. "He thinks I'm dramatizing," she says to Jeremy, indicating our father.

"I do not, dear!" my father protests. "I'm listening. I'm interested." And he was. It's just that it was so painful for him to hear the whole story, the true story.

"Everybody kept telling us that they couldn't do anything to us because that would turn world opinion against them," Catherine says. "But when people are walking up and down with guns, you don't think of the practical side."

"*You* don't," I mutter, my inability to absorb my big sister's fear again manifesting as disdain.

"*I* don't, all right?" Catherine reverts again to speaking only for herself, refusing the invitation to forget.

Jeremy turns to me and tries once more. "Were you—"

"I was scared, but I—I don't know, I—" Faltering again, stumbling, I'm still unable to complete a sentence, and then the conversation moves on, and we are talking about why Catherine told our captors we were Jewish ("When somebody comes up to you, and he's got a gun, and he says 'What religion are you?' you don't think about lying").

Later on, Catherine tells Jeremy that at times she felt safe. She wasn't contradicting herself, only being honest about how the sense of danger fluctuated. But when Catherine said that—when the vision of my big sister as unafraid reemerged—that made room for me to say a bit more, if still haltingly.

"I don't know, I sort of knew they couldn't do any—I knew it would turn out all right, sometimes."

Another time I say, "I don't know if I should say this, but I felt like God was with us," and another time, when Jeremy's friend A. J. asks if I ever wondered if we would be harmed, I say, "I *did*, I mean, I don't know—" yet again breaking off the sentence, and the thought.

"Now that it's all over, what sort of feeling do you have toward the whole thing?" Jeremy asks.

"It was scary sometimes," I say, at last completing a sentence, at last naming my own fear.

Trouble was, it was *all over* only in the most literal sense.

These conversations, recorded by an older cousin I hardly knew, but who asked the most important questions, and asked them with genuine compassion, captured the ways that each of us—my father, Catherine, and I—wished to understand the hijacking for the rest of our lives. This I discover only all these years later, when I go back to figure out why I remembered so little. That's when I discover my own utter determination to forget the hijacking, not just after I came home, but also while held hostage, a twelve-year-old girl who steadfastly refused—who needed desperately to refuse—to absorb so much of what was going on around her.

That day, Catherine fought for us to remember. Together my father and I fought back, but Catherine didn't give up, not yet. When Sylvia Jacobson came to visit a few weeks later, Catherine told her, in front of my father and me, how she had "expected the ring of women and children to be shot," that she had "waited to die." The Jacobson Papers don't reveal the responses of my father or me to this pronouncement.

Two summers later, Catherine told the kids at camp our hijacking story. More than fifty years after that, a friend from the summer of 1972 reaches out, writing to me, "Do you remember the two sisters who had been on a hijacked plane? That wasn't you, was it?" Dina, who recalls that we were visiting one parent and flying unaccompanied, remembers that Catherine told the story to a group of campers in our bunk, while I listened, that it was all quiet as Catherine spoke. Dina remembers the part about the plane's clogged toilets and that our trip out of the desert was "exciting and scary"—she must have been recalling the exploding planes. She remembers that Catherine spoke "a bit breathlessly," though mostly calmly. "I remember it was an emotional experience," Dina tells me, evidence that my sister had not given up on expressing the truth, even if her listeners were outside our family.

All these years later, I'm still unable to recapture a real memory of fear. When I call up the image of Palestina pointing her gun at me, I see a twelve-year-old girl, head down, deliberately slowing her steps, but the memory of any emotion still eludes me. When I think about standing outside the plane at night, surrounded by armed commandos, I see an impassive expression on my face, again with no accompanying emotion. When I think about Friday night on the plane, after the commandos took away the rest of the men, the most I can summon is a sense of unease. Yet within mere days after our return, the memory of my fear remained vivid to Catherine. I didn't want to believe her then, but I believe her now. Historians always count evidence closest to the event as the most convincing.

After Jeremy and A. J. packed up their equipment and went home, I opened my diary. In orange Magic Marker I wrote—as I often did on days when I decided not to enumerate my activities—"Hi—Bye." I didn't want to remember the conversation with Jeremy because I didn't want to remember the week on the plane in the desert. I didn't want to remember the conversation because I didn't want to remember Catherine's insistence that we were both afraid that we might never get home. I didn't want to remember that anyone thought I was ever really *that* scared.

My mission to forget did not fail. When I find the issue of the *Boston*

Phoenix in my father's filing cabinet, the interview condensed and re-arranged, I find that I can't remember ever talking to my cousin Jeremy about the hijacking. That had been the exact purpose of my diary entry that day: "Hi—Bye."

I write to Catherine, "Do you remember being interviewed by Jeremy Cole in our living room after we got back from the hijacking? Does that ring any bells for you?" Her answer: "Nope, no bells." When I send her a copy of the newspaper interview, she allows, "I remember saying those things, but not to whom. I remember seeing the picture of the two of us, but not the interview."

When I ask my father if he remembers the interview, he answers, "No. Do not. Racking brains but nothing comes to mind." ("'The grown-ups are very strange,' the little prince said to himself, as he continued on his journey.")

All of us had, after all, forgotten.

The diary and the tape: these are the two documents that reveal why I remember so little about the hijacking.

The diary that I, the historian, approached as my prized then-and-there document has turned out instead to be a record and a relic of era-sure. In the desert, I worked so hard to remember so little because I didn't want to have to tell my father about the bad parts. Instead, alongside the lean record I maintained in the pages of my daily log, I assembled nar-ratives of good cheer for my father (We sang songs and jumped rope!). Just so, my diary well illuminates the experience of the hijacking that I constructed for myself at the time.

Safely at home, it felt more vital than ever to forget. In conversation with Jeremy and my father, I denied Catherine the feelings she dared to express and denied that I'd been afraid too. When Catherine told me I was lying, I fought back ("I wasn't terrified!"). Before Catherine gave up, though, before my father and I colluded to silence her, she said it one more time, into the tape recorder, putting it on record: "Yes you were!" It would take a half century for me to believe my sister, for me at last to agree with her. In that way, the tape, in tandem with the diary, perfectly illuminates my experience of the hijacking.

There was one more step in my quest to remember or, more accurately, to understand why there was so much I didn't remember, why there was so much I didn't want my father to know, and to find out what remembering could tell me. What might I discover if I returned to the places where everything happened?

27

For my first trip to Israel in forty-eight years, Catherine has given me a leather notebook in which to record my travels. Jody has given me a bright white blouse to keep me cool in the Mediterranean heat. My mother, eighty-eight years old, has answered countless questions about Tel Aviv and Netanya during my childhood: the names of streets, the locations of the beaches and restaurants we frequented. Now she gives me a filmy scarf to cover my shoulders against the hot summer sun, and she writes me a rhyming poem that begins, "With no huge party/Or fancy feast/You'll take a trip/To the Middle East./With childhood summers/All around you/Memories will surround you." I write a poem back to her: "All those memories from being a child/May be still unreconciled/And so I head to Tel Aviv/To remember, to marvel, and to grieve."

It is my first trip to Israel since the summer of 1971. In high school Catherine and I joined summer programs and worked summer jobs, and during my first year of college, my mother and Tal moved to New York after my stepfather died in a car accident. Neither Catherine nor I ever went back.

I'm returning now to reckon with my childhood summers, and Bruce is coming with me. When I ask how he will cope with the possible intensity of my emotions, he smiles. "I can handle anything you throw at me," he says. My father, ninety-four years old, says only, "Forgive me for wishing you were already home."

In Tel Aviv, I trace and retrace the neighborhood that had been my world, and Catherine's. The corner of Ben-Zion and King George, once graced by a movie theater and falafel stand, is now a plaza of shops. From there, I follow the familiar wall of uneven reddish-tan stones up the hill, until I come to Number 19. There it is, the boxy detached four-story building, typical of 1960s Tel Aviv architecture. Newly built then, its modern elegance has faded a bit, the balconies now a facade of mismatched shutters. Unchanged, though, is the wide set of stone steps leading to the long stone walkway that ends in three more steps, the white ones where Catherine and I sat with Nurit and our other friends every day. A locked gate, not there in my childhood, blocks entry to the front doors.

The man who now owns my mother's apartment is expecting us, and while it's all different inside, it's small enough to summon the ghost of my childhood self moving about, alongside Catherine, my mother, my stepfather, baby Tal, Nurit. Farther up the street, the stores my mother called the Little Man and the Little Lady are now a single grocery, and ghosts easily greet me there too. At the top of Ben-Zion, the gray pavers and white railings of Habima Garden look the same, our former selves amiably haunting the places where my sister and I used to go to write poems together. The girl I conjure is happy, carefree.

The beach at the end of our street is right near the former American embassy, where my mother and stepfather rushed with the new baby as soon as the news of the hijacking came. Now you have to cross a busy road to get to the water, and a seaside promenade reaches south, all the way to Jaffa. Beachgoers still play paddleball by the water's edge, just like we did as kids, now against a necklace of high-rise hotels and a string of restaurants, their low tables and chairs set evenly on the fine white sand.

Tal and her family have joined Bruce and me for part of the trip, and one night we all dine on the Jaffa waterfront, watching the sun drop into the sea, just as it had so many years ago, prompting Catherine to draw and label a picture that remains faithful: *sunset, the sea, our table.*

Nurit and I have arranged to meet in front of our old apartment building. She has retired from the Ministry of Education where she worked with special-needs children; now she writes children's books and poetry. Rooted to the sidewalk in front of the building, we exchange long-ago

memories and grown-up insights. Eventually we walk up the steps together and venture into the back garden to find the grave of Nurit's cat
from decades past, then sit together on the white steps remembering the
games we played there: *Goomy*, *Dookim*, Five Stones. We talk on and
on, then talk more at dinner with her family (she has three children
and three grandchildren), and talk more another day, over coffee at
Steimatsky, the English-language bookstore we frequented as children,
now a café of the same name. As children, we never discussed why my
mother lived in Israel, why Catherine and I saw her only for summers.
Nurit tells me that back then she was afraid to ask.

One day I go back to the building with Tal's daughter, Quinn, who is
just about the age I was the summer of the hijacking. I'd shown Quinn
a photograph of me taken that summer, standing at the top of the white
steps, and that morning Quinn has taken it upon herself to dress just as
I'm dressed in the picture: dark shorts, light-colored T-shirt, sandals. She
stands for a photograph, copying my pose from 1970, my ghost coming
to life. *There I am*, I think, as she leans against the wall, ankles crossed,
the girl from half a century ago.

*Me at our apartment
building in Tel Aviv, the
summer of the hijacking.*
[EHUD BEN-DAVID]

I return to the building almost every day that I'm in Tel Aviv, sometimes several times in one day. Mostly I sit on the white steps, and the

last time I make the pilgrimage I understand that I could sit there every day for a year, or forever, without finding the answers to what living in that city, on that street, in that building, in that apartment, meant to me as a child. ("And the little prince went away, thinking of his flower.") For both Catherine and me, the hijacking was part of a larger upheaval in our lives: the repeated cycle of the long overseas journey to visit our mother, the attendant separation from our father, then saying goodbye to our mother for another year, and the long journey back to our father. No one ever talked about that either.

I send photographs of the apartment and the neighborhood, the beach and Jaffa and Netanya, to my mother. "Apartment looks so different," she writes back. "The beach looks more like Rio than Tel Aviv, but I guess that's an improvement. Everything looks familiar, but not."

I send the pictures to Catherine too. She chose not to join me on the trip, and from her home in western Massachusetts, where she lives with her partner, Holly, she scrolls through the images over morning coffee, "in silent reverence, tears streaming," she tells me, pondering "memories of joy and grief and fun and loss." That strikes me as exactly right. Just as Catherine wrote to our mother anticipating the summer of 1970, there was "so *much* to look forward to!"—the "sun and fun" and everyone we loved. I was happy and carefree those summers in Israel. There was grief and loss too. I was sad there too.

"Wow," Susie writes to me after I reach out to her via social media. "I would love to meet with you." Susie Hirsch had transferred from Barnard College to make aliyah to Israel, where her brother Howie joined her a number of years later. When I meet them, along with their spouses, for dinner in the Tel Aviv suburb of Ra'anana, Susie says she talks about the hijacking "sometimes," while Howie's wife, Lea, jokes that Howie pulls out the story "like a parlor trick"—if a conversation is growing dull, he'll sometimes whisper, "You think I should tell my story?" and she'll ask, "Are you up for it?" Recounting the story of their parents, at Heathrow Airport after the foiled hijacking of El Al Flight 219, as they learned that their three children were on the successfully commandeered TWA flight, Howie warns me, "This is probably going to make me cry."

When I mention the room Catherine and I shared with Susie at the Shepherd Hotel in Amman, Susie admits that she remembers very little about that night, when the three of us and the girl named Rina talked and sang songs, for she was too worried about her brothers, taken to a different hotel. I'm not sure Susie remembers Catherine and me at all, another reminder of our seemingly phantasmic presence on the plane in the desert.

"Wow!!!" Fran Chesler writes to me, "what a blast from the past!!"

When I'd asked Catherine, decades after we came home, which hostages she remembered, she'd answered right away, "Foozie, of course."

A social media scouring has led me back to her. It doesn't surprise me that, at first, Foozie doesn't remember us. For one thing, she cared for so many children on the plane, even if her boundless generosity made each of us feel as if we were her sole concern. For another, it was all so long ago, and Fran—she no longer goes by Foozie—almost never thinks about the hijacking anymore. But after I contact her, she digs out the account she wrote when she returned home, which instantly jogs her memory of "two lovely little girls" who were "traveling from one parent to another," and everything comes back to her. Fran made aliyah in 2005, selecting September 6 as her arrival date, closing the circle for herself.

On a July morning, Fran and I both arrive early at a restaurant in Petah Tikvah, outside Tel Aviv. Widowed with no children, she's now sixty-eight years old, her once long black hair gray and cut short. "Why do you remember me?" she asks more than once, genuinely puzzled. When I describe all that she did for Catherine and me, she seems uncomprehending. We talk through lunch, then coffee, then dessert, about our memories of the week in the desert ("You were children! Alone!" she says over and over), about the hostages we remember, about the postcard to our father that she wrote for us. She shows me her collection of mementos, arranged on the pages of an enormous scrapbook that she has brought along: her boarding pass, a landing card distributed by the commandos, a personal letter from the airline's president. We talk about her extra weeks of captivity, about Middle East politics—finding common ground only in that prospects for peace seem tragically distant—and about her long-ago visit to our New York apartment.

Back then my father had been pleased to meet the fellow hostage who took such good care of his girls, and yet Fran recalled sensing something else that day. It wasn't that she felt unwelcome, or in any way uncomfortable. It was more an awareness that my father wished to protect his daughters, and himself, from any reminders of the hijacking. Underneath his sincere warmth, he seemed to convey, *If you could leave now, that would be all right.* That's why she never came to visit us again. Maybe that's why my father has no memory of that visit, or of Foozie, at all.

"I love you," Fran says when we hug goodbye.

"I love you," I say, finally, after so many years.

Before we part, she hands me the account she wrote when she got home, several typed pages followed by many leaves of small, close handwriting, recognizable from the message Catherine and I sent to our father from the desert. I demur. She needn't give me the original, for I can easily scan the pages on my phone. She insists, pressing it into my hands, saying, "I saved it for forty-nine years, apparently for you."

When I plot the latitude and longitude of Dawson's Field online, up comes Jadara Equipment and Defence Systems. The plant was built in 2013, burying the old airstrip, which emanates from under the buildings on the satellite image.

"So this is your first official visit to Jordan," says our guide, Salah Khleifat, trim in his blue jeans and green short-sleeved shirt. Though his degree is in economics, Salah has a special interest in travelers who care about history and politics. The car ride takes Bruce and me past abandoned military buildings, a sign for Hashemite University (built in 1991), and a sign pointing toward the Syrian border. At the security station that blocks the entrance to the defense plant, Salah speaks through the car window, then gets out of the car. Men emerge, shake hands, speak in Arabic. I can see Salah gesturing toward me, explaining why I'm there. He comes back to say that the plant is a completely restricted area, that it's impossible to gain entry. The runway doesn't exist anymore. "There is nothing left," he says. "They have built over everything."

The security men have given Salah directions to an unrestricted high point, and we head south, then west, our driver pulling onto a narrow paved road, then a dirt road, until we come to a stop near a trash dump with feral dogs scrounging in the detritus. It is 8:30 in the morning, and it is already hot as we crunch across the powdery lime that covers our shoes in white dust. ("You were on your way back to the place where you landed?" the aviator asked the little prince.)

"At your time, in 1970, this was just desert," Salah says.

Indeed, in 1970 a reporter wrote, "There is not a single building of any sort at the airstrip." Almost fifty years later, I stand on a ledge, looking north over a flat expanse of scrub. A steel factory and parts of a petroleum refinery rise to our west. The newest part of the city of Zarqa spreads out behind us.

"The sand, I think, would be in that area," Salah says, pointing to a low ridge and the hills farther on. ("Then you don't remember," said the little prince. "This is not the exact spot.") Inside the right-angled walls of the defense plant, visible in the distance, lies the disappeared runway. Comparing the coordinates of the satellite image to his cell phone compass, Bruce determines that we're less than half a mile away. We're standing on the crest where reporters coming from Amman caught sight of the three airplanes, laid out like children's toys or three dots on a domino. Envisioning Catherine and me, two young hostages, Bruce loses his composure behind his sunglasses.

An occasional brush of wind relieves the solid morning heat, which seems suddenly familiar. "I remember that it was hot like this," I say. "The airplane doors were open, and sometimes the breeze would come in." Bruce is taking pictures, panning with his camera.

"Take your time, guys, not to rush," Salah says. "You can tag the photos with your location." ("And, if you should come upon this spot," said the aviator in *The Little Prince*, "please do not hurry on.")

"Yes, they'll be GPS tagged," Bruce says, steadying his voice. "This is where the sun came up," he tells me, pointing to the east.

"After such a nightmare," Salah says, "to come back and see the place where these things happened is something. This is the advantage of being a child at that time, because you hadn't any idea about what's going on."

We have stood on the ledge for a little more than half an hour. ("Look at it carefully so that you will be sure to recognize it in case you travel some day to the . . . desert," said the aviator in *The Little Prince*.) I'm ready to leave. The thought comes to me: *I don't ever need to come back here again.*

"It feels like it happened to someone else," I say.

"Regards from beautiful Amman," the general manager of the Jordan Intercontinental has written to me. "I am very pleased to know you are coming back to visit after all these years. Your story is very emotional." Carlos Malliaroudakis upgrades Bruce and me to a suite and graciously arranges a personal tour of the hotel.

Driving up, everything looks different. In the newsmen's raw footage from that Saturday afternoon forty-nine years ago, Catherine stood up to look out the windows of our van, the sight of fluttering flags signaling the possibility of release. Now I see the flags again, but the building has been remodeled. No longer white with gridded balconies, its exterior is tan and smooth instead.

The staff is expecting us. As Bruce and I head toward the reception area, someone swoops upon us and ushers us to the VIP Ambassador's Desk. That's when the flashback comes on, transporting me to the moment Catherine and I were ushered to the TWA desk amid the tumult ("I wanted to grab your hand and run," Catherine said, "but there was chaos and a crush of people"). This time, in the lobby's serene elegance, I fold my arms on the desk and rest my head in an effort to subdue the spiral of hallucinations. Also I'm crying.

To be sure, I'd shed tears before: listening to Peter, Paul and Mary's "Leaving on a Jet Plane," or coming upon my father's telegram at the Red Cross archives, or my father's words, captured on Jeremy's tape, that Foozie was still missing. But this time is different. Maybe it's the way the hotel staff steered Bruce and me to the desk, which felt like the way an unknown man had propelled Catherine and me inside the hotel, the replication of that swift movement bringing me back to who I was before. ("I have suffered too much grief in setting down these memories," said the aviator in *The Little Prince*.)

All those years ago, the twelve-year-old girl had willed herself to remain dry-eyed, determined to prove that everything was fine. Now my out-pouring lasts a long time, as if making amends for decades of dammed-up emotion. Tears for Catherine, who took it upon herself to protect us both. Tears for my father, who did not know if his girls would die. Tears for my absent mother, who did the best she could, even if it wasn't good enough. Tears for the twelve-year-old girl, who was me and yet is no longer me.

A fragment of consciousness surfaces with the realization that I need to explain myself to the woman seated behind the desk. When I lift my head, I see that she is patiently waiting out my spell.

"I was here as a child—" I begin haltingly.

The woman stops me, her sympathetic face framed by long black hair. "I know everything," she says.

A man in a robe and headdress places a box of tissues before me.

The woman at the table is Dima Assad, manager of guest relations. Behind us, equally forbearing, staff members stand in a row. On the seventh floor of the remodeled original building, they have filled our spacious suite with fresh flowers, fruit, wine, sweets, cheese, bowls of olive oil and ground spices. A note from Mr. Malliaroudakis reads, "We know that the last time you have visited us was 50 years ago, but rest assured Intercontinental Jordan will always be your home in Amman."

The hotel has quadrupled its number of guest rooms since 1970, adding buildings as the city expanded. Instead of the surrounding brown hills, a carpet of white structures now extends all the way to the horizon. The old facade's design is still evident in adjacent wings, and the pool still lies behind the original building, its mosaic tiles now tinting the water an opulent indigo. Visitors to the hotel must place their bags on a conveyor belt before walking through a metal detector, and the basement nightclub-turned-bomb shelter is gone. From the windows of our room, I can see the terrace where Catherine and I found a spot of calm and helped ourselves to food.

The Philadelphia Hotel was torn down years ago, but the Shepherd still stands on Zeid Bin Haritha Street, a short walk from the Intercontinental. Opened in 1967 by George Shalhoub, a Jordanian of Lebanese descent, it was the only other hotel in the Jebel Amman neighborhood (and the third of the city's trio of hotels) in 1970. "It gives me a shiver when I recall that experience of September 1970," Nader Shalhoub told me after I reached out to him. Working as the night manager of his father's business back then, he had one more semester left to complete his degree at the American University of Beirut. "I would like to welcome you back again in Amman, and hope I could be of help to you."

Two stories tall with thirty beds then, the hotel now boasts four stories and sixty beds. The recently built rooftop restaurant, run by Nader's sons, lights up at night, crowded with young people drinking and socializing in one of the city's trendiest hotspots. Nader, now seventy-two, shows Bruce and me the patched bullet holes on the outer walls, and another right inside the hotel entryway, from the September 1970 war. Joining us that day is Franz Zauner, the Austrian farmer from our plane. Driven out of the desert that first Monday night, he'd spent the week at the Shepherd Hotel and has remained friends with Nader across all these years.

Nader shows us to the room that Catherine and I shared with Susie and Rina and Patsy, which he recognizes from my description, and which now serves as his office. As we sip coffee, I look to the balcony (since enclosed, holding a grand desk) from which we witnessed the flashes of war, and I peek into the attached bath where I threw away my dust-caked clothing.

When I give Nader an article written by one of the BBC reporters in 1970, he exclaims, "David Lomax, my friend! He stayed with me months and months." Also staying at the Shepherd that fall, he tells us, were two Russian filmmakers, one of whom would later be shot from the very room in which we are sitting—"your room," Nader calls it. Out on the balcony, recording the war's soundscape, the man had held a microphone that a sniper mistook for a weapon.

Over the next days, Nader treats Bruce and me to dinner at the hotel's rooftop restaurant and to lunch at his private club, where we sip arak on a terrace ringed with blooming red geraniums. He invites us to his home for a meal of lamb and stuffed grape leaves with his family, grandchildren included, the walls filled with his wife's artwork.

"Do you think we encountered you in 1970?" I ask. As night manager, he worked the desk from 5:00 p.m. until midnight.

"Most likely, yes," he says.

When I tell him about throwing away my favorite pair of pants, the ones I wore all week in the desert, he says ruefully, the same warm and generous man now as then, "We could have washed them for you."

There is one more place to go.

"Welcome back after all these years," says Chris Betz, the events manager and curator of memorabilia at the Eero Saarinen terminal at Kennedy Airport. "It looks a little different, but it also feels the same."

Closed for nearly twenty years and almost torn down, the building has been reincarnated as the TWA Hotel and Museum, the hassle of present-day airport security replaced by mid-century modern nostalgia. The looping soundtrack plays Frank Sinatra ("Come Fly with Me") and the Beatles ("Ticket to Ride"). The shop sells TWA slippers just like the ones we got for free on the flight home. A Volkswagen bus, just like my father's, is parked out front as one of the museum's artifacts, as if my father is still there, waiting for his daughters to land.

"That's where you would have come through, right here," says Chris, as we proceed along what used to be called Flight Wing #1, explaining that the carpeting is chili-pepper red, the original Eero Saarinen color.

Bruce films the length of the walkway, a windowless two-hundred-plus-foot tube with curving walls of white concrete, "an elongated cave," as one architectural critic called it, that "beckons to the wondering child in all of us." We come to the spot where the walkway deposits us into the terminal, the place where Catherine and I first caught sight of my father. There are our ghosts again, and there is the girl, smiling for her father ("No crying, no tears, ready to go," said my stepmother).

"I'm just trying to imagine it," I say. Here, unlike the happy phantoms of summers in Israel, the ghost who greets me still feels like the ghost of someone else.

Maybe the hijacking feels like it happened to someone else because it did. Maybe that twelve-year-old girl, the one who was unable to absorb so much, and who worked so hard to forget, was a different person from the grown-up searching to understand what happened and why she remembered so little. Maybe that's why a meticulous reconstruction of my experiences of the hijacking can connect me only faintly to the fear with which Catherine contended, both her own and mine: a yoke of responsibility that made my sister's terror so much more acute.

No reconstruction can connect me to my own feelings of fear back then because I had so fully obliterated those feelings, and then so completely disconnected that girl in the desert from the rest of my life.

28

There's one last fellow hostage I want to find. In my diary, when I listed our grown-up friends, I wrote Mitch Meltzer's name first. I never mentioned Mitch in my diary again, but I always remembered him as a young man around the same age as Mark Shain and Mimi Beeber. In Sylvia Jacobson's papers, I'd come upon a questionnaire that Mitch had returned to Sylvia from his home in Florida. For her inquiry, "What were your feelings regarding helping others?" Mitch had checked off the box next to the answer, "I wanted to help others." Rob Hirsch, ten years old at the time, recalled that Mitch took it upon himself to take care of some of the young boys who were flying without their parents. Mitch was nineteen that summer, returning from Israel, where he'd worked on a couple of communal farms.

Searching for Mitch, I learn that he became a designer for Walt Disney World before he died of leukemia in the mid-1990s, in his early forties. Then, after Rob Hirsch puts me in touch with Mitch's son, I receive a heavy carton in the mail. Fanning out the accordion folders inside a latched case, I find the typed pages of a manuscript that Mitch started writing within weeks of his return from Jordan (he was among those held two weeks longer), both from notes he'd taken at the time and from memory.

In the early pages, Mitch re-creates a conversation he had at the airport gate in Tel Aviv with "two little girls" who were "sitting there looking scared and lonely." To my astonishment, I find that this is Catherine and me. He calls us "Mary and Kathy," either to shield our names or because that's what he remembered by the time he got home.

A self-described muscular two-hundred-plus pounds, Mitch asked if he could help carry a suitcase, to which Catherine assented, "managing a smile." When he asked how we liked flying, Catherine said ("her mouth firm") that she didn't like it, to which I added, "It scares her to death when we take off and land." There I was, acknowledging my big sister's fears, but that was before everything changed, before I needed her to save both our lives.

Up in the air, after the pilot turned the plane around to head back to the Middle East, when all of us passengers sat tensely quiet in our seats, Mitch walked back a couple of rows to check on the children he'd assisted at the airport.

"Where are you two girls going?" he asked.

"We don't know," Catherine said, interpreting the question differently, since New York was no longer our immediate destination. She added, perhaps hopefully, "Do you know?"

"We thought that we were going to New York," said Mitch's row mate, who had joined him in the aisle.

"We're going there too," I said. "Why is everybody so frightened? Can that man up there do anything?" Looking toward the front of the plane, I must have spied Rudi Swinkels or Frank Allen, since the pursers were the only male crew members not inside the cockpit. Maybe I was already scouting out a substitute for my father, a man who would fix everything, which meant there would be no reason for everybody to be so scared, which meant I wouldn't have to tell my father that I'd been scared too.

Mitch sensed panic from both of us and wondered what he could say to alleviate it. "We just have to wait a while," he tried, doing his best to keep his voice calm.

"My dad is going to meet us in New York," I said ("she seemed firm about that," Mitch wrote). I knew that the day my father picked us up at the airport was always the most important day of his whole summer, and I didn't want to disrupt that.

"He'll be there," Mitch's row mate said, also trying to reassure us.

Mitch produced the seat-pocket map. "See! These are mountains, the Alps—and this is the Adriatic—and this—"

"We know those are mountains," I said. "We just flew over them. Can't see them anymore—too many clouds."

"Where do you think we are now?" Catherine asked, bringing us back to the circumstances at hand.

Mitch suggested Turkey, prompting the other man to clap him on the back, which made Mitch feel like he was doing all right with the two girls who were alone and afraid.

Mitch's drafted scene ends there, but we show up once more in his narrative, this time on Monday night, right after the "most frightening moment." Mitch had been among those instructed to remain inside the aircraft, and as the hostages returned from the dark desert floor, he saw that one of us was crying, no doubt Catherine.

"Don't worry," Mitch comforted both of us, explaining that there hadn't been enough room at the hotel in Amman—that's what he'd heard people around him saying, about why some of us were ordered out of the vans and back onto the plane.

"Are you sure?" Catherine was doubtful.

"Got to believe in something," Mitch said.

"Yes," Catherine said, "but not in fairy stories." There she was, from the start, coaxing everyone, even the grown-up hostages, to face the fearful circumstances.

Although I remember none of these interactions, I now understand why I listed Mitch first among our adult friends: he had been our first one, beginning at the Tel Aviv airport, when he noticed us looking lonely after saying goodbye to our mother.

As I pore over Mitch Meltzer's words, one thought keeps surfacing. I've now spent years talking with Catherine, my parents, and my friends, parsing the entries of my diary, communicating with fellow hostages, locating my name and Catherine's on passenger lists, watching images of the two of us in news footage. I've collected plenty of evidence from which to reconstruct our experiences, yet at that moment it's as if I, the historian, have found the last piece of a puzzle definitively proving my hypothesis. *My God*, I think, *we were really on that hijacked plane.*

When Catherine told our cousin Jeremy how scared we were in the Jordan desert, I contradicted her because it felt imperative to appear unchanged for my father. Listening to the conversation from that day in our living room, I see that my father did in fact extend an opening to support Catherine when he said, "I'm listening. I'm interested." Still I recoiled, afraid of venturing toward the truth. The best way to keep the knowledge of our suffering from my father was to not think about the hijacking, so that I wouldn't want to talk about it, and to not talk about the hijacking, so that I wouldn't have to think about it.

Despite my best efforts, though, there had always been images that refused to dissipate, visions that loosened my grip on the narratives I so carefully formulated, even if I couldn't find the emotions to go with them: the gun at the neck, the gun pointed at me, the dynamite, the armed captors surrounding me. A half century later, lingering for the first time—and for a long time—over those images, I unbury something else too.

I didn't want to think about the hijacking back then because that would mean thinking about why my sister and I were on that plane at all. Just the same, talking about the hijacking to my friends at school would mean explaining why my mother lived in a faraway place. I didn't want to talk about the hijacking because I didn't want to have to explain to my friends why my family was so strange.

Why did it feel so urgent to protect my father from his daughters' suffering? I worried so much about him because his world revolved around us. My mother at least had the new baby, and she had already proven that she could survive without us. I worried so much about my father because it felt as though, if he knew how much we had suffered, he might die of the anguish. And since my mother had already left, I needed my father to survive.

Fifty years to the day of the hijacking, on September 6, 2020, former hostages from TWA 741 gather for a video reunion in the midst of a worldwide pandemic, signing on from the United States, Israel, and Europe. There are nearly forty of us, joined by more than twenty relatives, and Bruce sits by my side. I've extended an invitation to Catherine, but she has declined.

It is Sunday, the same day of the week as in 1970. We begin at 10:30 a.m. New York time, just about the hour that Captain C. D. Woods was attempting to land on that darkened desert runway. Babies and children have grown up, young adults have slid past middle age. David Raab has organized the event, and he is, he says right away, *verklempt*: overcome. Many of us are. David suggests that we each recount "the most poignant moment in our hijack experience," and I choose my memory of commandos jumping rope with the children. Then I add: "I've come to realize that I tended to hold onto cheerful scenes more than frightening ones."

After the reunion, a new question comes to me. Along with *Why did I remember so little?* and *What could remembering tell me?* I wonder for the first time, *What would have happened if I'd allowed myself to remember?*

The answer to my new question lies in the feelings that, at long last, keep me company when I think about the hijacking now, the feelings that emerged as I at last settled in with the images I never managed to erase; as I immersed myself in the brittle pages that began with the words "Ladies and Gentlemen"; as I gazed over the landscape where Catherine and I sat imprisoned inside a plane; as I sank back into the past at the Ambassador's Desk in the Intercontinental Hotel.

Most of all, the answer lies in the feelings that came over me as I sat on the white steps of my mother's apartment building in Tel Aviv, wishing to understand something I might never understand: what took my mother so far away from her children. Although I can never recapture the fear of the hijacking, I can recapture the sadness of childhood, symbolized and manifested in the experience of the hijacking. While the fear remains nearly impossible to access, the sadness has become my friend. From the beginning, I didn't want to remember the hijacking, not because of the fear but because of the sadness. I had really been there, in the desert, and when I was there—and before I got there and after I came home—I felt so sad. ("I have been having some trouble with a flower," said the little prince.)

That sadness was the source of the choked-back tears whenever I entered an airport, or when the wheels of an aircraft thudded to the ground. Twenty years after the hijacking, when I told the writer Jeffrey Simon "I don't like to fly, but I don't connect it to the hijacking," Simon

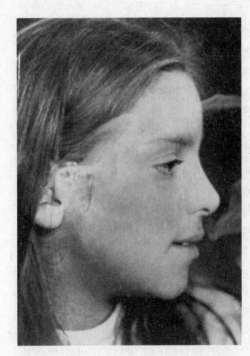

My stepfather took this double-exposure photograph in Tel Aviv. If you look closely, I appear to be thinking about my mother dancing.
[EHUD BEN-DAVID]

assumed I was evading feelings of fear, and when I first listened to the tape of that interview, I assumed the same. But in fact my answer wasn't entirely evasive. I didn't like to fly not simply because of the hijacking but because of why Catherine and I were on a plane from Tel Aviv to New York, by ourselves, in the first place. Flying fanned feelings of deep-rooted sadness more than anything else, as we left one parent to be with the other. Each time, I choked back tears. If I didn't stop the tears before they began, surely they would never cease.

In September 1970, *Life* magazine called the hijackings "the most audacious air piracy coup in history," but after September 11, 2001, a reporter called September 1970 "a big story for a little while." The 9/11 hijackers were different from our hijackers. Popular Front commandos were Marxist-Leninists, not Muslim jihadists, and the Front's leader, George Habash, was a Christian. Indeed, 1970 narratives of anti-Semitism tended to invoke not "Muslims" but "Arabs," just like the old woman sitting in our row up in the air, who cried out, "I hope it's not the Arabs!"

One particular parallel, though, always unsettled me. Passengers on one of the 9/11 planes reported via airphones and cell phones that the hijackers promised no harm to anyone. Our hijackers had promised the same. That was the way I always told the story of my hijacking: *They promised no harm, and they did not harm us.* But the 9/11 hijackers had not kept their word. They killed everybody. That's what impelled me to think back. Even if our captors never intended to harm us, the threat was necessary to their mission. The promise of no harm was the key to the story I'd so carefully constructed, and also the key to the fortress I'd built around my feelings, a key I had long ago discarded.

Catherine remembers the rope-jumping commandos too, along with the twinkling eyes of the Palestinian man who spied the heart she'd drawn on the back cover of her summer diary. She remembers our captors as desperate and as human, and when the hijacking resurfaces in her mind, she also—again, still—refuses to forget the fear. "We were afraid," she tells me all these decades later. "It was overwhelming." She had felt vulnerable, "overcome by helplessness, powerlessness, fear," wondering if she was "brave enough, smart enough" to take care of everything for both of us. What would she have done, she still wonders, if something else had happened, something worse than what did happen? Decades later, Catherine is willing to imagine what it was like for our father, "trying to remain calm, working as usual, not panicking," yet "dying inside," wishing even now that she could have "protected him from this."

The hijacking, at least obliquely, guided the choices that Catherine and I made when we grew up. Catherine first became an actress, freely expressing the conflicts and emotions of characters on a stage, before an audience whose sole purpose was to listen. After that, she became a social worker, dedicating her life to survivors of domestic violence, never looking away from the terrible things that happen to people inside their families. For my part, I studied comparative religion, ever searching for ways to reckon with the divine, then became a historian, delving into the lives of other people, writing books that made meaning out of other people's stories, other people's fears and grief, before turning, finally, to my own. ("I have never yet told this story," said the aviator who befriended the little prince.)

My story of the hijacking is a story about grown-ups not listening to children because they thought silence would better serve us. By encouraging Catherine and me to forget, the grown-ups silenced us, a silence that also encompassed my mother's departure. As children, Catherine and I coped with my mother's absence, the divorce, my father's pain, the hijacking, and the aftermath of the hijacking by staying close, as sisters. We never talked about any of it because no one encouraged us to, but I relied on my sister's bravery and protection. As we grew up, the distance that marked our adult relationship took root in those silences. My voyage into forgetting and remembering is also a story of my own complicity in that silence. My voyage is a story of empathy for Catherine and a journey of empathy for that twelve-year-old child unable to break the silence, a child who was, in the distant past, me.

After I return from Israel and Jordan, my mother gives me a handmade card. Inside I find another of her rhyming verses. "Little Martha took a vacation/and ended up in an Arab nation/Six long days soon passed by/with a tear and a sigh/And so she writes another book/all about the toll it took." *The toll it took.* In a way, my mother was willing to understand this better than my father. I think she means everything: the hijacking, and all that led up to it, and all that came after. ("This flower is a very complex creature," the little prince said to himself.)

All these years later when I ask my father what it was like for him, he repeats a line from the script he has never discarded: "I always knew you were coming home." Then he leaps ahead in time, his face lighting up with happiness, to the instant he caught sight of Catherine and me emerging from the airport walkway. "You were home!" he says. "Nothing else really mattered."

Except that it did. Everything mattered. At the very end of *The Little Prince*—my favorite book that summer, the one I read, reread, and memorized, the one we talked about with Foozie on the plane in the desert—the aviator closed his own tale this way: "And no grown-up will ever understand that this is a matter of so much importance."

ACKNOWLEDGMENTS

———

A book written from memories and archives cannot be written alone. Although I am solely responsible for this book's content, I am grateful to many people and institutions who showed me so much generosity along the way.

I thank Fabrizio Bensi at the archives of the International Committee of the Red Cross; Meghan Lee-Parker and Ryan Pettigrew at the Richard Nixon Library; Gary Zola, Ken Proffitt, and Joe Weber at the American Jewish Archives; Andrew Lee at New York University; Robert Congleton at Rider University; and Eugene Lim and Jana Lucash at Hunter College High School. I thank curators, archivists, and librarians at the National Archives, the Library of Congress, and the New York Public Library, including the Library for the Performing Arts. For gathering and sending documents, I thank the National Archives of the United Kingdom, the Swiss Federal Archives, the Vanderbilt News Archive, the University of Exeter Special Collections, the University of Miami Libraries Special Collections, and the Wisconsin Historical Society.

So many people connected to Trans World Airlines helped me out, beginning with staff at the State Historical Society of Missouri. I thank as well Chris Betz and Erica Hornung of the TWA Hotel and Museum in

New York; Beth Holcombe, president of Silver Wings International; Pamela Blaschum and John Mays at the TWA Museum in Kansas City; and Gene York. I also thank Marnix Groot of AirportHistory.org for sharing knowledge of the TWA Flight Center at Kennedy Airport.

For their translation skills working with poor-quality video and challenging handwriting, I thank Mohamed Abdou, Hadas Binyamini, and Ellis Garey. Thanks also to David Bell, Faith Hillis, and Moshe Sluhovsky for impromptu assistance with (respectively) French, German, and Hebrew words, and to Larry Wolff for assistance with an instance of puzzling German handwriting.

For sharing sources, I thank Jeffrey Simon for the tapes of his interviews with Catherine and me, Sheila Salenger and Rawn Salenger for Ken Salenger's dissertation, Dick Meyer and Jill Rosenbaum for tracking down a CBS special report, David Raab for hard-to-find BBC footage, and Howie Hirsch for footage of *Instant Recall*. I thank Victoria Phillips for her work on Martha Graham and the Cold War, and Rena Gluck for her work as a historian of the Batsheva Dance Company.

For sharing crucial personal sources, I thank Jody Goodman, Evelyn Goodman, and Nurit Peri for childhood letters; Toni Fitzpatrick for her diary entries; Ray Madrigal for gathering and transcribing Uncle Alfred's memories; and A. J. Sullivan for photographs of Catherine and me a half century ago. Jeremy Cole, thank you for keeping, finding, and converting the old reel-to-reel tapes.

Audiences at a variety of venues asked critical questions and offered illuminating reflections. I thank Adam Arenson and the members of the Writing History Seminar held at Columbia University; Kendra Field and everyone at the Mellon-Sawyer Seminar symposium "Writing Family, Reconstructing Lives" at Tufts University; Sarah Schulman and the audience at New Adventures in Nonfiction, at Performance Space New York; and Stéphane Gerson and everyone at the "Scholars and Their Kin" symposium at New York University. I thank Kate Brown and Alex Lichtenstein for encouraging my *American Historical Review* essay, "As If I Wasn't There: Writing from a Child's Memory."

Fellowships are a scholar's dream and a writer's balm. For giving their time to make both of those possible, I thank David Blight, Eric Foner,

James Goodman, Karl Jacoby, and Richard White. I thank Sebastian Jobs and the John F. Kennedy Institute for North American Studies at the Free University of Berlin for a residency that gave me time to craft the book proposal. I am honored to thank the John Simon Guggenheim Memorial Foundation for supporting this project, and the Dorothy and Lewis B. Cullman Center for Scholars and Writers at the New York Public Library for a truly unparalleled fellowship year there. For that year, I thank Salvatore Scibona, Lauren Goldenberg, and Paul Delaverdac, and my incredible cohort of fellows for their beautiful companionship and brightly lit minds: David Bell, Jennifer Croft, Mary Dearborn, Ada Ferrer, Vona Groarke, francine j. harris, Faith Hillis, Brooke Holmes, Karan Mahajan, Corey Robin, Marisa Silver, Kirmen Uribe, Amanda Vaill, and Frances Wilson.

How extraordinarily lucky I was to return to the Cullman Center for two more years. Thank you, Salvatore Scibona and William Kelly, for appointing me as interim director, once again bringing the library's incomparable resources into my daily life. I thank the terrific 2021–22 cohort of fellows: Rich Benjamin, David Wright Faladé, Julia Foulkes, Kaiama L. Glover, David Greenberg, Lewis Hyde, Karl Jacoby, Matthew Karp, Jonas Hassen Khemiri, Maaza Mengiste, Nara Milanich, Michael Prior, Josephine M. Rowe, Avi Steinberg, and Madeleine Thien. Thank you, Rich, for inviting me to present the book-in-progress, and thank you all for your support and reflections. Maaza, two very specific suggestions of yours made a difference. The equally terrific 2022–23 cohort, along with Catherine Nichols, accompanied me as I took the difficult steps of finishing the manuscript: Rozina Ali, Daphne A. Brooks, Colin Channer, Raghu Karnad, Margaret Kelleher, Claire Luchette, Neil Maher, Sarah Maza, Patrick Phillips, Daniel Saldaña Paris, Maurice Samuels, Brandon Taylor, Erin L. Thompson, Francesca Wade, and C Pam Zhang. To all of these Cullman fellows, your own research and writing inspired me in so many ways. Speaking of inspiration at the Cullman Center and the New York Public Library, I thank Jean Strouse and Brent Reidy too.

I can't believe how fortuitous it was that I made my return trip to Israel and Jordan the summer before Covid-19 covered the globe. Thank you, Tal Ben-David, Kevin Brady, Quinn Brady, and Lesley Goldman for being there too, and thank you Quinn for inhabiting my twelve-year-old self at the old apartment building. For generosity and compassion, I thank Nurit Peri and Nati Peri, Moshe Sluhovsky, Yael Sternhell, and Yonatan Levin. Roy and Mazal Ben-David, thank you for hosting the family reunion, and thank you to Ofra and Avner Greenberg, Moishe and Rachel Ben-David, Shahar Ben-David and Haim Yafim Sankov, and all the children and grandchildren. In Amman, I thank Jocelyn DeJong and Tariq Tell for a valuable dinner conversation; Carlos Malliaroudakis, Lucie Aslou, Dima Assad, Odai Qahwaji, and the entire staff of the Intercontinental Hotel; and Franz Zauner for joining us. I offer very special gratitude to Nader Shalhoub and his entire lovely family for treating Bruce and me like old friends, and to the knowledgeable and empathetic Salah Khleifat for guiding us back to the desert.

Many fellow hostages communicated and conversed willingly and generously. I am enormously grateful to Sarah (Malka) Bliner, William Burmeister, Fran Chesler, Eva Grubler, June Haesler, Howie Hirsch, Rob Hirsch, Daniel Kahn, Judy Kahn, Tova Lev Kahn, Alice Kessler-Harris, Jim Majer, Rita Manevitz, Barbara Mensch, Mimi (Beeber) Nichter (who is writing her own book about the hijacking), Nancy Porter, David Raab, Susie (Hirsch) Rosenrauch, Sheila Warnock, Tikva (Raab) Yudkowitz, and Franz Zauner. I thank the late Sylvia Jacobson for all her good work—I only wish I could have met her once again.

For very kindly sharing their own written accounts, I thank William Burmeister, Fran Chesler, Howie Hirsch, Susie (Hirsch) Rosenrauch, Sheila Warnock (for reading hers aloud to me), and Franz Zauner. I thank June Haesler for Rudi Swinkels's missing crew report and Matthew Meltzer for the invaluable manuscript pages of his late father, Mitch Meltzer.

Three fellow hostages deserve special gratitude. I thank David Raab for his book and his encouragement, and for organizing the fiftieth anniversary virtual reunion, including the video he created with Aaron Ovadia. I thank Fran Chesler, with love, for everything she did, both then and now. I feel immensely fortunate to be able to exchange messages of deep affection with her after so many years. Finding Jim Majer was an amazing gift, and I am so grateful for our nearly three years of steady correspondence. I remain bereft at his recent passing and hold his beloved Roz in my heart.

For reconnecting me to some of the people named here, I thank Tal Ben-David, David Greenberg, Rob Hirsch, Jim Majer, Barbara Mensch, David Raab, Ann Starer, Christine Tomasino, Miron Weinreb, and Armando Zetina.

For responding to queries so readily, I thank science teacher Fran Salzman, guidance counselor Allan McLeod, social studies teacher Irv Steinfink, and especially music teacher Helen Finegold Friedman. Clay Taliaferro, thank you for sharing memories of my father at the Delacorte Theater. McFeely Sam Goodman, thank you for our conversation about what it's like when terrible things happen to you at twelve years old.

A great many friends, colleagues, and friends-of-friends took an interest in this book. For caring and reflecting, I thank Susan Abulhawa, Edward Ball, Thomas Bender, Julie Berebitsky, David Blight, Nicholas Boggs, Ava Chin, Katharina Dahl, Matthew Dennis, Konstantin Dierks, Hasia Diner, Jim Downs, Marc Fisher, Ruth Franklin, Michel Gobat, Linda Gordon, Laura Gotkowitz, Steven Hahn, Leslie Harris, Mary Huissen, Maya Jasanoff, Carla Kaplan, Monica Kim, Sarah Knott, Karen Kupperman, Megan Marshall, Jürgen Martschukat, Jennifer McFeely, Ramsey McPhillips, Shana Minkin, Eva Moseley, Kevin Mumford, Timothy Naftali, James Oakes, David Oshinsky, Rachel Pastan, Fritz Read, Woody Register, Elizabeth Reis, Sarah Schulman, Gigi Simeone, Bryant Simon, Sheba Veghte, Richard White, and Nell Zink. To the late Tony Horwitz and the late Amy Kaplan, I thank you in sorrow.

For unending conversation, wisdom, and encouragement, I offer special gratitude to Laurie Bernstein, Ada Ferrer, James Goodman, Jody Goodman, Marisa Silver, and Ben Yagoda.

For generous and candid memories of our younger selves, I thank Sharon Achinstein, Peter Bancel, Jeffrey Barnes, Mary Kay (Gunning) Bonfante, Amanda Broun, Gregory Evans Dowd, Bea Fitzpatrick, Wilma Friedman, Ann Fries, Evelyn Goodman, Loren Chodosh Harkin (thank you for being at Performance Space that night too), Jamie Jamieson, Richard Kaye, Lisa (Grinberg) McManus, Dick Meyer, Lisa Morgan, Ted Osius, Lyman Page, Ed Redlich, Marsha Rich, Leanne Robbin, Ann

Starer, Dina Towbin, Mark van Roojen, Barbara Walker, Rachel Weil, Judith Weisenfeld, Susan Whitlock, Tiana Wimmer, and Duke Wiser.

Three special childhood friends reached back far into the past and supported me in particularly meaningful ways: Toni Fitzpatrick, Jody Goodman, and Nurit Peri.

Writing is both a privilege and a burden. James Goodman and Jennifer McFeely spent weeks reading and thinking about the manuscript, then held a virtual writer's workshop with Bruce and me during the pandemic—thank you so much, Jim and Jenny. Susan Whitlock, genius editor and dear friend, read the manuscript at the very end and offered her signature insights in a thousand ways. Wendy Strothman, my literary agent and friend, envisioned this book before I did, then stood by me with unwavering confidence. Jonathan Jao, my editor, had a vision too. Jonathan understood this book far better than I did and brought me around with a remarkable combination of patience and brilliance. At HarperCollins, I also thank David Howe for his overabundance of gracious guidance through the book's production and Miranda Ottewell for her copyediting.

My gratitude to family encompasses history, memories, documents, conversations, and above all, love. I thank Jeremy Cole for that long-ago interview in which he asked the right questions with so much kindness. I thank Ofra and Avner Greenberg for sustaining my connection to family in Israel. For always being there, I thank Tal Ben-David, Kevin Brady, and Quinn Brady; Matthew Choi; Holly Richardson; Tim and Sarah Dorsey, and Kate and Jay Petel; Dalen Cole and Julietta Cole; Jack Gescheidt, Andy Gescheidt, and Karen Balacek; Stephen Margolies (especially for family history); Ken Tosti and David O'Keefe; Betty and David Dorsey, Connie Cashman, Jon and Stacy Dorsey, and Ruth and Chris Purcell, and all the children and grandchildren. With immense sorrow I thank the late great Danielle Abrams.

It is difficult to find words to thank those most deeply affected: Stuart Hodes, Linda Hodes, Elizabeth Hodes, and Ehud Ben-David, the last in loving memory. Dad, Mom, Liz, Ehud: I love you.

Two people I have saved for last.

Catherine, you supported me, answered so many questions, and read the manuscript with such care. Back then, you took care of both of us. You were brave and strong and smart. Most of all, you fought for honest emotion, and I am sorry I was unable to do the same. You were my hero then, and you are my hero now.

Bruce, without you I would not have written this book. You joined me in puzzling out the meaning of the hijacking and the meaning of writing about it, and you read every word and every draft so many times. You were with me in Berlin, Geneva, Israel, Amman, and the Jordan desert, and you are by my side and in my heart every single day. I love you so much, and I am so grateful for your love.

To everyone named here, and to you, my readers: Thank you for listening.

NOTES

ABBREVIATIONS: NAMES

CH: Catherine Hodes
EB: Ehud Ben-David
EH: Elizabeth Hodes
LH: Linda Hodes
MH: Martha Hodes
SH: Stuart Hodes

ABBREVIATIONS: SOURCES

CH diary: Catherine Hodes diary, September 1970, transcribed in Sylvia R. Jacobson, "Children's Attitudinal and Behavioral Responses to Skyjack and Hostage Experiences," 1976, typescript draft, folder 9, box 1, SRJ-AJA
FBIS: Foreign Broadcast Information Service
FRUS: Foreign Relations of the United States
ICRC: Archives of the International Committee of the Red Cross, Comité International de la Croix Rouge, Geneva, Switzerland
IDP: International Documents on Palestine, Institute for Palestine Studies, Beirut
MA-UEL: Michael Adams Papers Relating to Middle Eastern Politics, MS 241, Special Collections, University of Exeter Library, Devon, England
NARA: National Archives and Records Administration, Washington, DC, and College Park, MD
Pan Am: Pan American Airways Records, ASM0341, Special Collections, University of Miami Libraries
RNL: Richard Nixon Presidential Library and Museum, Yorba Linda, CA
SRJ-AJA: Sylvia R. Jacobson Papers, MS-681, Jacob Rader Marcus Center, American Jewish Archives, Cincinnati
Swissair: Flugzeugentführung Swissair-Kurs 100/(50)/42/420, Federal Department of Home Affairs, Swiss Federal Archives, Bern
TARPA: TWA Active Retired Pilots' Association
TNA: The National Archives of the United Kingdom, Kew, Richmond, England
TWA: Trans World Airlines Records, box 168, KO453, Manuscript Collection, State Historical Society of Missouri, Columbia
VTNA: Vanderbilt Television News Archive, Nashville, TN

Note: For the sake of privacy, I have omitted details of citations to hostages' lawsuits against the airlines.

WHAT HAPPENED?

---

3 "years and years," thinking and talking, shake: CH written responses to MH questions, August 3, 2015.
7 "everybody": CH and MH with SH, interview by Jeremy Cole and A. J. Sullivan, New York, September 20, 1970, original tape.
7 studiously avoided: Raab, *Terror in Black September*.
7 "how the hijacking": David Raab email, March 3, 2019.
8 "two children": Raab, *Terror in Black September*, 54.
8 original document: Washington to Amman #146692, September 8, 1970, boxes 683–84, RG59, State Department, NARA.
8 "first three days," and following: CH and MH with SH, Cole interview.

1

---

13 "Of course I love you": Saint-Exupéry, *Little Prince*, 40.
13 "FANTASTIC!": MH diary, July 8, 1970.
14 nonsmoking section: CH written responses to MH questions, August 3, 2015; CH conversation, New York, March 27, 2016.

14   bought them: MH diary, March 22, 1969.

14   *Phaedra*: Clive Barnes, "Martha Graham, Love and 'Phaedra' . . . Matt Turney and Linda Hodes Are Starred," *New York Times*, April 10, 1969.

14   "In the evening," "She's leaving": MH diary, April 19, 1969.

14   "Mom left": MH diary, April 21, 1969.

14   "Good luck": "Ani" to CH and MH, September 1970.

14   "Darlings": LH to CH and MH, Tel Aviv [September 24, 1969].

14   "This whole flight": MH diary, September 6, 1970.

15   11:02 a.m.: Statement of Capt. C. D. Woods, 1, TWA; statement of Flight Engineer A. Kiburis, 1, TWA.

15   altitude, Brussels: Woods statement, 1; Kiburis statement, 1; "Combined Statement of Hostesses: B. McCarthy, R. Metzner, V. McVey, L. Jensen," 1, TWA.

15   headsets: Rudolf Swinkels crew report, 1, courtesy of June Haesler; "Combined Statement of Hostesses," 1.

15   stewardesses: "Combined Statement of Hostesses," 1.

15   A man: Statement of hostess J. Haesler, 1, TWA; statement of passenger R. L. Morris, 1, TWA; "Memo Concerning Hijacking Flight 741," 1, TWA.

15   argument: Richard Morse as told to Jeremiah V. Murphy, "From Andover to Amman: 20 Days in Desert—Part 1," *Boston Globe*, October 4, 1970.

15   airsick: Fran Chesler, "The Saga of a Flight: TWA Flight 741, September 6–September 28, 1970," unpublished ms., Fall 1970, part I, 1.

15   gun: CH diary; CH conversation, March 27, 2016.

15   nickel-plated: "Memo Concerning Hijacking," 1.

15   woman's finger: Sylvia R. Jacobson, "Speech Delivered at Temple Israel, Tallahassee, Florida, September 18, 1970," 2, folder 8, box 2, SRJ-AJA.

15   "not the Arabs!," "My pills!": CH responses to MH questions; CH conversation, March 27, 2016.

15   warns my sister: CH telephone interview by Jeffrey D. Simon, March 21, 1992, original tape; CH responses to MH questions.

15   fighting, "Get back!": Swinkels crew report, 1; Mitchell Meltzer as told to Howard Southgate, "Thumbs Up: Twenty-One Days as a Hijack Hostage," unpublished ms.,1970.

15   "Oh, my God!": Michael T. Kaufman, "Hijacked to the Desert: Account by Passengers," *New York Times*, September 17, 1970; Arnold C. Ropeik, "Day-by-Day . . . The Ordeal of the Raabs," *Trenton Sunday Times Advertiser*, September 20, 1970.

15   "Hijack!": Morris statement, 1.

15   "This is a hijack": "Memo Concerning Hijacking," 1.

15   raps out: Kiburis statement, 1.

15   rattled: Woods statement, 1; Kiburis statement, 1; Jim Majer, "Black September, 1970," *TARPA Topics*, November 2009, 11.

16   Monty Python's Flying Circus: "Hijacked Plane (to Luton)" sketch, *Monty Python's Flying Circus*, episode 16, series 2, recorded July 16, 1970.

16   Castro: "Hijack Hijinks," *New York Times*, March 17, 1968.

16   Maybe: Morris statement, 2; Hyman Kenneth Salenger, "Stress, Anxiety and Certain Characteristics of Cohesion: A Study of Relationships and Implications" (PhD diss., Laurence University, 1972), 118, 120; Wendy Schuman, "Sheila Warnock—Hijacked to Jordan," *DDB News*, October 1970.

16   Kids imagine: Howie Hirsch, "My Hijacking Story," unpublished ms., 2004.

16   Two men: John R. Pherson, "Americans Detained by PFLP," September 14, 1970, folder marked "10/1/1970," boxes 683–84, RG59, State Department, NARA; Ropeik, "Day-by-Day."

16   little boy: Tova Lev Kahn conversation, New York, April 2, 2019.

16   Passengers: Morris statement, 2; Jacobson, "Individual and Group Responses," 459, 460.

16   parents, own deaths: Salenger, "Stress," 129–30, 123.

16   "Where": Swinkels crew report, 1.

16   A stewardess: CH and MH with SH, interview by Jeremy Cole and A. J. Sullivan, New York, September 20, 1970, original tape.

16   maps, geography: Morris statement, 2; Swinkels crew report, 2; Meltzer, "Thumbs Up"; Yosef Trachtman as told to Steven Pratt, "Captive in the Desert: Yosef's Own Story," *Chicago Tribune*, September 20, 1970; Jacobson, "Speech Delivered," 3; Schuman, "Sheila Warnock"; Barbara Mensch conversation, New York, February 14, 2019.

16   "Good afternoon": MH diary, September 7, 1970.

17   "*3* acting classes": CH to LH and EB, New York, postmarked January 24, 1970.

17   eight hours: CH and MH with SH, Cole interview.

17   coastline: Morris statement, 2.

17   out of first class: Kiburis statement, 1; "Combined Statement of Hostesses," 1.

17   four or five: Morris statement, 1.

17   The hijacker: Woods statement, 2; Kiburis statement, 1; Swinkels crew report, 2; Morris statement, 1, 2; "Report: Hijacking of Flight 741," 1, TWA.

17   beverage service: Woods statement, 2; Swinkels crew report, 1; Haesler statement, 1; "Combined Statement of Hostesses," 1.

17   drinks, policy: Haesler statement, 1; "Report: Hijacking of Flight 741," 3; James E. Goodman, "June Haesler 'Wasn't Bored,' Plans to Fly Again," *Trenton Sunday Times Advertiser*, September 20, 1970.

18   Headsets, projector: Haesler statement, 1; "Report: Hijacking of Flight 741," 3.

18   landing: Statement of First Officer J. A. Majer, 2, TWA; Morris statement, 2; Majer, "Black September," 11–12.

18   male hijacker: Rodney C. Campbell, "TWA Flight 741—Hijacked September 6, 1970," *TARPA Topics*, November 2007, 57.

18   flares: Franz Zauner conversation, Amman, Jordan, July 8, 2019.

18   smudge pots: Woods statement, 1; Kiburis statement, 1.

18   "greaser": Majer statement, 2.

18   no damage: Carroll D. Woods, "Hijacking Report of TWA Flt. 741 of September 6, 1970," Prairie Village, Kansas, October 16, 1970, TWA.

18   Local time: Woods statement, 1; Majer statement, 2.
18   billows: CH responses to MH questions.
18   barrels, torches: Swinkels crew report, 2; Raab, *Terror in Black September*, 14 (quoting 1970 recollections); Meltzer, "Thumbs Up"; Burmeister, *Sky-Jacked*, 19.
19   absence: Sheila Warnock conversation, New York, September 23, 2019, including reading from journal kept September 6–14, 1970.
19   celebration: Goodman, "June Haesler 'Wasn't Bored'"; Majer, "Black September," 13; Campbell, "TWA Flight 741," 58.
19   ladder: Swinkels crew report, 4; Jacobson, "Individual and Group Responses," 460; CH responses to MH questions.
19   triumphant: Majer, "Black September," 13.
19   People: Majer statement, 2; "Combined Statement of Hostesses," 2; Goodman, "June Haesler 'Wasn't Bored'"; Swinkels crew report, 2.
19   short hair: Trachtman, "Captive in the Desert."
19   "safe and welcome": Sylvia R. Jacobson, untitled notes, folder 10, box 1, SRJ-AJA.
19   sorry too: Abu-Sharif and Mahnaimi, *Best of Enemies*, 83.
19   *We're sorry*: CH and MH with SH, Cole interview.
19   batteries: Swinkels crew report, 3.
19   Armed: "Combined Statement of Hostesses," 2.
19   landing cards, passports: Kiburis statement, 1; "Combined Statement of Hostesses," 2; Haesler statement, 2; Swinkels crew report, 2–3.
20   slogan cards: Folder marked "10/1/1970," boxes 683–84, NARA.
20   lanterns: Jacobson, "Individual and Group Responses," 460.
20   engines: Kiburis statement, 1; Majer, "Black September," 13.
20   dinner: Kaufman, "Hijacked to the Desert."
20   milk and water: "Combined Statement of Hostesses," 2; Morris statement, 5.
20   ambulance, doctor: Haesler statement, 2–3.
20   cabin crew: "Combined Statement of Hostesses," 2; Haesler statement, 2.

2

22   miles of nothing: CH and MH with SH, interview by Jeremy Cole and A. J. Sullivan, New York, September 20, 1970, original tape.
22   "At sunrise," "One sits": Saint-Exupéry, *Little Prince*, 97, 92.
23   Viewed: William Tuohy, "Jets Dominate Site of Desert Standoff," *Washington Post*, September 8, 1970.
23   Up close: "Hijacking," FOH 81220, September 8, 1970, FCO 14/778, TNA; David Zenian, "Plane Hostages Exercise in Desert," *Washington Post*, September 9, 1970; Rudolf Swinkels crew report, 3, courtesy of June Haesler; archival footage in "Hijacked," written and directed by Ilan Ziv, *American Experience*, PBS, 2006; Jacobson, "Individual and Group Responses," 461; CH telephone interview by Jeffrey D. Simon, March 21, 1992, original tape, quoted in Simon, *Terrorist Trap*, 99; CH written responses to MH questions, August 3, 2015.
23   graves: Deposition in lawsuit brought by hostage against Trans World Airlines.
23   representative: Swinkels crew report, 3; Sheila Warnock conversation, New York, September 23, 2019, including reading from journal kept September 6–14, 1970.
23   radio: Mitchell Meltzer as told to Howard Southgate, "Thumbs Up: Twenty-One Days As a Hijack Hostage," unpublished ms., 1970; Sylvia R. Jacobson, "Speech Delivered at Temple Israel, Tallahassee, Florida, September 18, 1970," 12, folder 8, box 2, SRJ-AJA.
23   college student: Sarah (Malka) Bliner telephone conversation, April 12, 2020.
23   select group: "Combined Statement of Hostesses: B. McCarthy, R. Metzner, V. McVey, L. Jensen," 2, TWA; statement of passenger R. L. Morris, 3, TWA.
23   hot meal: "Combined Statement of Hostesses," 2; statement of hostess J. Haesler, 3, TWA.
23   "most frightening": MH diary, September 8, 1970.
24   clipped English, questions: CH, "Motherlode," unpublished ms., 2015, 44.
24   three girls: CH, Simon telephone interview; CH responses to MH questions.
24   nearly a hundred: Swinkels crew report, 5; Raymond O. Miller, "Aircraft Hijackings," September 8, 1970, folder 3, box 330, Subject Files: Hijacking, National Security Council Files, Nixon Presidential Materials Staff, RNL.
24   radio reports, commandos: Michael T. Kaufman, "Hijacked to the Desert: Account by Passengers," *New York Times*, September 17, 1970; deposition in lawsuit against TWA.
25   Gathered: Richard Morse as told to Jeremiah V. Murphy, "From Andover to Amman: 20 Days in Desert—Part 1," *Boston Globe*, October 4, 1970.
25   order copilot: Jim Majer, "Black September, 1970," *TARPA Topics*, November 2009, 13.
25   dot: [Walter Jost] narrative, 49, English translation of Jost, *Rufzeichen*, folder 5, box 2, SRJ-AJA.
25   expert landing: "Report from F/O T. R. Cooper," September, 1970, 6, FCO 14/785, TNA.
25   cheer: Arnold C. Ropeik, "Day-by-Day . . . The Ordeal of the Raabs," *Trenton Sunday Times Advertiser*, September 20, 1970.
25   Armored vehicles: "Report from Cooper," 6.
25   enthusiastic welcome: CH and MH with SH, Cole interview; Raab, *Terror in Black September*, 70 (quoting 1970 recollections); Meltzer, "Thumbs Up"; Jacobson, "Individual and Group Responses," 464.
25   hasten the release, feel bad: Morris statement, 4; "Portrait of a Guerrilla Hijacker: Passenger's Diary Recalls Debates, Suspense," *Los Angeles Times*, September 14, 1970; Yosef Trachtman as told to Steven Pratt, "Captive in the Desert: Yosef's Own Story," *Chicago Tribune*, September 20, 1970; Jacobson, "Individual and Group Responses," 464.
25   visit: CH and MH with SH, Cole interview.
25   shed jackets, ties, and socks: Swinkels crew report, 7.

25   sleeveless shifts: "Hijacks/US/Demands/Airline Industry," *CBS Evening News*, September 9, 1970, #212640, VTNA.

25   sleeves: Deposition in lawsuit against TWA.

25   shoes: June Haesler conversation, New York, October 14, 2019.

25   temperatures plunge: Claude Frascani, "Report on the Mission in Jordan from 6–30 September, 1970," January 11, 1971 (English translation; original document in French dated December 14, 1970), 2, B AG 226 106-003, ICRC.

25   curtains: Jacobson, "Individual and Group Responses," 462.

25   Nighttime's, daytime's: Frascani, "Report on the Mission in Jordan," 3; Swinkels crew report, 3.

26   sandstorms: Ralph S. Sanford, "First Hand Experiences on a Swissair Flight—Which Took a Side Trip to the Jordanian Desert," speech at New York University and Post Graduate Hospital Alumni Association, October 20, 1970, 5, folder 4, box 2, SRJ-AJA; Jacobson, "Speech Delivered," 12; CH responses to MH questions.

26   suffocating: Fran Chesler, "The Saga of a Flight: TWA Flight 741, September 6–September 28, 1970," unpublished ms., Fall 1970, part II, 9.

26   airline food: "Combined Statement of Hostesses," 2.

26   boxed lunches: CH and MH with SH, Cole interview; Raab, *Terror in Black September*, 51 (quoting 1970 recollections).

26   food: MH diary, September 8, 1970; CH and MH with SH, Cole interview; Meltzer, "Thumbs Up"; "'Not Knowing if Anyone Knew Was the Worst Part,'" *Tallahassee Democrat*, September 20, 1970; Swinkels crew report, 4, 5, 6, 8; Morris statement, 3; Kaufman, "Hijacked to the Desert."

26   "hard as a rock": MH diary, September 8, 1970.

26   "Mainly": MH diary, September 10, 1970.

26   "bread & water": MH diary, September 10, 1970.

26   two trucks: "Combined Statement of Hostesses," 6; Zenian, "Hostages Exercise in Desert."

26   half cup: Morse, "Andover to Amman."

26   single bottle: Jacobson, "Speech Delivered," 13; CH, Simon telephone interview.

26   diapers: CH and MH with SH, Cole interview.

26   sanitary napkins: Jacobson, "Individual and Group Responses," 461; Susie (Hirsch) Rosenrauch, "Resilience and Coping in the Face of Trauma: A Retrospective Account Thirty Years after a Skyjacking," unpublished ms., 1999, 17.

26   containers, flush: Swinkels crew report, 4.

26   "This is how": CH telephone interview, quoted in Simon, *Terrorist Trap*, 99–100.

27   "Our children": Sylvia R. Jacobson, "Background" (notes), 10, folder 10, box 1, SRJ-AJA; CH responses to MH questions.

27   one big family: CH and MH with SH, Cole interview.

27   "We have many," and following: MH diary, September 8, 1970.

27   met Mark, "alternative": Mimi (Beeber) Nichter video conversation, September 27, 2020.

27   seek guidance: Hyman Kenneth Salenger, "Stress, Anxiety and Certain Characteristics of Cohesion: A Study of Relationships and Implications" (PhD dissertation, Laurence University, 1972), 121.

27   hubbub: CH and MH with SH, Cole interview.

28   nice: CH and MH with SH.

28   head commando: Jim Majer email, January 14, 2020; James E. Goodman, "June Haesler 'Wasn't Bored,' Plans to Fly Again," *Trenton Sunday Times Advertiser*, September 20, 1970.

28   "Romantic!": CH responses to MH questions; CH conversation, New York, February 6, 2017.

28   "Don't cry": Jacobson, "Children's Attitudinal and Behavioral Responses," 11.

28   grown-up friends, "your government": CH and MH with SH, Cole interview.

28   forgotten: Salenger, "Stress," 121.

28   does not care: Deposition in lawsuit against TWA.

28   angry: Frascani, "Report on the Mission in Jordan," 3.

28   "to Washington": CH and MH with SH, Cole interview.

28   "Israeli soldier!," "Oh the way," "walking around": CH and MH with SH, Cole interview.

29   screwed over, applaud: CH, Simon telephone interview.

29   stars: CH email, September 25, 2019.

29   kerosene lamps: Swinkels crew report, 4.

29   children stretch, kneel: Meltzer, "Thumbs Up"; "Welcome Home, Connie!" *South Amboy Citizen*, September 17, 1970; Tikva (Raab) Yudkowitz conversation, Teaneck, NJ, March 18, 2019; Rob Hirsch, "How I Survived a Plane Hijacking 50 Years Ago," *Newsday*, September 5, 2020.

29   "give up": MH diary, September 8, 1970.

29   "not pronounced," and following: MH to Jody Goodman, Tel Aviv, postmarked August 23, 1970.

30   a thousand: CH and MH with SH, Cole interview.

30   twenty-five children: Amman to Washington #4553, September 10, 1970, boxes 683–84, RG59, State Department, NARA.

30   seven babies: Statement of First Officer J. A. Majer, 1, TWA; statement of Flight Engineer A. Kiburis, 1, TWA.

30   unaccompanied: "Combined Statement of Hostesses," 1.

30   Parents, teenage girls, back of the plane: CH and MH with SH, Cole interview; Jacobson, "Individual and Group Responses," 465; Kaufman, "Hijacked to the Desert."

30   machine-gun emplacements: Morse, "Andover to Amman"; Meltzer, "Thumbs Up."

30   fuselage: Michael Adams, "Visit to Jordan, September 1970," 10, MA-UEL; Jacobson, "Individual and Group Responses," 463.

31   soda: CH and MH with SH, Cole interview; Meltzer, "Thumbs Up."

31   hose down: Kiburis statement, 3; Haesler statement, 6.

31   Grown-ups stroll: Haesler statement, 6.

31   Children: Jesse W. Lewis Jr., "'They Awoke Him . . . and Took Him,'" *Washington Post*, September 13, 1970.

31   puddle, sneak through: Gliksman, *Nouri*, 415; CH and MH with SH, Cole interview.

31   jogs: Ropeik, "Day-by-Day."

31   shade: "Combined Statement of Hostesses," 3; Haesler statement, 6.

31 lakes, sailboats: Haesler quoted in Rodney C. Campbell, "TWA Flight 741—Hijacked September 6, 1970," *TARPA Topics*, November 2007, 63; Patricia Parker Ridenhour, "Hijacked to Jordan," *Alumni News*, University of North Carolina–Greensboro, Winter 1971, 11.

31 pointing out: [Jost] narrative, 34.

31 piggyback rides: Meltzer, "Thumbs Up."

31 Frank Allen: "Hijacked Bridegroom Missed the Wedding," *Los Angeles Times*, October 1, 1970.

31 "Can't wait": Fran Chesler conversation, Petah Tikvah, Israel, July 5, 2019.

32 life rafts: Kiburis statement, 3; Swinkels crew report, 6; "Combined Statement of Hostesses," 4; Majer, "Black September," 14; Kiburis quoted in Campbell, "TWA Flight 741," 62; Jim Majer email, February 13, 2020.

32 candy and gum, balls, joins in: Meltzer, "Thumbs Up"; Kiburis statement, 3.

32 jump ropes: CH and MH with SH, Cole interview; Kiburis statement, 3; Swinkels crew report, 6; "Combined Statement of Hostesses," 4; Meltzer, "Thumbs Up"; CH responses to MH questions.

3

33 crying: MH diary, September 11, 1970.

33 ten more, David, Mark: MH diary, September 11, 1970; "Three Stewardesses Describe Week aboard Hijacked Plane," *Danville (VA) Bee*, September 14, 1970; Raab, *Terror in Black September*, 89–90 (quoting 1970 recollections); Jim Majer, "Black September, 1970," *TARPA Topics*, November 2009, 14–15.

33 devastated: Mimi (Beeber) Nichter video conversation, September 27, 2020.

33 powerful sandstorm, and following: Mitchell Meltzer as told to Howard Southgate, "Thumbs Up: Twenty-One Days As a Hijack Hostage," unpublished ms., 1970; "Combined Statement of Hostesses: B. McCarthy, R. Metzner, V. McVey, L. Jensen," 4, TWA; Rudolf Swinkels crew report, 7, courtesy of June Haesler.

33 made of sand: McVey quoted in Rodney C. Campbell, "TWA Flight 741—Hijacked September 6, 1970," *TARPA Topics*, November 2007, 63.

33 270 of us: Reuters, Amman, September 11, 1970, PREM 15/201, TNA.

33 vans arriving: "Portrait of a Guerrilla Hijacker: Passenger's Diary Recalls Debates, Suspense," *Los Angeles Times*, September 14, 1970.

33 on edge, brusque: Statement of passenger R. L. Morris, 5, TWA; "Hijack Victims Safe Now, but Left Loved Ones," *Daily News*, September 14, 1970; Sylvia R. Jacobson, "Thursday, September 10th" (notes), 1, folder 10, box 1, SRJ-AJA.

33 commandos instruct: Swinkels crew report, 7.

33 perfume: Arnold C. Ropeik, "Day-by-Day . . . The Ordeal of the Raabs," *Trenton Sunday Times Advertiser*, September 20, 1970.

33 talent show: McCarthy quoted in Campbell, "TWA Flight 741," 63.

34 Sabbath-eve: Fran Chesler, "The Saga of a Flight: TWA Flight 741, September 6–September 28, 1970," unpublished ms., Fall 1970, part II, 9.

34 wonder: Deposition in lawsuit brought by hostage against Trans World Airlines.

34 distribute: CH and MH with SH, interview by Jeremy Cole and A. J. Sullivan, New York, September 20, 1970, original tape; "Combined Statement of Hostesses," 4.

34 propaganda: CH telephone interview by Jeffrey D. Simon, March 21, 1992, original tape; CH and MH with SH, Cole interview.

34 "so many": CH and MH with SH, Cole interview.

34 "Tonight": MH diary, September 11, 1970.

34 candles: Jacobson, "Individual and Group Responses," 467; Raab, *Terror in Black September*, 99; Gliksman, *Nouri*, 429–30.

34 Dinner: "Combined Statement of Hostesses," 4.

34 candy: CH and MH with SH, Cole interview.

34 "guten Shabbos": Chesler, "Saga of a Flight," part I, 4.

35 "Poor man!": MH diary, September 11, 1970.

35 about a hundred: CH and MH with SH, Cole interview.

35 Some feel: Patricia Parker Ridenhour, "Hijacked to Jordan," *Alumni News*, University of North Carolina–Greensboro, Winter 1971, 12; June Haesler conversation, New York, October 14, 2019.

35 Others worry: Sylvia R. Jacobson, "Speech Delivered at Temple Israel, Tallahassee, Florida, September 18, 1970," 16, folder 8, box 2, SRJ-AJA.

35 Catherine and I sit: Chesler, "Saga of a Flight," part II, 5.

35 We talk: CH email, September 25, 2019; Chesler, "Saga of a Flight," part II, 5.

35 "When we cry," "wall space": Chesler, "Saga of a Flight," part II, 5, 10.

35 middle seat: Fran Chesler conversation, Petah Tikvah, Israel, July 5, 2019.

35 pink pill: Chesler.

35 climbs over: Chesler, "Saga of a Flight," part II, 9.

36 amicable, addresses, hug: Michael T. Kaufman, "Hijacked to the Desert: Account by Passengers," *New York Times*, September 17, 1970; "Hijacked Hostages," #2002, Moving Images Relating to Intelligence and International Relations, RG263, CIA, NARA.

36 sign, answer questions: Jacobson, "Speech Delivered," 17.

36 grandparents: CH email, February 22, 2015.

36 apologizes: "Three Stewardesses Describe Week."

36 lack of exultation: "Hijacked Hostages," #2002.

36 first van, driver: CH and MH with SH, Cole interview.

36 passenger seat: Alamy stock photo, #E0YM2C, alamy.com.

36 dragonflies: CH, "Motherlode," unpublished ms., 2015, 48.

36 a figure, afraid: CH written responses to MH questions, August 3, 2015.

36 crying: CH, "Motherlode," 48.

36 unsanitary, hotel or prison: CH and MH with SH, Cole interview; CH, Simon telephone interview.

36   torture: CH and MH with SH, Cole interview.

36   separate us: CH, Simon telephone interview.

37   dusty sand: "Hijacked Sep 6th Hostages Released Sep 11, 1970," YouTube, uploaded by Jessica Lamb, May 29, 2015, no longer available, accessed November 9, 2018.

37   crouch: CH, Simon telephone interview.

37   convoy: Michael Adams, "Visit to Jordan, September 1970," 10, MA-UEL.

37   Catherine wonders: CH and MH with SH, Cole interview.

37   smack: CH, Simon telephone interview.

37   prisoner of war: CH and MH with SH, Cole interview.

37   seen pictures: "U.S. Prisoners in North Vietnam," *Life*, October 20, 1967, 24–25.

37   first to arrive, army truck, woman sings: "Palestinian Hijacks/Releases," *NBC Evening News*, September 13, 1970, #453129, VTNA; archival footage in "Hijacked," written and directed by Ilan Ziv, *American Experience*, PBS, 2006; "Hijacked Hostages," #2002; Snow and Phillips, *Leila's Hijack War*, 60.

37   flags: CH and MH with SH, Cole interview; CH conversation, New York, September 16, 2019.

37   beautiful: CH and MH with SH, Cole interview.

37   camera lenses: MH diary, September 12, 1970.

37   "This morning": MH diary.

38   pandemonium: "Report from F/O T. R. Cooper," September 1970, 14, FCO 14/785, TNA; Murray Sayle, "Confusion as British Reach Hotel," *Sunday Times* (London), September 13, 1970.

38   threaten, hold babies: "Freed Hostages Tell of Chaos in Amman, Terror in Desert," *Jerusalem Post*, September 14, 1970; Jesse W. Lewis Jr., "'They Awoke Him . . . and Took Him,'" *Washington Post*, September 13, 1970; Sayle, "Confusion as British Reach Hotel."

38   young children: "Hijacked Hostages," #2002.

38   "At first," and following: Eric Pace, "Released Hostages Tell of Their Ordeal in Desert," *New York Times*, September 13, 1970; "Quotation of the Day, *New York Times*, September 13, 1970.

38   "got scared," be quiet: Pace, "Released Hostages."

38   "got inside": MH diary, September 12, 1970.

38   food, terrace: "Hijacked Hostages," #2002; CH, Simon telephone interview.

39   relieved and numb: CH telephone interview.

39   "nutritious meal!": MH diary, September 12, 1970.

39   leave the Intercontinental: MH diary, September 12, 1970.

39   Five beds: Nader Shalhoub conversation, Amman, Jordan, July 8, 2019.

39   balcony: CH, Simon telephone interview; CH responses to MH questions; CH email, April 9, 2019.

39   preoccupied: Susie (Hirsch) Rosenrauch and Howie Hirsch conversation, Ra'anana, Israel, July 7, 2019.

39   "really nice," cross out: MH diary, September 12, 1970.

39   telephone rings, driver informs: MH diary, September 13, 1970; CH diary.

39   "AIRPLANE": MH diary, September 13, 1970.

40   bougainvillea: CH responses to MH questions; CH email, April 9, 2019.

40   operators, will remember: CH email, July 15, 2016.

40   she had to go: LH conversation, New York, 2015.

40   too late: LH conversations, New York, June 24 and July 7, 2008, and July 19, 2015.

40   letter to God, "only thing": MH diary, September 13, 970.

40   dresses: "Palestinian Hijacks/Hostages/Israel/US," *NBC Evening News*, September 14, 1970, #453135, VTNA.

40   complimentary treats: CH and MH with SH, Cole interview; Haesler conversation; CH responses to MH questions.

40   "Hi, Jack!," "Open up!," latched, "very careful": CH and MH with SH, Cole interview; Ropeik, "Day-by-Day."

40   movie: CH and MH with SH, Cole interview.

41   "wheels": MH diary, September 14, 1970.

41   press conference: "Hijacked Sep 6th Hostages."

41   passageway: Carl Foster, "Walkway to Gate Structure" in "Trans World Airlines Flight Center," Landmarks Preservation Commission, Designation List 259, LP-1916, July 19, 1994.

41   waving: CH responses to MH questions.

41   "Oh, Dad!": SH conversation, New York, May 6, 2017; SH email, June 5, 2017; Hodes, *Onstage*, 250.

41   "no crying, no tears": EH telephone conversation, August 5, 2015.

41   "Nothing about him": Saint-Exupéry, *Little Prince*, 8.

42   hum: MH telephone interview by Jeffrey D. Simon, April 15, 1992, original tape.

42   "millions of things": MH to Jody Goodman, Tel Aviv, postmarked August 23, 1970.

42   "Hodes (child)": "Passengers on TWA Jet," *New York Times*, September 8, 1970.

42   "quiet things down": CH, Simon telephone interview.

4

45   read reports: "Jordan Army and Terrorists Pull Back from Amman," *Jerusalem Post*, September 6, 1970.

45   *Thank God*, and following: LH conversations, New York, June 24 and July 7, 2008; LH email, July 16, 2016.

46   Suddenly, and following: LH conversation, New York, July 19, 2015.

47   "already dead": LH conversation.

47   Dance Festival: New York Dance Festival program, September 5, 6, 1970, New York Shakespeare Festival Records, *T-Mss 1993-028, Billy Rose Theatre Division, New York Public Library for the Performing Arts.

47   skies: "Weather Reports and Forecast," *New York Times*, September 6, 1970.

47   "hijack desk": Rodney C. Campbell, "TWA Flight 741—Hijacked September 6, 1970," *TARPA Topics*, November 2007, 54; Frank Parisi, "'Became Very Close,'" *TWA Today*, September 21, 1970.

48   "on occasion": Parisi, "'Became Very Close.'"

48   Davis: Christopher Lydon, "Nixon Names Gen. Davis to Head Hijacking Fight," *New York Times*, September 22, 1970; Richard Goldstein, "General Benjamin O. Davis Jr. Dies at 89," *New York Times*, July 6, 2002.

48 Bighinatti: Adam Bernstein, "WWII Veteran, Red Cross Relief Official Enso Bighinatti," *Washington Post*, June 23, 2004.

48 more information: SH email, April 15, 2017; LH conversation, New York, January 9, 2018.

48 travel to Jordan, and following: SH conversation, New York, July 17, 2018.

49 father decided, and following: EH to CH and MH, New York, ca. September 9, 1970; SH, "Part Real—Part Dream," unpublished ms., ca. 2011, 267; SH, "Listen Up and Fly Right: Flying, Dancing, & the Meaning of Life," unpublished ms., 2015, 115–16; SH conversation, July 17, 2018; SH emails, August 20, 2008, and July 4, 2016; Hodes, *Onstage*, 249.

49 Clay Taliaferro: Jennifer Brewer, "The Protegé, the Professor," *Dance Teacher* 25 (2003): 50–53.

49 "On Sunday": MH email to Clay Taliaferro, April 19, 2019.

49 That afternoon, and following: Clay Taliaferro email, April 20, 2019.

49 "I'd love to," "You let us": SH email, August 20, 2008; Hodes, *Onstage*, 249–50; SH, "Part Real—Part Dream," 267; SH, "Listen Up," 116.

50 misfortune: LH conversation, June 24, 2008.

50 "I think": Tiana Wimmer email, April 29, 2019.

51 "eraser," polite guest: LH, "Notes from the Last Century," unpublished ms., part II (2000), 4, part I (1999), 20.

51 "Finitch," "Ignoramuses": LH, part I, 34.

51 crying, "Do you know": LH, part I, 48, 50.

51 *If she were*: LH, part II, 2.

51 dance class: LH, part II, 56.

51 "Deep gratitude," "With deep affection": Inscriptions in Leroy Leatherman and Martha Swope, *Martha Graham: Portrait of the Lady as an Artist* (New York: Alfred A. Knopf, 1966), and Martha Graham, *The Notebooks of Martha Graham* (New York: Harcourt Brace Jovanovich, 1973), MH personal copies.

51 "most important": LH interview by John Gruen, New York, April 14, 1976, Jerome Robbins Dance Division Oral History Project, New York Public Library for the Performing Arts, 39.

52 "Sure": Alfred Gescheidt childhood memories, ca. 1992, edited by Ray Madrigal, unpublished ms., 2014, 33.

52 accepted: Alfred Gescheidt, "An Interview with Stuart Hodes," New York, December 16, 20, 1996, January 17, 1997, 73; SH email, January 30, 2009.

52 "adding machine," "dared him": Gescheidt, "Interview with Stuart Hodes," 46, 28.

52 "half nerd": Christine Jowers, "A Person You Should Meet—Stuart Hodes," The Dance Enthusiast, December 10, 2007, www.dance-enthusiast.com/features/day-in-the-life/view/A-Person-You-Should-Meet-Stuart-Hodes-2007 -12-10.

52 "eighteen": SH interview by John Gruen, New York, April 27, May 4, 1976, Jerome Robbins Dance Division Oral History Project, New York Public Library for the Performing Arts, 3.

52 he returned: SH, Gruen interview; Gescheidt, "Interview with Stuart Hodes"; Hodes, *Onstage*, 1–20.

53 "All my love": Martha Graham to LH and SH, New York [March 12, 1953].

53 magnificent: Richard Buckle, "Martha Graham," *Observer* (London), March 7, 14, 1954, reprinted in Arnold L. Haskell, ed., *The Ballet Annual, 1955: A Record and Year Book of the Ballet* (London: Adam and Charles Black, 1954), 96.

53 "Wish I could": SH to LH, "Tuesday 17th," n.d.

53 "beside myself": LH to SH, n.d.

53 "can't do enough": LH to Albert and Lily Margolies, London, "Sunday," postmarked March 8, 1954.

53 "a riot": LH to "Dear family," "Sat.," n.d.

53 "terrific bang": LH to Albert and Lily Margolies, Zurich, June 1 [1954].

54 "sparkling city," *not done*: LH, "Notes," part III (ca. 2000–2001), 18, 19.

54 "miss you": LH to SH, "Thurs.," n.d.

54 "good night": LH to SH, "Mon. night," n.d.

54 "All that I": SH to LH, Boston, April 20, n.d.

54 "seedy": LH, "Notes," part III, 22.

54 "honor": SH, "Listen Up," 93.

54 "dangerous name": Hodes, *Onstage*, 234.

55 "very grateful," and following: SH to Martha Graham, draft, New York, October 4 [1958].

55 she wondered: LH, "Notes," part III, 9.

55 Yet my mother: "The Plight of the Young Mother," *Ladies' Home Journal*, February 1956, 61–63, 107–8, 110–13.

55 "runaway wife": Jhan and June Robbins, "The Mother Who Ran Away," *McCall's*, July 1956, 105.

55 magazine feature: Jhan and June Robbins, "Why Young Mothers Feel Trapped," *Redbook*, September 1960, reprinted in *Why Young Mothers Feel Trapped*, ed. Robert Stein (New York: Pocket Books, 1966).

55 "Go and look": Saint-Exupéry, *Little Prince*, 86.

56 "I think," and following: LH, "Notes," part III, 40.

57 "I love you": EH conversation, New York, 2017.

57 "shattering dullness": Howard Taubman, "The Theater: 'Sophie,'" *New York Times*, April 16, 1963.

57 "elaborate dud": "Shows on Broadway," *Variety*, April 17, 1963, 64.

57 "Truly Elizabeth": SH to Elizabeth Wullen, St. Louis, July 7, 1965.

57 "Among the teachers": Giora Manor, *Ehud Ben-David, Israeli Dancer, 1939–1977* (Tel Aviv: Israel Dance Society, 1978), 7.

57 to teach, "destroyed": Program, Batsheva Dance Company, ca. 1970.

57 Landing, and following: LH, "Notes," part III, 41–45.

58 *a million miles*, "visceral": LH, part III, 44, 46.

58 lead male dancer: Dora Sowden, "Ehud Ben David: A Home-Grown Star," *Dance Magazine*, May 1975, 67–69; "In Memoriam: Ehud Ben-David: Our Finest Male Dancer," *Jerusalem Post*, March 29, 1977.

58 "finest": Clive Barnes, "Dance: Batsheva Troupe Stages a Robbins Classic," *New York Times*, December 16, 1970.

58 "cutting": LH, "Notes," part III, 46.

58 "School": MH to LH, New York [December 1964].

59 "an offer," and following: SH to Mary Gallagher, ca. 1965.

59 "live with you": Hodes, *Onstage*, 243.

59   "disputes," alimony, custody: "Agreement, Linda Hodes with Stuart Hodes," Sydney D. Bierman, Attorney at Law, New York, July 1965.

59   "cleaned up": LH oral history interview by Victoria Phillips, April 11, 2017, 5, courtesy of Phillips.

5

60   "world-class": Alfred Gescheidt childhood memories, ca. 1992, edited by Ray Madrigal, unpublished ms., 2014, 23.

61   "Jewish extraction": Manor, "Batsheva," 110.

61   "miss you," "Not much more": CH to SH and EH, Tel Aviv, summer 1967.

62   "*so free!*": CH to SH and EH, Tel Aviv, June 24, 1969.

62   "longest": CH El Al Certificate, June 15, 1966.

64   "Don't cringe": LH to SH, Tel Aviv, May 21 [1965].

64   horse-drawn carriages: CH conversation, Brooklyn, March 17, 2017.

64   Ehud's parents: LH conversation, New York, May 1, 2017.

64   rarely talked: LH conversations, New York, March 15, 2017, and January 9, 2018.

65   "so happy": MH to SH, Tel Aviv [1965].

65   "things aren't": SH to LH, New York, September 9, 1965.

65   "eloquent": Clive Barnes, "Dance: 'Clytemnestra': Martha Graham Troupe Offers Drama of Greek Myths and Tragedies," *New York Times*, November 6, 1965.

65   "remarkable," "brilliant": Walter Terry, "Martha Graham—The Consummate Artists Still," *New York Herald Tribune*, November 6, 1965.

65   "wonderful triumph": Walter Terry, "Martha Graham Makes More Dance History," *New York Herald Tribune*, November 22, 1965.

65   closing night: Clive Barnes, "Martha Graham's Adieu," in "Dance: Washington's Stage Shortage," *New York Times*, November 22, 1965.

65   divorce: LH and SH divorce decree, Second Civil Court of District of Bravos, Chihuahua, Mexico, October 28, 1965 (translated Spanish to English, April 15, 1968).

65   "miss them": LH to SH, "Friday," Tel Aviv, ca. Fall 1965.

65   "fooling myself": SH to Elizabeth Wullen, St. Louis, May 29, 1965.

66   "get the hell": EH conversation, New York, 2017.

66   "howling": EH conversation.

66   "on account": CH to SH and EH, Tel Aviv, June 24, 1969.

67   shells: CH to SH and LH, MH to SH and LH, Tel Aviv, August 10, 1968.

67   "glorious": CH and MH to SH and LH, Tel Aviv, August 3, 1969.

67   married: LH and EB marriage license, Register Office, Kensington District, entry 52, July 10, 1968; LH conversation, May 1, 2017.

67   "beautiful place": CH to SH and EH, Tel Aviv [1969].

68   "always thinking": Saint-Exupéry, *Little Prince*, 24.

68   "so *much*": CH to LH, EB, Lily and Bert Margolies, New York, postmarked May 31, 1970.

69   "Dearest Darling": LH to CH and MH, Tel Aviv, "Saturday" [late 1969].

69   "What news!": CH to LH, EB, Lily and Bert Margolies, New York, December 4, 1969.

69   "smart girl": CH telephone conversation, October 10, 2022.

69   "Congratulations!": MH to LH, EB, Lily and Bert Margolies, New York [December 1969].

69   favorite: Miriam E. Mason, *The Middle Sister* (New York: Macmillan, 1947).

69   "legs tingling": MH diary, July 22, 1970.

69   "soap opera": MH to Nurit Weinreb [summer 1970].

69   "I was right": Nurit Weinreb to MH [summer 1970].

70   "It was great": MH diary, June 25, 1970.

70   "welcomed me": MH diary, August 2, 1970.

71   our last day: MH diary, September 5, 1970; photographs of Netanya beach, Israel.

6

72   "spectacular": "Mass Hijacking," *Jerusalem Post*, September 7, 1970.

72   sources: LH conversations, New York, March 15, 2017, and July 13, 2018; LH email, July 15, 2016.

73   "no new information: LH conversations, New York.

73   "hazardous": "100 'Weak' Passengers Freed," *Jerusalem Post*, September 8, 1970.

73   "deteriorating": "Growing Concern in Jerusalem," *Jerusalem Post*, September 8, 1970.

73   scoffing, "evacuation": "International Blackmail," *Jerusalem Post*, September 8, 1970.

73   "grueling": "Barter Talks in Amman," *Jerusalem Post*, September 9, 1970.

73   "half-way mark": David Zenian, "Hijack Hostages Stroll in Desert as Deadline Nears," *Jerusalem Post*, September 9, 1970.

73   "probable cost," "possibility," "helpless": "Papers Urge Strong Action on Hijacks," *Jerusalem Post*, September 10, 1970.

73   "blur": LH conversation, New York, June 24, 2008; LH email, July 15, 2016.

73   "Tell me": Saint-Exupéry, *Little Prince*, 103.

73   "We heard": LH in family conversation, New York, June 28, 2015.

73   "highly emotional": LH conversation, New York, July 19, 2015.

73   "very tense": Dora Sowden, "Concert Pitch as Batsheva Ballet Prepares for American Tour," *Jerusalem Post Magazine*, September 25, 1970.

73   no recollection: LH conversation, July 19, 2015.

73   "didn't know": LH oral history interview by Victoria Phillips, April 11, 2017, 12, courtesy of Phillips.

74 "Good evening," and following: "Palestinian Hijacks," *CBS Evening News*, September 6, 1970, #212586, VTNA.

74 radios: SH email, August 20, 2008.

74 Suspended animation: SH email.

74 "Imaginative": Don McDonagh, "Dance: Choreographers Have Their Day at Park," *New York Times*, September 7, 1970.

74 headline: "4 Jets Hijacked; One, a 747, Is Blown Up," *New York Times*, September 7, 1970.

74 map, "did not know": "4 Jets Hijacked."

74 another headline: "US Aides Express Helpless Feeling," *New York Times*, September 7, 1970.

74 "Unless": Linda Charlton, "2 Craft in Jordan," *New York Times*, September 8, 1970.

74 photograph: Eric Pace, "Life on Jets in Desert is Harsh," *New York Times*, September 9, 1970.

74 "uncertainty": Linda Charlton, "4 Nations Agree on Joint Effort to Free Hostages," *New York Times*, September 9, 1970.

74 "held hostage": "Ordeal in the Desert," *New York Times*, September 9, 1970.

75 all the stations: EH email, March 30, 2017.

75 enjoying: CH and MH with SH, interview by Jeremy Cole and A. J. Sullivan, New York, September 20, 1970, original tape.

75 "They threatened": "Palestinian Hijack/Demands," *CBS Evening News*, September 7, 1970, #212600, VTNA.

75 "Arabs now threaten": "Palestinian Hijacks/UAR/Jordan/Demands," *NBC Evening News*, September 7, 1970, #453492, VTNA.

75 "commandos": "Palestinian Hijacks/Demands," *ABC Evening News*, September 7, 1970, #12306, VTNA.

75 newspaper headlines: *Daily Mirror* (London); *Sun* (London), in "Palestinian Hijacks/Hostages/US/Britain," *ABC Evening News*, September 8, 1970, #12322, VTNA.

75 "Four explosions": "Palestinian Hijacks/Demands," *ABC Evening News*.

75 newsstand: Harry A. Dunphy, "Hijackers Set 'Final' Deadline: The Guerrillas Explain Why," *New York Post*, September 10, 1970.

75 "Oh, no!": Saint-Exupéry, *Little Prince*, 28.

75 temporarily: "Hijacks/US/Demands/Airline Industry," *CBS Evening News*, September 9, 1970, #212640; "Hijacks/United Nations/Israel/PFLP/Fighting," *ABC Evening News*, September 9, 1970, #12341; and "Hostages/Prisoners/Deadline," *NBC Evening News*, September 9, 1970, #453527, all VTNA.

75 "conflicting": "Palestinian Hijack," *CBS Evening News*, September 9, 1970, #212638, VTNA.

75 "probably": Alec Efty, "'Women, Children are Terrified . . .'" *Boston Globe*, September 9, 1970.

75 "Arabs said": "Palestinian Hijacks/BOAC/Threats," *NBC Evening News*, September 9, 1970, #453523, VTNA.

76 "Very serious": Amman to Geneva, 11:15Z, September 11, 1970, B AG 226 106-001, ICRC.

76 telegrams: "Messages pour les otages transmis par la Croix-Rouge américaine," September 11, 12, 1970, B AG 226 106-004, ICRC.

76 instructed: J. P. Maunoir, "Concerne: Jordanie—avion détournés," September 11, 1970, B AG 226 106-001, ICRC.

76 Unfurling, and following: "Messages pour les otages transmis par la Croix-Rouge américaine," September 11, 12, 1970.

77 "Keep your hearts": Sylvia R. Jacobson, "Observations on Follow-Up on Attitudes and Behaviors," 1–2, folder 10, box 1, SRJ-AJA.

77 "Okay, enough": SH email, July 7, 2016.

77 "Parents request": "Messages pour les otages transmis par la Croix-Rouge américaine," September 11, 1970.

77 "Dear Catherine & Martha," and following: EH to CH and MH, New York, ca. September 9, 1970.

78 phone rang, didn't want: SH conversation, New York, May 6, 2017.

78 anxiety: Toni Fitzpatrick email August 18, 2015.

79 impossible: Bea Fitzpatrick conversation, New York, November 5, 2015.

79 same day: Jody Goodman written responses to MH questions, August 2015; Jody Goodman conversation, New York, December 22, 2015; Evelyn Goodman, *My Forgiveness Journey: Changing My Destiny As I Traveled Worlds—A Memoir* (Lemont, Pa.: Eifrig Publishing, 2020), 92; SH conversation, May 6, 2017.

79 my name, "missed you": Goodman responses to MH questions; Jody Goodman telephone conversation, August 9, 2018.

79 my name: Marsha Rich telephone conversation, April 21, 2018.

80 starving: Lisa Grinberg telephone conversation, May 30, 2019.

80 confiscate: Tiana Wimmer email, April 29, 2019.

80 intrigued: Loren Chodosh Harkin to MH, "My recollections about Martha, at the start of 7th Grade," May 19, 2019.

80 "big deal": Rich telephone conversation.

80 "shocked": Helen Finegold Friedman emails, June 11, 22, 23, 24, 2020.

80 "hapless": cover photograph caption, *Jerusalem Post Week-End Magazine*, September 11, 1970.

81 "Tonight": "Palestinian Hijacks," *NBC Evening News*, September 11, 1970, #453109, VTNA.

81 "placed dynamite": "Palestinian Hijacks/Demands/US," *ABC Evening News*, September 11, 1970, #11966, VTNA.

81 "Arab guerrillas": "Palestinian Hijacks/Organization Change/Hostages," *CBS Evening News*, September 12, 1970, #212090, VTNA.

81 front-page: "Terrorists Blow Up Three Airliners," *Jerusalem Post*, September 13, 1970.

81 wondering, *now what happens*: LH conversation, July 19, 2015.

82 headlines: John L. Hess, "Arabs Blow Up 3 Jets in Desert After Taking Off Passengers," *New York Times*, September 13, 1970.

82 "thank God": Quotation of the Day, *New York Times*, September 13, 1970.

82 image: "Palestinian Hijacks/Releases," *NBC Evening News*, September 13, 1970, #453129, VTNA.

82 "six days": "Palestinian Hijacks/Releases."

82 "ever think," "certainly must": LH conversation, July 19, 2015.

82 "ever think," "No": SH conversation, May 6, 2017; SH, "Listen Up and Fly Right: Flying, Dancing, & the Meaning of Life," unpublished ms., 2015, 116.

83 "another planet": EH telephone conversation August 5, 2015.

7

87   timetable: "'Round the World/Trans Pacific Services, Effective September 1, 1970," *TWA System Timetable*, Bonus Adventure Tours, Trans World Airlines, 30, box 231A, KO453, TWA.

87   cockpit crew: Jim Majer, "Black September, 1970," *TARPA Topics*, November 2009, 11.

88   "prison," "how cute!": June Haesler conversation, New York, October 14, 2019.

88   our crew: Haesler conversation; "Combined Statement of Hostesses: B. McCarthy, R. Metzner, V. McVey, L. Jensen," 1, TWA.

88   new passengers, surprised: Telex Eingang #16012, September 17, 1970, folder 187/2/54, Swissair.

89   security guard: Statement of passenger R. L. Morris, 1, TWA.

89   metal detector: Haesler conversation; Abigail Klein Leichman, "'I Didn't Know if My Wife and Daughter were Alive,'" *Jerusalem Post Magazine*, September 4, 2020, 11.

89   Reboarding: Howie Hirsch, "My Hijacking Story," unpublished ms., 2004; Susie (Hirsch) Rosenrauch and Howie Hirsch conversation, Ra'anana, Israel, July 7, 2019.

89   "went up": Haesler conversation; James E. Goodman, "June Haesler 'Wasn't Bored,' Plans to Fly Again," *Trenton Sunday Times Advertiser*, September 20, 1970.

89   outfit, suit: Rudolf Swinkels crew report, 1, courtesy of June Haesler.

89   recognized: Rosenrauch and Hirsch conversation.

89   "keep joking," liquor cart: Haesler conversation; Goodman, "June Haesler 'Wasn't Bored'"; "Combined Statement of Hostesses," 1.

89   "stumbling": Haesler conversation.

90   "revolver": Statement of Capt. C. D. Woods, 1, TWA.

90   "a man": Statement of First Officer J. A. Majer, 1, TWA.

90   revolver, new captain: Statement of Flight Engineer A. Kiburis, 1, TWA.

90   "not try": Kiburis statement, 1.

90   crew assured: Majer statement, 1.

90   no question: "Palestinian Hijacks/BOAC/Threats," *NBC Evening News*, September 9, 1970, #453523, VTNA.

90   suicide mission: "Report: Hijacking of Flight 741," 7, TWA.

90   oxygen masks: Woods statement, 1; Majer statement, 1; Kiburis statement, 1.

90   jump seat: Kiburis statement, 1; "Memo Concerning Hijacking Flight 741," 1, TWA.

90   ordered the plane: Woods statement, 1; "Memo Concerning Hijacking," 2.

90   "Gaza Strip," and following: Woods statement, 1; Majer statement, 1; Kiburis statement, 1.

91   Jeppesen: Majer, "Black September," 11.

91   rudimentary: "Report: Hijacking of Flight 741," 2; "Memo Concerning Hijacking," 2.

91   segments: Woods statement, 1; Majer statement, 1; "Report: Hijacking of Flight 741," 2; Majer, "Black September," 11.

91   "Down with Israel": Majer statement, 1.

91   "middle finger," exact position: Woods statement, 2.

91   "junior geographers," "Gee": Fran Chesler, "The Saga of a Flight: TWA Flight 741, September 6–September 28, 1970," unpublished ms., Fall 1970, part I, 2, 1.

91   exciting, *Here I am*: Raab, *Terror in Black September*, 11 (quoting 1970 recollections).

91   asked himself: Franz Zauner conversation, Amman, Jordan, July 8, 2019.

92   "I expected," and following: Sacks, "Fallibility of Memory," quotations 102, 103, 110.

93   "grenade and pistol," and following: Majer statement, 1.

93   "Hello": Jim Majer email, January 8, 2020.

93   "desperate need": Jim Majer email, January 10, 2020.

94   "new pilot": CH written responses to MH questions, August 3, 2015.

94   "new captain": Woods statement, 1.

94   "new pilot": Swinkels crew report, 1.

94   "Female hijacker": "Combined Statement of Hostesses," 1.

94   "new captain": Statement of hostess J. Haesler, 1, TWA; Morris statement, 1.

94   repeated: Peter T. Chew, "Hostage Tells It As It Was," *National Observer*, October 5, 1970; "SM Stewardess Recounts 7-Day Hijack Ordeal," *Redwood City Tribune*, September 14, 1970; "Mrs. Falldine Describes Hijacking of Airplane," *Hattiesburg (MS) American*, September 30, 1970; Wendy Schuman, "Sheila Warnock—Hijacked to Jordan," *DDB News*, October 1970.

94   wrote it down: Chesler, "Saga of a Flight," part I, 1; Mitchell Meltzer as told to Howard Southgate, "Thumbs Up: Twenty-One Days as a Hijack Hostage," unpublished ms., 1970; Patricia Parker Ridenhour, "Hijacked to Jordan," *Alumni News*, University of North Carolina–Greensboro, Winter 1971, 10; Burmeister, *Sky-Jacked*, 16; Raab, *Terror in Black September*, 11 (quoting 1970 recollections); Sylvia R. Jacobson, "Speech Delivered at Temple Israel, Tallahassee, Florida, September 18, 1970," 3, folder 8, box 2, SRJ-AJA.

94   in lawsuits: Depositions in lawsuits brought by hostages against Trans World Airlines.

94   "We're going": Tikva (Raab) Yudkowitz conversation, Teaneck, NJ, March 18, 2019.

94   "We're taking you": Barbara Mensch conversation, New York, February 14, 2019.

94   "We will take you": Rob Hirsch, "How I Survived a Plane Hijacking 50 Years Ago," *Newsday*, September 5, 2020.

94   "Ladies and Gentlemen": Leila Khaled as told to Godfrey Jansen, "'This Is Your New Captain Speaking,'" *Life*, September 18, 1970, 34–35.

95   *Who are*: Susie (Hirsch) Rosenrauch, "Resilience and Coping in the Face of Trauma: A Retrospective Account Thirty Years after a Skyjacking," unpublished ms., 1999, 15–16.

95   "quite terrified": Raab, *Terror in Black September*, 13 (quoting 1970 recollections).

95   warning: Majer statement, 1.

95   "prepare": Majer, "Black September," 12.

95   "landing surface," "Unaccompanied": Jim Majer email, February 5, 2020.

95   Dusk: Woods statement, 1; Kiburis statement, 1.

96   "drag the field": Woods statement, 1; Majer statement, 2.

96 "fuel dump": Majer statement, 1.
96 "unsafe": Woods statement, 1; Kiburis statement, 1.
96 trick them: Kiburis statement, 1; "Report: Hijacking of Flight 741," 2.
96 *What else*: Woods quoted in Rodney C. Campbell, "TWA Flight 741—Hijacked September 6, 1970," *TARPA Topics*, November 2007, 58.
96 "her hands": Kiburis quoted in Campbell, "TWA Flight 741," 58.
96 "lower 41": Majer statement, 2; Kiburis statement, 1.
96 *get this plane*: McCarthy quoted in Campbell, "TWA Flight 741," 57.
96 smoother: Swinkels crew report, 2.
96 "painted": Morris quoted in Campbell, "TWA Flight 741," 54.
96 ordered: Majer statement, 2.
96 Dawson's Field: "Airstrip of the Guerrillas Was Once R. A. F. Field," *New York Times*, September 10, 1970.
96 variously estimate: "Arabs Hijack 3 Jetliners, Blow One Up, Try for 4th," *Washington Post*, September 7, 1970 (15 miles, 20 miles); Jerusalem International Service, September 8, 1970, folder 2, box 330, Subject Files: Hijacking, National Security Council Files, Nixon Presidential Materials Staff, RNL; J. F. S. Phillips, "The Dawson Field Hijackings," Diplomatic Report No. 567/70, Jordan, December 22, 1970, 1, FCO 17/1374, TNA (25 miles); "Situation Report as of 0600 Hours EST," September 7, 1970, Near Eastern Affairs Working Group, folder 2, box 330, RNL (30 miles); "Palestinian Hijacks/Demands/Rights/USSR," *NBC Evening News*, September 10, 1970, #453086, VTNA; "Angry Men, Desperate Days," *Newsweek*, September 21, 1970, 24 (40 miles); "Palestinian Hijacks/Hostages/US/Britain," *ABC Evening News*, September 8, 1970, #12322, VTNA (60 miles); David Zenian, "Plane Hostages Exercise in Desert," *Washington Post*, September 9, 1970 (nearly 80 miles).
97 "a little lonely": Saint-Exupéry, *Little Prince*, 72.
97 geologist, "We were afraid": "Hijacked," written and directed by Ilan Ziv, *American Experience*, PBS, 2006.
97 "dangerous place": "Airstrip of the Guerrillas."
97 well served: Wilson quoted in Campbell, "TWA Flight 741," 64.
97 "in Jordan," and following: Abu-Sharif and Mahnaimi, *Best of Enemies*, 83.
97 "None of you": "Hijacked Sep 6th Hostages Released Sep 11, 1970," YouTube, uploaded by Jessica Lamb, May 29, 2015, no longer available, accessed November 9, 2018.
97 Revolution Airport: "Airstrip of the Guerrillas."
97 "very worried," "dual passport": Morris statement, 2.
97 air-sickness bag: Gliksman, *Nouri*, 418.
97 blockage: Abu-Sharif and Mahnaimi, *Best of Enemies*, 86; MH telephone interview by Jeffrey D. Simon, April 15, 1992, original tape.
98 Arabic: Sarah (Malka) Bliner telephone conversation, April 12, 2020.
98 "not to worry": Raab, *Terror in Black September*, 25 (quoting 1970 recollections).
98 "fear for our lives," He watched: Kiburis statement, 2.
98 "Forget": Kiburis quoted in Campbell, "TWA Flight 741," 59.
98 "Don't worry," and following: Abu-Sharif and Mahnaimi, *Best of Enemies*, 85.

8

99   air traffic control: "F741/05 September P8715 Hijacked to Jordan," Fiumicino Airport, Rome, October 27, 1970, TWA; "Flight Dispatch Shift Summaries, Rome, shifts 1–3," September 6, 1970, TWA.
100 radar code: Jörg Andrees Elten, "'This is a Hijacking!'" *Reader's Digest*, July 1971 (translated and condensed from "Die Entführung," *Stern*, serialized December 1970–February 1971), 221.
100 Wiser, public relations: "The Frustrating Case of TWA Flight 741," *Business Week*, October 10, 1970, 34, 36.
100 In Amman: Rodney C. Campbell, "TWA Flight 741—Hijacked September 6, 1970," *TARPA Topics*, November 2007, 56.
100 "TWA Flight 741": Paris to Washington #12039, September 6, 1970, boxes 683–84, RG59, State Department, NARA.
100 "possibly planning": Washington to Amman #146334, September 6, 1970, boxes 683–84, NARA.
100 "to continue": "Convention on Offences and Certain other Acts Committed on Board Aircraft Signed at Tokyo, on 14 September 1963, In force 4 December 1969," United Nations, Treaty Series, vol. 704, No. 10106, chapter 4, article 11, 230.
100 Situation Room: Dave Clark, White House Situation Room, "Aircraft Hijackings," September 6, 1970, folder 2, box 330, Subject Files: Hijacking, National Security Council Files, Nixon Presidential Materials Staff, RNL.
100 "most advanced": Kissinger, *White House Years*, 315, 601–2.
100 composure: Michael Donley, Cornelius O'Leary, and John Montgomery, "Inside the White House Situation Room: A National Nerve Center," *Studies in Intelligence* (1997), Central Intelligence Agency Library online.
100 Yugoslavia: Clark, "Aircraft Hijackings.
100 Gaza Strip: E. O. Martin, "Aircraft Hijackings," September 6, 1970, folder 2, box 330, RNL.
100 off course: Chart of hijackings, 1900 EDT [September 6, 1970], folder 2, box 330, RNL.
100 Syria, Lebanon: Clark, "Aircraft Hijackings."
100 Jordan: Beirut to Washington #7404, September 6, 1970, boxes 683–84, NARA.
101 Popular Front, coordinated, coincidental: Clark, "Aircraft Hijackings."
101 El Al plane: E. O. Martin, "Aircraft Hijackings."
101 "I write": MH to Alice Kessler-Harris email, April 1, 2017.
101 "blown away!": Alice Kessler-Harris email, April 2, 2017.
101 flying home, a woman: Alice Kessler-Harris conversation, New York, May 11, 2017.
101 stood up, startled: "Palestinian Hijacks," *CBS Evening News*, September 6, 1970, #212586, VTNA.
101 trade, jumped up: Arlene Van Breems, "Hadassah President Recounts Hijack Plane Experiences," *Los Angeles Times*, September 24, 1970.

102   "lovely coast": "The Making of a Hijacker," *Sunday Times* (London), September 13, 1970.

102   Arguello: Metropolitan Police telegram, September 12, 1970, FCO 14/780, TNA; "Slain Airliner Hijacker a U.S. Citizen," *New York Times*, September 15, 1970.

102   passports: "Rapport de Henssler, inspecteur principal," December 9, 1970, folder 187/3/130, Swissair; Khaled, *My People Shall Live*, 191.

102   grenades, gun, cockpit: Khaled interview in MacDonald, *Shoot the Women First*, 116–17; "Hijacked," written and directed by Ilan Ziv, *American Experience*, PBS, 2006; "Hijack," produced and directed by Dominic Sutherland, *Timewatch*, BBC/Open University, 2007.

102   negative-G mode: "Hijacked," PBS, 2006; "Hijack," BBC, 2007.

102   plane dropped: "4 Jets Hijacked; One, a 747, Is Blown Up," *New York Times*, September 7, 1970; Kessler-Harris conversation.

102   lost her balance: "The Guerilla's Story," UK Confidential, BBC News, World Edition, January 1, 2001; Peter Hopkirk, "Miss Khaled Speaks Well of Police in Britain," *London Times*, October 6, 1970.

102   "amazed me": "Leila Khaled Mystified by Failure of Bombs," *London Times*, October 5, 1970.

102   tackle: Khaled, *My People Shall Live*, 195–96; "Palestinian Hijacks," *NBC Evening News*, September 6, 1970, #453478," VTNA.

102   Arguello fired: "Hijack," BBC, 2007.

102   El Al guard: "The Two El Al Security Guards: Police Action," September 11, 1970, FCO 14/786, TNA.

102   Amid the blasts: Elten, "'This Is a Hijacking!,'" 218–19.

102   "You mean": Kessler-Harris conversation.

103   press descended: Kessler-Harris.

103   wounded steward: "Two El Al Security Guards," 1.

103   pronounced dead: Khaled, *My People Shall Live*, 197.

103   police custody: Clive Borrell, "Yard Keeps Girl Hidden," *London Times*, September 8, 1970.

103   delighted: Reuters, Amman, September 7, 1970, folder 2, box 330, RNL ("girl commando"); "Palestinian Hijack/Demands," *CBS Evening News*, September 7, 1970, #212600, VTNA ("girl-guerrilla"); "100 'Weak' Passengers Freed," *Jerusalem Post*, September 8, 1970 ("girl terrorist"); Henry Maule, "British Defer Freeing Gal Terrorist," *Daily News*, September 10, 1970 ("gal terrorist").

103   "black-eyed": "Hijacking is 'Normal' to Her," *Boston Globe*, September 8, 1970.

103   "beauty": "Israel-Hijacking," September 10, 1970, news report, MS Jerusalem Bureau: Series I, AP18.10, item 12, folder 162, 18 of pdf, box 7, Associated Press Corporate Archives online.

103   "active": "Hijacks/Demands/US/Europe," *NBC Evening News*, September 7, 1970, #453494, VTNA.

103   Stanley and Miriam Hirsch: *Instant Recall*, television newsmagazine, King World Productions, September 12, 1990; Howie Hirsch, "My Hijacking Story," unpublished ms., 2004; Susie (Hirsch) Rosenrauch and Howie Hirsch conversation, Ra'anana, Israel, July 7, 2019.

103   same plane: "Aircraft Hijackings: Situation Report as of 07:30 EDT," CIA, September 7, 1970, folder 3, box 330, RNL; Tel. No. 391, September 6, 1970, FCO 14/778, TNA; Kessler-Harris conversation.

103   jubilant: "Palestinian Hijacks/Demands," *ABC Evening News*, September 7, 1970, #12306, VTNA.

103   three children: *Instant Recall*, September 12, 1990.

104   "hijack-proof": Kessler-Harris conversation.

104   "Lightning": SH conversation, New York, May 6, 2017.

104   "fragmentary": Dave Clark, White House Situation Room, "Aircraft Hijackings Information as of Noon EDT," September 6, 1970, folder 2, box 330, RNL; Haig to Nixon, "Middle East Developments," September 6, 1970, folder marked "September 1–7, 1970, 1 of 2," box 971, Alexander M. Haig Chronological Files, National Security Council Files, Nixon Presidential Materials Staff, RNL.

104   two men: Cairo to Washington #2095, September 12, 1970, boxes 683–84, NARA; Regional Security Officer, Rome, to Director Security, "Hijacking—Amsterdam/Cairo-5, September 1970—Flt. 93," September 11, 1970; George J. Politi to James O. Leet, "Hijacking Report Regional Security Officer, Rome," September 17, 1970; and Report No. PA.111, transmitted on I.T.N.—"News at Ten, Pan Am Hijacking," September 7, 1970, all Cairo Hijacking Materials, Pan Am.

104   paid cash: Note to J. O. L., "Booking Details Alleged Hijackers—Flight 093/06 Sep.," September 8, 1970, Cairo Hijacking Materials, Pan Am.

104   pat-down: John Barbour and Jules Loh, "Pilot of 747 Frisked Hijackers Before Takeoff," *Boston Globe*, September 13, 1970; "How to End Skyjacking: Interview with a Top Airline Executive," *U.S. News and World Report*, October 12, 1970, 48.

104   "What's going to happen," and following: "Hijacked," PBS, 2006; Peter Gelzinis, "1970 Hijacking Survivor Has Watched Terror Grow," *Boston Herald*, September 30, 2001.

104   too heavy: Dave Clark, White House Situation Room, "Aircraft Hijackings Information as of 1800 EDT," September 6, 1970, folder 2, box 330, RNL.

104   Eight minutes: "Hi-Jacked Boeing," September 8, 1970, FCO 14/778, TNA.

105   4:30: Raymond H. Anderson, "Hijackers in Cairo Say They Blew Up 747 in Retaliation for US Support of Israel," *New York Times*, September 8, 1970.

105   chutes, first explosion: "Hi-Jacked Boeing."

105   Reporters: Raymond Wilkinson, "'We All Ran Like Hell,'" *Guardian*, September 8, 1970.

105   "Where was": "Palestinian Hijack/Demands," *CBS Evening News*.

105   "seized": Haig to Nixon, "Middle East Developments."

105   hijackers: Radio-Schweiz AG, Flugsicherungsdienst Zürich, Auszug aus der Tonbandaufnahme (air traffic control, excerpt from tape recording), September 6, 1970, September 10, 1970, folder 187/2/62, Swissair.

105   "really moving!": "Article: Hijacked! The People Involved and Affected," *American Experience*, PBS, www.pbs.org/wgbh/americanexperience/features/people-involved-and-affected/.

105   "Haifa": Statement of Flight Engineer A. Kiburis, 1, TWA; Radio-Schweiz AG recording, 187/2/62, Swissair.

105   "destination": Radio-Schweiz AG recording, Swissair; Brigitte Moser testimony, September 23, 1970; Ernst Renggli testimony, September 28 and November 1, 1970; Peder Sollie testimony, September 17, 1970; Attila Janosha testimony, December 9, 1970; and Hans Sticher testimony, November 27, 1970, all Einvernahmeprotokolle der Besatzungsmitglieder und Geiseln, Kantonspolizei Zurich, Offiziersposten Flughafen (Interrogation

Records of Crew and Hostages, Cantonal Police Zurich, Airport), Beilagen B (Exhibit B), folder 189/2/3, Swissair.

105 Dim lights, obstacle: Ernst Vollenweider testimony, October 23, 1970, Einvernahmeprotokolle der Besatzungsmitglieder und Geislen, Kantonspolizei Zurich, Offiziersposten Flughafen (Interrogation Records of Crew and Hostages, Cantonal Police Zurich, Airport), Beilagen B (Exhibit B), folder 189/2/3, Swissair.

105 landed hard: Vollenweider testimony; Ralph S. Sanford, "First Hand Experiences on a Swissair Flight—Which Took a Side Trip to the Jordanian Desert," speech at New York University and Post Graduate Hospital Alumni Association, October 20, 1970, 3–4, folder 4, box 2, SRJ-AJA.

105 Armed commandos: Sollie testimony.

105 landing cards, passports: Moser testimony; Sanford, "First Hand Experiences," 4.

105 apologized: Sollie testimony.

105 "Israeli Air Force": Tel Aviv to Washington #4869, September 6, 1970, boxes 683–84, NARA.

105 H–5: "Military Deployment: Periodic Occupational and Environmental Monitoring Summary: Prince Hassan Air Base (H5) and Vicinity, Jordan," Department of Defense, 2018.

105 "Iraqi and guerillas": "Flight Dispatch Shift Summaries," TWA.

105 "still confused": Beirut to Washington #7406, September 6, 1970, boxes 683–84, NARA.

106 Foreign correspondents: Gerald Seymour, "The Middle East, September–October 1970," *Contemporary Review* 217 (December 1, 1970): 303–4.

106 "Yes": Seymour, "Middle East," 304.

106 "military dirt strip": Clark, "Aircraft Hijackings Information as of 1800 EDT."

106 "technical facilities": Amman to Washington #4351, September 6, 1970, boxes 683–84, NARA.

106 "doors": Amman to Washington #4532, September 6, 1970, folder 2, box 330, RNL.

106 send troops: Rome to Washington #4883, September 6, 1970, boxes 683–84, NARA.

106 "blow up": E. O. Martin, "Aircraft Hijackings."

106 army's tanks: Edward R. F. Sheehan, "In the Flaming Streets of Amman," *New York Times*, September 27, 1970.

106 surround: Kissinger to Nixon, "Status of Mid-East Hijacking" [September 7, 1970], folder marked "September 1–7, 1970, 1 of 2," box 971, RNL.

106 "powerless": "Richard E. Undeland, Public Affairs Officer, USIS, Amman," interview by Charles Stuart Kennedy, July 1994, in *Jordan Country Reader* (Arlington, VA: Association for Diplomatic Studies and Training), no pagination, www.adst.org/Readers/Jordan.pdf.

106 Beyond: Jim Majer, "Black September, 1970," *TARPA Topics*, November 2009, 15.

106 assemble a list: Raymond O. Miller, "Aircraft Hijackings," September 7, 1970, folder marked "September 1–7, 1970, 1 of 2," box 971, RNL.

106 no easy task: Bonn to Washington #10205, September 7, 1970, "List of Passengers Boarding Hijacked TWA 741 at Frankfurt Airport," folder 2, box 330, RNL.

106 "No info": Frankfurt to Washington #3264, September 7, 1970, boxes 683–84, NARA.

107 "respected": Washington to Amman #146337, September 6, 1970, boxes 683–84, NARA.

107 Cain: Chart of hijackings, folder 2, box 330, RNL; Michael T. Kaufman, "Hijacked to the Desert: Account by Passengers," *New York Times*, September 17, 1970.

107 Hirsch children: Washington to Amman #146405, September 7, 1970, boxes 683–84, NARA.

107 compiling: Amman to Geneva, 17:02Z, September 8, 1970, B AG 226 106-001, and "Bulletin d'information concernant avions détournés en Jordanie," Département des Opérations, September 8, 1970, B AG 226 106-004, both ICRC.

107 "Hodes, Miss," "Hodes (child)": "Passengers on TWA Jet," *New York Times*, September 8, 1970.

107 "According to reports": "Passengers on TWA Jet."

107 "Request you send": Washington to Amman #146368, September 7, 1970, boxes 683–84, NARA.

107 no one: "David E. Zweifel, Consular Officer, Amman," interview by Thomas J. Dunnigan, September 3, 1996, *Jordan Country Reader*, no pagination.

107 "You will see": Saint-Exupéry, *Little Prince*, 99.

107 "remarkable": Phillips, *Skyjack*, 140.

107 "frisson," "big story": John de St. Jorre, *Darling Baby Mine: A Son's Extraordinary Search for His Mother* (London: Quartet, 2016), 110.

9

108 150 passengers and ten crew: Statement of Flight Engineer A. Kiburis, 1, TWA; "Combined Statement of Hostesses: B. McCarthy, R. Metzner, V. McVey, L. Jensen," 1, TWA; "121 Hijack Victims Return; Seek Release of All," *TWA Today*, September 21, 1970; "Original number of hostages held by PFLP" [September 1970], FCO 14/784, TNA.

108 Our Boeing 707: Kiburis statement, 1; TWA 707-331 US domestic and international seating chart, August 27, 2018, Museum Photo of the Week, TWA Museum Guides blog, twamuseumguides.blogspot.com/2017/02/weekly-museum-photo-each-monday-well.html.

109 "Dear Claire," and following: MH diary, September 7, 1970.

110 "serious," "quiet," "shy": MH report cards, Hunter College Elementary School, New York, 1966, 1969.

110 "We leaned": Jacobson, "Children's Attitudinal and Behavioral Responses," 10.

111 article: Jacobson, "Individual and Group Responses," 459–69.

111 I learn: Sylvia R. Jacobson Papers finding aid, SRJ-AJA.

112 "kept diaries," "copied exactly": Jacobson, "Children's Attitudinal and Behavioral Responses," 4, 8.

112 "Dora's Diary," "copied": Jacobson, 5.

112 "A man ran," and following: CH diary.

113 Right away: CH and MH with SH, interview by Jeremy Cole and A. J. Sullivan, New York, September 20, 1970, original tape.

113 alert and afraid: CH written responses to MH questions, August 3, 2015.

113 chosen passengers: Arnold C. Ropeik, "Day-by-Day . . . The Ordeal of the Raabs," *Trenton Sunday Times Advertiser*,

September 20, 1970; Rodney C. Campbell, "TWA Flight 741—Hijacked September 6, 1970," *TARPA Topics*, November 2007, 59.

114   photograph: Linda Charlton, "Arabs Release Some Passengers, but Hold Many on Jets in Desert," *New York Times*, September 12, 1970.

114   "You seem," and following: "Hijacked Hostages," #3025, Moving Images Relating to Intelligence and International Relations, RG263, CIA, NARA; "Palestinian Hijacks/Demands/US," *CBS Evening News*, September 8, 1970, #212618, VTNA.

115   "pretty cool": William Tuohy, "In Middle of Desert Stood 2 Giant Jetliners," *Los Angeles Times*, September 8, 1970.

115   lined up: Deposition in lawsuit brought by hostage against Trans World Airlines.

115   "asked": "Drama on the Desert: The Week of the Hostages," *Time*, September 21, 1970, 25.

115   Catholic: Sheila Warnock conversation, New York, September 23, 2019, including reading from journal kept September 6–14, 1970.

115   commando asked: Fran Chesler, "The Saga of a Flight: TWA Flight 741, September 6–September 28, 1970," unpublished ms., Fall 1970, part II, 6; Fran Chesler conversation, Petah Tikvah, Israel, July 5, 2019.

116   six-year-old: Michael T. Kaufman, "Hijacked to the Desert: Account by Passengers," *New York Times*, September 17, 1970; "Welcome Home, Connie!" *South Amboy Citizen*, September 17, 1970.

116   "helped everybody": CH and MH with SH, Cole interview.

116   "poster child": Chesler conversation.

116   "Honey," and following: Chesler.

116   "he hoped": Sylvia R. Jacobson, "Speech Delivered at Temple Israel, Tallahassee, Florida, September 18, 1970," addenda, 2, folder 8, box 2, SRJ-AJA.

116   Outside the vans: Deposition in lawsuit against TWA.

116   "And now": Saint-Exupéry, *Little Prince*, 47.

116   assisting women: Jacobson, "Speech Delivered," addenda, 2.

116   "surrounded": Tikva (Raab) Yudkowitz conversation, Teaneck, NJ, March 18, 2019.

116   "crying": Deposition in lawsuit against TWA.

116   chill, *My God*: Warnock conversation.

117   "non-Jewish": Yosef Trachtman as told to Steven Pratt, "Captive in the Desert: Yosef's Own Story," *Chicago Tribune*, September 20, 1970.

117   "those of us": Susie (Hirsch) Rosenrauch, "Resilience and Coping in the Face of Trauma: A Retrospective Account Thirty Years after a Skyjacking," unpublished ms., 1999, 16.

117   name, determined: Warnock conversation.

117   "That moment": Raab, *Terror in Black September*, 39 (quoting 1970 recollections). On the release of Swissair Jews, see also United Press International, September 8, 1970, folder 2, box 330, Subject Files: Hijacking, National Security Council Files, Nixon Presidential Materials Staff, RNL; Gliksman, *Nouri*, 410n.

117   pediatrician: "Paid Notice: Deaths, Meldola, Rosemarie," *New York Times*, November 7, 1998.

118   *Why us*: Chesler, "Saga of a Flight," part II, 1.

118   "selection": Chesler conversation.

118   "all my life": "Hijacked," written and directed by Ilan Ziv, *American Experience*, PBS, 2006.

118   "mass murder": Eva Grubler video conversation, December 13, 2020.

118   "20 were taken," "hotel space": Statement of hostess J. Haesler, 4, TWA.

118   "stumbling back": Mitchell Meltzer as told to Howard Southgate, "Thumbs Up: Twenty-One Days as a Hijack Hostage," unpublished ms., 1970.

118   "started boarding": Richard Morse as told to Jeremiah V. Murphy, "From Andover to Amman: 20 Days in Desert—Part 1," *Boston Globe*, October 4, 1970.

118   "forgot to say": CH diary.

119   "most frightening": MH diary, September 8, 1970.

10

120   "All the non-Jews": CH diary.

120   Inside: Sheila Warnock conversation, New York, September 23, 2019, including reading from journal kept September 6–14, 1970.

121   "began reading": "Angry Men, Desperate Days," *Newsweek*, September 21, 1970, 24.

121   wept: William Tuohy, "'Innocents' Sweat, Fear Mistreatment," *Louisville (KY) Courier-Journal*, September 8, 1970.

121   first time: Jörg Andrees Elten, "'This is a Hijacking!'" *Reader's Digest*, July 1971 (translated and condensed from "Die Entführung," *Stern*, serialized December 1970–February 1971), 232.

121   "because": "Hijacked," written and directed by Ilan Ziv, *American Experience*, PBS, 2006.

121   "released," "crying": CH telephone interview by Jeffrey D. Simon, March 21, 1992, original tape.

121   agrees: Nancy Porter email, February 26, 2019.

122   not "hostile": "Newspaper Interview Statements by Secretary-General Habbash of the PFLP on Theoretical, Political and Military Questions Related to the Palestinian Movement," mid-May 1970 (*Al-Ahrar*, May 22, 1970), in *IDP 1970*, ed. Walid Khadduri (Beirut: Institute for Palestine Studies, 1973), 802.

122   "We always": "Statement by the Popular Front for the Liberation of Palestine to the People of Switzerland," Amman, February 18, 1969, in *IDP 1969*, ed. Walid Khadduri (Beirut: Institute for Palestine Studies, 1972), 597.

122   "nothing against": CH and MH with SH, interview by Jeremy Cole and A. J. Sullivan, New York, September 20, 1970, original tape.

122   "liked the Jews": Eric Pace, "Freed U.S. Hostages Tell of Desert Ordeal," *Tucson Star Citizen*, September 13, 1970.

122   "live together": "Portrait of a Guerrilla Hijacker: Passenger's Diary Recalls Debates, Suspense," *Los Angeles Times*, September 14, 1970.

122   "knew I was": Friedman, *Beirut to Jerusalem*, 57.

122   "took Palestine": Khaled interview in MacDonald, *Shoot the Women First*, 98.

122   "At first": Khaled, *My People Shall Live*, 67, 54.

123   "against Zionists": Khaled interview in MacDonald, *Shoot the Women*, 119.

123   "Israeli is Jewish": Edwin H. Baker Pratt Jr., "Arab Attitudes," letter to the editor, *New York Times*, September 20, 1970.

123   *Jews* and *the Jews*: Susan Abulhawa conversation, Philadelphia, July 16, 2021.

123   "no enmity": Sylvia R. Jacobson, "Speech Delivered at Temple Israel, Tallahassee, Florida, September 18, 1970," addenda, 2, folder 8, box 2, SRJ-AJA.

123   "Words": Saint-Exupéry, *Little Prince*, 84.

123   "would naturally": Abu-Sharif, *Arafat and the Dream of Palestine*, 27.

123   far fewer: "Jordan: Situation Report as of 06:00 EDT," CIA, September 9, 1970, folder 3, box 330, Subject Files: Hijacking, National Security Council Files, Nixon Presidential Materials Staff, RNL; "Re le Vice-Président Frey-mond," handwritten, September 14, 1970, B AG 226 106-001, and "Opération Jordanie, Septembre–Décembre 1970: Journal des évènements," Département des Opérations, Comité International de la Croix-Rouge, Geneva, March 1971, 31–32, B AG 226 106-003, both ICRC.

123   "*except*": Michael Adams, "Visit to Jordan, September 1970," 5, MA, UEL.

123   "Israel is America": Schmidt, *Armageddon in the Middle East*, 164.

124   dual citizenship: Rogers to Nixon, "Dual U.S.-Israeli Nationals," September 9, 1970, and "Hal" to "Al" [Saunders to Haig], September [9?], 1970, both folder 3, box 330, RNL.

124   "to separate": "All the Hostages Must Be Quickly Freed," *Washington Post*, September 11, 1970.

124   "the Jews": "Press Comment on Hijacking Issue Continues," *Daily Report*, FBIS, No. 176, September 10, 1970, H2.

124   "particularly": "Mideast Crisis and American Credibility," *Congressional Record*, September 10, 1970, 31180.

124   "terrorists'": "Hijacking," *Congressional Record*, September 10, 1970, 31326.

124   "somehow focused": "Hijacked," PBS, 2006.

124   "their fight": Roy Innis, "The Jews Must Not Stand Alone," *Manhattan Tribune*, September 19, 1970.

124   "My wife": "Palestinian Hijacks/US/USSR/Families," *CBS Evening News*, September 10, 1970, #212045, VTNA.

125   "Prayers": "Mideast Crisis and American Credibility," *Congressional Record*.

125   "reminiscent": "Hijacking," *Congressional Record*.

125   "Auschwitz": Chalmers M. Roberts, "Israelis Balking at Swap Plan," *Washington Post*, September 11, 1970.

125   "air field": News report, September 6–12, 1970, MS Jerusalem Bureau: Series I, AP18.10, folder 162, 11 of pdf, box 7, Associated Press Corporate Archives online.

125   "Why are you," "They are not": "Palestinian Hijacks/BOAC/Threats," *NBC Evening News*, September 9, 1970, #453523, and "Hijacks/United Nations/Israel/PFLP/Fighting," *ABC Evening News*, September 9, 1970, #12341, both VTNA.

125   "Jews on Jets": William Tuohy, "Jews on Jets Held for 'Interrogation' on Dual Citizenship," *Los Angeles Times*, September 9, 1970.

125   free to leave: Amman to Washington #4430, September 8, 1970, "Onward Travel of Released Hostages," folder 2, box 330, RNL.

125   concurred: "Situation Report as of 1800 Hours EST," September 7, 1970, Near Eastern Affairs Working Group, folder 2, box 330, RNL; Linda Charlton, "2 Craft in Jordan," *New York Times*, September 8, 1970.

125   reversed: Kissinger to Nixon, "Hijacking Status," September 9, 1970, folder marked "Middle East and Hijacking, 9/9/70," box H–077, Meetings Files, 1968–74, Washington Special Actions Group Meetings, National Security Council Institutional "H" Files, Nixon Presidential Materials Staff, RNL.

125   passports: Linda Charlton, "4 Nations Agree on Joint Effort to Free Hostages," *New York Times*, September 9, 1970; Eric Pace, "Life for Hostages On Jets Eases a Bit," *New York Times*, September 10, 1970; Wendy Schuman, "Sheila Warnock—Hijacked to Jordan," *DDB News*, October 1970.

125   airport: Amman to Geneva, 5:01Z, September 10, 1970, B AG 226 106-001, ICRC.

125   Anarchy: E. O. Martin, "Aircraft Hijackings," September 7, 1970, folder 3, box 330, RNL.

125   fedayeen: Amman to Washington #4486, September 9, 1970, "Hijacking," folder 2, box 330, RNL.

125   Tanks: Footage in "Jordan/Fighting/Hijackers' Demands," *CBS Evening News* September 10, 1970, #212047, VTNA.

125   Gunfire: "Situation Report as of 1600 hours EDT," Near Eastern Affairs Working Group, September 9, 1970; Haig to Kissinger, "Middle East Situation," September 9, 1970; and Kissinger to Nixon, "Morning Report on Hijacking Situation," September 10, 1970, all folder 2, box 330, RNL.

125   offices, schools, shopkeepers: Amman to Washington #4486, September 9, 1970, boxes 683–84, RG59, State Department, NARA.

125   megaphones: Amman to Washington #4486, September 9, 1970, "Hijacking," folder 2, box 330, RNL.

126   rubble: "Jordan: Situation Report as of 06:00 EDT."

126   "battlefield": "Guerrillas Surrounded by Troops," *Guardian*, September 10, 1970.

126   "no front line": "Palestinian Hijacks/Demands/Rights/USSR," *NBC Evening News*, September 10, 1970, #453086, VTNA.

126   king claimed: "Speech by King Hussein of Jordan on Relations with the Palestinian Resistance," Amman, September 6, 1970, in Khadduri, *IDP 1970*, 903–4.

126   state within a state: "Developments up to September 1970: Relations Between the Regime and the Fidā'iyyūn," *Middle East Record*, vol. 5, *1969–70*, ed. Daniel Dishon (Jerusalem: Israel Universities Press, 1977), 792–96.

126   Red Crescent: "The Individual Organizations: Al-Fath," Dishon, *Middle East Record*, 5:253; Bern to Washington #2248, September 14, 1970, folder 2, box 330, RNL.

126   Intercontinental Hotel: Kissinger to Nixon, "Mid-Day Report on the Hijacking Situation," September 10, 1970, folder 2, box 330, RNL.

126   "most famous": Ibrahim Noori, "To Remove a Bomb Call Room Service," *Boston Globe*, September 15, 1970.

126   From the streets: Gerald Seymour, "The Middle East, September–October 1970," *Contemporary Review* 217 (December 1, 1970): 306; Warnock conversation.

126   mortar: "Palestinian Hijacks/Demands/Rights/USSR," *NBC Evening News*.

126   Windows: Seymour, "Middle East," 306.

126   crawled: Archival footage, "Hijacked," PBS, 2006.

126   corridors, stairwells: Adams, "Visit to Jordan," 6; "Jordan: Situation Report as of 06:00 EDT"; Warnock conversation.

126   beds: Jerusalem International Service, September 8, 1970, folder 2, box 330, RNL.

126   lobby furniture: "'I Never Want to Go Back There,'" *Newsday*, September 14, 1970.
126   Jordanian soldiers: Adams, "Visit to Jordan," 7.
126   Hotel staff: Patrick Massey, "Hussein's Troops Flatten Amman in Six Days," *Guardian*, September 24, 1970.
126   Waiters, bomb shelter: Kissinger to Nixon, "Evening Report on the Hijacking Situation," September 9, 1970, and Amman to Washington #4531, September 10, 1970, "Situation at Jordan Intercontinental," both folder 2, box 330, RNL; "Jordan: Situation Report as of 06:00 EDT"; "Guerrillas Surrounded by Troops," *Guardian*, September 10, 1970; Jackie Ross, "Hijack Victims' Kin Wait in Nightmare," *Hartford Courant*, September 12, 1970; "'I Never Want to Go Back There.'"; Edward R. F. Sheehan, "In the Flaming Streets of Amman," *New York Times*, September 27, 1970; Adams, "Visit to Jordan," 9.
126   "sweep up": Henry Luce, "A Letter from the Publisher," *Time*, September 21, 1970, 9.
126   "sort of": "Palestinian Hijacks/Demands/Rights/USSR," *NBC Evening News*.
127   "frying pan": Pace, "Life for Hostages On Jets Eases a Bit."
127   pocketed: "Hostages Tell Story of Ordeal," *Washington Post*, September 12, 1970.
127   safer: "Drama on the Desert: The Week of the Hostages," *Time*, September 21, 1970, 25.
127   valuable: Amman to Washington #4532, September 10, 1970, "Possible Evacuation of TWA/Swissair Passengers Now in Amman," folder 2, box 330, RNL.
127   persuade: Paul Hodge, "School a Big Letdown to Hijack Victim, 13," *Washington Post*, September 14, 1970.
127   declined: Schuman, "Sheila Warnock."
127   interview: Warnock conversation.
127   "didn't know": "'I Never Want to Go Back There.'"
127   typewriters: Hampton, *War in the Middle East*, 12.
127   hounded: Eric Pace, "Released Hostages Tell of Their Ordeal in Desert," *New York Times*, September 13, 1970.
127   shouted: Warnock conversation.
127   taxis: Adams, "Visit to Jordan," 7.
127   "boys pointed": Hess, *My Times*, 77.
127   Pipes: Amman to Washington #4531, September 10, 1970, "Situation at Jordan Intercontinental," folder 2, box 330, RNL.
127   water gushing: Seymour, "Middle East," 306.
127   bathtub: Sheehan, "In the Flaming Streets of Amman."
127   headed out: Warnock conversation.
128   traded places: Raab, *Terror in Black September*, 45.
128   commandos awakened: "Combined Statement of Hostesses: B. McCarthy, R. Metzner, V. McVey, L. Jensen," 3, TWA.
128   "They'd like," wouldn't sleep: McCarthy and McVey quoted in Rodney C. Campbell, "TWA Flight 741—Hijacked September 6, 1970," *TARPA Topics*, November 2007, 60.
128   "You better": "Hijacked," PBS, 2006.
128   "That's me": McVey quoted in Campbell, "TWA Flight 741," 60.
128   Robert Schwartz and James Wood: John R. Pherson, "Americans Detained by PFLP," September 14, 1970, folder marked "10/1/1970," boxes 683–84, NARA; Patricia Sullivan, "Robert Schwartz, Defense Official Was Hostage in Hijacking," *Washington Post*, June 18, 2007.
128   "Sir": Gliksman, *Nouri*, 411.
128   dual: "Situation Report as of 0700 hours EDT," Near Eastern Affairs Working Group, September 15, 1970, folder 3, box 330, RNL.
128   "Don't worry": Gliksman, *Nouri*, 41,1–12.
129   tranquilizers: Michael T. Kaufman, "Hijacked to the Desert: Account by Passengers," *New York Times*, September 17, 1970.
129   "We sat": "Hijacked," PBS, 2006.
129   headline: "Correspondent Confirms Guerrillas Removed Jewish Passengers From Hijacked Planes," *JTA Daily News Bulletin*, Jewish Telegraphic Agency, September 10, 1970.
129   he wondered: Abigail Klein Leichman, "'I Didn't Know if My Wife and Daughter were Alive,'" *Jerusalem Post Magazine*, September 4, 2020, 11.
129   distinctions: Richard Morse as told to Jeremiah V. Murphy, "From Andover to Amman: 20 Days in Desert—Part 1," *Boston Globe*, October 4, 1970.
129   "very well": "Dawson's Field Drama: Life in a Hijacked Hothouse," *Sunday Times* (London), September 13, 1970.
129   "no different": "Freed Hostages Fear for Lives of Captives," *Ogden Standard-Examiner*, September 12, 1970.
129   "all the others," not "singled out": "Palestinian Hijacks/Hostages/US/Britain," *ABC Evening News*, September 8, 1970, #12322, VTNA.
129   "no differentiation": "Palestinian Hijacks/BOAC/Threats," *NBC Evening News*.
129   "News": MH diary, September 9, 1970.
129   "God-knows-where": CH diary.
129   "tightly focused": John de St. Jorre, *Darling Baby Mine: A Son's Extraordinary Search for his Mother* (London: Quartet, 2016), 111.

11

131   Comrade Ibrahim: "Palestinian Hijacks/Demands/US," *CBS Evening News*, September 8, 1970, #212618, VTNA.
131   "plastic toys," shouted: Gerald Seymour, "The Middle East, September–October 1970," *Contemporary Review* 217 (December 1, 1970): 304, 305.
131   communicate: Abu-Sharif and Mahnaimi, *Best of Enemies*, 61.
131   "tell me": "Palestinian Hijacks/Demands/US," *CBS Evening News*.
131   "any violence": "Hijacked Hostages," #3025, Moving Images Relating to Intelligence and International Relations, RG263, CIA, NARA.
132   "people's faces," "praying": MH diary, September 7, 1970.
132   "these people," and following: "Hijacked Hostages," #3025.

132 "world opinion," "Marxist-Leninists": Edward R. F. Sheehan, "In the Flaming Streets of Amman," *New York Times*, September 27, 1970.

133 "convince": Archival footage in "Terrorism at Home and Abroad," *The Seventies*, episode 7, CNN, 2015.

133 "destroy," "hedged": United Press International-Cairo, September 7, 1970, folder 2, box 330, Subject Files: Hijacking, National Security Council Files, Nixon Presidential Materials Staff, RNL.

133 "PFLP colleagues": Abu-Sharif and Mahnaimi, *Best of Enemies*, 85.

133 "Don't worry," "Not for you": Abu-Sharif and Mahnaimi, 85.

133 "Speedbird": Jim Majer, "Black September, 1970," *TARPA Topics*, November 2009, 13; statement of First Officer J. A. Majer, 2, TWA.

134 "that chap," pointing a gun: "Stewardess Tells of Worst Moment of All," *London Times*, September 14, 1970.

134 "sit down": "Palestinian Hijacks/Organization Change/Hostages," *CBS Evening News*, September 12, 1970, #212090, VTNA.

134 "have a talk," spoke Arabic: "Report from F/O T. R. Cooper," September 1970, 1, FCO 14/785, TNA.

134 announced, "wasn't sorry": "Report from Cooper," 2; Campbell Page, "Hijacked 58 Return to Heathrow Rain," *Guardian*, September 14, 1970.

134 fuel supply: "Report from Cooper," 3, 4.

134 "I hope": "Report from Cooper," 4.

134 "joining": "Report from Cooper," 5.

134 scene appeared: "Report from Cooper," 6.

134 Swissair captain: Fritz Schreiber testimony, October 27, 1970, Einvernahmeprotokolle der Besatzungsmitglieder und Geislen, in Kantonspolizei Zurich, Offiziersposten Flughafen (Interrogation Records of Crew and Hostages, Cantonal Police Zurich, Airport), Beilagen B (Exhibit B), folder 189/2/3, Swissair.

134 nearly 150: Amman to Washington #4520, September 9, 1970, "ICRC Hijack Negotiations," September 8–10, folder 2, box 330, RNL; Amman to Geneva, 17:32Z, September 9, 1970, B AG 226 106-001, ICRC; "BOAC List of Passengers," *London Times*, September 10, 1970.

134 almost 300: Amman to Geneva, 17:50Z, September 9, 1970, B AG 226 106-001, ICRC; Kissinger to Nixon, "Evening Report on the Hijacking Situation," September 9, 1970, folder 2, box 330, RNL.

134 quickly identified: "Hijacked BOAC Aircraft," Tel. No. 428, September 10, 1970, FCO 14/779, TNA; "Report from Cooper," 7.

134 immediately wired: "Report from Cooper," 6.

134 later glimpsed: Tel. No. 558, September 14, 1970, FCO 14/781, TNA.

135 nine hundred: Amman to Geneva, 13:02Z, September 9, 1970, B AG 226 106-001, ICRC.

135 "URGENTI": Amman to Geneva, 17:32Z, September 9, 1970, ICRC.

135 "type of trade": Raab, *Terror in Black September*, 70 (quoting 1970 recollections).

135 BOAC 775, new plane: "The Guerilla's Story," UK Confidential, BBC News, World Edition, January 1, 2001; Abu-Sharif, *Arafat and the Dream of Palestine*, 27; Michael Adams, "Visit to Jordan, September 1970," 5, MA-UEL.

135 wondered: Richard Morse as told to Jeremiah V. Murphy, "From Andover to Amman: 20 Days in Desert—Part 1," *Boston Globe*, October 4, 1970.

135 tightened: Robert Lindsay, "Airports Tighten Security, Intensify Luggage Search," *New York Times*, September 9, 1970; "Hijacks Prompt Security Measures," *Washington Post*, September 9, 1970.

135 security forces: Michael Lake, "Dynamite Hidden in Raiders' Clothing," *Guardian*, September 10, 1970.

135 "conceal": "Report from Cooper," 4.

136 Airport security: "Presentation to International Civil Aviation Organization Committee on Unlawful Interference with Air Transport," Montreal, September 3, 1969, 3, 4, folder 26, box 140, "Airline Hijackings," William Proxmire Papers, Wisconsin Historical Society; Jane Engle, "U.S. Aviation Security Timeline," *Los Angeles Times*, June 12, 2011.

136 airports and airlines, ramps and runways: Davis, *Benjamin O. Davis*, 359, 361.

136 "the guns": SH email, January 22, 2019.

136 recommended: Richard H. L. Reighard, "FAA Goal: Stop Inflight Crime at the Gate," *Air Line Pilot*, May 1970, 18–20.

136 immediately after: "Hijacks/Demands/US/Europe," *NBC Evening News*, September 7, 1970, #453494, and "Hijacks/US/Demands/Airline Industry," *CBS Evening News*, September 9, 1970, #212640, both VTNA; Lindsey, "Airports Tighten Security"; Robert M. Smith, "President Asks Wider Use of Electronic Surveillance," *New York Times*, September 12, 1970.

136 identification: "Security Checks Increased at World's Major Airports," *Irish Times*, September 11, 1970.

136 "special checks": European Airports Sharpen Lookout for Terrorists," *Jerusalem Post*, September 8, 1970.

136 departing Israel: "Careful Searches at Lod Airport," *Jerusalem Post*, September 22, 1970.

136 ticket agents: Lindsey, "Airports Tighten Security."

136 "really bitched": Laird-Kissinger telephone conversation, September 8, 1970, 7:50pm, Kissinger Telephone Conversation Transcripts, box 6, Chronological File, Digital National Security Archive, RNL.

136 foolproof: Adam Raphael, "New Ways to Stop Hijacks," *Guardian*, September 9, 1970; "What To Do About the Skyjackers?" *Time*, September 21, 1970, 25.

136 "pair of hands": Richard Ray, "Ideas to Stop Hijackings: Immobilize Passengers with Drugs, Handcuffs," *Boston Globe*, September 13, 1970.

136 armed guards: "The Nixon Announcement," *New York Times*, September 12, 1970.

136 visions: David Fairhall, "What Are the Dangers of Armed Guards on Planes?" *Guardian*, September 11, 1970; Richard Halloran, "Air Crewmen Tell Congress Unit Armed Guards May Be Perilous," *New York Times*, September 18, 1970.

136 bomb: Carleton K. Lewis, "Letters to the editor: Reader Reaction to Hijackings," *Washington Post*, September 16, 1970.

136 oven cleaner: Geneva Mendenhall to Ron Ziegler, Pennington, NJ, September 18, 1970, box 43, Subject Files: Judicial–Legal Matters, White House Central Files, Nixon Presidential Materials Project, RNL.

136 "monumental task": "Palestinian Hijacks/US/Britain/Future Prevention," *ABC Evening News*, September 9, 1970, #12339, VTNA.

137   "unclear": "Situation Report as of 0600 Hours EST," September 7, 1970, Near Eastern Affairs Working Group, folder 2, box 330, RNL.
137   "total control": Amman to Washington #4372, September 7, 1970, boxes 683–84, RG59, State Department, NARA.
137   "loaded": United Press International, September 8, 1970, folder 2, box 330, RNL.
137   "gun": Amman to Washington #4377, September 7, 1970, boxes 683–84, NARA.
137   terms: Kissinger to Nixon, "Status of Mid-East Hijacking" [September 7, 1970], folder marked "September 1–7, 1970, 1 of 2," box 971, Alexander M. Haig Chronological Files, National Security Council Files, Nixon Presidential Materials Staff, RNL; "Hijacking," Tel. No. 466, September 7, 1970, FCO 14/778, TNA; Linda Charlton, "2 Craft in Jordan," *New York Times*, September 8, 1970; Tad Szulc, "US and 4 Nations Seek Joint Stand on Detention," *New York Times*, September 8, 1970; J. F. S. Phillips, "The Dawson Field Hijackings," Diplomatic Report No. 567/70, Jordan, December 22, 1970, 4, FCO 17/1374, TNA; "Situation Report as of 0600 Hours EST," September 7, 1970, Near Eastern Affairs Working Group, folder 2, box 330, RNL.
137   Khaled: "Hijacking," Tel. No. 469, September 7, 1970, FCO 14/778, TNA.
137   American hostages: Amman to Washington #4372, September 7, 1970, boxes 683–84, NARA.
137   Israeli hostages: Bern to Washington #2163, September 11, 1970, folder 2, box 330, RNL.
137   Countdown began: Washington to Amman #4372, September 7, 1970, boxes 683–84, NARA.
137   "including remaining": Amman to Washington #4367, September 7, 1970, boxes 683–84, NARA.
137   "Time period": Amman to Washington #4372, September 7, 1970, boxes 683–84, NARA.
138   reiterated: Kissinger to Nixon, "Status of Mid-East Hijacking."
138   Television news: "Palestinian Hijacks/Demands," *ABC Evening News*, September 7, 1970, #12306, VTNA.
138   newspapers: Charlton, "2 Craft in Jordan."
138   "level-headed," "blood-bath": "Hi-Jacking," Tel. No. 220, September 7, 1970, PREM 15/201, TNA.
138   "For God's sake": SH conversation, New York, July 17, 2018.
138   "As parents": Joseph Chesler to Nixon, Brooklyn, September 7, 1970, White House Central Files, Alphabetical Name Files, RNL.
138   "My Daddy": Lini Kadaba to Nixon, Atlanta, September 8, 1970, folder marked "Hijacking, October 1969–September 10, 1970," box 42, Subject Files: Judicial–Legal Matters, White House Central Files, Nixon Presidential Materials Project, RNL.
138   on his mind: H. R. Haldeman Diaries Collection, September 11, 15, 1970, RNL.
138   "dramatic": Haldeman Diaries, September 7, 1970.
138   "closely informed": Kissinger to Nixon, "Status of Mid-East Hijacking."
138   "suggesting," weather: "Hijacked," written and directed by Ilan Ziv, *American Experience*, PBS, 2006.
138   Bern Group: Thomas J. Hamilton, "4-Nation Geneva Group Guides the Negotiations," *New York Times*, September 12, 1970.
138   Switzerland and West Germany: London to Washington, #7095, September 7, 1970, folder 2, box 330, RNL; "Middle East—Hi Jacking," Tel. No. 2588, September 7, 1970, FCO 14/778, TNA.
139   Great Britain: London to Washington, #7095, September 7, 1970, and "Situation Report as of 1800 Hours EST," September 7, 1970, Near Eastern Affairs Working Group, both folder 2, box 330, RNL.
139   Israel: "Situation Report as of 1800 Hours EST," September 7, 1970; "Hijacks/Demands/US/Europe," *NBC Evening News*; "Middle East—Hi Jacking"; Raab, *Terror in Black September*, 57, 73.
139   special mission: "Message transmis," Geneva, September 14, 1970, B AG 226 106-001, ICRC; "ICRC Action in Jordan," *International Review of the Red Cross* 10 (1970): 543–44.
139   opposed: "National Societies at Information Meeting," *International Review of the Red Cross* 10 (1970): 558–59.
139   "purely humanitarian": "Message No. 1094," Courvoisier to Marti [Geneva], September 8, 1970, B AG 226 106-001, and "Communiqué de presse No. 1077: Une mission spéciale du CICR part pour Amman," Geneva, September 7, 1970, B AG 226 106-004, both ICRC.
139   everyone released: "ICRC Action in Jordan," 544.
139   intermediary: "Hi-Jacking," Tel. No. 223, September 7, 1970, FCO 14/778, TNA.
139   "channel": "National Societies at Information Meeting," 560.
139   delegates departed: "Opération Jordanie, Septembre–Décembre 1970: Journal des évènements," Département des Opérations, Comité International de la Croix-Rouge, Geneva, March 1971, 31–32, B AG 226 106-003, ICRC; "ICRC Action in Jordan," 543.
139   Leading: Thomas J. Hamilton, "Red Cross Aide Far from Bland," *New York Times*, September 10, 1970.
139   "prickly," "difficult": "Hijacking," Tel. No. 515, September 11, 1970, FCO 14/779, TNA.
139   "inflated idea": Phillips, "Dawson Field Hijackings."
139   "flamboyant": "Angry Men, Desperate Days," *Newsweek*, September 21, 1970, 26.
139   "Lawrence of Arabia," camaraderie: Hella Pick, "Why the Red Cross Switched Front Men," *Guardian*, September 14, 1970.
139   imperious: Jesse W. Lewis Jr., "Personalities, Pride Enter Hostage Talks," *Washington Post*, September 15, 1970.
139   Olympic Airways: Tel Aviv to Washington #4877, September 7, 1970, folder 2, box 330, RNL; "Athens Agrees to Free 7 after Arabs Seize Airliner," *New York Times*, July 23, 1970.
139   boarded: "Middle East," International Committee of the Red Cross, *Annual Report 1970*, 62–63.
139   trickiest: "National Societies at Information Meeting," 559.
139   *sans discrimination*: "Opération Jordanie," 8.
140   no divisions: "Message No. 1094," Courvoisier to Marti [Geneva], September 8, 1970, B AG 226 106-001; "Communiqué de presse No. 1077: Une mission spéciale du CICR part pour Amman," Geneva, September 7, 1970, B AG 226 106-004.
140   withdraw and depart: Kissinger to Nixon, "Hijacking Status," September 9, 1970, folder marked "September 8–14, 1970, 2 of 2," box 971, and Kissinger to Nixon, "Hijacking Status," September 9, 1970, folder marked "Middle East and Hijacking, 9/9/70," box H–077, Meetings Files, 1968–74, Washington Special Actions Group Meetings, National Security Council Institutional "H" Files, Nixon Presidential Materials Staff, both RNL; "Confidentielle: Note," Geneva, September 9, 1970, B AG 226 106-001, ICRC; "Jordan: Situation Report as of 06:00 EDT," CIA, September 9, 1970, folder 3, box 330, RNL.
140   "great uneasiness": Rochat, *L'homme à la croix*, 417.

140 task force: Amman to Washington #4436, September 8, 1970, folder 2, box 330, RNL; "121 Hijack Victims Return; Seek Release of All," *TWA Today*, September 21, 1970.
140 "extreme tension": "The Frustrating Case of TWA Flight 741," *Business Week*, October 10, 1970, 34.
140 "on the moon": Bell quoted in Rodney C. Campbell, "TWA Flight 741—Hijacked September 6, 1970," *TARPA Topics*, November 2007, 67.
140 modes, Morse Code: Alex Hendry, "Room Where News Comes from Amman," *London Times*, September 12, 1970.
140 "all hours": "David E. Zweifel, Consular Officer, Amman," interview by Thomas J. Dunnigan, September 3, 1996, in *Jordan Country Reader* (Arlington, VA: Association for Diplomatic Studies and Training), no pagination, www .adst.org/Readers/Jordan.pdf.
140 taxi drivers or pedestrians: Bell quoted in Campbell, "TWA Flight 741," 67.
140 blockaded: Amman to Geneva, 18:52Z, September 9, 1970, B AG 226 106-001, ICRC.
140 neglected: Geneva to Washington #3085, September 9, 1970, boxes 683–84, NARA; Bern to Washington #2141, September 9, 1970, folder 2, box 330, RNL.
141 "encourages": "Hijacks/United Nations/Israel/PFLP/Fighting," *ABC Evening News*, September 9, 1970, #12341, VTNA.
141 "haste in accepting": "Israel-Hijacking," Tel Aviv, September 8, 1970, News Report, MS Jerusalem Bureau: Series I, AP18.10, folder 162, 57 of pdf, box 7, Associated Press Corporate Archives online.
141 "broil": "Hijacking," Tel. No. 789, September 8, 1970, PREM 15/201, TNA.
141 exasperated: Bern to Washington #2170, September 11, 1970, "Negative Israeli Position," and Amman to Washington #4576, September 11, 1970, both folder 2, box 330, RNL; Kissinger to Nixon, "Overnight Developments on Hijacking," September 11, 1970, box 331, Subject Files: Hijacking, National Security Council Files, Nixon Presidential Materials Staff, RNL; Tel Aviv to Washington #4977, September 11, 1970, boxes 683–84, NARA.
141 come to believe: "Hi-Jacking," Tel. No. 480, September 9, 1970, PREM 15/201, TNA.
141 "sentencing": Tel. No. 2594, September 8, 1970, PREM 15/201, TNA.
141 Blowing up: Amman to Washington #4521, September 9, 1970, folder 2, box 330, RNL.
141 "Were you so sad": Saint-Exupéry, *Little Prince*, 27.
141 "tremendous urgency": Washington to Amman #149954, September 13, 1970 [re: September 7], boxes 683–84, NARA.
141 "carry out": Washington to Amman #147006, September 8, 1970, RG59, State Department, NARA, in *FRUS*, vol. E-1, *Documents on Global Issues* (Washington, DC, 2005), document #49, 356.
142 "extremely serious," "one chance": Kissinger to Nixon, "Evening Report on the Hijacking Situation," September [9], 1970, folder marked "September 8–14, 1970, 2 of 2," box 971, RNL.
142 "three planes": E. O. Martin, "Situation in Jordan," September 9, 1970, folder 3, box 330, RNL.
142 "conclusive evidence": Kissinger to Nixon, "Mid-Day Situation Report on Hijacking Situation," September 9, 1970, folder 3, box 330, RNL.
142 "planes and passengers": Richard T. Kennedy and Harold H. Saunders to Kissinger, "WSAG Meeting on Hijacking Contingencies," September 9, 1970, folder marked "Middle East and Hijacking, 9/9/70," box H–077, RNL.
142 "great concern," "some disaster": *The Hijack Conspiracy*, part 1, September 9, 1970, CBS News special report with Walter Cronkite.
142 "lives": "Arab States—Israel," *Central Intelligence Bulletin*, September 10, 1970, 1, Crest: CIA database of declassified intelligence documents, NARA.
142 "human cargo": "Mideast Crisis and American Credibility," *Congressional Record*, September 10, 1970, 31180.

12

143 "Palestine?": June Haesler conversation, New York, October 14, 2019.
143 "national home": Balfour Declaration (1917) quoted in Stanislawski, *Zionism*, 41.
143 "irrepressible": Peel Report (1937), quoted in Black, *Enemies and Neighbors*, 79.
144 "deeply," "guilt": "Historical Document: The Case against a Jewish State in Palestine: Albert Hourani's Statement to the Anglo-American Committee of Enquiry of 1946," *Journal of Palestine Studies* 35 (2005): 89, 84.
144 "You realize": Crum, *Behind the Silken Curtain*, 87–91.
144 "one hope": Crossman, *Palestine Mission*, 79.
144 "still alive?": Quoted in Whitehouse, *People on the Beach*, 51.
144 "co-ordination": Khaled, *My People Shall Live*, 25.
145 Zionist story: Herman A. Gray, "In Defense of Israel," *Jewish Newsletter*, New York, July 28, 1958; "Golda Meir: 'Who Can Blame Israel?'" *Sunday Times* (London), interview by Frank Giles, June 15, 1969; M. Shertok, "Reply of the Provisional Government of Israel to the Proposal Regarding the Return of Arab Refugees," August 1, 1948, in *The Palestinian Refugees: A Collection of United Nations Documents* (Institute for Palestine Studies, 1970), 7–9.
145 "Israeli family," "sat down," PFLP: Abu-Sharif and Mahnaimi, *Best of Enemies*, 7, 28, 43, 50–51.
146 "Painters": CH to SH and EH, Tel Aviv, June 28, 1968 or 1969.
146 "many Americans": Tolan, *Lemon Tree*, xviii.
146 "whole story": Quoted in Shipler, *Arab and Jew*, 475.
146 "never existed": Shavit, *My Promised Land*, 160.
146 "lived": Bartov, "National Narratives of Suffering," 198.
146 "ardent tourist": Joan Comay, *Everyone's Guide to Israel* (New York: Doubleday, 1966), 204.
146 "came to a country," "blind spots": Elon, *Israelis*, 26, 157.
147 toys: Central Zionist Archives A202/97, Custodian of Absentee Property report, February 22, 1953, cited in Fischbach, *Records of Dispossession*, 74.
147 "we had to leave": Confino, "When Genya and Henryk Kowalski Challenged History," 135.
147 "coffee and pita": Protocol of meeting of Jewish Agency Executive, May 6, 1948, Central Zionist Archive 45/2, Jerusalem, quoted in Morris, *Palestinian Refugee Problem Revisited*, 310.
147 "We came": S. Yizhar [Yizhar Smilansky], *Khirbet Khizeh* (1949; New York: Farrar, Straus and Giroux, 2008), 104,

108. See also William Zukerman, "Arab Refugees—A Moral Problem: A Summary of a Tragedy," *Jewish Newsletter* (New York), December 1, 1958.

147 "no good": Gluck, *Batsheva Dance Company*, 101.

148 "Nixon": MH diary, November 7, 1968.

148 Moratorium Day: MH diary, October 15, 1969; MH scrapbook, 1968–70.

148 "really neat": MH diary, May 12, 1970.

148 "Shirley Chisolm": MH to LH, New York, January 16, 1970.

148 collected donations: MH to LH and EB, New York, postmarked May 15, 1970.

148 "Power to the People": "Newton, at Panther Parley, Urges Socialist System," *New York Times*, September 6, 1970.

148 "could NEVER": MH diary, September 4, 1969.

148 Few: Burmeister, *Sky-Jacked*, 20; Barbara Mensch conversation, New York, February 14, 2019; Haesler conversation; Sheila Warnock conversation, New York, September 23, 2019, including reading from journal kept September 6–14, 1970.

148 yearning: "'Not Knowing if Anyone Knew Was the Worst Part,'" *Tallahassee Democrat*, September 20, 1970.

149 "fast becoming": "Marxist Leader of Commandos: George Habash," *New York Times*, June 13, 1970.

149 "fastest-growing": Dana Adams Schmidt, "Sensational Claims Win Recruits For Palestinian Commando Unit," *New York Times*, September 17, 1969.

149 "most extreme": Dana Adams Schmidt, "At Least 100 Die in Amman Clashes with Guerrillas," *New York Times*, June 11, 1970.

149 "every": "Founding Statement of the Popular Front for the Liberation of Palestine—December 11, 1967," pflp-documents.org/documents/PFLP-FoundingStatementEnglish1967.pdf

149 Armed resistance: "First Political Statement Issued by the Popular Front for the Liberation of Palestine," *Al-Hurriyah*, November 12, 1967, in *IDP 1967*, ed. Fuad A. Jabber (Beirut: Institute for Palestine Studies, 1970), 723–26.

149 "guerrilla warfare," "striking": *The Military Strategy of the PFLP* (Beirut: Information Department PFLP, 1970), 85.

149 "totally against": George Habash interview by Lee Griggs, "A Voice of Extremism," *Time*, June 13, 1969, 42.

150 "mastermind": John M. Lee, "Hijacking Mastermind is No. 2 in the Popular Front," *New York Times*, September 14, 1970; Abu-Sharif, *Arafat and the Dream of Palestine*, 26.

150 "traveled": Abu-Sharif, *Arafat and the Dream of Palestine*, 18.

150 "excellent English": James E. Goodman, "June Haesler 'Wasn't Bored,' Plans to Fly Again," *Trenton Sunday Times Advertiser*, September 20, 1970.

150 working classes: "The Political, Organizational and Military Report of the Popular Front for the Liberation of Palestine, February 1969," in *Basic Political Documents of the Armed Palestinian Resistance Movement*, ed. Leila S. Kadi (Beirut: Palestine Liberation Organization Research Center, 1969), 194–99.

150 "excellent jobs": Georgie Anne Geyer, "The Palestinian Refugees—A New Breed: Smart, Skilled, Fanatical," *New Republic*, November 21, 1970, 18.

150 "bourgeois": Brian Moynahan and William Shawcross, "Rival Faces of Terrorism," *Sunday Times* (London), September 13, 1970.

150 influential: Don Peretz, "Arab Palestine: Phoenix or Phantom?" *Foreign Affairs* 48 (1970): 328–29.

150 "refugees": Dana Adams Schmidt, "An Arab Guerrilla Chief Emerges," *New York Times*, March 4, 1969.

150 notably absent: Lee, "Hijacking Mastermind."

150 presumably: "Plan for Hijacking Called a Month Old," *New York Times*, September 11, 1970; John M. Lee, "Tension Termed Guerrillas' Aim," *New York Times*, September 16, 1970.

150 "third world war": "Guerrillas 'Would Risk World War,'" *London Times*, September 16, 1970.

150 "socialist": "Guerrillas 'Would Risk World War.'"

150 call attention: J. F. S. Phillips, "The Dawson Field Hijackings," Diplomatic Report No. 567/70, Jordan, December 22, 1970, 4, FCO 17/1374, TNA.

150 "media operation": "Hijack," produced and directed by Dominic Sutherland, *Timewatch*, BBC/Open University, 2007.

150 "We said": "Hijacked," written and directed by Ilan Ziv, *American Experience*, PBS, 2006.

151 "Suddenly": Karmi, *In Search of Fatima*, 387.

152 Rogers plan: "The Revised Rogers Peace Plan," "President Nasser's Reply," "Israel's Reply," and "UN Security Council Resolution of 22 November 1967," all in *Survival: Global Politics and Strategy* 12 (1970): 336–42, 345; "Press Conference Statements by Secretary-General Habbash of the PFLP on the Front's Attitude towards the Rogers Plan and Its Acceptance by Certain Arab Governments," Tripoli, July 25, 1970, in *IDP 1970* ed. Walid Khadduri (Beirut: Institute for Palestine Studies, 1973), 878–82.

152 chose Dawson's Field: "Interview Statements by Two Officials of the PFLP on the Plane Hijackings Carried Out by Them," Amman, September 7, 1970, in Khadduri, *IDP 1970*, 904.

152 Jordan's borders: "Guerrillas Fight Jordan's Troops in Amman Region," *New York Times*, June 10, 1970; Eric Pace, "Hussein's Tanks Clearing Guerrillas from Amman," *New York Times*, September 18, 1970.

152 King Hussein: "Master of Survival: Hussein Ibn Talal el-Hashim," *New York Times*, September 22, 1970.

152 "trying to divide": "Richard E. Undeland, Public Affairs Officer, USIS, Amman," interview by Charles Stuart Kennedy, July 1994, in *Jordan Country Reader* (Arlington, VA: Association for Diplomatic Studies and Training), no pagination, www.adst.org/Readers/Jordan.pdf.

152 Hussein voiced: "Speech by King Hussein of Jordan on Relations with the Palestinian Resistance," Amman, September 6, 1970, in Khadduri, *IDP 1970*, 903–4.

152 tensions escalating: Phillips, "Dawson Field Hijackings."

152 Kissinger worried: Washington Special Actions Group Minutes, September 10, 1970, box H–114, National Security Council Files, Nixon Presidential Materials, NARA, in *FRUS*, vol. 24, *Jordan, September 1970* (Washington, DC, 2008), document #222, 642.

153 "Nixon and Kissinger": O'Connell, *King's Counsel*, 107–8.

153 "thrust back": *The Hijack Conspiracy*, part 1, September 9, 1970, CBS News special report with Walter Cronkite.

153 "non-rational": Amman to Washington #4571, September 10, 1970, folder 2, box 330, Subject Files: Hijacking, National Security Council Files, Nixon Presidential Materials Staff, RNL.

153 "shame": "Hussein: 'Every Day Jordan is Collapsing,'" *Washington Post*, September 17, 1970.

153 "harm done": Washington to Amman #147976, September 10, 1970, RG59, State Department, NARA, in *FRUS*, vol. 24, document #219, 539.

153 not responsible: Tad Szulc, "Plea on Hostages Is Made by Rogers," *New York Times*, September 9, 1970.

153 "minimally": Amman to Geneva #4591, September 11, 1970, RG59, State Department, NARA, in *FRUS*, vol. E-1, *Documents on Global Issues* (Washington, DC, 2005), document #62, 408.

153 personal appeal: Kissinger to Nixon, "Hijacking Status," September 9, 1970, folder marked "Middle East and Hijacking, 9/9/70," box H–077, Meetings Files, 1968–74, Washington Special Actions Group Meetings, National Security Council Institutional "H" Files, Nixon Presidential Materials Staff, RNL.

153 "humanitarian": Szulc, "Plea on Hostages."

153 "savage and inhuman": "Hi-Jacking," Tel. No. 1879, September 8, 1970, FCO 14/778, TNA; "Ordeal in the Desert," *New York Times*, September 9, 1970.

153 Support, disapproval: "Al Ahram Says Hijacking Harms Guerrilla Cause," *New York Times*, September 9, 1970; David Hirst, "How the Arab World Divides," *Guardian*, September 9, 1970; "And What Next?" *Egyptian Gazette*, September 10, 1970; "For the Record . . . From Cairo's Controlled Press," *Washington Post*, September 10, 1970; "Official Arab Views Mixed on Hijackings," *New York Times*, September 10, 1970; "Symptoms," *Egyptian Gazette*, September 11, 1970; "Darkness in the Desert," *Guardian*, September 12, 1970; "Reaction of Arab Countries to Hijacking," September 14, 1970, FCO 14/781, TNA; "Summary of Reactions of Arab Countries to Hi-jacking," September 18, 1970, FCO 14/781, TNA; "Comment from the World's Newspapers," in Julian Critchley, *Crisis Paper No. 10: Hijacking* (London: Atlantic Educational, 1970), 9–16.

153 *Pravda*, Communist regimes: "Hijacking," Tel. No. 1034, September 10, 1970, FCO 14/779, TNA; "Communist Press Condemns Hijacks," *Boston Globe*, September 11, 1970; Bernard Gwertzman, "Moscow Ambiguous in Reaction to the Hijackings," *New York Times*, September 20, 1970.

154 "fanatical": Washington to Amman #147006, September 8, 1970, RG59, State Department, NARA, in *FRUS*, vol. E-1, document #49, 356.

154 "wasteland": "Mideast Crisis and American Credibility," *Congressional Record*, September 10, 1970, 31180.

154 "Maoist": "Peace Possible in Mideast," *Congressional Record*, September 22, 1970, 33180, quoting *Peoria Journal Star* editorial, September 18, 1970.

154 "madmen": "Concurrent Resolution for Extradition of Airline Hijackers," *Congressional Record*, September 9, 1970, 30900.

154 "wild men": "Hi-Jacking," Tel. No. 554, September 14, 1970, PREM 15/202, TNA.

154 "tragedy," uncivilized: "Aircraft Hijacking," *Congressional Record*, September 9, 1970, 31039.

154 "shuffling": Eric Pace, "Hostages on BOAC Jet Say Food Is Not Provided," *New York Times*, September 11, 1970.

154 "barbarity": "Ordeal in the Desert," *New York Times*, September 9, 1970.

154 "To dismiss": Stephen S. Rosenfeld, "The Commandos in Perspective," *Washington Post*, September 11, 1970.

154 "beautiful": "The New Barbarians," *Berkeley Tribe*, September 11–18, 1970, 3.

154 "Why?": "Palestinian Hijacks/Demands/US," *CBS Evening News*, September 8, 1970, #212618, VTNA.

154 "opponents": Said, *Question of Palestine*, 122.

155 *my fault?*: CH telephone interview by Jeffrey D. Simon, March 21, 1992, original tape.

155 "impressing," "show us": CH and MH with SH, interview by Jeremy Cole and A. J. Sullivan, New York, September 20, 1970, original tape.

155 "And once again": Saint-Exupéry, *Little Prince*, 98.

13

156 "hot and uncomfortable": CH diary.

156 "sweatboxes": "Arabs Threaten to Blow up 2 Jets," *Boston Globe*, September 8, 1970.

156 "sun-scorched": William Tuohy, "Hostages Brace for 2 More Days," *Los Angeles Times*, September 11, 1970.

156 temperatures: "Urgent: Départ d'un second avion spécial du CICR," Geneva, September 10, 1970, B AG 226 106-004, ICRC.

156 high of 131: Claude Frascani, "Report on the Mission in Jordan from 6–30 September, 1970," January 11, 1971 (English translation; original document in French dated December 14, 1970), 2, B AG 226 106-003, ICRC.

156 generator: Statement of passenger R. L. Morris, 4, 5, TWA.

156 plastic cups: Patricia Parker Ridenhour, "Hijacked to Jordan," *Alumni News*, University of North Carolina–Greensboro, Winter 1971, 11; Rudolf Swinkels crew report, 5, courtesy of June Haesler.

156 "What the hell": June Haesler conversation, New York, October 14, 201.

157 "Jerry Koosman": Jim Majer, "Black September, 1970," *TARPA Topics*, November 2009, 14.

157 chlorine: Jacobson, "Individual and Group Responses," 465.

157 bribe: Roni Raab, "The Day My Plane Was Hijacked," *Jewish Press*, September 14, 2018; Tikva (Raab) Yudkowitz conversation, Teaneck, NJ, March 18, 2019.

157 "scarcely enough," "extremely serious": Saint-Exupéry, *Little Prince*, 6, 27.

157 dinner rolls, commandos provided: Swinkels crew report, 3; "Combined Statement of Hostesses: B. McCarthy, R. Metzner, V. McVey, L. Jensen," 2, TWA.

157 deliveries: CH and MH with SH, interview by Jeremy Cole and A. J. Sullivan, New York, September 20, 1970, original tape; Swinkels crew report, 5; "Combined Statement of Hostesses," 6; statement of hostess J. Haesler, 5, TWA.

157 burner: Swinkels crew report, 4; Haesler statement, 4.

157 "first two days": "Hijacked," written and directed by Ilan Ziv, *American Experience*, PBS, 2006.

157 exactly: Morris statement, 4.

157 "really gave us": CH and MH with SH, Cole interview.

157 Hoarding: Morris statement, 3.

157 justified: Deposition in lawsuit brought by hostage against Trans World Airlines.

157 "'me first'": Statement of Flight Engineer A. Kiburis, 2, TWA.

157 watermelon seeds: Raab, *Terror in Black September*, 67.

157 kept kosher: Kiburis statement, 2; "Combined Statement of Hostesses," 3, 5; Jacobson, "Individual and Group

Responses," 461; Susie (Hirsch) Rosenrauch, "Resilience and Coping in the Face of Trauma: A Retrospective Account Thirty Years after a Skyjacking," unpublished ms., 1999, 21.

157   commissary: Swinkels crew report, 1.

157   looked askance: Jacobson, "Individual and Group Responses," 461.

157   expressed frustration: Swinkels crew report, 8; Kiburis statement, 2.

158   "Don't ask me": "Rav Isaac Hutner & The TWA Hijacking," on "Luke Ford: Stay in Your Lane," August 4, 2017, lukeford.net/blog/, summarizing online class by Professor Marc B. Shapiro, Weinberg Chair of Judaic Studies, University of Scranton; Marc B. Shapiro email, December 17, 2018.

158   rabbi implored: Sylvia R. Jacobson, "Speech Delivered at Temple Israel, Tallahassee, Florida, September 18, 1970," addenda, 4, folder 8, box 2, SRJ-AJA.

158   exchanges: Mitchell Meltzer as told to Howard Southgate, "Thumbs Up: Twenty-One Days as a Hijack Hostage," unpublished ms., 1970.

158   menu: Box 232, KO453, TWA.

158   fruit, cake: MH diary, July 3, 25, 1970.

158   candy: Jacobson, "Speech Delivered," 12.

158   booze: Hyman Kenneth Salenger, "Stress, Anxiety and Certain Characteristics of Cohesion: A Study of Relationships and Implications" (PhD diss., Laurence University, 1972), 134.

158   walked the aisles: Swinkels crew report, 4.

158   "Pick up": CH and MH with SH, Cole interview.

158   edging: Peter T. Chew, "Hostage Tells It As It Was," *National Observer*, October 5, 1970.

158   items: Morris statement, 3.

158   pigpen: George B. Freda, "Death Often Next Door for Airline Hijack Hostages," *Orlando Evening Star*, September 28, 1970.

158   slobs: Morris statement, 3.

159   rubbing alcohol: Haesler statement, 5.

159   jerry cans: "Combined Statement of Hostesses," 2.

159   "hardly": Sylvia R. Jacobson, "Thursday, September 10th" (notes), 2, folder 10, box 1, SRJ-AJA.

159   "true": Jacobson, "Children's Attitudinal and Behavioral Responses," 13.

159   diapers: Jacobson, "Individual and Group Responses," 461.

159   "prying": Rosenrauch, "Resilience and Coping," 20.

159   "drop dead": Deposition in lawsuit against TWA.

159   cleaning: Swinkels crew report, 4.

159   reserves: "Combined Statement of Hostesses," 2.

159   a tap: Deposition in lawsuit against TWA.

159   water and electricity: CH and MH with SH, Cole interview.

159   "excrement": Frascani, "Report on the Mission in Jordan."

159   commandos joined: Frascani.

159   clothes hangers: James E. Goodman, "June Haesler 'Wasn't Bored,' Plans to Fly Again," *Trenton Sunday Times Advertiser*, September 20, 1970.

159   odor: Majer, "Black September," 14.

159   "nauseatingly": Deposition in lawsuit against TWA.

159   pitch-dark: CH and MH with SH, Cole interview.

159   generator: McCarthy quoted in Rodney C. Campbell, "TWA Flight 741—Hijacked September 6, 1970," *TARPA Topics*, November 2007, 61; Swinkels crew report, 4.

160   recirculated: Jacobson, "Speech Delivered," 11.

160   sanitation details: CH and MH with SH, Cole interview; Swinkels crew report, 6; "Combined Statement of Hostesses," 4.

160   toilet brigade: Michael T. Kaufman, "Hijacked to the Desert: Account by Passengers," *New York Times*, September 17, 1970.

160   pumping a stick: CH and MH with SH, Cole interview.

160   passed out: MH notes from group conversation, TWA 741, 50th anniversary video reunion, organized by David Raab, September 6, 2020.

160   "don't shove": Fran Chesler, "The Saga of a Flight: TWA Flight 741, September 6–September 28, 1970," unpublished ms., Fall 1970, part II, 1; Raab, *Terror in Black September*, 105; Yudkowitz conversation.

160   drain handles: Jim Majer email, January 12, 2020.

160   ditch: Kiburis quoted in Campbell, "TWA Flight 741," 61.

160   "huge flood": Majer, "Black September," 14.

160   *rapidement*: Amman to Geneva, 17:02Z, September 8, 1970, B AG 226 106-001, ICRC.

160   "paradise": Fritz Schreiber testimony, October 27, 1970, Einvernahmeprotokolle der Besatzungsmitglieder und Geislen, in Kantonspolizei Zurich, Offiziersposten Flughafen (Interrogation Records of Crew and Hostages, Cantonal Police Zurich, Airport), Beilagen B (Exhibit B), folder 189/2/3, Swissair.

160   lists: Amman to Geneva, "Suite mon dix," handwritten, 18:37Z, September 9, 1970, B AG 226-004, and Amman to Geneva, 18:37Z, September 9, 1970, B AG 226-003, both ICRC; "Combined Statement of Hostesses," 5.

160   pharmacists and shopkeepers: Hella Pick, "What do the Jet Captives Need?" *Guardian*, September 11, 1970.

161   cigarettes: Swinkels crew report, 5.

161   suffered: Washington to Amman #146417, September 8, 1970, boxes 683–84, RG59, State Department, NARA; Geneva to Amman, 10:45Z, September 10, 1970, B AG 226 106-001, and Geneva to Amman, 9:55Z, September 11, 1970, B AG 226 106-001, both ICRC; William Montgomery, "Mrs. Burnett Recounts Her Ordeal," *Albuquerque Journal*, September 16, 1970; "WSA Pleads Release of UW Hostage," *Wisconsin State Journal*, September 25, 1970; Morris statement, 5; Frascani, "Report on the Mission in Jordan," 2, 4; Sylvia R. Jacobson, "Observations on Follow-Up on Attitudes and Behaviors," 5, folder 10, box 1, SRJ-AJA; Jacobson, "Individual and Group Responses," 465; affidavits, depositions, and other material in lawsuits brought by hostages against Trans World Airlines.

161   sparkling: [Walter Jost] narrative, 24, English translation of Jost, *Rufzeichen*, folder 5, box 2, SRJ-AJA.

161   mobile clinic: David Zenian, "Plane Hostages Exercise in Desert," *Washington Post*, September 9, 1970.

161   all found: Kaufman, "Hijacked to the Desert"; Goodman, "June Haesler 'Wasn't Bored.'"

161   "medicine or comfort": CH and MH with SH, Cole interview.
161   "understanding": Swinkels crew report, 7.
161   "superb": Jacobson, "Speech Delivered," 7.
161   "beautiful eyes," "best of all": Arnold C. Ropeik, "Day-by-Day . . . The Ordeal of the Raabs," *Trenton Sunday Times Advertiser*, September 20, 1970.
161   "every type": Haesler statement, 5.
161   informed TWA: Washington to Amman #146692, September 8, 1970, and Amman to Washington, #4419, September 8, 1970, boxes 683–84, NARA.
161   supplied us: CH conversation, New York, March 27, 2016.
161   singled out: "Urgent: Départ d'un second avion spécial du CICR," Geneva, September 10, 1970, B AG 226 106-004, ICRC; "Translation of ICRC press release forwarded in Geneva 3092," September [10], 1970, folder 3, box 330, Subject Files: Hijacking, National Security Council Files, Nixon Presidential Materials Staff, RNL; Alec Efty, "'Women, Children are Terrified . . . ,'" *Boston Globe*, September 9, 1970.
161   "main problem": "Ordeal for the Innocent: Story of Hijack Victims," *U.S. News and World Report*, September 21, 1970, 20.
161   very much wanted: Amman to Geneva, 17:04Z, September 10, 1970, B AG 226 106-001, ICRC.
162   "some action": H. R. Haldeman Diaries Collection, September 8, 1970, RNL.
162   "Kidnapping": "Blackbeard Is Alive and Well in the Middle East," *Congressional Record*, September 15, 1970, 31715.
162   "For your info": Bern to Washington #2162, 00:40Z, September 11, 1970, folder 2, box 330, RNL.
162   letter, bouquet: Marcel A. Naville to "Madame," Geneva, September 11, 1970, B AG 226 106-004, and Courvoisier to Rochat, Geneva, 22:30Z, September 10, 1970, B AG 226 106-001, both ICRC; "A Red Cross Greeting Is Sent to New Mother," *New York Times*, September 13.
162   "Number": Amman to Washington #4576, September 11, 1970, folder 2, box 330, RNL.
162   "happy moment": "Palestinian Hijacks/US/USSR/Families," *CBS Evening News*, September 10, 1970, #212045, VTNA.
162   "quite well": "Palestinian Hijacks/US/USSR/Families."
162   disseminated: "Palestinian Hijacks/Birth/US/UAR," *ABC Evening News*, September 10, 1970, #11948, VTNA; William Tuohy, "Baby Born on Hijacked Jet in Desert," *Washington Post*, September 11, 1970; "Baby Born Aboard Hostage Jet," *Boston Globe*, September 11, 1970; "Birth in Desert," *London Times*, September 11, 1970; "Child Born to US Hostage," *Guardian*, September 11, 1970; "A Red Cross Greeting is Sent to New Mother," *New York Times*, September 13, 1970.
162   "modern history's": "Lead baby," Reuters, September 13, 1970, and "Urgent: Hijack-Baby," Reuters, Geneva, September 13, 1970, in B AG 226 106-004, ICRC.
162   correction: "Urgent: Piraterie Aérienne," Agence-France Press, September 13, 1970, B AG 226 106-004, ICRC.
162   retracted: "No Hostage Gave Birth, Red Cross Aide Reports," *New York Times*, September 14, 1970; "'Hijack Baby' False Alarm, Red Cross Says," *Chicago Tribune*, September 14, 1970; "Doctor Says No Baby Was Born," *London Times*, September 14, 1970.
162   "bad joke": Hella Pick, "ICRC Role Change," *Guardian*, September 14, 1970.
162   tonsilitis: Swinkels crew report, 6; Majer quoted in Campbell, "TWA Flight 741," 61.
162   through the night: Majer quoted in Campbell, "TWA Flight 741," 62.
162   "to hold": Majer, "Black September," 15.
162   "*Everybody*": Haesler conversation.
162   "I love you": Majer quoted in Campbell, "TWA Flight 741," 61–62.
163   "a father": CH and MH with SH, Cole interview.
163   "cholera shot": MH diary, September 8, 1970.
163   "spectacle": Rochat, *L'homme à la croix*, 437.
163   "six passengers": Rochat, 440.

14

164   "We've stopped": MH diary, September 6, 1970.
164   "Do you eat?": EH to CH and MH, New York, ca. September 9, 1970.
165   obligations: Statement of Flight Engineer A. Kiburis, TWA, 5.
165   "something to do": Statement of Capt. C. D. Woods, 2, TWA.
165   "a million": McCarthy quoted in Rodney C. Campbell, "TWA Flight 741—Hijacked September 6, 1970," *TARPA Topics*, November 2007, 54.
165   three hours: Statement of hostess J. Haesler, 4, TWA; James E. Goodman, "June Haesler 'Wasn't Bored,' Plans to Fly Again," *Trenton Sunday Times Advertiser*, September 20, 1970.
165   "Everybody": Haesler quoted in Campbell, "TWA Flight 741," 60.
165   "beautiful": Metzner quoted in Campbell, 63.
165   "no idea": CH conversation, New York, 2015.
165   "tried to recall": "'Not Knowing if Anyone Knew Was the Worst Part,'" *Tallahassee Democrat*, September 20, 1970.
166   "did nothing": Fran Chesler, "The Saga of a Flight: TWA Flight 741, September 6–September 28, 1970," unpublished ms., Fall 1970, part II, 2.
166   "a statue": Mitchell Meltzer as told to Howard Southgate, "Thumbs Up: Twenty-One Days as a Hijack Hostage," unpublished ms., 1970.
166   Conversation: Hyman Kenneth Salenger, "Stress, Anxiety and Certain Characteristics of Cohesion: A Study of Relationships and Implications" (PhD diss., Laurence University, 1972), 135.
166   join others: CH and MH with SH, interview by Jeremy Cole and A. J. Sullivan, New York, September 20, 1970, original tape.
166   talked about: Ralph S. Sanford, "First Hand Experiences on a Swissair Flight—Which Took a Side Trip to the Jordanian Desert," speech at New York University and Post Graduate Hospital Alumni Association, October 20, 1970, 7, folder 4, box 2, SRJ-AJA.

166   gallows humor: Jacobson, "Individual and Group Responses," 466.

166   "cigarettes": Raab, *Terror in Black September*, 65 (quoting 1970 recollections).

166   puzzles: Patricia Parker Ridenhour, "Hijacked to Jordan," *Alumni News*, University of North Carolina–Greensboro, Winter 1971, 11; Paul Martin, "Biscuits and Water Diet for Hijacked Britons," *London Times*, September 11, 1970.

166   word games: Campbell Page, "Hijacked 58 Return to Heathrow Rain," *Guardian*, September 14, 1970.

166   study guide, *Coffee*: Barbara Mensch conversation, New York, February 14, 2019.

166   "uninhibited memoirs": Trudy Baker and Rachel Jones, *Coffee Tea or Me: The Uninhibited Memoirs of Two Airline Stewardesses* (New York: Bantam, 1968).

166   *Manchild*: Deposition in lawsuit brought by hostage against Trans World Airlines.

166   cards: Sanford, "First Hand Experiences," 7.

166   chess: Raab, *Terror in Black September*, 65 (quoting 1970 recollections).

166   checkers: Sylvia R. Jacobson, "Background" (notes), 6, folder 10, box 1, SRJ-AJA.

166   guessing games: Meltzer, "Thumbs Up."

166   backgammon: Eva Grubler video conversation, December 13, 2020.

166   Birthdays: "Combined Statement of Hostesses: B. McCarthy, R. Metzner, V. McVey, L. Jensen," 4, TWA; "Three Stewardesses Describe Week Aboard Hijacked Plane," *Danville (VA) Bee*, September 14, 1970; Goodman, "June Haesler 'Wasn't Bored'"; Ridenhour, "Hijacked to Jordan," 11–12; Sylvia R. Jacobson, "Speech Delivered at Temple Israel, Tallahassee, Florida, September 18, 1970," 14, folder 8, box 2, SRJ-AJA; William Tuohy, "Jet Hostage Tells of His Birthday Fete," *Los Angeles Times*, September 13, 1970; McCarthy quoted in Campbell, "TWA Flight 741," 63.

167   "Yankee Doodle": Jesse W. Lewis Jr., "'They Awoke Him . . . and Took Him,'" *Washington Post*, September 13, 1970.

167   "I'll Never Fall in Love Again": McCarthy quoted in Campbell, "TWA Flight 741," 63.

167   "Sealed with a Kiss": Susie (Hirsch) Rosenrauch and Howie Hirsch conversation, Ra'anana, Israel, July 7, 2019.

167   "Show Me the Way," "Up, Up and Away": Lewis, "'They Awoke Him.'"

167   "How many days": "'We Were Hijacked!'" *Seventeen*, December, 1970, 170.

167   "white TWA": Fran Chesler WhatsApp message, July 5, 2019.

167   "One hundred": Susie (Hirsch) Rosenrauch, "Resilience and Coping in the Face of Trauma: A Retrospective Account Thirty Years after a Skyjacking," unpublished ms., 1999, 17.

167   "Living on a Jet Plane": "Life on Jet in Desert Had Lighter Moments," *Orlando Sentinel*, September 13, 1970.

167·   "you wouldn't": Yosef Trachtman as told to Steven Pratt, "Captive in the Desert: Yosef's Own Story," *Chicago Tribune*, September 20, 1970.

167   snarling: Jacobson, "Children's Attitudinal and Behavioral Responses," 10.

167   "pent-up": CH and MH with SH, Cole interview.

167   food, water: Peter T. Chew, "Hostage Tells It As It Was," *National Observer*, October 5, 1970.

167   appointed themselves: Jacobson, "Individual and Group Responses," 463–64.

167   Elderly: Jacobson, 466.

167   Europeans: Jacobson, "Speech Delivered," B6.

167   Holocaust survivors: Jacobson, "Individual and Group Responses," 466.

167   "don't know": Michael T. Kaufman, "Hijacked to the Desert: Account by Passengers," *New York Times*, September 17, 1970.

167   beautiful: CH email, September 25, 2019.

167   unreal, *What a place*: Chesler, "Saga of a Flight," part II, 5.

167   "twisted": Meltzer, "Thumbs Up."

167   Crying: Raab, *Terror in Black September*, 76.

167   pacing: Jacobson, "Individual and Group Responses," 466.

167   snoring: [Walter Jost] narrative, 29, English translation of Jost, *Rufzeichen*, folder 5, box 2, SRJ-AJA.

168   coughing: Jacobson, "Individual and Group Responses," 465.

168   intrusive: Sylvia R. Jacobson, "Life on Board" (notes), W-5, folder 10, box 1, SRJ-AJA.

168   cried: Tova Lev Kahn conversation, New York, April 2, 2019.

168   "prison": Chesler, "Saga of a Flight," part II, 5.

168   prayer book: Rosenrauch, "Resilience and Coping," 18.

168   *Now, you can't*: Raab, *Terror in Black September*, 79 (quoting 1970 recollections).

168   "When you are": Kaufman, "Hijacked to the Desert."

168   "magnificence": [Jost] narrative, 52.

169   "I've continued": MH diary, September 9, 11, 1970.

169   magazine: *Ambassador* magazine, September 1970, box 224, KO453, TWA.

169   mail-order, and following: *TWA Flight Shop: Gifts, Souvenirs & Travel Accessories*, box 227, KO453, TWA.

171   "Be my friends," "Come and play": Saint-Exupéry, *Little Prince*, 76, 78.

171   "mile upon mile": Edward R. F. Sheehan, "In the Flaming Streets of Amman," *New York Times*, September 27, 1970.

171   "bumping along," and following: "Hijacked," written and directed by Ilan Ziv, *American Experience*, PBS, 2006.

171   forbade, closer: Gerald Seymour, "The Middle East, September–October 1970," *Contemporary Review* 217 (December 1, 1970): 304–5.

171   "three dots": Phillips, *Skyjack*, 146.

171   "fantastic": Henry Luce, "A Letter from the Publisher," *Time*, September 21, 1970, 9.

171   "glassy mirage": Sheehan, "Flaming Streets of Amman."

171   "surreal": Hampton, *War in the Middle East*, 4.

171   got closer: AP Archive, "Guerrilla Hijackings: Deadline at Dawson's Field," uploaded September 23, 1970, YouTube video.

172   *never*: David Hirst, "Jets, Dust, and the Press," *Guardian*, September 11, 1970.

172   "We demand," and following: "Hijacks/United Nations /Israel/PFLP/Fighting," *ABC Evening News*, September 9, 1970, #12341; "Hijacks/US/Demands/Airline Industry," *CBS Evening News*, September 9, 1970, #212640; and "Palestinian Hijacks/BOAC/Threats," *NBC Evening News*, September 9, 1970, #453523, all VTNA; "1970 Rev-

olution Airport Press Conference," YouTube, uploaded by Catzotto, September 25, 2010; Eric Pace, "Life on Jets Held in Desert Is Harsh," *New York Times*, September 9, 1970.

172 "jokes," admits: June Haesler conversation, New York, October 14, 2019.

174 "keep everyone": Kiburis statement, 3.

174 "disgust": "Hijacked," PBS, 2006.

175 "dangers": Seymour, "Middle East," 306.

175 "My name": "Palestinian Hijacks/US/USSR/Families," *CBS Evening News*, September 10, 1970, #212045, VTNA; Tova Lev Kahn telephone conversation, March 28, 2019.

175 big smile: AP Archive, "Guerrilla Hijackings."

175 getting us home: Ridenhour, "Hijacked to Jordan," 11.

175 get us out: David Zenian, "Hijack Hostages Stroll in Desert as Deadline Nears," *Jerusalem Post*, September 9, 1970.

175 care: Raab, *Terror in Black September*, 65.

175 forgotten: Deposition in lawsuit against TWA.

175 know about us: Zenian, "Hostages Stroll in Desert."

175 "blackout," "you are": Haesler conversation, recalling Kiburis.

175 ten-second: AP Archive, "Guerrilla Hijackings."

176 window seat: AP Archive.

15

177 "thinking": June Haesler conversation, New York, October 14, 2019, recalling Kiburis.

177 assured us, echoed: CH diary; statement of Flight Engineer A. Kiburis, TWA, 3.

177 tell the world: Statement of passenger R. L. Morris, 4, TWA.

177 "frightened": Leila Khaled, as told to Godfrey Jansen, "'This Is Your New Captain Speaking,'" *Life*, September 18, 1970, 34.

177 admire: Sylvia R. Jacobson, "Seizure" (notes), II, folder 10, box 1, SRJ-AJA.

178 "remarkable": J. F. S. Phillips, "The Dawson Field Hijackings," Diplomatic Report No. 567/70, Jordan, December 22, 1970, 8, FCO 17/1374, TNA.

178 amiable: Claude Frascani, "Report on the Mission in Jordan from 6–30 September, 1970," January 11, 1971 (English translation; original document in French dated December 14, 1970), 3, B AG 226 106-003, ICRC; "Hi-Jacking," Tel. No. 499, September 10, 1970, FCO 14/779, TNA; "Dawson's Field Drama: Life in a Hijacked Hothouse," *Sunday Times* (London), September 13, 1970.

178 crazy: "Dawson's Field Drama"; Yosef Trachtman as told to Steven Pratt, "Captive in the Desert: Yosef's Own Story," *Chicago Tribune*, September 20, 1970.

178 "brothers and sisters": Morris statement, 4.

178 Ohio State: Ernst Vollenweider testimony, October 23 1970, Einvernahmeprotokolle der Besatzungsmitglieder und Geislen, in Kantonspolizei Zurich, Offiziersposten Flughafen (Interrogation Records of Crew and Hostages), Cantonal Police Zurich, Airport), Beilagen B (Exhibit B), folder 189/2/3, Swissair.

178 sunset walk: "Portrait of a Guerrilla Hijacker: Passenger's Diary Recalls Debates, Suspense," *Los Angeles Times*, September 14, 1970.

178 "kindhearted": Ralph S. Sanford, "First Hand Experiences on a Swissair Flight—Which Took a Side Trip to the Jordanian Desert," speech at New York University and Post Graduate Hospital Alumni Association, October 20, 1970, 7, folder 4, box 2, SRJ-AJA.

178 sister, imprisoned: John R. Pherson, "Americans Detained by PFLP," September 14, 1970, folder marked "10/1/1970," boxes 683–84, RG59, State Department, NARA.

178 "beautiful": Kathryn Johnson, "UK Prof Held Hostage Used Yoga for Aid," *Lexington (KY) Leader*, October 1, 1970.

178 *Do I hate*, "such pain": Fran Chesler, "The Saga of a Flight: TWA Flight 741, September 6–September 28, 1970," unpublished ms., Fall 1970, part II, 5, 9.

178 treated with care: Morris statement, 5.

178 "tough soldiers": "Angry Men, Desperate Days," *Newsweek*, September 21, 1970, 24.

178 guns were cool: Daniel Kahn video conversation, September 19, 2020.

178 cat's cradle: Jacobson, "Individual and Group Responses," 463.

178 "child cried": *The Hijack Conspiracy*, part 2, September 12, 1970, CBS News special report with John Hart.

178 "pretty nice": "Palestinian Hijacks/US/USSR/Families," *CBS Evening News*, September 10, 1970, #212045, VTNA.

178 captors and crew: Rudolf Swinkels crew report, 5, courtesy of June Haesler; "Combined Statement of Hostesses: B. McCarthy, R. Metzner, V. McVey, L. Jensen," 6, TWA.

178 disapproved: Jacobson, "Seizure" (notes), III–2.

179 "No thanks": Kiburis quoted in Rodney C. Campbell, "TWA Flight 741—Hijacked September 6, 1970," *TARPA Topics*, November 2007, 61.

179 "complete control": "Stewardess Tells of Stay in Desert," *Asbury Park Evening Press*, September 16, 1970.

179 "leaders": CH and MH with SH, interview by Jeremy Cole and A. J. Sullivan, New York, September 20, 1970, original tape.

179 Catherine observed: CH and MH with SH.

179 empathy: "'We Were Hijacked!'" *Seventeen*, December, 1970, 170.

179 "very sympathetic": "Passengers Now 'Sympathetic,'" *Winnipeg Free Press*, September 15, 1970.

179 "Naturally," and following: Abu-Sharif and Mahnaimi, *Best of Enemies*, 86–87.

179 "fair hearing": Kiburis statement, 3.

179 "I am a soldier," and following: [Walter Jost] narrative, 39, 48, English translation of Jost, *Rufzeichen*, folder 5, box 2, SRJ-AJA.

179 "*very* serious": Moss, *Girl on a Plane*, 111, 140, 226 (a fictionalized account; see 273–74).

180 "Why": Walter Reich, "Hostages and the 'Syndrome,'" *New York Times*, January 15, 1980.

180 engaged: Hyman Kenneth Salenger, "Stress, Anxiety and Certain Characteristics of Cohesion: A Study of Relationships and Implications" (PhD diss., Laurence University, 1972), 134.

180 crew cautioned: Sylvia R. Jacobson, "Speech Delivered at Temple Israel, Tallahassee, Florida, September 18, 1970," unpaginated questions and answers, folder 8, box 2, SRJ-AJA.

180 mostly listened: CH and MH with SH, Cole interview; Morris statement, 4; Jacobson, "Speech Delivered," unpaginated questions and answers.

180 "No, no,": CH and MH with SH, Cole interview.

180 indoctrination: "Freed Hostages Careful to Emphasise 'Good Treatment,'" *Jerusalem Post*, September 14, 1970.

180 "Yes, yes": CH and MH with SH, Cole interview.

181 ten-year-old: CH and MH with SH; Michael T. Kaufman, "Hijacked to the Desert: Account by Passengers," *New York Times*, September 17, 1970.

181 "deserve": CH and MH with SH, Cole interview.

181 admiration: CH and MH with SH.

181 confirms, and following: Sarah (Malka) Bliner telephone conversation, April 12, 2020.

181 connections: "Combined Statement of Hostesses," 3, 4; Jacobson, "Speech Delivered," unpaginated questions and answers.

181 paperwork: Pherson, "Americans Detained."

181 photograph: "'We Were Hijacked!'" 170.

182 hotel bills: Jacobson, "Speech Delivered," unpaginated questions and answers.

182 car-wash: Arnold C. Ropeik, "Day-by-Day . . . The Ordeal of the Raabs," *Trenton Sunday Times Advertiser*, September 20, 1970.

182 address book, uniform, ribbons: Kiburis statement, 2.

182 handed over: Raab, *Terror in Black September*, 50 (quoting 1970 recollections).

182 "grilling," "irate": Jim Majer, "Black September, 1970," *TARPA Topics*, November 2009, 14.

182 "How many," fiancé: Jim Majer email, January 14, 2020.

182 go-betweens: Kiburis statement, 2; "Combined Statement of Hostesses," 3; Majer, "Black September," 13.

182 "religious articles," "mountain": Swinkels crew report, 5.

182 "Don't lie": Chesler, "Saga of a Flight," part I, 3.

182 "list items": MH diary, September 8, 1970.

182 calling hostages: "Combined Statement of Hostesses," 7; Jacobson, "Individual and Group Responses," 465.

182 advised us: "Combined Statement of Hostesses," 3.

182 teenage girl: "'We Were Hijacked!'" 170.

182 "See?": Raab, *Terror in Black September*, 81.

183 prayer books, toys: Susie (Hirsch) Rosenrauch, "Resilience and Coping in the Face of Trauma: A Retrospective Account Thirty Years after a Skyjacking," unpublished ms., 1999, 18; Raab, *Terror in Black September*, 49.

183 model El Al airplane: Ropeik, "Day-by-Day."

183 jewelry: Tova Lev Kahn conversation, New York, April 2, 2019.

183 presents: Howie Hirsch, "My Hijacking Story," unpublished ms., 2004.

183 statue: Mitchell Meltzer as told to Howard Southgate, "Thumbs Up: Twenty-One Days as a Hijack Hostage," unpublished ms., 1970.

183 movie camera: Burmeister, *Sky-Jacked*, 27, 26.

183 "suitcases": CH diary.

183 "I cried": MH diary, September 10, 1970.

183 "secret place": Saint-Exupéry, *Little Prince*, 31.

183 didn't believe: Fran Chesler conversation, Petah Tikvah, Israel, July 5, 2019.

183 wasn't scared: Barbara Mensch conversation, New York, February 14, 2019.

183 "fantasies": Rosenrauch, "Resilience and Coping," 25.

184 "state of mind": Johnson, "UK Prof Held Hostage."

184 traumatic: Exhibit annexed to lawsuit brought by hostage against Trans World Airlines.

184 "entire world": Sanford, "First Hand Experiences," 8.

184 "collectively terrorized": Frascani, "Report on the Mission in Jordan," 2.

184 "terrified": Frascani quoted in Alec Efty, "'Women, Children are Terrified . . . ,'" *Boston Globe*, September 9, 1970.

184 "didn't understand": "Passenger Advises No Force: 'These Guys Mean Business!'" *Boston Globe*, September 14, 1970.

184 "controlled fear": Mario S. Modiano, "Freed U.S. Citizens Tell of Their Fears," *New York Times*, September 14, 1970.

184 "lingering memory": Elon, *Israelis*, 199.

184 "brought me": Erna [rendered as "Erma"] Jankelovits interview by Sherry Amatenstein, Forest Hills, NY, November 24, 1996, tape #4, Visual History Archive, USC Shoah Foundation.

185 "I know": Jerry Berkowitz in "In Our Own Words: TWA 741, 50th Anniversary Reunion, September 6, 1970–September 6, 2020," organized and compiled by David Raab, private video.

185 one person: CH and MH with SH, Cole interview.

185 "angriest": Deposition in lawsuit brought by hostage against Trans World Airlines.

185 "one lady": Raab, *Terror in Black September*, 30 (quoting 1970 recollections).

16

186 "parade": CH telephone interview by Jeffrey D. Simon, March 21, 1992, original tape. See also statement of passenger R. L. Morris, 3, TWA; Jim Majer, "Black September, 1970," *TARPA Topics*, November 2009, 12.

186 dignified: Sylvia R. Jacobson, "Speech Delivered at Temple Israel, Tallahassee, Florida, September 18, 1970," 9, folder 8, box 2, SRJ-AJA.

186 pretended: CH and MH with SH, interview by Jeremy Cole and A. J. Sullivan, New York, September 20, 1970, original tape.

186 Sometimes: CH and MH with SH.

186 pointed: Deposition in lawsuit brought by hostage against Trans World Airlines.

186 tourists: "Combined Statement of Hostesses: B. McCarthy, R. Metzner, V. McVey, L. Jensen," 4, TWA; Raab, *Terror in Black September*, 29 (quoting 1970 recollections); Tova Lev Kahn conversation, New York, April 2, 2019.

186 "freak": Susie (Hirsch) Rosenrauch, "Resilience and Coping in the Face of Trauma: A Retrospective Account Thirty Years after a Skyjacking," unpublished ms., 1999, 20.

186 "attraction": Fran Chesler, "The Saga of a Flight: TWA Flight 741, September 6–September 28, 1970," unpublished ms., Fall 1970, part II, 1.

186 inmates: Mitchell Meltzer as told to Howard Southgate, "Thumbs Up: Twenty-One Days as a Hijack Hostage," unpublished ms., 1970.

186 barter: Claude Frascani, "Report on the Mission in Jordan from 6–30 September, 1970," January 11, 1971 (English translation; original document in French dated December 14, 1970), 2–3, B AG 226 106-003, ICRC.

186 "feel exactly": CH and MH with SH, Cole interview.

186 requested: "Combined Statement of Hostesses," 4; Woods quoted in Rodney C. Campbell, "TWA Flight 741—Hijacked September 6, 1970," *TARPA Topics*, November 2007, 60.

187 machine guns: Rudolf Swinkels crew report, 4, courtesy of June Haesler.

187 wouldn't harm, "when people": CH and MH with SH, Cole interview.

187 nice commandos: Hyman Kenneth Salenger, "Stress, Anxiety and Certain Characteristics of Cohesion: A Study of Relationships and Implications" (PhD diss., Laurence University, 1972), 130.

187 "trust": Deposition in lawsuit against TWA.

187 "shoot": June Haesler conversation, New York, October 14, 2019.

187 "Here, catch": McVey quoted in Campbell, "TWA Flight 741," 60.

187 "manned": Paul Martin, "Biscuits and Water Diet for Hijacked Britons," *London Times*, September 11, 1970.

187 surrounded: Intelligence Information Cable, "Government of Jordan intentions regarding hijacked TWA and Swissair airliners," September 8, 1970, folder 2, box 330, Subject Files: Hijacking, National Security Council Files, Nixon Presidential Materials Staff, RNL.

187 "From time to time": Saint-Exupéry, *Little Prince*, 46–47.

187 "We're glad," "Thanks": Raab, *Terror in Black September*, 51 (quoting 1970 recollections).

187 "Explosives": "Hijacking," Tel. No. FOH, September 8, 1970, FCO 14/778, TNA.

187 "reputation": Near Eastern Department, "Hijacking of Aircraft," September 9, 1970, FCO 14/778, TNA.

188 "We must," "because of you": Tikva (Raab) Yudkowitz conversation, Teaneck, NJ, March 18, 2019.

188 explosion-ready: Jacobson, "Individual and Group Responses," 465.

188 "cannot wait": Burmeister, *Sky-Jacked*, 28.

188 "Don't": Haesler conversation.

188 "frightened": Leila Khaled, as told to Godfrey Jansen, "'This Is Your New Captain Speaking,'" *Life*, September 18, 1970, 34.

188 "think about": CH and MH with SH, Cole interview.

188 lounge: Swinkels crew report, 5; "Three Stewardesses Describe Week aboard Hijacked Plane," *Danville (VA) Bee*, September 14, 1970.

189 red-rimmed: Deposition in lawsuit against TWA.

189 "have coffee": Kahn conversation.

189 "want to die": Kahn.

189 questioned Sara Raab, and following: Raab, *Terror in Black September*, 58, 74–75; Arnold C. Ropeik, "Day-by-Day . . . The Ordeal of the Raabs," *Trenton Sunday Times Advertiser*, September 20, 1970.

190 brought Mimi, and following: Mimi (Beeber) Nichter video conversation, September 27, 2020.

190 army shirt, photo, "Israeli army": Beeber quoted in Simon, *Terrorist Trap*, 100.

191 did not believe: "Jordan Hostages," *CBS Evening News*, September 27, 1970, #212445, VTNA.

191 "very intense": Nichter conversation.

191 pleasant messages: Deposition in lawsuit against TWA.

191 *both okay*: CH and MH to SH and EH, Jordan desert, September 1970.

192 "fear and efforts," "expressions": Jacobson, "Children's Attitudinal and Behavioral Responses," 9, 11. On 11, Jacobson mixes me up with a much younger child to whom the Palestinian doctor fed baby food.

192 "didn't really": CH and MH with SH, Cole interview.

17

195 "most frightening": MH diary, September 8, 1970.

195 "hysterical": MH diary, September 11, 1970.

195 around 2:30, and following: Raab, *Terror in Black September*, 1–2, 89–90.

196 stop crying: Tikva (Raab) Yudkowitz conversation, Teaneck, NJ, March 18, 2019.

196 sandstorm: Rudolf Swinkels crew report, 7, courtesy of June Haesler; "Combined Statement of Hostesses: B. McCarthy, R. Metzner, V. McVey, L. Jensen," 4, TWA; statement of hostess J. Haesler, 7, TWA.

196 arriving vans: "Portrait of a Guerrilla Hijacker: Passenger's Diary Recalls Debates, Suspense," *Los Angeles Times*, September 14, 1970.

196 270 of us: Reuters, Amman, September 11, 1970, PREM 15/201, TNA.

196 guards: Statement of passenger R. L. Morris, 5, TWA; "Hijack Victims Safe Now, but Left Loved Ones," *Daily News*, September 14, 1970; Sylvia R. Jacobson, "Thursday, September 10th" (notes), 1, folder 10, box 1, SRJ-AJA.

196 doctor: Jacobson, "Individual and Group Responses," 466.

196 halted: Amman to Geneva, 8:06Z, September 12, 1970,'B AG 226 106-001, ICRC; Bern to Washington #2187, September 11, 1970, folder 2, box 330, Subject Files: Hijacking, National Security Council Files, Nixon Presidential Materials Staff, RNL; "Middle East," International Committee of the Red Cross, *Annual Report 1970*, 62.

196 ordered: Amman to Geneva, 8:06Z, September 12, 1970, and "Département des Opérations: Chronologie de l'action du CICR en Jordanie du 6 au 30 Septembre 1970 (détournements d'avions et actions de secours)," October 14, 1970, 1, B AG 226 106-003, both ICRC; Bern to Washington #2187, September 11, 1970, folder 2, box 330, RNL; "Combined Statement of Hostesses," 6.

196 no longer, instructed, "threw": Swinkels crew report, 7.

196   *Something*: [Walter Jost] narrative, 61, English translation of Jost, *Rufzeichen*, folder 5, box 2, SRJ-AJA.
196   Abu-Fadi: Fritz Schreiber testimony, October 27, 1970, Einvernahmeprotokolle der Besatzungsmitglieder und Geislen, in Kantonspolizei Zurich, Offiziersposten Flughafen (Interrogation Records of Crew and Hostages, Cantonal Police Zurich, Airport), Beilagen B (Exhibit B), folder 189/2/3, Swissair.
196   possibly dictated: Murray Sayle, "Confusion as British Reach Hotel," *Sunday Times* (London), September 13, 1970.
196   "already loaded," "don't play games," "desperate": "23 Hostages Taken to Amman; Fate of Others Still Uncertain," *Los Angeles Times*, September 12, 1970.
196   "Conditions": Bird, *Crossing Mandelbaum Gate*, 263–64.
197   dynamite: Bern to Washington #2187, September 11, 1970, folder 2, box 330, RNL.
197   distributed: "Combined Statement of Hostesses," 4.
197   "Ladies and gentlemen": Address of Dr. George Habash, Secretary General of the Central Committee of the Popular Front for the Liberation of Palestine at the Jordan Intercontinental Hotel," Amman, June 12th 1970," 1, folder marked "10/1/1970," boxes 683–84, RG59, State Department, NARA. For a different translation from the Arabic, in *Al-Nahar* in Beirut, June 13, 1970, see "Speech by Secretary-General Habbash of the PFLP to Foreign Hostages Held in the Intercontinental Hotel in Amman," June 12, 1970, in *IDP 1970*, ed. Walid Khadduri (Beirut: Institute for Palestine Studies, 1973), 836–37.
198   "old dream": Peter Young, "Soldiers of a Phantom Nation on the March," *Life*, June 12, 1970, 26D, 28.
198   Habash apologized: Dana Adams Schmidt, "Hussein Accepts Guerrilla Terms; Ousts 2 Generals," *New York Times*, June 12, 1970; Dana Adams Schmidt, "The World: Hussein Yields Under Commando Pressure," *New York Times*, June 14, 1970; Eric Pace, "155 U.S. Citizens in Jordan Leave as Fighting Ends," *New York Times*, June 13, 1970; "Arab Guerrillas v. Arab Governments," *Time*, June 22, 1970, 22–23; Abu-Sharif, *Arafat and the Dream of Palestine*, 26.
198   "Believe me": Pace, "155 U.S. Citizens in Jordan Leave."
198   "I hope," and following: Address of Dr. George Habash, June 12th 1970, 1.
199   "Anything," and following: Habash, 3.
199   "I know," and following: Address of Dr. George Habash, June 12th 1970, 4.
199   *my fault*: CH telephone interview by Jeffrey D. Simon, March 21, 1992, original tape.
200   "swamp," and following: "Road to Surrender: From the Security Council Resolution . . . to the Rogers' Plan: A Study Presented by the PFLP," quotations on 1, folder marked "10/1/1970," boxes 683–84, NARA.
200   "I stopped": Saint-Exupéry, *Little Prince*, 100.
200   "It's hard": CH written responses to MH questions, August 3, 2015; CH conversation, New York, February 6, 2017.
200   drawing paper: Gliksman, *Nouri*, 426.
200   packed the pages: John R. Pherson, "Americans Detained by PFLP," September 14, 1970, folder marked "10/1/1970," boxes 683–84, NARA; Susie (Hirsch) Rosenrauch and Howie Hirsch conversation, Ra'anana, Israel, July 7, 2019.
200   commandos served, *What the hell*: June Haesler conversation, New York, October 14, 2019.
201   "all the men": MH diary, September 11, 1970.
201   climbed down: Swinkels crew report, 8.
201   ironic: Morris statement, 5.
201   "every remaining": CH diary.
201   "See you!": Haesler conversation.
201   "Don't worry": Michael T. Kaufman, "Hijacked to the Desert: Account by Passengers," *New York Times*, September 17, 1970.
201   felt sad: Burmeister, *Sky-Jacked*, 30, 31.
201   told the men, crowded into: Swinkels crew report, 8.
201   rumor: Schreiber testimony, October 27, 1970, Swissair; Mario S. Modiano, "Freed U.S. Citizens Tell of Their Fears," *New York Times*, September 14, 1970.
201   "My friends": Ralph S. Sanford, "First Hand Experiences on a Swissair Flight—Which Took a Side Trip to the Jordanian Desert," speech at New York University and Post Graduate Hospital Alumni Association, October 20, 1970, 9, folder 4, box 2, SRJ-AJA.
201   *ripped*: [Jost] narrative, 69.
201   Louma, young male: [Jost], [66a]–67.
202   pilot-cousin: Susie (Hirsch) Rosenrauch, "Resilience and Coping in the Face of Trauma: A Retrospective Account Thirty Years after a Skyjacking," unpublished ms., 1999, 16.
202   Israeli Air Force: Raab, *Terror in Black September*, 45.
202   airworthy: Statement of Flight Engineer A. Kiburis, TWA, 3; "Report: Hijacking—Flight 741," 4, TWA; Jim Majer, "Black September, 1970," *TARPA Topics*, November 2009, 12.
202   "enough": Kiburis quoted in Rodney C. Campbell, "TWA Flight 741—Hijacked September 6, 1970," *TARPA Topics*, November 2007, 58–59.
202   blankets: Statement of First Officer J. A. Majer, 2, TWA; "Report: Hijacking of Flight 741," 4, TWA.
202   "These men": MH diary, September 11, 1970.
202   Shabbat program: Fran Chesler, "The Saga of a Flight: TWA Flight 741, September 6–September 28, 1970," unpublished ms., Fall 1970, part II, 9.
202   talent show: "Three Stewardesses Describe Week Aboard Hijacked Plane," *Danville (VA) Bee*, September 14, 1970.
202   talking softly: Kaufman, "Hijacked to the Desert."
202   sentry duty: Jacobson, "Individual and Group Responses," 467; Sylvia R. Jacobson, "Leadership Patterns and Stress Adaptations Among Hostages in Three Terrorist Captured Planes," International Conference on Psychological Stress and Adjustment in Time of Peace and War, Tel Aviv, Israel, January 7, 1975, 11, folder 9, box 1, SRJ-AJA.
202   reassuring: "'Not Knowing if Anyone Knew Was the Worst Part,'" *Tallahassee Democrat*, September 20, 1970.
203   "flirting," "You know," "Don't worry": Tova Lev Kahn conversation, New York, April 2, 2019.
203   "touching": "Combined Statement of Hostesses," 5.
203   "Get off": CH and MH with SH, interview by Jeremy Cole and A. J. Sullivan, New York, September 20, 1970, original tape; Kaufman, "Hijacked to the Desert."

203 Palestina: Deposition in lawsuit brought by hostage against Trans World Airlines.

203 "If you": Deposition.

203 overheard, Rumors: "Combined Statement of Hostesses," 5.

203 stayed awake: James E. Goodman, "June Haesler 'Wasn't Bored,' Plans to Fly Again," *Trenton Sunday Times Advertiser*, September 20, 1970.

203 "Good-bye": Sylvia R. Jacobson, "Speech Delivered at Temple Israel, Tallahassee, Florida, September 18, 1970," 17, folder 8, box 2, SRJ-AJA.

203 "Don't worry," *kill us*: Deposition in lawsuit against TWA.

203 convoy: "Hijacking," Tel. No. 508, September 11, 1970, FCO 14/779, TNA.

203 updated proposal: Amman to Geneva, 9:21Z, September 10, 1970, B AG 226 106-001; Amman to Geneva, 22:45Z, September 10, 1970, B AG 226 106-001; and Amman to Geneva, 17:04Z, September 10, 1970, B AG 226 106-004, all ICRC; "Hi-Jacking," Tel. No. 496, September 10, 1970, FCO 14/779, TNA; Kissinger to Nixon, "Mid-Day Report on the Hijacking Situation," September 10, 1970, and Amman to Washington #4576, September 11, 1970, both folder 2, box 330, RNL; "Opération Jordanie, Septembre–Décembre 1970: Journal des évènements," Département des Opérations, Comité International de la Croix-Rouge, Geneva, March 1971, 17, B AG 226 106-003, ICRC.

204 remaining hostages, "particularly important": "Hi-Jacking," Tel. No. 502, September 10, 1970, PREM 15/201, TNA.

204 "clever": Washington Special Actions Group Minutes, September 10, 1970, box H–114, National Security Council Files, Nixon Presidential Materials, NARA, in *FRUS*, vol. 24, *Jordan, September 1970* (Washington, DC, 2008), document #222, 643.

204 uninterested: "Hijacking: Secretary of State's telephone conversation with Mr. Rogers," September 11, 1970, FCO 14/779, TNA; Peter Grose, "Mrs. Meir Indicates Israel Won't Free Guerrillas," *New York Times*, September 11, 1970.

204 "crimes": Tel Aviv to Washington #4977, September 11, 1970, "Hijacking," folder 2, box 330, RNL.

204 Instead, strong statement: Mordechai Kidron telephone message to Geneva, 9h45, September 11, 1970, B AG 226 106-001, ICRC.

204 force: Tel Aviv to Washington #4977.

204 "Jewish law": Saul Jay Singer, "Rav Moshe Feinstein, Golda Meir, and Redeeming Skyjacked Hostages," *Jewish Press*, August 8, 2018.

204 objections: Amman to Washington #4576, 8:25Z, September 11, 1970, folder 2, box 330, RNL; Tel. No. 242, September 11, 1970, FCO 14/779, TNA.

204 Fourth Geneva: Geneva to Amman, 5:00Z, September 11, 1970, B AG 226 106-004 ICRC.

204 "discriminative": "Middle East," *Annual Report 1970*, 59–60.

204 "fantastic tension": Kissinger to Nixon, "Mid-Day Report on Hijacking Situation," September 11, 1970, folder 2, box 330, RNL.

204 "failed," "mad hope": Rochat, *L'homme à la croix*, 452, 453.

204 increasing strains: "Rapport de M. Freymond," Geneva, September 14, 1970, 2, B AG 226 106-003, ICRC; J. F. S. Phillips, "The Dawson Field Hijackings," Diplomatic Report No. 567/70, Jordan, December 22, 1970, 3, FCO 17/1374, TNA.

205 "except the PFLP": Paraphrased in Michael Adams, "Visit to Jordan, September 1970," 13, MA-UEL.

205 PLO leadership: "SITREP up to 0800 Saturday 12 September 1970," PREM 15/202, TNA; Snow and Phillips, *Leila's Hijack War*, 51.

205 military intervention: Amman to Geneva, 7:46Z, September 11, 1970, B AG 226 106-001, ICRC; "Palestinian Hijacks/Demands/US," *ABC Evening News*, September 11, 1970, #11966, VTNA.

205 broadcast: "BBC News Broadcasts," September 11, 1970, FCO 14/779, TNA; "Hi-Jacking," Tel. No. 512, September 11, 1970, FCO 14/779, TNA.

205 why the commandos: "Secretary of State's telephone conversation with Mr. Rogers," September 11, 1970, FCO 14/779, TNA; Claude Frascani, "Report on the Mission in Jordan from 6–30 September, 1970," January 11, 1971 (English translation; original document in French dated December 14, 1970), 4, B AG 226 106-003, ICRC.

205 military planes: Kissinger to Nixon, "Hijacking Status," September 9, 1970, folder marked "September 8–14, 1970, 2 of 2," box 971, Alexander M. Haig Chronological Files, National Security Council Files, Nixon Presidential Materials Staff, RNL; Tad Szulc, "6 U.S. Transports Wait in Turkey," *New York Times*, September 10, 1970; Kissinger, *White House Years*, 605.

205 "U.S. Sixth Fleet": Reuters, Amman, September 11, 1970, PREM 15/201, TNA.

205 telegram and radio messages: Geneva to Amman, 11:55, September 11, 1970, B AG 226 106-001, and "Radio-message," Geneva to Amman, 13:00Z, September 11, 1970, B AG 226 106-001, both ICRC; Bern to Washington #2187, September 11, 1970, folder 2, box 330, RNL.

205 "so confusing": "Telephone conversation between the Foreign and Commonwealth Secretary and Mr. Rogers," September 11, 1970, FCO 14/779, TNA.

205 "purely humanitarian": Washington to Amman #147080, September 9, 1970, and Washington to Ankara #147083, September 9, 1970, both folder 2, box 330, RNL.

205 evacuation: "Telephone conversation between the Foreign and Commonwealth Secretary and Mr. Rogers."

205 "calm": "Hijacking," Tel. No. 516, September 11, 1970, FCO 14/779, TNA.

205 massacre: R. Hanbury-Tenison, "Hijacking," September 11, 1970, PREM 15/201, TNA; R. Hanbury-Tenison, "Hijacking," September 11, 1970, FCO 14/779, TNA.

205 After midnight: Geneva to Amman, 1:30, September 12, 1970, B AG 226 106-001, and Geneva to Amman, 1:50Z, September 12, 1970, B AG 226 106-004, both ICRC.

206 "international crisis": "Piraterie confusion sur le sort des otages de Zarka," Agence-France Press, Geneva, September 12, 1970, B AG 226 106-004, ICRC.

206 wanted to know: "Hijacking," September 12, 1970, PREM 15/202, TNA; "SITREP up to 0800."

206 Frantic: Hella Pick, "What do the Jet Captives Need?" *Guardian*, September 11, 1970.

206 "threatening": Kissinger, *White House Years*, 608.

206 "critical stage": Kissinger to Nixon, "Mid-Day Report on Hijacking Situation," September 11, 1970.

206 "No!": Kissinger-Rogers telephone conversation transcript, September [11 or 12], 1970, Jordan File, box 30, Nixon Presidential Materials Staff, RNL.

206   "Dead or alive": Nixon-Kissinger telephone conversation transcript, September 11, 1970, Chronological Files, box 30, Nixon Presidential Materials, NARA, in *FRUS*, vol. 24, document #226, 658.

206   thought plenty, and following: "Hijacked Hostages," #2002, Moving Images Relating to Intelligence and International Relations, RG263, CIA, NARA.

18

207   Together: Amman to Washington #4537, September 10, 1970, folder 2, box 330, Subject Files: Hijacking, National Security Council Files, Nixon Presidential Materials Staff, RNL.

207   vans escorted: David Hirst, "Guerrillas Let Hostages Leave Desert," *Guardian*, September 12, 1970; A. D. Horne, "Hijackers Blow Up 3 Jetliners," *Washington Post*, September 13, 1970.

207   quizzed: "Combined Statement of Hostesses: B. McCarthy, R. Metzner, V. McVey, L. Jensen," 5, TWA.

207   "Do you believe": Yosef Trachtman as told to Steven Pratt, "Captive in the Desert: Yosef's Own Story," *Chicago Tribune*, September 20, 1970.

207   plastic explosives: "The Diary of Sergeant Ernest Hartill," *Sunday Times* (London), September 27, 1970.

207   "dynamite": William Tuohy, "Hostages Moved, 3 Planes Blown Up," *Los Angeles Times*, September 13, 1970.

207   confiscated: Sylvia R. Jacobson, "Speech Delivered at Temple Israel, Tallahassee, Florida, September 18, 1970," addenda, 2, folder 8, box 2, SRJ-AJA.

208   "How many times": Raab, *Terror in Black September*, 106; Arnold C. Ropeik, "Day-by-Day . . . The Ordeal of the Raabs," *Trenton Sunday Times Advertiser*, September 20, 1970.

208   Stationed: Statement of hostess J. Haesler, 8, TWA; Haesler quoted in Rodney C. Campbell, "TWA Flight 741—Hijacked September 6, 1970," *TARPA Topics*, November 2007, 69.

208   commandos shepherded: Fran Chesler, "The Saga of a Flight: TWA Flight 741, September 6–September 28, 1970," unpublished ms., Fall 1970, part I, 4.

208   called out names: "Report from F/O T. R. Cooper," September 1970, 12, FCO 14/785, TNA.

208   sorting everyone: "Report from Cooper," 12; Peder Sollie testimony, September 17, 1970, and Jean-Michel Weiss testimony, October 21, 1970, both Einvernahmeprotokolle der Besatzungsmitglieder und Geislen, in Kantonspolizei Zurich, Offiziersposten Flughafen (Interrogation Records of Crew and Hostages, Cantonal Police Zurich, Airport), Beilagen B (Exhibit B), folder 189/2/3, Swissair.

208   moved quickly: "Diary of Sergeant Hartill"; "On This Day in History: September 6," ITN Source, YouTube, uploaded by Jessica Lamb, May 29, 2015, no longer available, accessed September 19, 2022.

208   at Dawson's Field: Archival footage in "Hijacked," written and directed by Ilan Ziv, *American Experience*, PBS, 2006; archival footage in "Black September: Three Planes Were Hijacked by the PFLP," YouTube, uploaded by Global Entertainment, May 20, 2017, no longer available, accessed September 19, 2022; AP Archive, "Guerrilla Hijackings: Deadline at Dawson's Field," uploaded September 23, 1970, YouTube video.

208   Dalal: Terry Gallacher, "Dawson's Field 1970," January 3, 2012, in "Terence Gallacher's Recollections of a Career in Film: A Series of Articles on Documentary Film Making," terencegallacher.wordpress.com/2012/01/03/dawsons-field-1970/.

209   saw and heard: Fritz Schreiber testimony, October 27, 1970, and Janosfia testimony, December 9, 1970, Swissair.

209   open their mouths: "Diary of Sergeant Hartill."

209   "extraordinary": Raab, *Terror in Black September*, 109.

209   "spectacular": "Jordan/Released Hostages," *CBS Evening News*, September 26, 1970, #212424, VTNA.

209   swayed violently: "Report from Cooper," 13.

209   "pieces of metal": Barbara Mensch conversation, New York, February 14, 2019.

209   *fanatics*: [Walter Jost] narrative, 74, English translation of Jost, *Rufzeichen*, folder 5, box 2, SRJ-AJA.

209   "school kids": Beeber quoted in Simon, *Terrorist Trap*, 100.

209   "beautiful": Tuohy, "Hostages Moved."

209   "home": Patricia Parker Ridenhour, "Hijacked to Jordan," *Alumni News*, University of North Carolina–Greensboro, Winter 1971, 12.

209   caught off guard: "Pour Comité Naville de Freymond," Geneva, 9:30, September 13, 1970, B AG 226 106-001, and "Séance Plénière Extraordinaire," 15h30, September 14, 1970, 3, B AG 226 106-003, both ICRC.

210   meeting, blown up: Bern to Geneva, quoting Amman to Bern, September 12, 1970, 21h00, B AG 226 106-001, and "Message reçu de M. Freymond, via Beyrouth," 16h00, September 12, 1970, B AG 226 106-001, both ICRC; "Pour Comité Naville de Freymond."

210   displeased: "Pour Comité Naville de Freymond."

210   return the planes: "Arab States—Israel," *Central Intelligence Bulletin*, September 14, 1970, 2, Crest: CIA database of declassified intelligence documents, NARA; "PFLP Asks Central Committee to Rescind Suspension," *Daily Report*, FBIS, No. 179, September 15, 1970, A1; "Jordan-Fedayeen: Situation Report," *Weekly Summary*, September 18, 1970, 12, Crest, NARA.

210   "exposing": Radio Baghdad, Voice of Central Committee, September 13, 1970, quoted in "Relations Up to and During the Civil War (June–September 1970)," *Middle East Record*, vol. 5, *1969–70*, ed. Daniel Dishon (Jerusalem: Israel Universities Press, 1977), 316.

210   expel: "Arab States—Israel," 2; "PFLP Asks Central Committee," A1; "Jordan-Fedayeen."

210   intimidate, frustration: "Rapport de M. Freymond," Geneva, September 14, 1970, 3, B AG 226 106-003, ICRC.

210   provoke panic: Snow and Phillips, *Leila's Hijack War*, 57.

210   "rage": "Note de dossier: Téléphone de M. Courvoisier a M. Max Petitpierre," 15:45h, September 12, 1970, B AG 226 106-001, ICRC.

210   "unjustifiable," "imperialist": "Statement by the PFLP on Its Conditions for the Release of the Hostages Held on the Planes Hijacked by the Front," September 15, 1970, in *IDP 1970*, ed. Walid Khadduri (Beirut: Institute for Palestine Studies, 1973), 915.

210   "utter lack": "Statement by the Press Spokesman for the PFLP on Some of the Circumstances Attendant on the Blowing Up of the Planes Hijacked by the Front," September 12, 1970, in Khadduri, *IDP 1970*, 908.

210   "blown up": Nixon-Kissinger telephone conversation transcript, September 12, 1970, Chronological Files, box

30, Nixon Presidential Materials, NARA, in *FRUS*, vol. 24, *Jordan, September 1970* (Washington, DC, 2008), document #232, 664.

210   "giant jetliners": *The Hijack Conspiracy*, part 2, September 12, 1970, CBS News special report with John Hart.

210   Catherine pondered: CH and MH with SH, interview by Jeremy Cole and A. J. Sullivan, New York, September 20, 1970, original tape.

210   internment camp: Raab, *Terror in Black September*, 107.

211   live through: Moss, *Girl on a Plane*, 212 (a fictionalized account; see 273–74).

211   "shot": "Stewardess Tells of Stay in Desert," *Asbury Park Evening Press*, September 16, 1970.

211   relieved: CH and MH with SH, Cole interview.

211   commandos jumped: "Report from Cooper," 13; Horst testimony, October 21 and 29, 1970, and Weiss testimony, October 21, 1970, Swissair; "Palestinian Hijacks/Releases," *NBC Evening News*, September 13, 1970, #453129, VTNA.

211   translated: Mensch conversation.

211   hand over: Schreiber testimony, October 27, 1970, Swissair; "Diary of Sergeant Hartill."

211   heard: Eric Marsden, "Israel Fears for the Missing Victims: Gunpoint Drama after the Planes Exploded," *Sunday Times* (London), September 13, 1970; Horne, "Hijackers."

211   Weapons: Schreiber testimony, October 27, 1970, Swissair.

211   Time: Deposition in lawsuit brought by hostage against Trans World Airlines.

211   prayed: Deposition.

211   faint: Deposition.

211   "lost contact": "Palestinian Hijacks/Israeli Retaliation/Hostages," *CBS Evening News*, September 13, 1970, #212110, VTNA.

211   doctor, drove away: [Jost] narrative, 76.

211   refugee camps: Mensch conversation; June Haesler conversation, New York, October 14, 2019.

211   "a long time": Saint-Exupéry, *Little Prince*, 76, 77.

211   mixture: Sarah (Malka) Bliner telephone conversation, April 12, 2020.

211   "Imperialists!": "U.S. Hostages Tell of Treatment," *Kingston (NY) Daily Freeman* , September 28, 1970.

211   "greeted warmly": "Palestinian Hijacks/Releases," #453129.

211   "indescribably horrible": Jacobson, "Speech Delivered," unpaginated questions and answers.

211   "indescribable confusion," no one possessed: "Jordan: Situation Report as of 06:00 EDT," CIA, September 9, 1970, folder 3, box 330, RNL.

212   Over the phone: "Liste reçue de TWA Zurich à 17h30 par téléphone et transmise à la Croix-Rouge américaine à 19h00," September 13, 1970, B AG 226 106-001, ICRC.

212   MISS HODES AND CHILD, MISS LIST: "Liste reçue de TWA Zurich."

212   120 hostages: Amman to Washington #4638, September 12, 1970, boxes 683–84, RG59, State Department, NARA.

212   proving impossible: "Rapport de M. Freymond."

212   humanitarian treatment: J. P. Tripp, "Hijacking" [ca. September 14, 1970], 2, PREM 15/202, TNA.

212   foreign military attack: "Arab States—Israel," 1.

212   worried: "Darkness in the Desert," *Guardian*, September 12, 1970.

212   off the planes: Kissinger to Nixon, "Overnight Developments on Hijacking," September 11, 1970, box 331, Subject Files: Hijacking, National Security Council Files, Nixon Presidential Materials Staff, RNL.

212   "threat": Rogers-Kissinger telephone conversation transcript, September 12, 1970, Chronological Files, box 30, NARA, in *FRUS*, vol. 24, document #231, 663.

212   "almost unthinkable": Hirst, "Guerrillas Let Hostages Leave."

212   No one knew: "Arab States—Israel," 1–2; London to Washington #7205, September 10, 1970, boxes 683–84, NARA.

212   returned passports: Amman to Geneva, 14:20Z, September 11, 1970, B AG 226 106-001, ICRC.

212   police escorted: Amman to Geneva.

213   hailed from: Linda Charlton, "Arabs Release Some Passengers, but Hold Many on Jets in Desert," *New York Times*, September 12, 1970.

213   some were Jews: Raab, *Terror in Black September*, 96.

213   US government: Tel. No. 2674, September 12, 1970, FCO 14/780, TNA.

213   "transferred": "Telex conference with Amman," September 12, 1970, PREM 15/202, TNA.

213   CIA wondered: "Arab States—Israel," 1.

213   Jordanian ambassador: Washington to Amman #149919, September 12, 1970, boxes 683–84, NARA.

213   "retaken": J. F. S. Phillips, "The Dawson Field Hijackings," Diplomatic Report No. 567/70, Jordan, December 22, 1970, 6, FCO 17/1374, TNA.

213   "free from," "as uncertain": *Hijack Conspiracy*, part 2.

213   In 1970: Nina Nelson, *Your Guide to Jordan* (London: Alvin Redman, 1966), 79–80; archival footage in "Hijacked," PBS, 2006.

213   Intercontinental: Dougherty, *Golden Memories*; Nelson, *Your Guide to Jordan*, 88.

213   *Lights!*: Haesler conversation.

213   hotel facade: Susie (Hirsch) Rosenrauch, "Resilience and Coping in the Face of Trauma: A Retrospective Account Thirty Years after a Skyjacking," unpublished ms., 1999, 22; Edward R. F. Sheehan, "In the Flaming Streets of Amman," *New York Times*, September 27, 1970.

213   couldn't believe: Susie (Hirsch) Rosenrauch and Howie Hirsch conversation, Ra'anana, Israel, July 7, 2019.

214   singing: "Hijacked Hostages," #2002, Moving Images Relating to Intelligence and International Relations, RG263, CIA, NARA.

214   "brought the planes": "Freed Hostages Careful to Emphasise 'Good Treatment,'" *Jerusalem Post*, September 14, 1970.

214   couple of hours: Amman to Geneva, 13:02Z, September 9, 1970 [#2], B AG 226 106-004, ICRC; Michael Adams, "Visit to Jordan, September 1970," 10, MA-UEL.

214   early afternoon: Amman to Washington #4637, September 12, 1970, and Amman to Washington #4638, September 12, 1970, both folder 2, box 330, RNL.

214   Watching: "Hijacked Hostages," #2002.
214   *How can*: CH telephone interview by Jeffrey D. Simon, March 21, 1992, original tape.
214   "Reporters," "This one guy": MH diary, September 12, 1970.
215   "Here they come!": Campbell, "TWA Flight 741," 68.
215   "C'mon": "Hijacked Hostages," #2002.
215   When our driver: "Hijacked Hostages."
216   "We urge": "Hijacked Hostages Freed," #895, Moving Images Relating to Intelligence and International Relations, NARA.
216   alights: "Hijacked Hostages," #2002.
216   "TWA," and following: "Hijacked Hostages."
216   "How about," "They are fine": "Palestinian Hijacks/Releases," #453129.
216   shaking, breaks down: "Freed Hostages Careful."
216   "caked": Tuohy, "Hostages Moved."
216   white dress: Jesse W. Lewis Jr., "'They Awoke Him . . . And Took Him,'" *Washington Post*, September 13, 1970.
216   luggage, porters, entrance: "Hijacked Hostages Freed," #895.
216   "wild confusion": "First Women and Children Freed—'Well Treated,'" *Egyptian Gazette*, September 13, 1970.
217   man materializing: CH and MH with SH, Cole interview.
217   footage: Unidentified BBC footage, in David Raab and Aaron Ovadia, "TWA 741 50th Anniversary Reunion, September 6, 1970–September 6, 2020," private video, courtesy of David Raab.
217   "grab your hand": CH written responses to MH questions, August 3, 2015.

19

218   "Go inside": "Hijacked Hostages Freed," #895, Moving Images Relating to Intelligence and International Relations, RG263, CIA, NARA.
218   "with TWA," faithful stewardesses: Rodney C. Campbell, "TWA Flight 741—Hijacked September 6, 1970," *TARPA Topics*, November 2007, 68.
218   "Richard Wilson": Michael T. Kaufman, "Hijacked to the Desert: Account by Passengers," *New York Times*, September 17, 1970.
218   "our responsibility": Campbell, "TWA Flight 741," 68.
219   emotional scenes: "Hijacked Hostages," #2002, Moving Images Relating to Intelligence and International Relations, NARA.
219   "rough day": "Hijacked Hostages."
219   Watching: Sheila Warnock conversation, New York, September 23, 2019, including reading from journal kept September 6–14, 1970.
219   "My son": Raab, *Terror in Black September*, 107.
219   couldn't find: Warnock conversation.
219   "registered": "Hijacked Hostages Freed," #895.
219   "Your husband": "Hijacked Hostages," #2002.
219   little Connie: Alamy stock photo, #E0YM41, alamy.com.
219   glass of water: Tova Lev Kahn conversation, New York, April 2, 2019.
219   long tables: Tikva (Raab) Yudkowitz conversation, Teaneck, NJ, March 18, 2019.
219   blacked out: Deposition in lawsuit brought by hostage against Trans World Airlines.
220   tourists: Eric Pace, "Amman Diary: Window on the War," *New York Times*, September 24, 1970.
220   reporters: Ibrahim Noori, "To Remove a Bomb Call Room Service," *Boston Globe*, September 15, 1970.
220   "hot lights": Bird, *Crossing Mandelbaum Gate*, 267.
220   "poured down": CH and MH with SH, interview by Jeremy Cole and A. J. Sullivan, New York, September 20, 1970, original tape.
220   hoping: Susie (Hirsch) Rosenrauch, "Resilience and Coping in the Face of Trauma: A Retrospective Account Thirty Years after a Skyjacking," unpublished ms., 1999, 22.
220   "certain things": *Instant Recall*, King World Productions television newsmagazine, September 12, 1990.
220   "Tired," hungry: "Hijacked Hostages," #2002.
220   "did everything": "Freed Hostages Careful to Emphasise 'Good Treatment,'" *Jerusalem Post*, September 14, 1970.
220   "on the verge": "Passengers Describe 'Nightmare' as Captives," *Boston Globe*, September 13, 1970.
220   "Help her": "Hijacked Hostages," #2002.
221   "this many Jews": Jesse W. Lewis Jr., "'They Awoke Him . . . And Took Him,'" *Washington Post*, September 13, 1970.
221   "happy to see": Eric Pace, "Released Hostages Tell of Their Ordeal in Desert," *New York Times*, September 13, 1970.
221   "Miss McCarthy," and following: "Hijacked Hostages," #2002.
221   caustic, motorcade, award: "Douglas Kiker, TV Journalist, 61; Was Correspondent for NBC News," *New York Times*, August 15, 1991.
221   cramping: June Haesler conversation, New York, October 14, 2019.
221   "Everyone": "Drama on the Desert: The Week of the Hostages," *Time*, September 21, 1970, 27.
222   "At first": "Freed Hostages Careful."
222   "good words": "Freed Hostages Careful."
222   "anything": William Tuohy, "Hostages Moved, 3 Planes Blown Up," *Los Angeles Times*, September 13, 1970.
222   "I don't know": "Hijacked," written and directed by Ilan Ziv, *American Experience*, PBS, 2006.
222   "six days," and following: Pace, "Released Hostages"; "Hijacked Hostages," #2002.
223   "rough," and following: "Palestinian Hijacks/Releases," *NBC Evening News*, September 13, 1970, #453129, VTNA.
223   "seen the stuff": "Hijack," produced and directed by Dominic Sutherland, *Timewatch*, BBC/Open University, 2007.
223   "Not these," and following: "Palestinian Hijacks/Releases," #453129; "Hijacked Hostages," #2002.

224 "only worry": William Tuohy, "Popular Front Seems Splintered by Anarchy," *Los Angeles Times*, September 15, 1970.

224 "must eat": "Report from F/O T. R. Cooper," September, 1970, 14, FCO 14/785, TNA.

224 "big question": "Hijacked Hostages," #2002.

224 "haunting": *The Hijack Conspiracy*, part 2, September 12, 1970, CBS News special report with John Hart.

224 "free to leave": Kissinger to Nixon, "Afternoon Report on the Hijacking Situation," September 12, 1970, box 330, Subject Files: Hijacking, National Security Council Files, Nixon Presidential Materials Staff, NARA, in *FRUS*, vol. E-1, *Documents on Global Issues* (Washington, DC, 2005), document #64, 415.

225 depart: Amman to Washington #4637, September 12, 1970, folder 2, box 330, Subject Files: Hijacking, National Security Council Files, Nixon Presidential Materials Staff, RNL.

225 "PFLP hostages": Amman to Washington #4637.

225 couldn't guarantee, *épreuve*: "Opération Jordanie, Septembre–Décembre1970: Journal des évènements," Département des Opérations, Comité International de la Croix-Rouge, Geneva, March 1971, 26, B AG 226 106-003, ICRC.

225 "great danger": Bern to Geneva, 21h00, September 12, 1970, B AG 226 106-001, ICRC.

225 enough space: CH and MH with SH, Cole interview.

225 Catherine: Pace, "Released Hostages."

225 gunfire: Ralph S. Sanford, "First Hand Experiences on a Swissair Flight—Which Took a Side Trip to the Jordanian Desert," speech at New York University and Post Graduate Hospital Alumni Association, October 20, 1970, 11, folder 4, box 2, SRJ-AJA.

225 "panic," "Very bad": Raab, *Terror in Black September*, 107–8.

225 outdoor area: Susie (Hirsch) Rosenrauch and Howie Hirsch conversation, Ra'anana, Israel, July 7, 2019.

225 told the boys: Howie Hirsch, "My Hijacking Story," unpublished ms., 2004.

225 "C & I," "conversed": MH diary, September 12, 1970.

225 "Father requests": "Messages pour les otages transmis par la Croix-Rouge américaine," September 12, 1970, B AG 226 106-004, ICRC.

226 "If you love": Saint-Exupéry, *Little Prince*, 103.

226 diary entries: MH diary, September 12, 1970; CH diary.

226 telephone call: MH diary, September 13, 1970.

226 "jubilant!": CH diary.

20

227 350 hostages: Kissinger, "Hijacking Situation Report, 10:30am Sunday Morning," September 13, 1970, box 331, Subject Files: Hijacking, National Security Council Files, Nixon Presidential Materials Staff, RNL.

227 officials urged, "complete hysteria": Raab, *Terror in Black September*, 116.

227 "Come on": Jacobson, "Children's Attitudinal and Behavioral Responses," 13.

227 "Move apart," laughed: Jacobson, 13.

227 Swiss plane: "Balair 1, chartered by TWA . . . ," 16h00 [September 13?, 1970], B AG 226 106-001, ICRC.

227 Red Cross pilot: "Note de dossier," 11h45, September 13, 1970, B AG 226 106-001, ICRC.

227 "Mr. and Mrs. Stanley Hirsch": "A Family Flies Separately—Still Is Hijack Victim," *International Herald Tribune*, September 9, 1970.

228 the first: Howie Hirsch, "My Hijacking Story," unpublished ms., 2004; Susie (Hirsch) Rosenrauch and Howie Hirsch conversation, Ra'anana, Israel, July 7, 2019.

228 Two hours: Sheila Warnock conversation, New York, September 23, 2019, including reading from journal kept September 6–14, 1970.

228 stylish: "The United Nations Protected Area and Old Nicosia Airport," United National Peacekeeping Force in Cyprus, unficyp.unmissions.org.

228 US ambassador: Sylvia R. Jacobson to William P. Rogers, Tallahassee, FL, December 13, 1971, folder 4, box 1, SRJ-AJA.

228 "I am a Jew," "schoolgirl": "Bride Is Among 254 Hostages Flown to Cyprus," *Guardian*, September 14, 1970.

228 Regina Palace: Map of Nicosia, Department of Lands and Surveys, Cyprus, 1966, rev. 1983, Map Division, New York Public Library.

228 deluxe: Hazel Thurston, *Travellers' Guide to Cyprus* (New York: Bobbs-Merrill, 1971), 110.

228 cigarettes: CH telephone interview by Jeffrey D. Simon, March 21, 1992, original tape; CH written responses to MH questions, August 3, 2015.

228 "Catherine & Sue & I": MH diary, September 13, 1970.

228 telephone lines: Philip Ward, *Touring Cyprus* (Stoughton, WI: Oleander, 1972), 130.

228 switchboards: CH responses to MH questions; CH email, July 15, 2016.

228 spoke to: CH responses to MH questions.

228 had to go: LH conversation, New York, 2015; LH email, July 15, 2016.

229 little kids: Warnock conversation.

229 "hanging": Tikva (Raab) Yudkowitz conversation, Teaneck, NJ, March 18, 2019.

229 drank and smoked: Warnock conversation.

229 champagne: June Haesler conversation, New York, October 14, 2019.

229 "My husband," and following: "Palestinian Hijacks/Hostages/Israel/US," *NBC Evening News*, September 14, 1970, #453135, VTNA.

230 "All said": "Palestinian Hijacks/Hostages/Israel/US."

230 moon: Weather Reports and Forecast, *New York Times*, September 14, 1970.

230 glow: Ken Macrorie, "Arriving and Departing," *Reporter*, September 13, 1962, 54.

230 airline had called: SH email, September 7, 2008.

230 two hours: EH telephone conversation, August 5, 2015.

230 madhouse: SH email, August 31, 2015.

230 8:30 p.m.: Dick Belsky, "Hostages Home Amid Joy, Fear," *New York Post*, September 15, 1970.

230   "Can you," and following: "Hijacked Sep 6th Hostages Released Sep 11, 1970," YouTube, uploaded by Jessica Lamb, May 29, 2015, no longer available, accessed November 9, 2018.
231   welcoming party: Tova Lev Kahn conversation, New York, April 2, 2019.
231   "so great": MH diary, September 14, 1970.
232   Catherine and I told: EH email, June 5, 2017.
232   Catherine did: SH email, September 7, 2008.
232   "whole family": MH diary, September 14, 1970.
232   "free now": Toni Fitzpatrick diary, September 13, 1970, in Fitzpatrick email, August 18, 2015.
232   *Wandering Jew:* CH responses to MH questions; CH email, June 5, 2017.
232   three minutes: "You can telephone all over the world," Bell System advertisement, 1965.
232   "'Goodbye'": Saint-Exupéry, *Little Prince*, 38, 40.
232   "Dear Catherine & Martha," and following: EH to CH and MH, New York, ca. September 9, 1970.
233   "so glad": MH diary, September 14, 1970.
233   "finally home!" and following: MH to Nurit Weinreb, New York, September 18, 1970.
233   "All is well," and following: CH to Nurit Weinreb, New York, postmarked September 28, 1970.
233   stepmother's family: EH telephone conversation, August 5, 2015; EH email, June 5, 2017; CH and MH with SH, interview by Jeremy Cole and A. J. Sullivan, New York, September 20, 1970, original tape (SH prompting us to repeat what we had talked about).
234   adventure story: SH email, August 12, 2018.
234   can recall: CH email, August 12, 2018.
234   "These children," regimen: EH telephone conversation, August 5, 2015.
234   "Good news!": MH to LH, New York, postmarked December 1, 1970.
234   "plugging away": CH to Lily and Bert Margolies, New York, October 30, 1970.
234   normal: CH email, August 12, 2018.
234   "pushing": CH to Lily and Bert Margolies, New York, postmarked January 25, 1971.
234   "great": MH diary, September 15, 1970.
234   I too loved: MH diary, September 21–22, 1970.
234   didn't bring it up: Loren Chodosh Harkin to MH, "My recollections about Martha, at the start of 7th Grade," May 19, 2019. Also Wilma Friedman conversation, New York, March 1, 2016; Wilma Friedman email, April 6, 2018.
235   I said: Jody Goodman written responses to MH questions, August 2015; Marsha Rich telephone conversation, April 21, 2018; Lisa Grinberg telephone conversation, May 30, 2019.
235   unchanged: Tiana Wimmer email, April 29, 2019.
235   "No harm done": Harkin, "My recollections."
235   "love school!": MH diary, September 22, 1970.
235   "*3* acting classes": CH to LH and EB, New York, postmarked January 24, 1970.
235   felt fragile: CH, Simon telephone interview.
235   jumper: CH responses to MH questions; CH email, June 5, 2017.
235   theater classes: CH to LH and Lily Margolies, New York, October 13, 1970.
235   "Martha and I": CH to Bert Margolies, October 1, 1970.
235   "Thank God": CH diary.
235   "not known": "List of Persons Presumed Held," *New York Times*, September 14, 1970.
235   baby: "A Red Cross Greeting Is Sent to New Mother," *New York Times*, September 13, 1970.
236   recognized, "guerrillas threatened": "In the Desert, Hostage Passengers Can Only Wait," *Life*, September 18, 1970, 36.
236   "strike savagely," "lives in jeopardy": "Chaos in the Sky," *Life*, September 18, 1970, 30.
236   military government: John L. Hess, "Martial Law Proclaimed," *New York Times*, September 17, 1970.
236   stray cats: MH diary, September 17, 1970.
236   photograph: "Pirates in the Sky," *Time* cover, September 21, 1970.
236   image: "The Hijack War," *Newsweek* cover, September 21, 1970.
236   "thinking & feeling": EH to CH and MH, ca. September 9, 1970.

21

237   fifty-six people: Mark R. Arnold, "New Violence Spins Hostages Out of Reach," *National Observer*, September 21, 1970.
237   "How are": Mike Majer to Nixon, September 21, 1970, box 43, Subject Files: Judicial–Legal Matters, White House Central Files, Nixon Presidential Materials Project, RNL.
237   "Hi, Henry," and following: Nixon-Kissinger telephone conversation transcript, September 12, 1970, Chronological Files, box 30, Nixon Presidential Materials, NARA, in *FRUS*, vol. 24, *Jordan, September 1970* (Washington, DC, 2008), document #233, 665–66.
238   familiar terms: "SITREP up to 0800, Saturday 12 September 1970," PREM 15/202, TNA; Bern to Geneva, 21h00, September 12, 1970, and "Message reçu de M. Freymond, via Beyrouth," 16h00, September 12, 1970, B AG 226 106-001, ICRC; "Note pour le Chef du Département," folder 189/4/28, Swissair; Kissinger to Nixon, "Afternoon Report on the Hijacking Situation," September 12, 1970, box 330, Subject Files: Hijacking, National Security Council Files Nixon Presidential Materials Staff, NARA, in *FRUS*, vol. E-1, *Documents on Global Issues* (Washington, DC, 2005), document #64, 415.
238   adamant: Kissinger to Nixon, "Hijacking Situation Report," September 13, 1970, box 331, Subject Files: Hijacking, National Security Council Files, Nixon Presidential Materials Staff, RNL; Kissinger to Nixon, "Mid-Afternoon Report on the Hijacking Situation," September 14, 1970, box 331, RNL; "Minister for Foreign Affairs Abba Eban Replies to Motions for the Agenda on Plane Hijackings," press bulletin, September 15, 1970, FCO 14/782, TNA.
238   "these people": "Palestinian Hijacks/US/Israel," *CBS Evening News*, September 14, 1970, #212127, VTNA.

238   in agreement: "Mrs. Meir Makes Statement on Arrival in New York," *Daily Report*, FBIS, No. 181, September 17, 1970, H1; Washington to Amman #154300, September 19, 1970, RG59, State Department, NARA, in *FRUS*, vol. E-1, document #73, 452; John P. MacKenzie, "Mrs. Meir Rejects Deal on Hostages," *Washington Post*, September 21 1970.

238   "our stand": "Mediation Refused," *Daily Report*, FBIS, No. 179, September 15, 1970, A1.

238   some feared: "Note de dossier, Concerne: téléphone de M. W. Jucker," 15h30, September 13, 1970, B AG 226 106-001, ICRC; Washington to Amman #149954, September 13, 1970, boxes 683–84, RG59, State Department, NARA; Amman to Washington #4672, September 13, 1970, folder 2, box 330, Subject Files: Hijacking, National Security Council Files, Nixon Presidential Materials Staff, RNL; Kissinger to Nixon, "Mid-Afternoon Report on the Hijacking Situation."

238   discontent: "Pour Comité Naville de Freymond," Geneva, 9:30, September 13, 1970, B AG 226 106-001, ICRC; "Jordan: Situation Report as of 06:00 EDT," CIA, September 9, 1970, folder 3, box 330, RNL.

238   ill will: Kissinger to Nixon, "Evening Report on the Hijacking Situation," September 15, 1970, box 331, RNL; "Opération Jordanie, Septembre–Décembre 1970: Journal des évènements," Département des Opérations, Comité International de la Croix-Rouge, Geneva, March 1971, 35, B AG 226 106-003, ICRC.

238   wavering: Bern to Washington #2248, September 14, 1970, and Geneva to Washington #3145, September 14, 1970, both folder 2, box 330, RNL; "Séance Plénière Extraordinaire," 15h30, September 14, 1970, 6, B AG 226 106-003, ICRC.

238   arrested 450: "Palestinian Hijacks/Israeli Counter-Hostages," *NBC Evening News*, September 13, 1970, #453127, and "Israel/Hijack Reaction," *ABC Evening News*, September 14, 1970, #11989, both VTNA; "Israelis Arrest 450 in Bid to Aid Hostages," *New York Times*, September 14, 1970; Peter Grose, "Raids a Surprise," *New York Times*, September 14, 1970; Walter Schwarz, "Arabs Arrested for Interrogation," *Guardian*, September 14, 1970; "Zionists Round-Up 450 Civilians," *Fateh*, September 17, 1970.

238   "security check," "collecting": Peter Grose, "Israel Clears and Frees 75 of 450 Arrested Arabs," *New York Times*, September 15, 1970.

238   government warned: "Talks with PFLP," *Daily Report*, FBIS, No. 179, September 15, 1970, H1; "Hi-Jacking," Tel. No. 573, September 15, 1970, PREM 15/202, TNA, also in FCO 14/781, TNA.

238   "barbaric," "unimaginable": "Israel Warned of Massive Reprisals," *Guardian*, September 14, 1970.

238   "ruthlessness": "Jordan: Situation Report as of 06:00 EDT."

238   seventy-five, all: Grose, "Israel Clears and Frees 75"; Peter Grose, "All 450 Seized by Israelis Now Free," *New York Times*, September 19, 1970.

238   "told Israel": LH conversations, New York.

239   "victims," "peace talks": Walter Schwarz, "The Death of the Desert Robin Hoods," *Guardian*, September 26, 1970.

239   Views: James Feron, "Arabs of West Bank Keeping a Close Eye on Strife in Jordan," *New York Times*, September 18, 1970; James Feron, "On the West Bank, the Mood is Pessimistic," *New York Times*, September 19, 1970; George C. Wilson, "Arabs in Occupied Jordan: Watching a Child Bleed to Death," *Washington Post*, September 23, 1970.

239   "courageous": "L. Dean Brown, Ambassador, Jordan," interview by Horace J. Torbert, May 1989, *Jordan Country Reader* (Arlington, VA: Association for Diplomatic Studies and Training), no pagination, www.adst.org/Readers/Jordan.pdf.

239   Kissinger agreed: Kissinger, *White House Years*, 612, 631.

239   massacre: "Protest," September 24, 1970, News Report, MS Jerusalem Bureau: Series I, AP18.10, folder 159, 80 of pdf, box 7, Associated Press Corporate Archives online.

239   Khaled agreed: Khaled, *My People Shall Live*, 206.

239   officially declared: "Palestinians Say Amman in Flames," *London Times*, September 19, 1970; Eric Pace, "Amman, from the Inside," *New York Times*, September 21, 1970; "Amman: City in Hiding," *Washington Post*, September 21, 1970; "The Battle for Amman," *Jerusalem Post*, September 22, 1970; David Hirst, "The Most Vicious of all Arab Conflicts," *Guardian*, September 24, 1970; "Tales of Terror, Hunger in Amman Told," *Fateh*, September 30, 1970; Alex Efty, "Battles Diary: Devastation Seen All Over Amman," *Fateh*, September 30, 1970; David Lomax, "A Diary of the Jordan Civil War," *Listener* (BBC), October 1, 1970, 444–47.

239   pawn, journalists: Pace, "Amman Diary: Window on the War," *New York Times*, September 24, 1970.

239   "dilapidated": Michael Adams, "Visit to Jordan, September 1970," 47, MA-UEL.

239   sounds, "black and bloated": Patrick Massey, "Hussein's Troops Flatten Amman in Six Days," *Guardian*, September 24, 1970.

239   "How many": Jenevizian quoted in Rodney C. Campbell, "TWA Flight 741—Hijacked September 6, 1970," *TARPA Topics*, November 2007, 75.

239   "rivers": Edward R. F. Sheehan, "In the Flaming Streets of Amman," *New York Times*, September 27, 1970.

239   "Where": Nixon-Kissinger telephone conversation transcript, September 17, 1970, NARA, in *FRUS*, vol. 24, *Jordan, September 1970* (Washington, DC, 2008), document #256, 718.

240   Bern Group: Thomas J. Hamilton, "Fears Voiced in Berne over Fate of the Hostages," *New York Times*, September 23, 1970.

240   "all the buses": Fran Chesler, "The Saga of a Flight: TWA Flight 741, September 6–September 28, 1970," unpublished ms., Fall 1970, part I, 4.

240   "Others also": Barbara Mensch conversation, New York, February 14, 2019.

240   Stopping: Chesler, "Saga of a Flight," part I, 5; Ernst Vollenweider testimony, October 23 1970, Einvernahmeprotokolle der Besatzungsmitglieder und Geiseln, in Kantonspolizei Zurich, Offiziersposten Flughafen (Interrogation Records of Crew and Hostages, Cantonal Police Zurich, Airport), Beilagen B (Exhibit B), folder 189/2/3, Swissair.

240   *Oh, my God*: "Hijacked," written and directed by Ilan Ziv, *American Experience*, PBS, 2006.

240   "prisoners of war" (in Arabic): AP Archive, "RR7038 Guerrilla Hijackings Deadline at Dawson's Field," YouTube video.

240   "more cozy place": "Telex conference with Amman," September 12, 1970, PREM 15/202, TNA.

240   "treat them": John L. Hess, "Arabs Blow Up 3 Jets in Desert after Taking Off Passengers," *New York Times*, September 13, 1970.

240   Swinkels: Rudolf Swinkels crew report, 11, courtesy of June Haesler; Tel. No. 5, September 14, 1970, FCO 14/781, TNA.

240   Dutch citizen: Raab, *Terror in Black September*, 121.

240   Gazing: Swinkels crew report, 12.
240   scattered, moved: "Hijacking," Tel. No. 2677, September 13, 1970, FCO 14/780, TNA; Abu-Sharif and Mahnaimi, *Best of Enemies*, 87–88.
240   pita: Mensch conversation.
240   canned: Patricia Parker Ridenhour, "Hijacked to Jordan," *Alumni News*, University of North Carolina–Greensboro, Winter 1971, 12.
240   sardine cans: Statement of Flight Engineer A. Kiburis, TWA, 4; Woods journal quoted in Campbell, "TWA Flight 741," 72.
240   chess, Scrabble, songs: Raab, *Terror in Black September*, 184 (quoting 1970 recollections); Jim Majer, "Black September, 1970," *TARPA Topics*, November 2009, 17.
240   soothing: Jim Majer email, November 20, 2021.
240   played cards: Statement of passenger R. L. Morris, 6, TWA; Richard Morse as told to Jeremiah V. Murphy, "From Andover to Amman: 20 Days in Desert—Part 1," *Boston Globe*, October 4, 1970; Burmeister, *Sky-Jacked*, 45.
240   poker: Burmeister, *Sky-Jacked*, 45.
240   "Marxist game": Majer, "Black September," 16.
240   "dings": Chesler, "Saga of a Flight," part II, 7; Majer, "Black September," 16.
240   books: Chesler, "Saga of a Flight," part I, 6.
240   birthday: Woods journal quoted in Campbell, "TWA Flight 741," 71; Chesler, "Saga of a Flight," part II, 6; Burmeister, *Sky-Jacked*, 48.
241   atheism, comfort: Raab, *Terror in Black September*, 184, 185 (quoting 1970 recollections).
241   friendship: Chesler, "Saga of a Flight," part II, 7.
241   "very proper": "Seven Terrorists Freed as Last Hijack Hostages Arrive Home," *Jerusalem Post*, October 4, 1970.
241   "we ate": Mario Modiano, "Guerrillas Kissed Last Six Goodbye," *London Times*, October 1, 1970.
241   "all treated": John M. Lee, "U.S. Hostages on Cyprus, Worn Out but Relieved," *New York Times*, September 28, 1970. See also "The Diary of Sergeant Ernest Hartill," *Sunday Times* (London), September 27, 1970 ("The seven Jews in the house were treated very well and the guerrillas were not antagonistic towards them").
241   "treated us," "demanding": Kathryn Johnson, "UK Prof Held Hostage Used Yoga for Aid," *Lexington (KY) Leader*, October 1, 1970.
241   "little more": Lee, "U.S. Hostages on Cyprus."
241   "just trying": Beeber quoted in Simon, *Terrorist Trap*, 101.
241   "situation": Dave Behrens, "Scriptural Greetings for Returning Hostages," *Newsday*, September 29, 1970.
241   "I learned": "Hostages Praise Treatment at Hands of Arab Captors," *Orlando Evening Star*, September 29, 1970.
241   "great many": Saint-Exupéry, *Little Prince*, 83.
241   bastard, letters: Chesler, "Saga of a Flight," part II, 3, 9.
241   "You know": Fran Chesler conversation, Petah Tikvah, Israel, July 5, 2019.
241   spirits, fear: Tel. No. 590 [message from BOAC captain], September 16, 1970, FCO 14/782, TNA.
241   "if anything": Lee, "U.S. Hostages on Cyprus."
241   never get home: "Jordan Civil War 'Very Scary,' Freed Shain Says," *Sheboygan Press*, September 29, 1970.
241   "had to": "Hijackers 'Would Have Killed Us,'" *Guardian*, September 28, 1970. See also "Hostages Home: 'We Were Knocking About Amman,'" *Sunday Times* (London), September 27, 1970.
242   "bringing back": Raab, *Terror in Black September*, 189.
242   the worst: Majer, "Black September," 17; "Captors Thought 'I Was Spy,'" *Jerusalem Post*, September 28, 1970; Raab, *Terror in Black September*, 188–89.
242   "under fire": Peter Hopkirk, "American Captives Saw Their Guards Killed," *Times* (London), September 28, 1970.
242   daily meals, distant gunfire: "'Diary of Sergeant Hartill.'"
242   smell: Raab, *Terror in Black September*, 179 (quoting 1970 recollections).
242   "If you don't": Mensch conversation.
242   "don't remember," "sixteen years old": Mensch.
242   twelve-by-sixteen: Woods journal quoted in Campbell, "TWA Flight 741," 71.
242   *waiting*: Chesler, "Saga of a Flight," part I, 6.
242   "so close": Mimi (Beeber) Nichter video conversation, September 27, 2020.
242   Hussein ordered: "Opération Jordanie," 60.
242   soldiers found: "Jordanian Soldiers Free 16 Hostages," *Egyptian Gazette*, September 26, 1970.
243   had invited: MH diary, September 25, 1970.
243   announced: Tel. No. 676, September 26, 1970, FCO 14/785, TNA; "PFLP to Free all Hostages," *Egyptian Gazette*, September 27, 1970; "Remaining Hostages," *Jerusalem Post*, September 27, 1970; Jonathan C. Randal, "Last Six Hijack Hostages Freed," *Washington Post*, September 30, 1970.
243   "All well," "Oh God," "Dearest Roz," "Honey": "Received from ICRC delegation Amman following message from liberated USA hostages," September 27, 1970, B AG 226 106-002, ICRC.
243   wedding: "Hijacked Bridegroom Missed the Wedding," *Los Angeles Times*, October 1, 1970.
243   sing: "First Hijacked, Then Hooked," *TWA Today*, October 19, 1970, 3.
243   "best possible," and following: "Jordan Hostages," *CBS Evening News*, September 27, 1970, #212445, VTNA.
243   "I suppose": Lee, "U.S. Hostages on Cyprus."
243   "exciting": "Hostages Describe Captivity as 'Exciting, Fantastic, Scary,'" *Miami Herald*, September 28, 1970; "32 American Tell of Joy Over Release," *Los Angeles Times*, September 28, 1970.
244   "affected me": David Raab in "In Our Own Words: TWA 741, 50th Anniversary Reunion, September 6, 1970–September 6, 2020," organized and compiled by David Raab, private video.
244   "F.A.I.T.H.": Majer, "Black September," 19.
244   "Nice," "signed up," "very moving": "Greetings of Released Hostages at Fiumicino Airport . . . September 28, 1970," *Weekly Compilation of Presidential Documents*, October 5, 1970, 1292–93, box 41, Subject: Judicial–Legal Matters, White House Central Files, Nixon Presidential Materials Project, RNL; Chesler identified in Raab, *Terror in Black September*, 222.
244   "Oh, yes": "Nixon/European Tour/Hostages," *ABC Evening News*, September 28, 1970, #12215, VTNA.
244   "big news story": H. R. Haldeman Diaries Collection, September 28, 1970, RNL.

244 Fan Club, the press, "wouldn't recommend": "Hostages Return Home with Mixed Feelings about Their Abductors; Cheered by Hundreds," *JTA Daily News Bulletin*, Jewish Telegraphic Agency, September 30, 1970.

244 filled my diary: MH diary, September 28, 1970.

22

246 last six: "Jordan/Hostages/US Aid," *CBS Evening News*, September 29, 1970, #212485, and "Jordan/Hostages/Prisoners," *NBC Evening News*, September 30, 1970, #453429, both VTNA; Thomas Hamilton, "Last 6 Hostages Are Released," *New York Times*, September 30, 1970; Jonathan C. Randal, "Last Six Hijack Hostages Freed," *Washington Post*, September 30, 1970; "Middle East Crisis: SITREP at 0700," October 1, 1970, FCO 14/786, TNA.

246 "God-knows-where": CH diary.

246 "didn't feel," remained sick: MH diary, September 30, 1970, and September 30–October 3, 1970.

246 "long journey": Saint-Exupéry, *Little Prince*, 42.

246 release, Khaled boarded: "Middle East Crisis: SITREP at 0700"; "Palestinian Prisoner Release," *CBS Evening News*, September 30, 1970, #212526; "Palestinian Prisoner Release," *ABC Evening News*, September 30, 1970, #12271; and "Hijacks/United Nations/Prisoner Release," *CBS Evening News*, October 1, 1970, #206332, all VTNA; "Britain Releases Woman Hijacker," *New York Times*, October 1, 1970; "3 Nations Free Arab Guerrillas," *Washington Post*, October 1, 1970; Christine Eade, "Leila on Her Way Home," *Guardian*, October 1, 1970; "Seven Terrorists Freed as Last Hijack Hostages Arrive Home," *Jerusalem Post*, October 4, 1970; Khaled, *My People Shall Live*, 210–12.

246 Nasser, wreath: "Les 7 fédayines au Caire," October 5, 1970, folder 187/3/101, Swissair; "Hijacking 'Part of Master Plan,'" *Egyptian Mail*, October 8, 1970.

247 "distressed": Khaled, *My People Shall Live*, 210.

247 grudging contribution: Tel. No. 943, October 5, 1970, FCO 14/786, TNA; Peter Grose, "Israelis Release Two Algerian Officials Removed from an Airliner," *New York Times*, October 15, 1970.

247 "rule of law": "Hi-Jacking," Tel. No. 359, October 1, 1970, FCO 14/786, TNA.

247 "aliases": "Chronology of Hijackings of U.S. Registered Aircraft and Legal Status of Hijackers," 17, in US Department of Transportation, Federal Aviation Administration, "Aircraft Hijackings and Other Criminal Acts Against Civil Aviation: Statistical and Narrative Reports," January 1, 1983.

247 "know them": CH and MH with SH, interview by Jeremy Cole and A. J. Sullivan, New York, September 20, 1970, original tape.

247 two-thirds: Kissinger, "Hijacking Situation Report, 10:30am Sunday Morning," September 13, 1970, box 331, Subject Files: Hijacking, National Security Council Files, Nixon Presidential Materials Staff, RNL; "Minister for Foreign Affairs Abba Eban Replies to Motions for the Agenda on Plane Hijackings," press bulletin, September 15, 1970, FCO 14/782, TNA; Raab, *Terror in Black September*, 193.

247 crew members, and following: Eric Pace, "Guerrillas Raise Their Price," *New York Times*, September 16, 1970; "College Girls, Rabbis among Hostages Held Captive by Hijackers in Jordan," *Danville (VA) Register*, September 15, 1970; "U.S. Hostages Include Rabbis, Businessmen," *Washington Post*, September 16, 1970; Kathryn Johnson, "UK Prof Held Hostage Used Yoga for Aid," *Lexington (KY) Leader*, October 1, 1970; Richard Morse as told to Jeremiah V. Murphy, "From Andover to Amman: 20 Days in Desert—Part 1," *Boston Globe*, October 4, 1970; William Montgomery, "Mrs. Burnett Recounts Her Ordeal," *Albuquerque Journal*, September 16, 1970; Beth Rickers, "To Nowhere and Back: Burmeister Shares Story of 1970 in Book," *Worthington (MN) Globe*, July 21, 2012; Patricia Sullivan, "Robert Schwartz: Defense Official Was Hostage in Hijacking," *Washington Post*, June 18, 2007; Amman to Washington #4757, September 15, 1970, box 331, Subject Files: Hijacking, National Security Council Files, Nixon Presidential Materials Staff, RNL (names of hostages held longer).

247 Israeli stamp: Raab, *Terror in Black September*, 93.

248 "not all": "Palestinian Hijacks/US/Israel," *CBS Evening News*, September 14, 1970, #212127, VTNA.

248 "54 other": "Hijacked," written and directed by Ilan Ziv, *American Experience*, PBS, 2006.

248 "PFLP segregated": "Dawson's Field Hijackings," Wikipedia, accessed August 28, 2022; followed by "Six hostages in particular were kept because they were men and American citizens, not necessarily Jews."

248 "56 passengers": "When September Turned Black," *Jerusalem Post Magazine*, September 4, 2020, 10.

248 "No longer": Theodore M. Hesburgh, "A Proposal for Mideast Peace . . . ," *New York Times*, October 1, 1970.

248 "gain": David Wilsworth, "Arab Exiles Learn to Live with Abuse," *London Times*, September 16, 1970. See also James A. Michener, "'What to Do About the Palestinian Refugees?'" *New York Times*, September 27, 1970; Jerome Caminada, "Land for Palestinians May Yet Be the Outcome," *Times* (London), September 28, 1970.

248 fanatics: Georgie Anne Geyer, "The Palestinian Refugees—A New Breed: Smart, Skilled, Fanatical," *New Republic*, November 21, 1970, 15–18; "Drama on the Desert: The Week of the Hostages," *Time*, September 21, 1970, 18; "The U.S. and the Skyjackers: Where Power is Vulnerable," *Time*, September 21, 1970, 12.

248 fanatics, barbarians: "Back to Barbarism," *New York Times*, September 15, 1970; "Help Israel Now," *Congressional Record*, September 18, 1970, 32702.

248 animals: "Current Palestinian Guerrilla Hijackings," *Congressional Record*, September 10, 1970, 31252.

248 strategic error: "Interview with Ghassan Kannafani," *New Left Review* 67 (1971): 53.

248 Jordan, masses: George Habash, "The Popular Front for the Liberation of Palestine," in *Palestine Lives: Interviews with Leaders of the Resistance*, ed. Clovis Maksoud (Beirut: Palestine Research Center, 1973), 69–82.

249 "killing": George Habash interview in *Aksam*, August 15, 1969, quoted in *Middle East Record*, vol. 5, 1969–70, ed. Daniel Dishon (Jerusalem: Israel Universities Press, 1977), 268.

249 "not one particle": PFLP statement, September 29, 1970, quoted in Dishon, *Middle East Record*, 5:268.

249 Habash explained: "Press conference statements by General Secretary Habash of the PFLP outlining the conclusions of the Front's Third National Conference and discussing the strategy of 'revolutionary violence,'" Beirut, March 14, 1972, in *IDP 1972*, ed. Jorgen S. Nielsen (Beirut: Institute for Palestine Studies, 1975), 288.

249 renounce: Paula Schmitt, "Interview with Leila Khaled," *+972* blog, May 17, 2014.

249 "can apologize": "Terror Through Time: Hijack!" narrated by Fergal Keane, produced by Polly Weston, BBC Radio 4, October 21, 2013.

249 package, peace talks: Abu-Sharif and Mahnaimi, *Best of Enemies*, ix–x, 97–99, 102, 161, 208, 215, 216; Abu-Sharif, *Arafat and the Dream of Palestine*, 45–51, 163–77; Bassam Abu-Sharif, "Arafat's Aide, on Israel: We Are Ready to Talk," *New York Times*, June 22, 1988; Anthony Lewis, "A Chance to Talk," *New York Times*, June 23, 1988; Flora Lewis, "Talking of Terror," *New York Times*, November 30, 1988.
249 "pattern": Khalidi, *Hundred Years' War*, 122.
249 "never": Murray Sayle, "Confusion as British Reach Hotel," *Sunday Times* (London), September 13, 1970.
249 "unlikely": Jesse W. Lewis Jr., "'They Awoke Him . . . And Took Him,'" *Washington Post*, September 13, 1970.
249 "press home": "Hijacked," PBS, 2006.
250 "break down," "no hostages": J. F. S. Phillips, "The Dawson Field Hijackings," Diplomatic Report No. 567/70, Jordan, December 22, 1970, 9, 2, FCO 17/1374, TNA.
250 "Why not?," "Yes": Jenevizian quoted in Rodney C. Campbell, "TWA Flight 741—Hijacked September 6, 1970," *TARPA Topics*, November 2007, 55, 65.
250 "many times": "Jordan Hostages," *CBS Evening News*, September 27, 1970, #212445, VTNA.
250 "not to hurt any": "Hijacked," PBS, 2006.
250 "not to hurt anyone": George Habash and Mahmoud Soueid, "Taking Stock: An Interview with George Habash," *Journal of Palestine Studies* 28 (1998): 93.
250 "Many": "We Will Not Be Silenced: Against the Censorship and Criminalization of Academic Political Speech," New York University webinar, October 23, 2020.
251 "kind of cool": Daniel Kahn video conversation, September 19, 2020.
251 "wasn't afraid": "In Our Own Words: TWA 741, 50th Anniversary Reunion, September 6, 1970–September 6, 2020," organized and compiled by David Raab, private video.
251 "collectively terrorized": Claude Frascani, "Report on the Mission in Jordan from 6–30 September, 1970," January 11, 1971 (English translation; original document in French dated December 14, 1970), 2, B AG 226 106-003, ICRC.
251 "didn't understand": "Passenger Advises No Force: 'These Guys Mean Business!'" *Boston Globe*, September 14, 1970.
251 "controlled fear": Mario S. Modiano, "Freed U.S. Citizens Tell of Their Fears," *New York Times*, September 14, 1970.
251 "explode": "Hijack," produced and directed by Dominic Sutherland, *Timewatch*, BBC/Open University, 2007.
251 "kill you": Beeber quoted in Simon, *Terrorist Trap*, 100.
251 "fiery death": Burmeister, *Sky-Jacked*, 28.
251 "None of": "Article: Hijacked! The People Involved and Affected," *American Experience*, PBS, www.pbs.org/wgbh/americanexperience/features/people-involved-and-affected/.
252 "destroy": United Press International-Cairo, September 7, 1970, folder 2, box 330, Subject Files: Hijacking, National Security Council Files, Nixon Presidential Materials Staff, RNL.
252 "frightened": Leila Khaled, as told to Godfrey Jansen, "'This Is Your New Captain Speaking,'" *Life*, September 18, 1970, 34.
252 "could have gone": MH notes from group conversation, TWA 741, 50th anniversary video reunion, organized by David Raab, September 6, 2020.

23

255 "None": F. C. Wiser to Fran Chesler, New York, September 29, 1970, in Chesler scrapbooks; F. C. Wiser to Mitchell Meltzer, New York, September 29, 1970, in Meltzer family papers.
255 "had spent": "Palestinian Hijacks/Releases," *ABC Evening News*, September 13, 1970, #453129, VTNA.
255 "this minute": "Nixon/European Tour/Hostages," *ABC Evening News*, September 28, 1970, #12215, VTNA.
255 "nothing": "Palestinian Hostages/Release," *ABC Evening News*, September 29, 1970, #12237, VTNA.
256 "Oh dear!": MH diary, September 10, 1970.
256 "ANYTHING!": MH diary, September 8, 1970.
256 captors took: MH diary, September 9, 11, 1970.
256 cried hard: MH diary, September 11, 1970.
256 "*all* the men," "Poor man!": MH diary.
256 "Gosh!": MH diary, September 12, 1970.
256 "really nice," "Neat!" "so great," "Glory!" "love school!": MH diary, September 12, 13, 14, 22, 1970.
257 "Literally?": CH written responses to MH questions, August 3, 2015; CH email, July 19, 2018.
257 birthday: inscription "*all* my Love, Foozie," in Samuel Tenenbaum, *The Wise Men of Chelm* (New York: Thomas Yoseloff, 1965).
257 "only thing": MH diary, September 13, 1970.
257 "Curiously," and following: Sylvia R. Jacobson, untitled notes, folder 10, box 1, SRJ-AJA.
257 "no longer": Jacobson, "Children's Attitudinal and Behavioral Responses," 20.
258 "Due to": Rosemary Aurichio to Cheslers, New York, September 30, 1970, in Chesler scrapbook. My father surely received the same letter.
258 "both okay": CH and MH to SH and EH, Jordan desert, September 1970.
258 pink dress: Tova Lev Kahn telephone conversation, March 28, 2019.
258 request: Emilio von Hofmannsthal to "Miss Hodes," New York, September 15, 1970; SH to Emilio von Hofmannsthal, New York, November 30, 1970.
258 plea: H. Kenneth Salenger to "Miss Hodes," Williamsville, NY, September 1971.
258 published article: Jacobson, "Individual and Group Responses," 459–69.
258 note: Sylvia R. Jacobson to SH, Tallahassee, FL, April 4, 1974.
258 meaningful: Kathryn Johnson, "UK Prof Held Hostage Used Yoga for Aid," *Lexington (KY) Leader*, October 1, 1970.
258 witnesses: Richard Morse, as told to Jeremiah V. Murphy, "Hostages in Middle as Guerrillas Face Army," *Boston Globe*, October 5, 1970.
258 Within days: Sylvia R. Jacobson, "Guest Speaker: since Fall 1970," folder 11, box 1, SRJ-AJA; Carrie Teegardin, "Hijack Expert Really Can Say She Knows How It Is," *Tallahassee Democrat*, September 8, 1970.

259 "emotional high": Court order in lawsuit brought by hostage against Trans World Airlines.
259 "sunny vacation": Ralph S. Sanford, "First Hand Experiences on a Swissair Flight—Which Took a Side Trip to the Jordanian Desert," speech at New York University and Post Graduate Hospital Alumni Association, October 20, 1970, 1, 16, folder 4, box 2, SRJ-AJA.
259 "Inside": Abigail Klein Leichman, "The Other 9/11," *Jerusalem Post Magazine*, September 4, 2020, 10.
259 other families: MH notes from group conversation, TWA 741, 50th anniversary video reunion, organized by David Raab, September 6, 2020.
259 parents: Sylvia R. Jacobson, "Observations on Follow-Up on Attitudes and Behaviors," 1, folder 10, box 1, SRJ-AJA.
259 short story: Susie Hirsch, "Hijacked!" unpublished ms., Fall 1970.
259 "state of mind": Susie (Hirsch) Rosenrauch email, March 26, 2019.
259 "pleased": MH diary, September 16, 1970.
259 Repercussions: Depositions in lawsuits brought by hostages against Trans World Airlines.
260 "came home": Sarah (Malka) Bliner email, April 12, 2020.
260 "didn't have words": Mimi (Beeber) Nichter video conversation, September 27, 2020.
260 write a paper: Susie (Hirsch) Rosenrauch, "Resilience and Coping in the Face of Trauma: A Retrospective Account Thirty Years after a Skyjacking," unpublished ms., 1999.
260 "very into": Susie (Hirsch) Rosenrauch email, March 26, 2019.
260 "We went back": Rosenrauch, "Resilience and Coping."
260 "didn't really": Howie Hirsch in "In Our Own Words: TWA 741, 50th Anniversary Reunion, September 6, 1970–September 6, 2020," organized and compiled by David Raab, private video.
260 "taken hostage," "acute stress disorder": "Diagnostic Features," "Trauma-and Stressor-Related Disorders," *Diagnostic and Statistical Manual*.
261 "The companions": Saint-Exupéry, *Little Prince*, 109.
261 "No": Mark Shain email, July 15, 2015.
261 obituary: "Mark Shain," *Milwaukee Journal Sentinel*, November 8, 9, 2008.
261 In April: MH diary, April 15–18, 1971; MH autobiography, unpublished ms., 1970–71, 27.
261 "look well": LH to Lily and Bert Margolies, New York, April 18, 1971.
262 "Occasionally": MH autobiography, 1.
262 "lobby," and following: MH autobiography, 1.
262 "Everything": Lisa Grinberg telephone conversation, May 30, 2019.
262 imagined: Rachel Weil email, May 10, 2019.

24

263 "Boarded": MH diary, July 25, 1971.
263 "we had gone," and following: MH autobiography, unpublished ms., 1970–71, 52.
264 "Flowers": Saint-Exupéry, *Little Prince*, 37.
264 "usual announcements," and following: MH autobiography, 52.
264 "weird-looking," and following: MH autobiography, 54.
265 "treat you": LH to CH and MH, Tel Aviv, postmarked September 22, 1971.
265 "No": MH to LH, EB, Lily and Bert Margolies, New York, September 27, 1971.
265 I dreamed: MH dream notebook, September 7, 1971.
265 "two lives," and following: MH, "So Far Away," English 8A6, Hunter College High School, New York, 1971.
265 "Well": MH diary, September 6, 1972.
265 headlines: "9 Israelis on Olympic Team Killed with 4 Arab Captors as Police Fight Band That Disrupted Munich Games," *New York Times*, September 6, 1972.
266 "can't really": SH email, June 5, 2017.
266 *Oh, Dad!*, stories: SH emails, July 4, 2016, June 5, 2017, and January 16, 2019; SH conversation, May 6, 2017, New York; Hodes, *Onstage*, 250.
266 favored stories: Hodes, *Onstage*, 249–50.
266 third story, and following: SH emails, August 20, 2008, and July 4, 2016; SH conversation, New York, July 17, 2018; SH, "Listen Up and Fly Right: Flying, Dancing, & the Meaning of Life," unpublished ms. 2015, 116.
266 offered: Sylvia R. Jacobson, untitled notes, folder 10, box 1, SRJ-AJA.
266 "commandeered": Memorandum: Sylvia R. Jacobson to Alvin Meadow, April 3, 1978, folder 6, box 1, SRJ-AJA.
267 "determined": "'Not Knowing if Anyone Knew Was the Worst Part,'" *Tallahassee Democrat*, September 20, 1970.
267 "kept watch": Sylvia R. Jacobson obituary, Interoffice Memorandum, Linda G. Miklowitz, Attorney and Counselor at Law, Tallahassee, FL, April 29, 1994, folder 7, box 1, SRJ-AJA.
267 "Curiously": Jacobson, untitled notes.
267 disturbing: Depositions in lawsuits brought by hostages against Trans World Airlines.
267 father declined: SH conversation, New York, September 16, 2015; SH email, March 30, 2017.
268 "no selection": Yossi Melman, "Setting the Record Straight: Entebbe Was Not Auschwitz," *Haaretz*, July 8, 2011.
268 "Hey!!" and following: Ed Redlich email, April 29, 2019.
268 "Did you know?" and following: Duke Wiser conversation, Princeton, NJ, May 25, 2017.
269 "I thought": Barbara Walker email, September 27, 2018.
269 "significant": Leanne Robbin email, April 29, 2019.
269 "blown away": Jody Banks email, April 29, 2019.
269 "vague memory": Peter Bancel emails, July 19, 20, 2020.
269 "only the vaguest": Jeffrey Barnes email, April 29, 2019.
269 "You told": Mark van Roojen conversation, Princeton, NJ, March 29, 2018.
269 "you had been": Susan B. Whitlock email, September 21, 2001 (following 9/11).
269 "Is it possible": Ted Osius email, December 22, 2019.
270 "By the way": Judith Weisenfeld conversation, New York, February 6, 2019.
270 "de-emphasizing": Gregory Dowd email, April 30, 2019.
270 kind to us: Sharon Achinstein email, March 23, 2019.

270   "very casual": Jamie Jamison conversation, New York, March 2019.
270   "don't like to fly," and following: MH telephone interview by Jeffrey D. Simon, April 15, 1992, original tape.
270   "trying": Simon, *Terrorist Trap*, 106, 105.
271   "I would say": CH telephone interview by Jeffrey D. Simon, March 21, 1992, original tape.

25

272   brittle issue: A. J. Sullivan and Jeremy Cole, "A half hour out, hijackers got the plane . . . ," *Boston Phoenix*, October 6, 1970. The paper gave our last name as "Hones" and spelled Catherine's name with a *K*, despite Jeremy's repeated attempts at correction.
272   "Amazing!": SH email, March 6, 2017.
272   "Wow," and following: Jeremy Cole email, March 6, 2017.
273   "You're on," and following: CH and MH with SH, interview by Jeremy Cole and A. J. Sullivan, New York, September 20, 1970, original tape.
276   "I am sorry": Address of Dr. George Habash, Secretary General of the Central Committee of the Popular Front for the Liberation of Palestine at the Jordan Intercontinental Hotel," Amman, June 12th 1970, 1, folder marked "10/1/1970," boxes 683–84, RG59, State Department, NARA.
278   "most frightening": MH diary, September 8, 1970.
280   "Children should": Saint-Exupéry, *Little Prince*, 17.

26

281   "What did": CH and MH with SH, interview by Jeremy Cole and A. J. Sullivan, New York, September 20, 1970, original tape.
281   "bewilderment": CH telephone interview by Jeffrey D. Simon, March 21, 1992, original tape.
281   "liberal": Claude Frascani, "Report on the Mission in Jordan from 6–30 September, 1970," January 11, 1971 (English translation; original document in French dated December 14, 1970), 3, B AG 226 106-003, ICRC.
281   dispensed: Jacobson, "Individual and Group Responses," 461.
281   Children: Mitchell Meltzer as told to Howard Southgate, "Thumbs Up: Twenty-One Days as a Hijack Hostage," unpublished ms., 1970.
282   "comatose": Raab, *Terror in Black September*, 65.
282   lost count: Deposition in lawsuit brought by hostage against Trans World Airlines.
282   "queer sort": Deposition.
282   Sleeping Pill Mike: [Walter Jost] narrative, 43, English translation of Jost, *Rufzeichen*, folder 5, box 2, SRJ-AJA.
282   "clarifying," "encouraging": Cohen, Berliner, and Mannarino, "Treating Traumatized Children," 32.
283   "first three days," and following: CH and MH with SH, Cole interview.
284   "Actually": "Hijacked Hostages," #3025, Moving Images Relating to Intelligence and International Relations, RG263, CIA, NARA.
286   "expected": Sylvia R. Jacobson, untitled notes, folder 10, box 1, SRJ-AJA.
287   "Do you remember": Dina Towbin social media message, June 21, 2022.
287   recalls, and following: Dina Towbin email, June 22, 2022; Dina Towbin conversation, New York, August 3, 2022.
287   "Hi—Bye": MH diary, September 20, 1970.
288   "Do you remember": MH and CH emails, March 6, 2017.
288   "No": SH email, March 6, 2017.
288   "grown-ups": Saint-Exupéry, *Little Prince*, 47.

27

290   "no huge party," "All those memories": LH and MH emails, June 12, 2019.
290   "Forgive me": SH conversation, New York, June 18, 2019.
293   "And the little prince": Saint-Exupéry, *Little Prince*, 66.
293   "so different": LH email, July 20, 2019.
293   "reverence": CH email, July 20, 2019.
293   "so *much*": CH to LH, EB, Lily and Bert Margolies, New York, postmarked May 31, 1970.
293   "Wow": Susie Hirsch social media message, March 25, 2019.
293   "sometimes," and following: Susie (Hirsch) Rosenrauch and Howie Hirsch conversation, Ra'anana, Israel, July 7, 2019
294   "wow!!!": Fran Chesler social media message, March 3, 2019.
294   "Foozie": CH written responses to MH questions, August 3, 2015.
294   "lovely": Fran Chesler conversation, Petah Tikvah, Israel, July 5, 2019.
294   "Why do you?" and following: Chesler.
295   no memory: SH conversation, New York, July 17, 2018.
295   "I love you," and following: Chesler conversation.
295   plant was built: "The Opening of Jadara's Factory," *Jadara News*, May 30, 2013, Jadara.jo.
295   "So this," and following: Salah Khleifat conversation, Amman and Zarqa, Jordan, July 10, 2019.
296   "You were": Saint-Exupéry, *Little Prince*, 98.
296   "single building": David Zenian, "Plane Hostages Exercise in Desert," *Washington Post*, September 9, 1970.
296   "Then you don't": Saint-Exupéry, *Little Prince*, 99.
296   "And, if you should": Saint-Exupéry, *Little Prince*, 113.
296   "Look at it": Saint-Exupéry, 113.
297   "Regards": Carlos Malliaroudakis email, March 26, 2019.

297   "grab your hand": CH responses to MH questions.
297   "I have suffered": Saint-Exupéry, *Little Prince*, 18.
298   "We know": Carlos Malliaroudakis to MH and Bruce Dorsey, Amman, Jordan, July 8, 2019.
299   "a shiver": Nader Shalhoub email, March 5, 2019.
299   night manager: Nader Shalhoub conversation, Amman, Jordan, July 8, 2019.
299   "welcome": Shalhoub email, March 5, 2019.
299   Zauner: "Young Austrian Farmer Visiting in Orland Tells of Amman Hijacking," unidentified newspaper clipping, September 1970, and "Austrian Visitor Tells of Plane Hijack Ordeal," *Orland (CA) Unit-Register*, September 17, 1970, both Zauner scrapbook.
299   "David Lomax," Russian filmmakers, "your room": Shalhoub conversation; Patrick Massey, "Hussein's Troops Flatten Amman in Six Days," *Guardian*, September 24, 1970.
299   "Do you think," and following: Shalhoub conversation.
300   "Welcome back," and following: Chris Betz conversation, New York, December 30, 2019.
300   "elongated cave": Ken Macrorie, "Arriving and Departing," *Reporter*, September 13, 1962, 54.
300   "No crying, no tears": EH telephone conversation, August 5, 2015.

28

302   Meltzer's name: MH diary, September 8, 1970.
302   "your feelings," "I wanted": Meltzer response, questionnaire, folder 89, box 2, SRJ-AJA.
302   recalled: Rob Hirsch, "How I Survived a Plane Hijacking 50 Years Ago," *Newsday*, September 5, 2020; Susie (Hirsch) Rosenrauch and Howie Hirsch conversation, Ra'anana, Israel, July 7, 2019.
302   Searching: Mike Oliver, "Orlandoan Suffers from Leukemia, No Health Insurance," *Orlando Sentinel*, August 22, 1993; Mitchell Meltzer obituary, *Orlando Sentinel*, June 16, 1994.
302   "two little girls," and following: Mitchell Meltzer as told to Howard Southgate, "Thumbs Up: Twenty-One Days as a Hijack Hostage," unpublished ms., 1970.
304   "most frightening": MH diary, September 8, 1970.
304   "Don't worry," and following: Meltzer, "Thumbs Up."
305   "I'm listening": CH and MH with SH, interview by Jeremy Cole and A. J. Sullivan, New York, September 20, 1970, original tape.
306   "most poignant": David Raab email, July 24, 2020.
306   "come to realize": MH in "In Our Own Words: TWA 741, 50th Anniversary Reunion, September 6, 1970–September 6, 2020," organized and compiled by David Raab, private video.
306   "Ladies and Gentlemen": Address of Dr. George Habash, Secretary General of the Central Committee of the Popular Front for the Liberation of Palestine at the Jordan Intercontinental Hotel," Amman, June 12th 1970, 1, folder marked "10/1/1970," boxes 683–84, RG59, State Department, NARA.
306   "I have been": Saint-Exupéry, *Little Prince*, 70.
306   "don't like to fly": MH telephone interview by Jeffrey D. Simon, April 15, 1992, original tape.
307   "most audacious": "Chaos in the Sky," *Life*, September 18, 1970, 30.
307   "big story": Peter Gelzinis, "1970 Hijacking Survivor Has Watched Terror Grow," *Boston Herald*, September 30, 2001.
308   rope-jumping, spied the heart: CH conversation, New York, February 6, 2017.
308   desperate: CH written responses to MH questions, August 3, 2015.
308   "We were afraid": CH conversation, February 6, 2017.
308   "overcome": CH responses to MH questions.
308   "remain calm": CH email, March 30, 2017.
308   "I have never": Saint-Exupéry, *Little Prince*, 109.
309   "Little Martha": LH to MH, July 2019.
309   "This flower": Saint-Exupéry, *Little Prince*, 35.
309   "always knew," "You were home!": SH conversation, August 11, 2018; SH email, August 11, 2018.
309   "And no grown-up": Saint-Exupéry, *Little Prince*, 111.

WORKS CONSULTED

———

A wide variety of sources assisted me in re-creating and understanding the larger context of my experience in September 1970. Here are some of them.

Abu Al-Hayja', Muhammad, and Rachel Leah Jones. "'Ayn Hawd and the 'Unrecognized Villages.'" *Journal of Palestine Studies* 31 (2001): 39–49.

AbuKhalil, As'ad. "Internal Contradictions in the PFLP: Decision Making and Policy Orientation." *Middle East Journal* 41 (1987): 361–78.

Abu-Odeh, Adnan. *Jordanians, Palestinians and the Hashemite Kingdom in the Middle East Peace Process.* Washington, DC: US Institute of Peace Press, 1999.

Abu-Sharif, Bassam. *Arafat and the Dream of Palestine: An Insider's Account.* New York: Palgrave Macmillan, 2009.

Abu-Sharif, Bassam, and Uzi Mahnaimi. *Best of Enemies: The Memoirs of Bassam Abu-Sharif and Uzi Mahnaimi.* Boston: Little, Brown, 1995.

Achcar, Gilbert. *The Arabs and the Holocaust: The Arab-Israeli War of Narratives.* New York: Metropolitan Books, 2009.

Adorjan, Michael, Tony Christensen, Benjamin Kelly, and Dorothy Pawluch. "Stockholm Syndrome as Vernacular Resource." *Sociological Quarterly* 53 (2012): 454–74.

Ahmad, Sa'di H., and Lila Abu-Lughod, eds. *Nakba: Palestine, 1948, and the Claims of Memory.* New York: Columbia University Press, 2007.

Alexander, David A., and Susan Klein. "Kidnapping and Hostage-Taking: A Review of Effects, Coping and Resilience." *Journal of the Royal Society of Medicine* 102 (2009): 16–21.

Alterman, Eric. *We Are Not One: A History of America's Fight Over Israel.* New York: Basic Books, 2022.

Anderson, Betty S. "September 1970 and the Palestinian Issue: A Case Study of Student Politicization at the American University of Beirut (AUB)." *Civil Wars* 10 (2008): 261–80.

Anziska, Seth. *Preventing Palestine: A Political History from Camp David to Oslo.* Princeton, NJ: Princeton University Press, 2018.

Ashkenazi, Ofer. "Hidden in Plain Sight: The Nakba and the Legacy of the Israeli Historians' Debates." *Zeithistorische Forschungen/Studies in Contemporary History* 16 (2019): 549–63.

Ashton, Nigel J. "Cold War, Hot War and Civil War: King Hussein and Jordan's Regional Role, 1967–73." In Ashton, *Cold War in the Middle East,* 188–209.

———, ed. *The Cold War in the Middle East: Regional Conflict and the Superpowers, 1967–73.* New York: Routledge, 2007.

———. "Introduction: The Cold War in the Middle East, 1967–73." In Ashton, *Cold War in the Middle East,* 1–15.

Bailey, Clinton. *Jordan's Palestinian Challenge, 1948–1983: A Political History.* Boulder, CO: Westview, 1984.

Bar-On, Dan, and Saliba Sarsar. "Bridging the Unbridgeable: The Holocaust and Al-Nakba." *Palestine-Israel Journal of Politics, Economics and Culture* 11 (2004): 63–70.

Bar-On, Mordechai. "Conflicting Narratives or Narratives of a Conflict: Can the Zionist and Palestinian Narratives of the 1948 War Be Bridged?" In Rotberg, *Israeli and Palestinian Narratives,* 142–73.

Barari, Hassan A. "Four Decades after Black September: A Jordanian Perspective." *Civil Wars* 10 (2008): 231–43.

Barlow, M. Rose, Kathy Pezdek, and Iris Blandón-Gitlin. "Trauma and Memory." In Gold, *Foundations in Knowledge,* 307–31.

Barnwell, Kristi N. "'Caught Between His Friends and His Enemies': The Evolution of American-Jordanian Collaboration in the 1960s." *Diplomacy and Statecraft* 22 (2011): 281–99.

Bartov, Omer. "National Narratives of Suffering and Victimhood: Methods and Ethics of Telling the Past as Personal Political History." In Bashir and Goldberg, *Holocaust and the Nakba,* 187–205.

Bashir, Bashir, and Amos Goldberg. "Deliberating the Holocaust and the Nakba: Disruptive Empathy and Binationalism in Israel/Palestine." *Journal of Genocide Research* 16 (2014): 77–99.

———, eds. *The Holocaust and the Nakba: A New Grammar of Trauma and History*. New York: Columbia University Press, 2019.

Beinin, Joel. "Forgetfulness for Memory: The Limits of the New Israeli History." *Journal of Palestine Studies* 34 (2005): 6–23.

Benvenisti, Meron. *Sacred Landscape: The Buried History of the Holy Land Since 1948*. Berkeley: University of California Press, 2000.

Beška, Emanuel, and Zachary Foster. "The Origins of the Term 'Palestinian' ('Filastīnī') in Late Ottoman Palestine, 1898–1914." *Academia Letters* (2021): article 1884, 1–22.

Bird, Kai. *Crossing Mandelbaum Gate: Coming of Age between the Arabs and Israelis, 1956–1978*. New York: Scribner, 2010.

Black, Ian. *Enemies and Neighbors: Arabs and Jews in Palestine and Israel, 1917–2017*. New York: Grove, 2017.

Blanga, Yehuda U. "Full Effort to Avoid Peace: The Failure of the First Rogers Plan." *Middle Eastern Studies* 54 (2018): 981–99.

Bliss, Edward Jr. *Now the News: The Story of Broadcast Journalism*. New York: Columbia University Press, 1991.

Blumenau, Bernhard. "The Other Battleground of the Cold War: The UN and the Struggle against International Terrorism in the 1970s." *Journal of Cold War Studies* 16 (2014): 61–84.

Boord, Ofer. "The War of Independence Exhibited: A Study of Three Israeli Museums." *Israel Studies* 21 (2016): 82–108.

Bowers, Peter M. *Boeing Aircraft since 1916*. London: Putnam, 1966.

Bradley, Doug, and Craig Werner. *We Gotta Get Out of This Place: The Soundtrack of the Vietnam War*. Amherst: University of Massachusetts Press, 2015.

Brand, Laurie A. *Palestinians in the Arab World: Institution Building and the Search for State*. New York: Columbia University Press, 1988.

Brandon, Henry, and David Schoenbaum. "Jordan: The Forgotten Crisis: Were We Masterful . . . or Lucky?" *Foreign Policy* 10 (1973): 158–81.

Bray, Jemma, Neil Brewer, Kate Cameron, and Reginald D. V. Nixon. "Comparing Children's Memories for Negative Versus Positive Events in the Context of Posttraumatic Stress Symptoms." *Behavior Therapy* 49 (2018): 32–45.

Bregman, Ahron. *Cursed Victory: Israel and the Occupied Territories—A History*. New York: Pegasus, 2014.

Bryant, Richard A. "Acute Stress Disorder and Posttraumatic Stress Disorder." In Gold, *Foundations in Knowledge*, 161–84.

Buber, Martin. *A Land of Two Peoples: Martin Buber on Jews and Arabs*, edited by Paul Mendes-Flohr. New York: Oxford University Press, 1983.

Bunton, Martin. *The Palestinian-Israeli Conflict: A Very Short Introduction*. New York: Oxford University Press, 2013.

Burmeister, William Lewis. *Sky-Jacked by PFLP Pirates: To Nowhere and Back*. Self-published, 2011.

Campbell, Karen M. "The Emotional Trauma of Hijacking: Who Pays?" *Kentucky Law Journal* 74 (1985): 599–622.

Chamberlin, Paul Thomas. *The Global Offensive: The United States, the Palestine Liberation Organization, and the Making of the Post-Cold War Order*. New York: Oxford University Press, 2012.

Christianson, Sven-Åke, and Torun Lindholm. "The Fate of Traumatic Memories in Childhood and Adulthood." *Development and Psychopathology* 10 (1998): 761–80.

Clarke, P. R. F., P. S. Eccersley, J. P. Frisby, and J. A. Thornton. "The Amnesic Effect of Diazepam (Valium)." *British Journal of Anaesthesia* 42 (1970): 690–97.

Cleaver, Kathleen Neal. "Back to Africa: The Evolution of the International Section of the Black Panther Party, 1969–1972." In *The Black Panther Party (Reconsidered)*, edited by Charles E. Jones, 211–54. Baltimore: Black Classic, 1998.

Clifford, Rebecca. *Survivors: Children's Lives after the Holocaust*. New Haven, CT: Yale University Press, 2020.

Cobban, Helena. *The Palestinian Liberation Organisation: People, Power and Politics*. New York: Cambridge University Press, 1984.

Cohen, Beth B. *Case Closed: Holocaust Survivors in Postwar America*. New Brunswick, NJ: Rutgers University Press, 2006.

Cohen, Hillel. *Year Zero of the Arab-Israeli Conflict: 1929*. Waltham, MA: Brandeis University Press, 2015.

Cohen, Judith A., Lucy Berliner, and Anthony P. Mannarino. "Treating Traumatized Children: A Research Review and Synthesis." *Trauma, Violence, and Abuse* 1 (2000): 29–46.

Confino, Alon. "When Genya and Henryk Kowalski Challenged History—Jaffa, 1949: Between the Holocaust and the Nakba." In Bashir and Goldberg, *Holocaust and the Nakba*, 135–53.

Cooley, John K. *Green March, Black September: The Story of the Palestinian Arabs*. London: Frank Cass, 1973.

Coontz, Stephanie. *A Strange Stirring: "The Feminine Mystique" and American Women at the Dawn of the 1960s*. New York: Basic Books, 2011.

———. *The Way We Never Were: American Families and the Nostalgia Trap*. New York: Basic Books, 1992.

Crais, Clifton. *History Lessons: A Memoir of Madness, Memory, and the Brain*. New York: Overlook, 2014.

Crossman, Richard. *Palestine Mission: A Personal Record*. New York: Harper and Brothers, 1947.

Crum, Bartley C. *Behind the Silken Curtain: A Personal Account of Anglo-American Diplomacy in Palestine and the Middle East*. New York: Simon and Schuster, 1947.

Danion, Jean-Marie, Marie-Agathe Zimmermann, Dominique Willard-Schroeder, Danielle Grangé, and Léonard Singer. "Diazepam Induces a Dissociation between Explicit and Implicit Memory." *Psychopharmacology* 99 (1989): 238–43.

Daoudi, Mohammed S. Dajani, and Zeina M. Barakat. "Israelis and Palestinians: Contested Narratives." *Israel Studies* 18 (2013): 53–69.

David, Saul. *Operation Thunderbolt: Flight 139 and the Raid on Entebbe Airport, the Most Audacious Hostage Rescue Mission in History*. New York: Little Brown, 2015.

Davies, R. E. G. *TWA: An Airline and Its Aircraft*. McLean, VA: Paladwr, 2000.

Davis, Benjamin O. *Benjamin O. Davis, Jr., American: An Autobiography*. Washington, DC: Smithsonian, 2000.

Dawidowicz, Lucy S. "The Arab-Israel War of 1967: American Public Opinion." *American Jewish Year Book* 69 (1968): 198–229.

de Muijnck, Deborah. "Narrative, Memory and PTSD: A Case Study of Autobiographical Narration After Trauma." *European Journal of Life Writing* 11 (2022): 75–95.

Diagnostic and Statistical Manual of Mental Disorders. 5th ed. Washington, DC: American Psychiatric Association, 2022.

Diner, Hasia R. *We Remember with Reverence and Love: American Jews and the Myth of Silence after the Holocaust, 1945–1962*. New York: New York University Press, 2009.

Dinnerstein, Leonard. *America and the Survivors of the Holocaust*. New York: Columbia University Press, 1982.

Dobbs, Michael. *The Unwanted: America, Auschwitz, and a Village Caught in Between*. New York: Alfred A. Knopf, 2019.

Doherty, Maggie. *The Equivalents: A Story of Art, Female Friendship, and Liberation in the 1960s*. New York: Alfred A. Knopf, 2020.

Don-Yehiya, Eliezer. "Memory and Political Culture: Israeli Society and the Holocaust." *Studies in Contemporary Jewry* 9 (1993): 139–62.

Dougherty, Pamela. *Golden Memories of InterContinental Jordan*. Amman: InterContinental Jordan, 2015.

Elon, Amos. *The Israelis: Founders and Sons*. 1971. Reprint, New York: Penguin, 1981.

Engel, David. *Zionism: A Short History of a Big Idea*. New York: Pearson Longman, 2009.

Ensalaco, Mark. *Middle Eastern Terrorism: From Black September to September 11*. Philadelphia: University of Pennsylvania Press, 2008.

Falah, Ghazi. "The 1948 Israeli-Palestinian War and Its Aftermath: The Transformation and De-Signification of Palestine's Cultural Landscape." *Annals of the Association of American Geographers* 86 (1996): 256–85.

Fang, J. C., J. V. Hinrichs, and M. M. Ghoneim. "Diazepam and Memory: Evidence for Spared Memory Function." *Pharmacology Biochemistry and Behavior* 28 (1987): 347–52.

Fass, Paula S. "Childhood and Memory." *Journal of the History of Childhood and Youth* 3 (2010): 155–64.

Fassin, Didier, and Richard Rechtman. *The Empire of Trauma: An Inquiry into the Condition of Victimhood*. Princeton, NJ: Princeton University Press, 2009.

Filkins, Dexter. "Shot in the Heart: When Yitzhak Rabin was Killed, Did the Prospects for Peace Perish, Too?" *New Yorker*, October 26, 2015.

Finkelstein, Norman G. *Image and Reality of the Israel-Palestine Conflict*. 2nd ed. London: Verso, 2003.

Fischbach, Michael R. *The Movement and the Middle East: How the Arab-Israeli Conflict Divided the American Left*. Stanford, CA.: Stanford University Press, 2019.

———. *Records of Dispossession: Palestinian Refugee Property and the Arab-Israeli Conflict*. New York: Columbia University Press, 2003.

Fischer, Yochi. "What Does Exile Look Like? Transformations in the Linkage Between the Shoah and the Nakba." In Bashir and Goldberg, *Holocaust and the Nakba*, 173–86.

Fivush, Robyn. "Children's Recollections of Traumatic and Nontraumatic Events." *Development and Psychopathology* 10 (1998): 699–716.

Flapan, Simha. *The Birth of Israel: Myths and Realities*. New York: Pantheon, 1987.

Franklin, Ruth. "The Diaries of Anne Frank." *Ghost Stories* (Substack), July 4, 2022. https://ruthfranklin.substack.com/p/the-diaries-of-anne-frank.

Friedman, Thomas L. *From Beirut to Jerusalem*. Rev. ed. New York: Anchor, 1995.

Fruchter-Ronen, Iris. "Black September: The 1970–71 Events and their Impact on the Formation of Jordanian National Identity." *Civil Wars* 10 (2008): 244–60.

Gabriel, Mary. *Ninth Street Women: Lee Krasner, Elaine de Kooning, Grace Hartigan, Joan Mitchell, and Helen Frankenthaler; Five Painters and the Movement that Changed Modern Art*. New York: Little, Brown, 2018.

Gage, Beverly. "Terrorism and the American Experience: A State of the Field." *Journal of American History* 98 (2011): 73–94.

Garfinkle, Adam M. "U.S. Decision Making in the Jordan Crisis: Correcting the Record." *Political Science Quarterly* 100 (1985): 117–38.

Gat, Moshe. "Military Power and Foreign Policy Inaction: Israel, 1967–1973." *Israel Affairs* 22 (2016): 69–95.

———. "Mission Impossible: William Rogers (Secretary of State, 1969–1973) and the Attempt to Reach a Peace Accord between Israel and Egypt." *Middle Eastern Studies* 55 (2019): 769–85.

Gazit, Shlomo. *Trapped Fools: Thirty Years of Israeli Policy in the Territories*. London: Frank Cass, 2003.

Gelvin, James L. *The Israel-Palestine Conflict: One Hundred Years of War*. 3rd ed. New York: Cambridge University Press, 2014.

Gerges, Fawaz A. "The 1967 Arab-Israeli War: U.S. Actions and Arab Perceptions." In *The Middle East and the United States: History, Politics, and Ideologies*, edited by David W. Lesch and Mark. L. Haas, 139–57. 6th ed. New York: Routledge, 2018.

Ghoneim, M. M., and S. P. Mewaldt. "Benzodiazepines and Human Memory: A Review." *Anesthesiology* 72 (1990): 926–38.

———. "Effects of Diazepam and Scopolamine on Storage, Retrieval and Organizational Processes in Memory." *Psychopharmacologia* 44 (1975): 257–62.

Gliksman, Devora. *Nouri: The Story of Isidore Dayan and the Growth of a Vibrant Community in America*. Brooklyn: Mesorah, 2016.

Gluck, Rena. *Batsheva Dance Company: My Story, 1964–1980*. Self-published, 2006.

Gold, S. N., ed. *Foundations in Knowledge*. Vol. 1 of *American Psychological Association Handbook of Trauma Psychology*. Washington, DC: American Psychological Association, 2017.

Goodman, Gail S., and Jodi A. Quas. "Predictors of Accurate and Inaccurate Memories of Traumatic Events Experienced in Childhood." *Consciousness and Cognition* 3 (1994): 269–94.

Gopnik, Adam. "The Strange Triumph of 'The Little Prince.'" New Yorker.com, April 29, 2014.

Gorenberg, Gershom. *The Accidental Empire: Israel and the Birth of the Settlements, 1967–1977*. New York: Times Books, 2006.

Gorny, Yosef. *Zionism and the Arabs, 1882–1948: A Study of Ideology*. New York: Oxford University Press, 1987.

Grabski, August, ed. *Rebels against Zion: Studies on the Jewish Left Anti-Zionism*. Warsaw: Jewish Historical Institute, 2011.

Graham, Martha. *Blood Memory: An Autobiography*. New York, Doubleday, 1991.

Grant, Elaine X. "TWA—Death of a Legend." *St. Louis Magazine*, July 28, 2006.

Gresh, Alain. *The PLO: The Struggle Within; Towards an Independent Palestinian State*. London: Zed, 1985.

Grossman, David. *The Yellow Wind*. Rev. ed. New York: Picador, 2002.

Grossmann, Atina. *Jews, Germans, and Allies: Close Encounters in Occupied Germany*. Princeton, NJ: Princeton University Press, 2007.

Haig, Alexander M., Jr., with Charles McCarry. *Inner Circles: How America Changed the World; A Memoir*. New York: Warner Books, 1992.

Hampton, Wilborn. *War in the Middle East: A Reporter's Story; Black September and the Yom Kippur War*. Cambridge, MA: Candlewick, 2007.

Haslam, Nick, and Melanie J. McGrath. "The Creeping Concept of Trauma." *Social Research: An International Quarterly* 87 (2020): 509–31.

Hattis, Susan Lee. *The Bi-National Idea in Palestine during Mandatory Times*. Haifa, Israel: Shikmona/Ben-Nun, 1970.

Hazkani, Shay. *Dear Palestine: A Social History of the 1948 War*. Stanford, CA: Stanford University Press, 2021.

———. "Israel's Vanishing Files, Archival Deception and Paper Trails." *Middle East Report* 291 (2019): 10–15.

Hermann, Tamar. "Zionism and Palestinian Nationalism: Possibilities of Recognition." *Israel Studies* 18 (2013): 133–47.

Hersh, Seymour M. *The Price of Power: Kissinger in the Nixon White House*. New York: Summit, 1983.

Herzberg, David. *Happy Pills in America: From Miltown to Prozac*. Baltimore: Johns Hopkins University Press, 2009.

Hess, John L. *My Times: A Memoir of Dissent*. New York: Seven Stories, 2003.

Hever, Hannan. "'The Two Gaze Directly into One Another's Face': Avot Yeshurun between the Nakba and the Shoah—An Israeli Perspective." *Jewish Social Studies: History, Culture, Society* 18 (2012): 153–63.

Hinrichs, James V., Steven P. Mewaldt, M. M. Ghoneim, and Janis L. Berie. "Diazepam and Learning: Assessment of Acquisition Deficits." *Pharmacology Biochemistry and Behavior* 17 (1982): 165–70.

Hodes, Stuart. *Onstage with Martha Graham*. Gainesville: University Press of Florida, 2021.

Hoffman, Bruce. *Inside Terrorism*. 3rd ed. New York: Columbia University Press, 2017.

Howe, Mark L. "Individual Differences in Factors that Modulate Storage and Retrieval of Traumatic Memories." *Development and Psychopathology* 10 (1998): 681–98.

Hyde, Lewis. *A Primer for Forgetting: Getting Past the Past*. New York: Farrar, Straus, Giroux, 2019.

Indyk, Martin. *Master of the Game: Henry Kissinger and the Art of Middle East Diplomacy*. New York: Alfred A. Knopf, 2021.

Irving, Sarah. *Leila Khaled: Icon of Palestinian Liberation*. London: Pluto Press, 2012.

Iyad, Abu, with Eric Rouleau. *My Home My Land: A Narrative of the Palestinian Struggle*. New York: Times Books, 1981.

Jacobson, Sylvia R. "Children's Attitudinal and Behavioral Responses to Skyjack and Hostage Experiences." Draft typescript, 1976. Folder 9, box 1, Sylvia R. Jacobson Papers, American Jewish Archives, Cincinnati.

———. "Individual and Group Responses to Confinement in a Skyjacked Plane." *American Journal of Orthopsychiatry* 43 (1973): 459–69.

Jain, Shaili. *The Unspeakable Mind: Stories of Trauma and Healing from the Frontlines of PTSD Science*. New York: Harper, 2019.

Jawad, Saleh Abdel. "The Arab and Palestinian Narratives of the 1948 War." In Rotberg, *Israeli and Palestinian Narratives*, 72–114.

Jensen, Meg. *The Art and Science of Trauma and the Autobiographical: Negotiated Truths*. Cham, Switzerland: Palgrave Macmillan, 2019.

Jost, Walter. *Rufzeichen: Haifa: Ein Passagier erlebt die Entführung der Swissair DC-8 "Nidwalden" und als Geisel den Krieg der Fedayin*. Zurich: Schweizer, 1972.

Judt, Tony. *Postwar: A History of Europe since 1945*. New York: Penguin Press, 2005.

Kadman, Noga. *Erased from Space and Consciousness: Israel and the Depopulated Palestinian Villages of 1948*. Bloomington: Indiana University Press, 2015.

Kallus, Rachel. "Patrick Geddes and the Evolution of a Housing Type in Tel-Aviv." *Planning Perspectives* 12 (1997): 281–320.

Kaplan, Amy. *Our American Israel: The Story of an Entangled Alliance*. Cambridge, MA: Harvard University Press, 2018.

Karmi, Ghada. *In Search of Fatima: A Palestinian Story*. London: Verso, 2002.

Katsiaficas, George. "Organization and Movement: The Case of the Black Panther Party and the Revolutionary People's Constitutional Convention of 1970." In *Liberation, Imagination, and the Black Panther Party: A New Look at the Panthers and Their Legacy*, edited by Kathleen Cleaver and George Katsiaficas, 141–55. New York: Routledge, 2001.

Kazziha, Walid. *Revolutionary Transformation in the Arab World: Habash and His Comrades from Nationalism to Marxism*. London: Charles Knight, 1975.

Khaled, Leila, as told to George Hajjar. *My People Shall Live: Autobiography of a Revolutionary*. Toronto: NC Press, 1975.

Khalidi, Rashid. *The Hundred Years' War on Palestine: A History of Settler Colonialism and Resistance, 1917–2017*. New York: Metropolitan Books, 2020.

———. *The Iron Cage: The Story of the Palestinian Struggle for Statehood*. Boston: Beacon, 2006.

———. "The 1967 War and the Demise of Arab Nationalism: Chronicle of a Death Foretold." In *The 1967 Arab-Israeli War: Origins and Consequences*, edited by William Roger Louis and Avi Shlaim, 264–84. New York: Cambridge University Press, 2012.

———. "Observations on the Right of Return." *Journal of Palestine Studies* 21 (1992): 29–40.

———. *Palestinian Identity: The Construction of Modern National Consciousness*. New York: Columbia University Press, 1997.

———. "The Palestinian People: Twenty-Two Years after 1967." In *Intifada: The Palestinian Uprising Against Israeli Occupation*, edited by Zachary Lockman and Joel Beinin, 113–26. Boston: South End Press, 1989.

———. "The Palestinians and 1948: The Underlying Causes of Failure." In Rogan and Shlaim, *War for Palestine*, 12–36.

Khalidi, Walid, ed. *All That Remains: The Palestinian Villages Occupied and Depopulated by Israel in 1948*. Washington, DC: Institute for Palestine Studies, 1992.

———. "The Fall of Haifa Revisited." *Journal of Palestine Studies* 37 (2008): 30–58.

———. "Why Did the Palestinians Leave, Revisited." *Journal of Palestine Studies* 34 (2005): 42–54.

Khoury, Nadim. "Holocaust/Nakba and the Counterpublic of Memory." In Bashir and Goldberg, *Holocaust and the Nakba*, 114–31.

Kimmerling, Baruch, and Joel S. Migdal. *The Palestinian People: A History*. Cambridge, MA: Harvard University Press, 2003.

Kissinger, Henry. *White House Years*. 1979. Reprint, London: Phoenix Press, 2000.

Koerner, Brendan I. *The Skies Belong to Us: Love and Terror in the Golden Age of Hijacking*. New York: Crown, 2013.

Korn, David A. "U.S.–Soviet Negotiations of 1969 and the Rogers Plan." *Middle East Journal* 44 (1990): 37–50.

Kreindler, Lee S. "Aviation Law: Hijacking and Emotional Trauma." *New York Law Journal*, June 21, 1974.

Krisch, Joshua A. "What is the Flight Management System? A Pilot Explains." *Popular Mechanics*, March 18, 2014.

Labelle, Maurice M., Jr. "'The American People Know So Little': The Palestine Arab Refugee Office and the Challenges of Anti-Orientalism in the United States, 1955–1962." *Mashriq and Mahjar: Journal of Middle East and North African Migration Studies* 5 (2018): 1–27.

Lalor, Paul. "Black September 1970: The Palestinian Resistance Movement in Jordan, 1967–1971." PhD diss., Saint Anthony's College, Oxford University, 1992.

Lang, Daniel. "A Reporter at Large: The Bank Drama." *New Yorker*, November 25, 1974.

Langer, Lawrence L. *Holocaust Testimonies: The Ruins of Memory*. New Haven, CT: Yale University Press, 1991.

Large, David Clay. *Munich 1972: Tragedy, Terror, and Triumph at the Olympic Games*. Lanham, MD: Rowman and Little-field, 2012.

Larson, George C. "How Things Work: Cabin Pressure; Why You Remain Conscious at 30,000 Feet." *Air & Space Magazine*, December 2001/January 2002.

Latner, Teishan A. "Take Me to Havana! Airline Hijacking, U.S.-Cuba Relations, and Political Protest in Late Sixties' America." *Diplomatic History* 39 (2015): 16–44.

LeBor, Adam. *City of Oranges: An Intimate History of Arabs and Jews in Jaffa*. 2006. Rev. ed., London: Head of Zeus, 2017.

Lentin, Ronit. "The Contested Memory of Dispossession: Commemorizing the Palestinian Nakba in Israel." In *Thinking Palestine*, edited by Ronit Lentin, 206–20. London: Zed Books, 2008.

Levin, Andrew P., Stuart Kleinman, and John S. Adler. "DSM-5 and Posttraumatic Stress Disorder." *Journal of the American Academy of Psychiatry and the Law* 42 (2014): 146–58.

Leys, Ruth. *Trauma: A Genealogy*. Chicago: University of Chicago Press, 2000.

Litvak, Meir, and Esther Webman. *From Empathy to Denial: Arab Responses to the Holocaust*. New York: Columbia University Press, 2009.

Lukacs, Yehuda, ed. *The Israeli-Palestinian Conflict: A Documentary Record, 1967–1990*. New York: Cambridge University Press, 1992.

Lustick, Ian S. "Israeli History: Who Is Fabricating What?" *Survival* 39 (1997): 156–66.

Lynn, John A. *Another Kind of War: The Nature and History of Terrorism*. New Haven, CT: Yale University Press, 2019.

MacDonald, Eileen. *Shoot the Women First*. New York: Random House, 1991.

Makdisi, Ussama. "'Anti-Americanism' in the Arab World: An Interpretation of a Brief History." *Journal of American History* 89 (2002): 538–57.

Mandel, Neville J. *The Arabs and Zionism before World War I*. Berkeley: University of California Press, 1976.

Manor, Giora. "Batsheva: The Flagship of Modern Dance in Israel." *Israel Dance Quarterly* 4 (1994): 106–11.

McAlister, Melani. *Epic Encounters: Culture, Media, and U.S. Interests in the Middle East, 1945–2000*. Berkeley: University of California Press, 2001.

McNally, Richard J. *Remembering Trauma*. Cambridge, MA: Harvard University Press, 2003.

Meichenbaum, Donald. "A Constructive Narrative Perspective on Trauma and Resilience: The Role of Cognitive and Affective Processes." In Gold, *Foundations in Knowledge*, 429–42.

Meiser-Stedman, Richard, Patrick Smith, and William Yule. "The Trauma Memory Quality Questionnaire: Preliminary Development and Validation of a Measure of Trauma Memory Characteristics for Children and Adolescents." *Memory* 15 (2007): 271–79.

Mewaldt, Steven P., James V. Hinrichs, and M. M. Ghoneim. "Diazepam and Memory: Support for a Duplex Model of Memory." *Memory and Cognition* 11 (1983): 557–64.

Meyerowitz, Joanne, ed. *Not June Cleaver: Women and Gender in Postwar America, 1945–1960*. Philadelphia: Temple University Press, 1994.

Miller, Sam. "Contribution of Flight Systems to Performance-Based Navigation." *Aero Quarterly*, February 2009.

Mitelpunkt, Shaul. *Israel in the American Mind: The Cultural Politics of U.S.-Israeli Relations, 1958–1988*. New York: Cambridge University Press, 2018.

Morris, Benny. *The Birth of the Palestinian Refugee Problem Revisited*. 2nd ed. New York: Cambridge University Press, 2004.

Moss, Miriam. *Girl on a Plane: Based on the True Story of a Hijacking*. Boston: Houghton Mifflin Harcourt, 2016.

Mukhar, Randa Nasri. "A Study in Political Violence: The Jordanian Internal War of 1968–1971." MA thesis, American University of Beirut, 1978.

Naftali, Timothy. *Blind Spot: The Secret History of American Counterterrorism*. New York: Basic Books, 2005.

Namnyak, M., N. Tufton, R. Szekely, M. Toal, S. Worboys, and E. L. Sampson. "'Stockholm Syndrome': Psychiatric Diagnosis or Urban Myth?" *Acta Psychiatrica Scandinavica* 117 (2008): 4–11.

Nasaw, David. *The Last Million: Europe's Displaced Persons from World War to Cold War*. New York: Penguin, 2020.

Neff, Donald. *Fallen Pillars: U.S. Policy towards Palestine and Israel since 1945*. Washington, DC: Institute for Palestine Studies, 1995.

———. "Nixon's Middle East Policy: From Balance to Bias." *Arab Studies Quarterly* 12 (1990): 121–52.

———. "U.S. Policy and the Palestinian Refugees." *Journal of Palestine Studies* 18 (1988): 96–111.

Nets-Zehngut, Rafi. "Israeli Memory of the Palestinian Refugee Problem." *Peace Review: A Journal of Social Justice* 24 (2012): 187–94.

———. "Israel's Publications Agency and the 1948 Palestinian Refugees." *Israel Studies* 21 (2016): 54–81.

Nevo, Joseph. "'Zionism' Versus 'Judaism' in Palestinian Historiography." In *Medieval and Modern Perspectives on Muslim-Jewish Relations*, edited by Ronald L. Nettler, 159–73. Oxford, England: Harwood, 1995.

Nixon, Richard M. *RN: The Memoirs of Richard Nixon*. New York: Grosset and Dunlap, 1978.

Novick, Peter. *The Holocaust in American Life*. Boston: Houghton Mifflin, 1999.

Noyes, Russell Jr., and Roy Kletti. "Depersonalization in Response to Life-Threatening Danger." *Comprehensive Psychiatry* 18 (1977): 375–84.

O'Ballance, Edgar. *Arab Guerilla Power, 1967–1972*. London: Faber and Faber, 1974.

O'Connell, Jack. *King's Counsel: A Memoir of War, Espionage, and Diplomacy in the Middle East*. New York: W. W. Norton, 2011.

O'Malley, Padraig. *The Two-State Delusion: Israel and Palestine; A Tale of Two Narratives*. New York: Viking, 2015.

Orange, Donna M. "Out of Time: Siblings as Trauma Transmitters, Protectors, Sources of Courage." *Psychoanalytic Inquiry* 34 (2014): 251–61.

Oz, Amos. *Under This Blazing Light*. New York: Cambridge University Press, 1995.

Pappé, Ilan. "The Bible in the Service of Zionism: 'We Do Not Believe in God, but He Nonetheless Promised Us Palestine'" In *The Bible, Zionism, and Palestine: The Bible's Role in Conflict and Liberation in Israel-Palestine*, edited by Michael J. Sandford, 7–19. Dunedin, New Zealand: Relegere, 2016.

Pennebaker, James W. "Writing about Emotional Experiences as a Therapeutic Process." *Psychological Science* 8 (1997): 162–66.

Peretz, Don. "Arab Palestine: Phoenix or Phantom?" *Foreign Affairs* 48 (1970): 322–33.

Phillips, David. *Skyjack: The Story of Air Piracy*. London: Harrap, 1973.

Phillips, Julie. *The Baby on the Fire Escape: Creativity, Motherhood, and the Mind-Baby Problem*. New York: W. W. Norton, 2022.

Phillips, Victoria. *Martha Graham's Cold War: The Dance of American Diplomacy*. New York: Oxford University Press, 2020.

Phillips-Fein, Kim. *Fear City: New York's Fiscal Crisis and the Rise of Austerity Politics*. New York: Metropolitan Books, 2017.

Ponce de Leon, Charles L. *That's the Way It Is: A History of Television News in America*. Chicago: University of Chicago Press, 2015.

Pranger, Robert J. *American Policy for Peace in the Middle East, 1969–1971: Problems of Principle, Maneuver and Time*. Washington, DC: American Enterprise Institute, 1971.

Press, Eyal. *Beautiful Souls: The Courage and Conscience of Ordinary People in Extraordinary Times*. New York: Picador, 2012.

Prose, Francine. *Anne Frank: The Book, the Life, the Afterlife*. New York: Harper, 2009.

Quandt, William B. *Decade of Decision: American Policy toward the Arab-Israeli Conflict, 1967–76*. Berkeley: University of California Press, 1977.

———. *Peace Process: American Diplomacy and the Arab-Israeli Conflict since 1967*. Washington, DC: Brookings Institution Press, 2005.

Quandt, William B., Fuad Jabber, and Ann Mosely Lesch, eds. *The Politics of Palestinian Nationalism*. Berkeley: University of California Press, 1973.

Raab, David. "Remembrance of Terror Past." *New York Times*, August 22, 2004.

———. *Terror in Black September: The First Eyewitness Account of the Infamous 1970 Hijackings*. New York: Palgrave Macmillan, 2007.

Reeve, Simon. *One Day in September: The Full Story of the 1972 Munich Olympics Massacre and the Israeli Revenge Operation "Wrath of God."* New York: Arcade, 2000.

Reeves, Richard. *President Nixon: Alone in the White House*. New York: Simon and Schuster, 2001.

Reich, Walter. "Hostages and the 'Syndrome,'" *New York Times*, January 15, 1980.

Rifai, Salwa Shtieh. "The Palestinian Guerrillas' Image in the *New York Times* during the Jordan Crisis, 1970." MA thesis, California State University–Northridge, 1987.

Ringli, Kornel. *Designing TWA: Eero Saarinen's Airport Terminal in New York*. Zurich: Park Books, 2015.

Rizo-Martínez, Lucía Ester. "El síndrome de Estocolmo: Una revisión sistemática." *Clínica y Salud* 29 (2018): 81–88.

Robinson, Shira. *Citizen Strangers: Palestinians and the Birth of Israel's Liberal Settler State*. Stanford, CA: Stanford University Press, 2013.

Rochat, André. *L'homme à la croix: Une anticroisade*. Vevey, Switzerland: Éditions de l'Aire, 2005.

Rogan, Eugene L., and Avi Shlaim, eds. *The War for Palestine: Rewriting the History of 1948*. New York: Cambridge University Press, 2007.

Rosenthal, Steven T. *Irreconcilable Differences? The Waning of the American Jewish Love Affair with Israel*. Waltham, MA: Brandeis University Press, 2001.

Rotberg, Robert I, ed. *Israeli and Palestinian Narratives of Conflict: History's Double Helix*. Bloomington: Indiana University Press, 2006.

Rothman, Joshua. "Annals of Inquiry: Becoming You—Are You the Same Person You Were When You Were a Child?" *New Yorker*, October 10, 2022.

Rouhana, Nadim N., and Daniel Bar-Tal. "Psychological Dynamics of Intractable Ethnonational Conflicts: The Israeli-Palestinian Case." *American Psychologist* 53 (1998): 761–70.

Rubinovitz, Ziv. "Blue and White 'Black September': Israel's Role in the Jordan Crisis of 1970." *International History Review* 32 (2010): 687–706.

Sacks, Oliver. "The Fallibility of Memory." In *The River of Consciousness*, 101-22. New York: Alfred A. Knopf, 2017.

Said, Edward W. "Afterword: The Consequences of 1948." In Rogan and Shlaim, *War for Palestine*, 248–61. New York: Cambridge University Press, 2007.

———. "Invention, Memory, and Place." *Critical Inquiry* 26 (2000): 175–92.

———. *The Politics of Dispossession: The Struggle for Palestinian Self-Determination, 1969–1994*. New York: Vintage, 1994.

———. *The Question of Palestine*. New York: Vintage, 1979.

Saint-Exupéry, Antoine de. *The Little Prince*. New York: Harcourt, Brace and World, 1943.

Salloukh, Bassel F. "State Strength, Permeability, and Foreign Policy Behavior: Jordan in Theoretical Perspective." *Arab Studies Quarterly* 18 (1996): 39–65.

Salmon, Karen, and Richard A. Bryant. "Posttraumatic Stress Disorder in Children: The Influence of Developmental Factors." *Clinical Psychology Review* 22 (2002): 163–88.

Sayigh, Yezid. *Armed Struggle and the Search for State: The Palestinian National Movement, 1949–1993*. New York: Oxford University Press, 1997.

———. "Struggle Within, Struggle Without: The Transformation of PLO Politics since 1982." *International Affairs* 65 (1989): 247–71.

Schacter, Daniel L. *Searching for Memory: The Brain, the Mind, and the Past*. New York: Basic Books, 1996.

Schalinski, Inga, Maggie Schauer, and Thomas Elbert. "The Shutdown Dissociation Scale." *European Journal of Psychotraumatology* 6 (2015): no. 25652.

Scham, Paul, Benjamin Pogrund, and As'ad Ghanem. "Introduction to Shared Narratives—A Palestinian-Israeli Dialogue." *Israel Studies* 18 (2013): 1–10.

Schiff, Stacy. *Saint-Exupéry: A Biography*. New York: Alfred A. Knopf, 1994.

Schiller, Kay, and Christopher Young. *The 1972 Munich Olympics and the Making of Modern Germany*. Berkeley: University of California Press, 2010.

Schmidt, Dana Adams. *Armageddon in the Middle East: Arab vs. Israeli through the October War*. New York: New York Times, 1974.

Schwartz, Vanessa R. *Jet Age Aesthetic: The Glamour of Media in Motion*. New Haven, CT: Yale University Press, 2020.

Seaton, Matt. "The Etymology of Terror." *New York Review of Books*, November 17, 2021.

Segev, Tom. *1949: The First Israelis*. New York: Free Press, 1986.

———. *1967: Israel, the War, and the Year that Transformed the Middle East*. New York: Metropolitan Books, 2007.

———. *The Seventh Million: The Israelis and the Holocaust*. New York: Hill and Wang, 1993.

Sela, Avraham, and Alon Kadish. "Israeli and Palestinian Memories and Historical Narratives of the 1948 War—An Overview," *Israel Studies* 21 (2016): 1–26.

Selzer, Michael, ed. *Zionism Reconsidered: The Rejection of Jewish Normalcy*. New York: Macmillan, 1970.

Sfard, Michael. *The Wall and the Gate: Israel, Palestine, and the Legal Battle for Human Rights.* New York: Metropolitan Books, 2018.

Shapira, Anita. *Land and Power: The Zionist Resort to Force, 1881–1948.* New York: Oxford University Press, 1992.

Shapira, Anita, and Ora Wiskind-Elper. "Politics and Collective Memory: The Debate over the 'New Historians' in Israel." *History and Memory* 7 (1995): 9–40.

Shapiro, Edward S. *A Time for Healing: American Jewry since World War II.* Baltimore: Johns Hopkins University Press, 1992.

Sharabi, Hisham. *Palestine Guerrillas: Their Credibility and Effectiveness.* Washington, DC: Georgetown University Center for Strategic and International Studies, 1970.

Shavit, Ari. *My Promised Land: The Triumph and Tragedy of Israel.* New York: Spiegel and Grau, 2013.

Shemesh, Moshe. *The Palestinian Entity, 1959–1974: Arab Politics and the PLO.* London: Frank Cass, 1988.

Shipler, David K. *Arab and Jew: Wounded Spirits in a Promised Land.* Rev. ed. New York: Penguin, 2002.

Shlaim, Avi. "The Debate about 1948." *International Journal of Middle East Studies* 27 (1995): 287–304.

Shumsky, Dmitry. *Beyond the Nation-State: The Zionist Political Imagination, from Pinsker to Ben-Gurion.* New Haven, CT: Yale University Press, 2018.

Siegal, Nina. "Researchers Uncover Two Hidden Pages in Anne Frank's Diary." *New York Times*, May 15, 2018.

Silverberg, Robert. *If I Forget Thee, O Jerusalem: American Jews and the State of Israel.* New York: William Morrow, 1970.

Simon, Jeffrey D. *The Terrorist Trap: America's Experience with Terrorism.* 2nd ed. Bloomington: Indiana University Press, 2001.

Slaughter, Joseph R. "Hijacking Human Rights: Neoliberalism, the New Historiography, and the End of the Third World." *Human Rights Quarterly* 40 (2018): 735–75.

Slyomovics, Susan. *The Object of Memory: Arab and Jew Narrate the Palestinian Village.* Philadelphia: University of Pennsylvania Press, 1998.

Small, Scott A. *Forgetting: The Benefits of Not Remembering.* New York: Crown, 2021.

Smith, Pamela Ann. "The Palestinian Diaspora, 1948–1985." *Journal of Palestine Studies* 15 (1986): 90–108.

Snow, Peter, and David Phillips. *Leila's Hijack War: The True Story of 25 Days in September, 1970.* London: Pan Books, 1970.

Sorby, Karol. "The War of Attrition in the Middle East, 1969–1970." *Asian and African Studies* 26 (2017): 127–47.

Sowden, Dora. "Building a New Dance in a New Country." *Dance Magazine*, January 1969, 62–64.

Stampnitzky, Lisa. *Disciplining Terror: How Experts Invented "Terrorism."* New York: Cambridge University Press, 2013.

Stanislawski, Michael. *Zionism: A Very Short Introduction.* New York: Oxford University Press, 2017.

Sternhell, Zeev. *The Founding Myths of Israel: Nationalism, Socialism, and the Making of the Jewish State.* Princeton, NJ: Princeton University Press, 1997.

Stocker, James. "Diplomacy as Counter-Revolution? The 'Moderate States,' the Fedayeen and State Department Initiatives towards the Arab-Israeli Conflict, 1969–1970." *Cold War History* 12 (2012): 407–28.

Stone, I. F. *Underground to Palestine and Reflections Thirty Years Later.* New York: Pantheon, 1978.

Terr, Lenore C. "Childhood Traumas: An Outline and Overview." *American Journal of Psychiatry* 148 (1991): 10–20.

———. "Children of Chowchilla: A Study of Psychic Trauma." *Psychoanalytic Study of the Child* 34 (1979): 547–623.

———. "Chowchilla Revisited: The Effects of Psychic Trauma Four Years after a School-Bus Kidnapping." *American Journal of Psychiatry* 140 (1983): 1543–50.

———. "Treating Childhood Trauma." *Child and Adolescent Psychiatric Clinics of North America* 22 (2013): 51–66.

———. "Using Context to Treat Traumatized Children." *Psychoanalytic Study of the Child* 64 (2009): 275–98.

Tolan, Sandy. *The Lemon Tree: An Arab, a Jew, and the Heart of the Middle East.* New York: Bloomsbury, 2006.

Tomeny, Carol Lynne. "Compensation under the Warsaw Convention for Victims of Hijackings and Terrorist Attacks." *Brooklyn Journal of International Law* 3 (1976): 31–56.

Tone, Andrea. *The Age of Anxiety: A History of America's Turbulent Affair with Tranquilizers.* New York: Basic Books, 2009.

Toth, Sheree L., and Dante Cicchetti. "Remembering, Forgetting, and the Effects of Trauma on Memory: A Developmental Psychopathology Perspective." *Development and Psychopathology* 10 (1998): 589–605.

Trimble, Michael R. "Post-traumatic Stress Disorder: History of a Concept." In *Trauma and Its Wake: The Study and Treatment of Post-traumatic Stress Disorder*, edited by Charles R. Figley, 5–14. New York: Brunner/Mazel, 1985.

Troen, S. Ilan. "Israeli Views of the Land of Israel/Palestine." *Israel Studies* 18 (2013): 100–14.

Twersky, Rebecca S., John Hartung, Bernard J. Berger, Jocelyn McClain, and Christian Beaton. "Midazolam Enhances Anterograde but not Retrograde Amnesia in Pediatric Patients." *Anesthesiology* 78 (1993): 51–55.

van der Hart, Onno, Ellert Nijenhuis, Kathy Steele, and Daniel Brown. "Trauma-Related Dissociation: Conceptual Clarity Lost and Found." *Australian and New Zealand Journal of Psychiatry* 38 (2004): 906–14.

Viana, Karolline A., Anelise Daher, Lucianne C. Maia, Paulo S. Costa, Carolina C. Martins, Saul M. Paiva, and Luciane R. Costa. "Memory Effects of Sedative Drugs in Children and Adolescents—Protocol for a Systematic Review." *Systematic Reviews* 5 (2016): 1–5.

Wade, Francesca. *Square Haunting: Five Women, Freedom and London between the Wars.* London: Faber and Faber, 2020.

Walker, Richard W., Rodney J. Vogl, and Charles P. Thompson. "Autobiographical Memory: Unpleasantness Fades Faster Than Pleasantness over Time." *Applied Cognitive Psychology* 11 (1997): 399–413.

Waxman, Chaim I. *America's Jews in Transition.* Philadelphia: Temple University Press, 1983.

Waxman, Dov. *Trouble in the Tribe: The American Jewish Conflict over Israel.* Princeton, NJ: Princeton University Press, 2016.

Whitehouse, Rosie. *The People on the Beach: Journeys to Freedom after the Holocaust.* London: Hurst, 2020.

Yaqub, Salim. "The Politics of Stalemate: The Nixon Administration and the Arab-Israeli Conflict, 1969–73." In Ashton, *Cold War in the Middle East*, 35–58.

Young, Allan. *The Harmony of Illusions: Inventing Post-Traumatic Stress Disorder.* Princeton, NJ: Princeton University Press, 1995.

Zakariah, Muhamad Hasrul. "The Uprising of the *Fedayeen* against the Government of Jordan, 1970–1971: Declassified Documents from the British Archive." *International Journal of West Asian Studies* 2 (2010): 47–64.

Zauner, Franz. *Entführung nach Jordanien.* Self-published, 2012.

Zeedani, Said. "Recognition of the Other and His Past." *Israel Studies* 18 (2013): 148–55.

Zernichow, Simen, and Hilde Henriksen Waage. "The Palestine Option: Nixon, the National Security Council, and the Search for a New Policy, 1970." *Diplomatic History* 38 (2014): 182–209.

ABOUT THE AUTHOR

———

Martha Hodes is professor of history at New York University. She is the author of the award-winning books *Mourning Lincoln*; *The Sea Captain's Wife: A True Story of Love, Race, and War in the Nineteenth Century*; and *White Women, Black Men: Illicit Sex in the Nineteenth-Century South*. She has presented her scholarship around the world and is the recipient of fellowships from the Guggenheim Foundation, the National Endowment for the Humanities, the Charles Warren Center at Harvard University, the Whiting Foundation, and the Cullman Center for Scholars and Writers at the New York Public Library.